Budgets and Bureaucrats: The Sources of Government Growth

Budgets and Bureaucrats: The Sources of Government Growth   *Edited by Thomas E. Borcherding*

Duke University Press   Durham, North Carolina   1977

© 1977, Duke University Press

Library of Congress Catalogue card no. 75–30407
I.S.B.N. 0–8223–0352–3

Printed in the United States of America
by Kingsport Press, Inc.

To Winston C. Bush, 1941–1973

Contents

Acknowledgments

Originally these essays were developed as papers given at the Wednesday evening Workshop on Non-Market Bureaucracy held at V.P.I.'s Center for the Study of Public Choice during the academic year 1972–73. Funds to support this research were generously provided by the Foundation for Research on Economics and Education in Los Angeles under the directorship of Dr. J. Clayburn LaForce.

Perhaps the most enthusiastic member of the seminar was Winston Bush. Not only did he deliver two of his own papers to this group, and circulated still a third written with me, but he cheerfully and efficiently read and criticized the rest, contributing much to their improvement. It was Winston, along with Gordon Tullock and James Buchanan, who first encouraged me to seek their publication as a book. When I left the Center in the summer of 1973 Winston carried much of the administrative burden of organizing these papers in suitable form. Winston was to have been listed as coeditor.

Those of us who were privileged to know Winston will share my sadness that he could not have seen *Budgets and Bureaucrats* enter that arena of ideas to which he contributed so tirelessly and with such good humor in his short professional life. Tragically, Winston died in an automobile accident on December 1, 1973 at the beginning of what his friends and colleagues felt was to have been a most productive and happy career.

Finally, I would like to express my personal thanks to the Earhart and Relm Foundations of Ann Arbor for providing me summer grants in 1973 and 1974 which enabled me to edit these papers and continue with my own research without other preoccupations.

T.E.B.

Foreword

This challenging and exciting book examines the forces that have been at work in influencing the dramatic growth in public expenditures over the past century. As Thomas Borcherding points out, only about half the increase in real government spending can be explained by changes in the standard economic variables of relative price, real income, and population. This collection of essays highlights an important factor largely neglected by economists and other researchers that explains a major fraction of the previously unexplained portion of the growth in the public sector. That factor is the role of the bureaucracy per se in the milieu of government.

As James Buchanan has eloquently reminded us, it is one of those stunning paradoxes that "Western societies have attained universal suffrage only after popular democracy has disappeared. The electorate, the ultimate sovereign, must, to an extent not dreamed of by democracy's philosophers, be content to choose its leaders." Obviously, the chasm between the voters and the elected has become larger and larger and the bureaucracy has become less and less responsive to the wishes, desires, and tastes of the citizenry. How could it be otherwise when out of some three million employees in the executive branch of the federal government, citizens may vote for but two of these individuals?

Fortunately, we have come a long way in the study of bureaucratic behavior since the publication in the twilight of the nineteenth century of Woodrow Wilson's famous article on bureaucracy, "The Study of Administration." In essence, Wilson assumed that government employees were robots who faithfully executed policy without influencing policy, who behaved as if they had no personal goals, desires, or feelings. Students of the study of public choice, however, as all of the contributors to this volume are, do not work on this rather implausible caricature of man. On the basis of the empirical study of individual human behavior in various institutional settings, modern scholars see no fundamental differences between bureaucrats (public or private) and nonbureaucrats in their reactions to social, political, and economic stimuli.

Basic research by such scholars as Armen Alchian, James Buchanan, Louis De Alessi, Harold Demsetz, Anthony Downs, Roland McKean, William Niskanen, and Gordon Tullock have led us to believe that property rights (or the lack thereof) and other features of implicit and explicit incentive systems are important. Individuals in the bureaucracy, like the rest of us, do react to different incentive schemes; they do have various

preferences and have the capacity, will, and desire to rank these preferences. They prefer more rather than less income, power, prestige, pleasant surroundings, and congenial employees.

The work of Alchian, Buchanan, and others has permitted us to view
and analyze the behavior of the bureaucrat in a different light. He is not
a robot, but he does importantly affect decision making and policy outcomes. To paraphrase Gordon Tullock's variation on Adam Smith's
theme, it is not due to the benevolence of the bureaucrat that we expect
our research grant, our defense contract, or our welfare check, but out of
his regard for his own personal interest. It is important to emphasize that
the intent of such behavior is not necessarily immoral or evil. The bureaucrat is simply behaving like a utility maximizing human being, just as the
rest of us do. Unfortunately, and unlike the marketplace where normally
there are alternatives, there is an almost complete lack of competition in
the government arena. Because of this noncompetitive structure, the
public interest is not likely to be served by each bureaucrat striving to
maximize his own income and satisfactions.

The writers in this volume build on the theoretical advances of Alchian,
Buchanan, and others and knowledge about governmental institutions of
the type developed by Roy Blough, Charles Lindbloom, and Aaron Wildavsky. It is by combining theory with knowledge about specific incentive
systems (rewards and costs) in public agencies that the scholar can derive
operational hypotheses concerning bureaucratic behavior in government
bureaus. An enormous amount of work still awaits us. This volume, however, represents a pioneering effort toward combining our theoretical and
empirical knowledge in order to develop a base on which we might ultimately achieve effective reform of institutions in the public sector. It is
through this approach that we may begin to restore some of the lost faith
in representative government.

The central theme which runs strongly through all the papers is the
theory and practice of public choice. The papers are about ideas that
economists and political scientists have discussed, reasoned over, built
theories about, and in some cases argued rather heatedly over; but rarely
have we gotten down to the hard, grubby work of digging for the facts
that are part of the real world in which we live. This empirical aspect of
the study of public choice is relatively new. As a result, the methodology
and research itself is relatively simple. But no matter, we are finally
launched on the way to the scientific and empirical testing of hypotheses
about governmental and bureaucratic behavior.

The fresh and original articles in this book will be welcomed by several
clienteles: economists, especially in public finance, human resources and
microeconomic theory; political scientists in public administration, urban
and state government, and political theory; management scientists; and

organizational theorists and practitioners (cutting across the disciplines of psychology, sociology, political science, business administration, and economics). Hopefully, those charged with policy making at all levels of government—elected, appointed, and career officials—will find this collection useful.

The editor is admirably qualified for the task at hand. He has been a postdoctoral fellow in the Thomas Jefferson Center for Studies in Political Economy at the University of Virginia and served as a research fellow at the Center for the Study of Public Choice at Virginia Polytechnic Institute and State University and at the Hoover Institution on War, Revolution and Peace at Stanford University. He has also taught courses in the relatively new discipline of public choice in three major universities. During all this time, he has acquired an intimate knowledge of the literature and has as well contributed liberally to it. He possesses a wide-ranging intellectual curiosity that is particularly manifested in his choice of topics and authors as well as in his own contributions to this valuable volume. I strongly suspect that in a few years many individuals will think of this stimulating book as an important milestone in the study of government.

David G. Davies
Department of Economics
Duke University
Durham, North Carolina

Contributors

Thomas E. Borcherding was with the Department of Economics and the Center for the Study of Public Choice at Virginia Polytechnic Institute and State University, Blacksburg, Virginia when these papers were initially written and presented. He is now Associate Professor at Simon Fraser University in Burnaby, British Columbia. He was on leave to the Hoover Institution on War, Revolution and Peace, Stanford University, when *Budgets and Bureaucrats* was edited.

James M. Buchanan is Director of the Center for Study of Public Choice at V.P.I. He is also University Professor at that institution and a member of its Department of Economics.

Winston C. Bush was Research Associate at the Center for the Study of Public Choice and Assistant Professor of Economics at V.P.I.

Arthur T. Denzau was an Assistant Professor of Economics at V.P.I. and Research Associate with the Center for the Study of Public Choice. He is now Associate Professor of Economics at the University of Arizona.

Charles J. Goetz was Professor of Economics and Research Associate at V.P.I.'s Center for the Study of Public Choice. He is now a Professor in the University of Virginia's School of Law.

Dennis J. Jacobe was a graduate student in Economics and Public Choice at V.P.I. and is now Assistant Economist with the United States League of Savings Associations, Chicago.

Cotton M. Lindsay is Associate Professor of Economics at University of California, Los Angeles.

Robert J. Mackay is Assistant Professor of Economics at V.P.I. and also Research Associate with the Center for the Study of Public Choice. Currently he is associated with the Federal Reserve in Washington, D.C.

Don Norman is a graduate economics student at U.C.L.A.

William Orzechowski was a graduate student at V.P.I., and taught at Jacksonville State University, Jacksonville, Alabama while writing his paper. Currently he is Assistant Professor of Economics at Oglethorpe University in Atlanta.

Robert M. Spann is Associate Professor of Economics at V.P.I. and Research Associate at the Center for the Study of Public Choice.

Robert J. Staaf is Assistant Professor of Economics at V.P.I. and Research Associate at the Center for the Study of Public Choice.

Gordon Tullock is University Professor and a member of the Economics Department at V.P.I. He edits *Public Choice,* a scholarly journal with offices in the Center for the Study of Public Choice.

Budgets and Bureaucrats: The Sources of Government Growth

1. Why Does Government Grow? *James M. Buchanan*

The explosive growth of government at all levels today is alarming. Even people who do not examine the simple statistics should be increasingly concerned about higher and higher taxes levied in support of governmental programs that become less and less efficient in providing benefits of real value. If a forward look is attempted, the picture seems horrendous. In a decade governments will be using up more than one-half of each dollar of national income generated, and well over a third of gross national product will be expended through governmental channels. The propensity of government to seize upon and to spend additional dollars of the income growth that the national economy generates cannot be questioned. But as the share of government in the economy grows, can the private and nongovernmental sector continue to provide the means of satisfying government's voracious appetite?

The need to understand why government grows so rapidly seems urgent. If alarm about the current spending explosion is to lead to effective political countermeasures, if the explosion is to be stopped or even slowed down, we must have some understanding, some explanation, of why it is occurring. We must explain the institutional and political processes that produce the results that we see, results that seem fully desirable only to the bureaucrats on the expanding public payrolls.

The research project undertaken by members of the staff of the Center for the Study of Public Choice, Virginia Polytechnic Institute and State University, and under the sponsorship of the Foundation for Research in Economics and Education, has such explanation as its primary objective. Preliminary results of this research are reported in detail in the following papers; this paper provides a summary overview.

Government growth clearly has a momentum all its own, quite independent of general growth in the national economy. Economists have devoted much attention to isolating the sources of economic growth, but, surprisingly, they have paid almost no attention to the problem of determining why governments' share in the national economy continues to increase.

Because of this relative neglect, the research here must be treated as exploratory and provisional. There are no widely accepted paradigms or models upon which specific hypotheses might be constructed and tested. Features of several models will appear in the papers attached, and no single and inclusive explanatory theory emerges full-blown from our efforts. Further research is clearly needed here, and if our preliminary results can stimulate this, one subsidiary purpose will have been accomplished. More importantly, if political leaders and their advisers can be informed of the significance as well as the difficulty of getting answers to the basic question posed, the first step toward corrective countermeasures may be closer than current observation suggests.

What Government Spending, When, and How?

Before we discuss explanations of why government grows, however, some disaggregation is in order. We must look, even if briefly, at the historical record. Growth in total government spending and taxation may exert differing effects with differing mixes among levels of government. Furthermore, growth rates that might be currently observed may be viewed quite differently if they are believed to be temporary phenomena than if they represent long-term patterns. Finally, growth in aggregate governmental activity, even at one level, may depend for its effects on just how this activity is organized, on just what functions are expanding within the public sector.

Borcherding's paper on the record of a century of public spending provides a historical perspective. Significant results emerge from the data presented for the period 1870 through 1970. In the nineteenth century the public sector, overall, was expanding, but it was growing less rapidly than national income. And equally, if not more, important, within the public sector itself decentralization was occurring, with local government spending expanding relative to that of the states, and with state-local spending combined expanding relative to that by the federal government. Both of these results turned around in this century. The twentieth century is characterized by both an increasing governmental share in the national economy and an increasing portion of this public-sector share occupied by the federal government. Centralization *and* growth have occurred, a much more fearsome pair than the converse, growth with decentralization.

Somewhat surprisingly perhaps, within the governmental budget itself, there has been no dramatic shift in spending patterns over the century. Transfers have increased slightly relative to resource-using expenditures, and notably during the 1960s. Furthermore, this element of spending seems most likely to rise during ensuing decades. And, notably, the United States pattern differs from that in other Western nations largely in the relatively smaller share of transfer expenditures undertaken.

The nineteenth century record suggests clearly that an increasing governmental share is not a necessary and inevitable accompaniment to national economic development. The explosion in taxation and public spending that we live with is a twentieth century phenomenon, and the pattern that was changed before can be reversed. Government need not grow more rapidly than the national economy; there is no such relationship written in our stars.

This is not to suggest that a reversal of the trend established over many decades will be easy to accomplish, even if the institutional means are discovered, the political leadership emerges, and the public support is mobilized. Simple and straightforward projections of current trends yield fearful results, as Jacobe's paper demonstrates for the federal government alone. This remains true regardless of the time period used for the basis of projection. As a supplemental note of pessimism, the record suggests that almost every projection of government growth made during the years since World War 2 has been woefully inaccurate, and always on the side of under- rather than overestimation. It is time to become concerned.

Government "By the People"? or Government "Against the People"?

Do governments expand in direct response to the demands of ordinary people for more and better public-service programs? Or do governments operate independently of the people, producing results that may not be related to the wishes of the citizens and which, on balance, do the people more harm than good? These questions get at the very heart of democracy, and they may not seem directly connected to problems of taxation and spending. But until they are answered, no progress at all can be made toward explaining government growth. In a democratic decision model, any explanation for observed high rates of growth in taxation and spending must be grounded on the demands of the citizens. Why do people want governmental agencies to do so much for them, things which they might do better privately?

Why are the people willing to pay onerous taxes for governmental programs? Are those goods and services normally offered by governments characteristically those that become relatively more important as income rises through time? Does the shift from a production to a service economy necessarily embody an expanded role for government? Does increasing population in general, and increasing concentration of this population in particular, generate pressures on governments to supply relatively more services and the private sector relatively less? Does the relatively lower productivity of resources used by governments generate the paradoxical pattern of relatively expanding governmental spending? These subsidiary questions, and more, will be discussed directly or indirectly in the research papers. These questions emerge from a "government by the people" or democratic model of politics. As the questions might indicate, and as the research results support, some part of the over-all expansion in the public sector of the national economy can be satisfactorily explained in this way.

But not all. Resort to a quite different and nondemocratic model of the political structure leads to quite different subsidiary questions, the answers to which yield further explanatory potential. Are the people misled into thinking that their taxes are low and that public spending benefits are high? Do they operate under a set of fiscal illusions? If they do, what are the institutions and instruments that foster these illusions, and what individuals and groups find it advantageous to maintain these institutions? Where does the political party, the aspiring politician, the working bureaucrat fit into the picture? What motivates the men who must provide the human bridge between "the people" — those who pay the taxes — and "the people" — those who may secure benefits from governmental programs? Are these two sets of people necessarily equivalent? Or is government increasingly becoming a means of making transfers among groups? What is the role of the political entrepreneur in all this? What are the effects of allowing bureaucrats to vote? Is not this a direct conflict of interest?

Once again, each of these subsidiary questions will be discussed, directly or indirectly, in the research papers here. Note, however, that such questions as these emerge only in a model that is nondemocratic in its essentials, a model that offers an explanation of observed results in terms of a perversion of the true demands of the people.

Neither of these two contrasting models of politics will be proved appropriate or inappropriate here. Any plausibly adequate explanation of the expansion of the governmental sector in the modern American economy requires both models, or some mixture of the two. Without doubt, some considerable part of the observed growth in the public sector, at all levels, is directly traceable to the demands of the citizenry, genuine demands for more services accompanied by an increased willingness to shoulder the tax burdens required for financing. But, once this is acknowledged, there can also be little doubt but that a significant and remaining part of the observed growth in the public sector can be explained only by looking at the motivations of those who secure direct personal gains from government expansion, gains that are unrelated to the benefits filtered down to the ordinary citizens.

The two contrasting models of politics provide a helpful means of presenting the research results in summary form. But they do more than that. The means toward checking the expansion of taxation and spending may depend critically on our ability to separate the two forces at work. Blunderbuss attempts to cut back on public spending programs, willy-nilly, and without recognition that such attempts may be subverted by the bureaucracy, may backfire. If the bureaucracy retains power to allocate general spending cuts among functions, it will, of course, direct the cuts to those areas that are most sensitive, those most in demand by the people. If we adopt the norm that government programs should be directly responsive to the demands of the citizenry, whether we might personally agree with the citizenry or not, but that government should not offer an instrument of enrichment for self-serving bureaucrats, the prospect for checking the expansion in the public sector may lie not so much in direct spending or taxing limitations but, instead, in structural-procedural reforms within the governmental structure itself. Rules that allow for more contracting out and for less direct provision by governments may do more toward reducing tax burdens than budgetary limits. Changes in pay schedules for teachers may produce more education at less cost more effectively than changes in the size of the educational budget at any governmental level.

Responsive Government

Inflation, Population, and Public Spending

The most obvious explanatory elements in the growth of gross public spending can be covered briefly and without detail. Defined in current dollar magnitudes, total spending, both for the private and the public sectors of the economy, increases as inflation occurs. Even when the gross figures are reduced to real terms, to dollars of constant purchasing power, however, we still are faced with the task of explaining more than 4300 percent increase in aggregate government spending over the years of this century.

One of the first explanations suggested is population growth. To what extent can we "explain" the growth of government as a direct consequence of the population increase over the period? Borcherding's computations suggest that some 25 percent of the increase in real spending by governments might be explained by population, on the presumption that the goods and services supplied by political units are demanded in the same fashion as those supplied in the private sector. That is to say, if there are really no net efficiency gains to be secured through providing the goods and services jointly through governments, we can then "explain" up to 25 percent of the increase in this way. But, somewhat paradoxically, if such efficiencies do not exist, there is no argument for having the goods provided by governments at all. Goods and services had as well be provided and supplied through ordinary markets. On the other hand, if there are clear net efficiency gains to be made through the joint-supply properties of governments, the explanatory potential for population increase falls below the 25 percent figure noted.

The Services Economy and Income Elasticity of Demand

In either case, our major explanatory task remains before us. What causes the growth in real government spending per capita?

As the general development in the national economy has taken place, there has been a pronounced shift in employment away from production and trade and into the services sector. Since government output is heavily weighted by services, this underlying shift in the structure of the economy would, in itself, explain some of the relative increase in the size of the public sector. When Borcherding examines the data, however, he finds that, even within the services sector, government has increased its relative share in employment. As with population increase, there remains much more to explain.

The growth in income itself will, of course, explain a large share of spending growth in absolute terms. But income will explain some of the relative increase in the government's share only if it can be demonstrated that the goods and services supplied publicly are those for which individuals' demands are highly responsive to income shifts, more responsive than for nongovernmental goods, considered as a package. If the income elasticity of demand is high, to slip into economists' jargon here, there will be a more than proportionate increase in demand consequent on an increase in incomes. Borcherding's estimates suggest that governmentally supplied goods and services possess no such characteristic features, and that the responsiveness in demand to income change is, if anything, somewhat less than that which characterizes private spending. We must look elsewhere for our explanation.

The Public Productivity Paradox

Most of us who use governmental services do not need to be informed that productivity is low relative to that in the nongovernmental sector. Anyone who doubts this statement need only call on his personal experience with the mails during the last Christmas holiday season. And Spann examines the data and he finds that for the five-year period 1962–67 there was no net increase in productivity in the state-local services covered in his study. If anything, productivity may have slightly declined over that period. Earlier work by Professor William Baumol of Princeton University suggested that extremely low rates of productivity growth are characteristic features of the goods and services that governments have traditionally supplied. We need not argue here about whether the relatively low productivity in government employment is inherent in the technology of the goods and services supplied or stems from the motivation system for employees in government. The facts are that, for whatever reason, we witness the phenomenon of increasing productivity in the private sector of the economy alongside stationary or even declining productivity in the public sector.

This unbalanced relationship between rates of productivity increase for the two sectors insures that, in real terms, the relative costs of goods and services supplied governmentally increase. In order to maintain a labor force, wages and salaries in the public sector employments will have to be roughly equivalent to wages and salaries obtainable in the private sector. But the latter, wages and salaries in the market sector, will tend to increase as productivity increases, without necessarily causing an increase in the prices of private-sector output. When governmental employers find it necessary to offer matching wages and salaries, but without the accompanying increase in productivity, the unit costs of goods and services supplied governmentally must rise relative to the costs of market-produced goods and services. To the individual demanders, and consumers, of governmental goods and services the "prices" of these, measured in units of privately produced goods that are given up, must increase.

With an increase in relative price, quantity demanded normally is expected to go down, other things remaining the same. This first principle of economic theory remains valid here. But even though price increases and quantity demanded decreases (if all other determinants of demand should remain unchanged), the buyer or demander may still *spend more* on the good than before. And since we measure the size of the public or governmental sector by total spending, there is nothing really inconsistent about the low productivity in this sector being one of the important causal factors in the growth of spending for goods and services supplied by this sector. The importance of this factor might be more accurately estimated if we did, in fact, have good measures for governmental output in physical terms. Lacking this, we must make do with what we have, and the evidence suggests that this effect, stemming from the combination of low productivity growth and a relatively low price elasticity of demand for publicly supplied goods and services, does add significantly to our explanation of government growth.

Urbanization and Congestion

As population has increased, and as the structure of the national economy has changed, urbanization has taken place. This increases the economic interdependence among persons, and with this the potential for conflict, because of common use of resources that have not historically been assigned as private property. With urbanization comes congestion in all its forms, and this opens up a role for governments in mitigating the evils if not eliminating them. One part of the hypothesis here can scarcely be questioned. More governmental action is required as congestion increases, and congestion is directly related to the concentration of people in space. But the type of governmental action suggested may not, and need not, give rise to large increases in government budgets. To reduce congestion, corrective regulatory measures may be in order (e.g., zoning, traffic controls, emission and effluent standards, etc.). These may require only nominal budgetary outlays.

On the other hand, increases in incomes that accompany urbanization should reduce economic interdependencies of the positive sort and thus should reduce the need for governmental action. In very poor communities, citizens may find it essential to join forces through governmental units to provide common facilities (e.g., swimming pools). As communities, and individuals, become richer, however, each family can afford to provide its own facilities. This should be a force working toward a reduction rather than an increase in the relative share of government in the economy.

Borcherding examines the evidence empirically. He finds that there is little or no explanatory value in urbanization as a cause for government growth.

Growth of Responsive Government

Any or all of the reasons discussed above might explain why governments would grow, even in an "ideal democracy," where the demands of the people are transmitted directly into observed budgetary outcomes. As we have indicated, a large part of any total explanation must take these demand-increasing influences into proper account. Borcherding attempts to make quantitative estimates, and he concludes that perhaps as much as one-half to two-thirds of the real growth in per capita government spending can be explained satisfactorily by combining all of the elements discussed to this point. As he puts it in his paper, all of these factors combined explain why we might observe an aggregate governmental sector spending about one-fifth of gross national product (GNP), but they do not help us in going beyond this and in explaining why we observe government spending more than one-third of GNP.

The gap that remains after we have exhausted all of the economic elements that might reflect genuine demands of the people for expanded governmental services is a large one. More importantly, this gap is the margin for potential correction, the margin for reduction that might be accomplished with net benefits to most of the citizenry. We need not, in fact, be greatly concerned if governmental growth could somehow be limited to the rates required to allow responsible and responsive adjustment to the demand-increasing factors. We become properly concerned when observed rates of increase clearly exceed these limits, in the current instance by as much as one-third. It is this margin that must be tackled with corrective measures, and, therefore it is essential that our analysis extend beyond those factors treated in part 1.

Excessive Government

Tax Consciousness and Fiscal Illusions

We need to introduce elements of a nondemocratic model of politics. We must search for reasons why budgetary results are not those desired by the citizens for whom spending programs are alleged to be undertaken, why these results are uniformly in the direction of excessively large outlays. Our research must examine possibilities of breakdowns in the transmission of individuals' demands through the political-fiscal process, including the possibility that the transmission institutions may be deliberately perverted by self-seeking politicians and bureaucrats who succeed in isolating themselves from the discipline imposed by the electoral process.

Perhaps the most significant finding in the unpublished 1972 survey of California citizens' attitudes conducted under the supervision of Professor W. C. Stubblebine for the Foundation for Research in Economics and Education concerns the failure of citizens to estimate properly the true tax costs of various state-local spending programs. These costs are underestimated, sometimes by a factor of two-thirds. The people who pay taxes do not realize how much they pay, and they think that they secure government goods and services at bargain prices. Suppose that we know the cost of an automobile to be $3000 and that we ask a buyer how much he paid. If he tells us $1000, we should indeed be amazed at his ignorance, and we should predict that he would foolishly spend too much on cars. Yet this is roughly what the situation is with respect to individuals' indirect "purchases" of governmental goods and services through the whole political budgetary process.

This prompts our research into the sources for such illusions. Why does the average citizen underestimate the costs of public services? In his paper Goetz suggests several parts of an answer, and details need not be elaborated here. Relatively large amounts of state-local taxes are at least partially concealed in the final market prices of goods and services. The consumer looks at the retail price of a good, and he rarely breaks this down into the "true price" and "tax" components. Income taxes, which have become increasingly important at the state level, and which (along with payroll taxes) dominate the federal revenue structure, are largely withheld at the income source. Withholding has the effect of making the individual unaware that he is paying for a slice of government before he has the opportunity to pay for anything else. He concerns himself with his net or take-home paycheck, and his consciousness of a tax obligation comes home to him only on tax accounting day in March or April of each year. With the property tax, traditionally the mainstay of local governmental revenue systems, the relatively high awareness of the taxpayer is reduced by the inclusion of tax obligations in monthly mortgage payments. And, for renters, property taxes are equivalent to excise taxes; they show up imbedded in rents.

Economists always return to a central principal, TANSTAAFL, "there ain't no such thing as a free lunch," by which they mean that someone must pay, even if a good seems to be costless to those who consume it. Many fiscal institutions have "free lunch" features built into them and foster the notion that some monies are free. The federal government's program of grants to states and localities increased dramatically in the 1960s. Recipient governments, as represented by their politicians, treat federal grants as if these are, in fact, free monies. The elementary fact that individuals who live in California are also federal taxpayers is lost in the shuffle between Washington and Sacramento.

Fortunately, the national economy continues to grow. National income goes up year by year. This growth insures that the base of taxation increases. From this it follows that, even without changes in tax rates, revenues collected will rise through time. Legislators, whether in the Congress or in the state assemblies, again treat this automatic revenue increase as free money, to be used for new spending programs if desired. Goetz estimates that only a third of the increase in state-local revenues is generated by new taxes and by increased tax rates. Two-thirds of the increase stems from the automatic increase in collections consequent on income growth in the economy.

Although we have included this brief treatment of fiscal illusions under nondemocratic models of politics, we should note that fiscal instruments that generate illusions may be chosen by the people. Taxpayers may, in fact, prefer to fool themselves (as witness Governor Reagan's unsuccessful fight to keep the California income tax on a nonwithholding basis). Even in a tolerably working democracy, individuals may be reluctant to accept tax instruments that will produce rational budgetary choices. This is a democratic dilemma; rational behavior in selecting among taxes may guarantee irrational budgetary results. All of this may be acknowledged, yet the primary explanation for the persistence of illusions may lie in the behavior of those who find it in their private interests to insure irrational budgetary outcomes.

Politics for Profit

Politicians are politicians because they want to be. They are no more robots than other men. Yet the politician who would do nothing other than reflect the preferences of his constituents would in fact, be robot-like in his behavior. Few, if any, politicians are so restricted. They seek office because they seek "profit," in the form of "political income," which will normally be obtained only if their behavior is not fully in accord with the desires of electoral majorities. Those men who are attracted to politics as a profession are likely to be precisely those who have considerable interest in promoting their own version of good government, along with those who see the potential opportunities for direct and indirect bribes, and those who evaluate political office as means toward other ends.

The electoral process offers, at best, a crude disciplinary check on those who depart too much from constituency preferences. Elections are held only at periodic intervals. Information is poor, and citizens have relatively little private interest in securing more. As a result, almost any politician can, within rather wide limits, behave contrary to the interests of his constituents without suffering predictable harm. If he departs far from these preferences, he may fail to be reelected. But if the stakes are high, if the potential gains to him in "political income" are sufficiently large, reelection may be willingly sacrificed. Bush et al. explore several of these possibilities in one of his papers.

If the behavior of politicians in seeking and securing "political income" while holding elective office does nothing but create some slack between the working of practical government and an idealized drawing-board model, there would be no cause for concern here. But if this behavior of politicians biases results consistently in the direction of larger governments, it becomes relevant for our purpose. The presence of such biases seems clearly established. Even such a straightforward item as the legislative salary level is directly related to budgetary size. It is much easier to justify a legislative salary increase item in a ten- than in a six-billion-dollar budget. It is much easier to increase legislative salaries for an assembly that meets for six months each year than for an assembly that meets for two months each biennium.

If we introduce the opportunities for potential bribes, whether these be illegal or sub rosa, it is equally clear that these opportunities increase, perhaps exponentially, with growth in governmental size. If, however, governments are excessively large for satisfying constituency demands, or at least for satisfying the preferences of the required majority of constituents, why do not political entrepreneurs find it profitable to appeal to those who would benefit, in the net, from budgetary reductions?

Why should platforms based on tax reduction, and spending reduction, not be observed? Why should those legislators, and coalitions of legislators, who seek indirect bribes not seek out those who might benefit from reductions in governmental size? The basic reason is that taxes are more general than spending programs. Spending projects tend to be concentrated so as to provide benefits to particular groups whereas taxes tend to be levied generally on all those who qualify in terms of a defined base. Furthermore, incumbent politicians, elected on a tax-and-spend program are becoming increasingly difficult to displace. The increasing costs of entry into politics serve to maintain incumbents in elected office. The analysis does not suggest that new political entrepreneurs appealing to those who seek limits on governmental growth must fail in their efforts. It suggests only that the task of this type of political entrepreneur is much more difficult than that faced by the aspiring, and especially incumbent, politicians who can appeal to specific constituency demands for new and expanded projects.

Conflict of Interest

When he became Deputy Secretary of Defense in 1969, David Packard was required to dispose of holdings in a company that maintained an interest in defense contracts. Conflict-of-interest rules have been rigorously applied to high-level governmental appointees during the last decade. Given this, it is perhaps somewhat surprising that the obvious conflict of interest presented by the extension of the voting franchise to members of the vast governmental bureaucracy, at all levels, has scarcely been noted. As Bush and Denzau, and Borcherding, Bush, and Spann remark in their papers, almost no one has analyzed this particular problem. And, unfortunately for our purposes, it seems that the initial disenfranchisement of bureaucrats located in the District of Columbia was not related to the conflict of interest discussed here. Even the Hatch Act, which did seek to reduce overt political activity of bureaucrats, is now under fire in the courts, and it may well be jettisoned if some federal judge decides that he likes his bureaucrat neighbor.

We must be specific. Why is there an obvious conflict of interest present when bureaucrats are allowed to vote in elections organized by the jurisdiction that employs them? Bureaucrats are no different from other persons, and, like others, they will rationally vote to further their own interests as producers when given the opportunity. Clearly their interests lie in an expanding governmental sector, and especially in one that expands the number of its employees. Salaries can be increased much more readily in an expanding agency than in a declining or stagnant one. Promotions are much more rapid in an organization that is increasing in size than in one that is remaining stable or declining in size. From this it follows directly that bureaucrats will vote for those politicians and parties that call for overall governmental expansion rather than for their opposites. This introduces yet another bias in voting outcomes, a bias that grows increasingly important as the sheer size of the bureaucracy grows.

Perhaps this conflict of interest need not be of major concern, even now, if all eligible voters chose to exercise their options. The nonbureaucrat, however, has relatively little private, personal interest in voting, per se, unless the alternatives involve issues that directly influence his well-being. He votes largely out of some sense of duty or obligation to democratic forms, and when voting is costly he may not vote at all. Often he does not; only fifty-five percent of eligible voters participated in the 1972 presidential election.

Things are quite different with the bureaucrat. He will have a much greater interest in exercising his franchise, because his own well-being is directly related to electoral outcomes. And, to the extent that a relatively larger proportion of bureaucrats vote, their individual votes have more value in determining outcomes than might be indicated from a simple head count. Bush et al. examine the data on voting behavior and find that the conflict-of-interest hypothesis is corroborated. From the data they compute a power index for bureaucrats which allows us to place effective weights on their votes, and indirectly to measure the bias that their exercise of the franchise introduces.

Education for the People or Education for the Educators?

We bring our discussion down to concrete terms if we look at one part of the bureaucracy. Educational outlays make up more than 40 percent of combined state and local budgetary expenditures. In his two research papers, Staaf carefully examines the data on recent changes in educational organization and asks: Have the changes been implemented for the benefit of the taxpaying public or for the benefit of those educators who make the organizational decisions? The evidence suggests that the changes have been designed to benefit the members of the educational bureaucracy. The taxpaying public has found itself burdened with significantly higher costs without getting demonstrable improvements in the quality of educational services.

The consolidation of school districts is a case in point. Major consolidation reduced the number of districts from 117,000 in 1940 to 18,000 in 1970. This change took place despite the absence of data suggesting that consolidation facilitates superior educational quality. Why, then, did it occur? How can we explain the institutional change? Once we look at the motivational structure within the educational bureaucracy the answer emerges. Consolidation is desired by educators because salary levels and promotion prospects, and notably those for educational administrators, depend directly on district size.

A by-product of consolidation is a reduction in the competitiveness among local school systems, and an increase in monopoly control of local education. One objective of the educational bureaucracy is to shield itself from competitive pressures, pressures that must work for efficiency in terms of results desired by the final consumers of education, even if not by those educators who supply it.

The absence of effective competition, the difficulty in defining output, and the absence of cost-reducing motivation in the governmental sector — these allow cost-increasing institutions to become imbedded in the bureaucratic structure. Staaf looks in one paper at data on teacher salary levels. He finds that salaries depend largely on educational attainment (higher degrees or work toward higher degrees) and on years of teaching experience. Salaries are unrelated to student achievement, and the data indicate that there is little or no relationship between these salary-making variables and achievement of students. Apparently, students do equally well under teachers who have attained only minimal levels of training and who are not experienced as they do under highly educated teachers with long years of experience. These results suggest that education, as a public service, is being purchased inefficiently in almost all jurisdictions. But what person or group in the education bureaucracy has any motive for changing the pattern? Quite the opposite. School system administrators find their own salaries to be related directly to the number of teachers with experience and with higher degrees. The cost-increasing features feed on themselves.

But why don't experience and training matter? Surely experience in teaching should lead to better teaching and surely education has some positive value. Staaf explains the paradox by examining the behavioral situation in which teachers find themselves. Since their rewards are not related in any way to the final output that they produce, which should be measurable in student achievement, teachers have no personal incentive to perform well. They are not so much bad teachers, as they are teachers who have no reason to be good.

Private Provision of Public Goods and Services: Reducing Spending (and Taxes) Without Reducing Benefits

Aspiring politicians who seek to dislodge incumbents from elective office often refer to major cost-savings that might be introduced by greater efficiencies in spending, cost-savings that may be utilized to provide additional goods without the necessity of imposing new taxes. The public accepts most of these arguments for what they are, and it does not expect the pattern of governmental growth to be changed much regardless of which politician or political party gains power. When we look carefully at the institutional structure of government, however, at the internal motivational system at work in the bureaucracy, the prospect of securing dramatic efficiency gains becomes exciting. If major institutional changes could be made, government budgets could be slashed (along with taxes) without reducing either the quantity or the quality of goods and services enjoyed by the final consumer, the taxpaying citizen.

But a shift in approach would be required to accomplish this. *Governmental financing of goods and services must be divorced from direct governmental provision or production of these goods and services.* There may be fully legitimate arguments for governmental financing but little or no argument for governmental provision. Through the simple device of introducing private provision under governmental financing, the growth in public spending may, figuratively speaking, be stopped in its tracks.

Why should this make so much difference? Why should private contractors be able to supply the same quality of goods and services at substantially lower costs? The motivational differences between the private firm, whose managers can secure direct monetary rewards from cost-savings, and the bureaucratic agency are clear enough, even without supporting empirical evidence. But the facts themselves are dramatic. Spann examines the results of the various studies that have compared the costs of private and public provision of similar services. Scottsdale, Arizona, gets its fire protection from a private firm at one-half the cost of the same quality protection under governmental provision. Monmouth County, New Jersey has its garbage collected by private contractors at two-thirds of the cost of doing it publicly. These are examples of what might be achieved by widespread introduction of private provision under governmental financing. The introduction of educational vouchers, with the education being supplied to families by private firms, might produce higher quality education at substantially lower costs. Even if parental choices through full voucher schemes should not be accepted, the willingness of local governments to purchase education through performance contracting with private firms offers substantial potential for cost reduction.

Such institutional changes may do much toward checking excessive government growth. But even the widespread introduction of the private provision of goods and services that are governmentally financed may not remove the basic bureaucratic influences in democratic decisions. Persons employed by private firms which supply goods on contract to governments may behave similarly to persons who work directly for governments.

Conclusions

We started out to explain why governments grow so rapidly. We end by zeroing in on the motivational structure of the governmental bureaucracy as the primary source for that part of governmental growth that does not represent response to the demands of citizens for goods and services. The policy implication is that attempts to reduce excessive governmental spending might be aimed at the motivational structure of bureaucracy rather than at aggregate budgetary or tax levels. On the other hand, if the bureaucracy is considered to be so firmly entrenched and its institutions so rigid that direct attack would be futile, alternative means may be required. It may prove possible to force through the internal structural changes that might be suggested by the analysis only if aggregate budget and tax limits are imposed on legislative bodies, at the constitutional level. Legislators respond to many constituencies, including that of the bureaucracy. And until the legislator is forced by constitutional restrictions to face up to the inherent conflict between the interests of the citizenry and those of the bureaucracy, he may continue to take the route which, to him, seems that of least resistance. This route has been, until now, that of allowing government budgets (and taxes) to grow.

2. One Hundred Years of Public Spending, 1870– 1970   *Thomas E. Borcherding*

Over the last ten decades public spending has been rising at an annual rate almost two or three percent faster than has the Gross National Product (GNP). What I intend to do in this paper is to document this increase and to develop the patterns of growth of the various components that make up the aggregates. In particular I am interested in the change in distribution of spending among the three levels of government, federal, state, and local; the changing character of the spending itself; changes over the various time periods; and the changes in relative importance of government expenditures to private spending. In addition, I wish to examine four other historical-statistical questions: what has been the behavior of government spending during the business cycle; has the expansion of federal spending during depression and war time accelerated the rate of growth of public spending and speeded up the tendency towards centralization in later periods; has government activity changed much as compared to the private services sector; and finally, to what extent has the production of public services been shifted from reliance on private suppliers to public production by government bureaucracies?

Reasons for this growth of government expenditure are explored not in this paper but in my accompanying essay, "The Sources of Growth of Public Spending in the United States, 1902–1970." It is hoped, however, that this document will give the reader a better understanding of the change in the role of the government over the last one hundred years. He can then decide for himself if the change has been sufficient to warrant the concern expressed by and debated among many economists, social scientists, commentators in the popular press, and public officials as to its appropriateness.

The Early Period, 1870 to 1902

The first thirty-two years of this fiscal history are difficult to study because of the lack of adequate data on nonfederal governments. (Actually, even the federal data before 1929 were not originally collected by the

Source note: I would like to thank the Earhardt Foundation of Ann Arbor and the Foundation for Research in Economics and Education of Los Angeles for financial support of this research in the winter of 1972 and the summer of 1973 respectively. My research assistant at that time, Roger Meiners of Virginia Polytechnic Institute and State University, is to be commended for his painstaking efforts.

U.S. Bureau of the Census as they are today. In fact, before 1921 there was no federal budget document as we now know it). Fortunately, economic historians have found the pre-1929 period of sufficient interest to work the data back into the nineteenth century. Still, the evidence they offer before 1902 for nonfederal spending is extremely crude and the error implicit in the estimates must be, to hazard a personal guess, in the order of 20% or so. Given this caveat let us pursue the question of what happened to public spending in the last thirty years of the past century.

Table 1 shows federal spending for 1870–1902. In per capita terms there clearly was no growth, while in absolute terms the increase was about 3.3% per year. Since GNP in real terms rose at a rate slightly more than 5%, the actual share of federal government spending in national income fell during the period. It is also instructive to remove the defense component from this spending, and I have done so using two methods. The first simply removes the spending of the various bureaus that would be strictly linked with defense: War and Navy. The second method is to remove all war and war-related expenditures (a technique suggested by Buchanan [6]), which include direct defense, international relations, veterans' benefits and interest on the largely war-incurred national debt. Using either definition it is clear that nondefense or "civilian" spending rose by rates smaller than GNP. (Table 15 at the end of the next section can be consulted for the precise increases. These federal data are reasonably good measures found in the Census publication, *Historical Statistics of the United States, Colonial Times to 1957*. It is the state and local data that are less reliable). Clearly, one gets the impression of a slowly growing, increasingly nonmilitary federal government—a role which was to be completely reversed in the twentieth century.

No completely consistent and comprehensive study of total government and nonfederal spending for this period has yet been done, but some smaller scale explorations are available which give us some pretty fair notions of what took place at these levels of government.

Five estimates of all public employment, federal and nonfederal, for the period involved, show increases that range between 1.8% and 4.1% per annum [7, 13, 14, 15, and 19]. Now spending must certainly have risen even more quickly since Rees [23] shows that real wages in manufacturing were rising about 1.4% for the slightly later period 1890–1914. If wages in the public sector were rising at about the same rate, it seems likely that government spending was growing at perhaps 5% per year in aggregate, or slightly more slowly than was GNP.[1] Given that federal

1. It is assumed that the growth of public spending is closely related to the growth of public employment weighed by wages. In other words, the growth of public spending is more or less equivalent to the growth in the public sector's wages bill. This has been established as approximately true using cross-sectional data for 1962 by Borcherding and Deacon

spending was increasing at the annual rate of 3.3%, the growth of state and local spending may have exceeded 3%. The difference was, however, rather moderate given the evidence that Davis and Legler [11] offer on the basis of regional estimates for the period 1871–1899. They show that per capita aggregate spending does not appear to have changed much at all, which may imply that government grew only slightly more than population, i.e., by 2.3% per year over the period. Table 2 shows regional estimates in nominal dollars by regions. No price deflator is necessary since the price level in 1870 was probably not terribly different from the 1899 level. (There was, in fact, deflation during part of the period as historians of the "Silver Question" have pointed out in some detail). Growth of public spending was largely in the Central parts with the East Coast unaffected and the Pacific and Mountain regions declining. It seems unlikely then that total government spending was rising even as fast as 2.5% per year, a figure obtained by a simple averaging of the regional growth rates (excluding the obvious outliers) in Table 2 and adding the population growth of 2.3%.[2] It would then appear from the Davis-Legler data that the government's claim on the economy was probably falling in relative terms by 1 or 2% per year.

Table 3 uses the Davis-Legler estimates to get a notion of what the relationship of federal to nonfederal spending was over this period. With the exception of two of the Central regions the role of the federal government was diminishing. Thus begins to emerge the picture of a public sector that was either stable or, more likely, decreasing its share of national income, but becoming less centralized as well.

As to the relative position of states to nonfederal governments, the evidence is not quite so clear. Studenski and Kroos [26] in their monumental (in scope) but controversial (in statistical reliability) study of public spending suggest that over the period 1869 to 1899 state spending rose by 70% and local spending by only 30%. This is highly questionable, however, since only the larger Eastern cities were surveyed and their

---

[5]. Since the wages bill is a product of employment and the wage rate, its growth over time is approximately equal to the annual percentage change of the former plus the yearly growth of the latter. Thus, if public employment was growing about 3% per year and wages at 1.5%, the wages bill was rising by less than 5%. Since the latter is a good proxy for government spending, it seems reasonable to say that public spending was in aggregate increasing at less than the economy-wide yearly growth rate of over 5%. This implies a relatively shrinking public sector.

2. The Davis-Legler data [11] suggest the growth in per capita government spending was about 0.5% per annum. This was obtained by simple averaging of the nine regions but dropping the outliers in the western United States where population was relatively low. Since population in aggregate was growing by 2.3% per annum, this implies that total government spending was growing by less than 3% annually. Again, a shrinking public sector is suggested.

Table 1. Federal spending, 1870 to 1902 (in 1929 prices)

Year	Total federal expenditures			Non-defense federal expenditure			"Civilian" federal expenditures[a]		
	Total (millions)	Per Capita	% of GNP	Total (millions)	Per Capita	% of GNP	Total (millions)	Per Capita	% of GNP
1870	419	10	4.5	316	7	3.4	136	3	1.5
1880	470	9	2.9	379	7	2.3	210	4	1.3
1890	636	10	2.4	502	8	2.0	430	7	1.6
1902	1100	14	2.4	783	10	1.7	325	5	0.8

Source: Federal spending, population, and income from U.S. Bureau of the Census, *Historical Statistics of the United States: Colonial Times to 1957* (Washington, D.C.: U.S. Government Printing Office, 1961).

a. "Civilian" is defined as total minus national security, veterans' payments and interest on the national debt.

Table 2. Per capita government spending by regions, 1871 and 1899 (in current dollars)

Year	New England	Middle Atlantic	East-North Central	West-North Central	South Atlantic
1871	35	22	13	15	17
1899	35	25	18	18	20

Year	East-South Central	West-South Central	Mountain	Pacific
1871	5	17	59	38
1899	7	11	27	32

Source: Lance Davis and John Legler, "Government in the American Economy, 1815–1902: A Quantitative Study," *Journal of Economic History* (Dec., 1966).

spending relative to their populations was used as the estimating ratio for the other cities. State estimates were based on a similar spotty sample. Davis and Legler use much more exhaustive sampling methods to get their data, and their estimates suggest just the opposite. Table 4 shows that except for the East (where Studenski and Kroos concentrated their studies) that the ratio of state to nonfederal spending was either constant or declining. Thus it appears that the decentralization of government was taking place at the nonfederal level too.

There are still other measures that shed light on the diffusion of spending. Tables 5 and 6 show the ratio of state and local government spending respectively to that of all government expenditures. These ratios suggest that not only was the federal share of government spending declining, but so also was that of the states. Since federal spending was growing more slowly than the economy as a whole, so too must have that of the states. Though local government was growing relative to the other levels of

Table 3. Percentage of federal to all public spending by regions, 1871 and 1899

Year	New England	Middle Atlantic	East-North Central	West-North Central	South Atlantic
1871	41	46	32	40	90
1899	31	43	42	38	63

Year	East-South Central	West-South Central	Mountain	Pacific
1871	17	39	85	68
1899	43	37	35	37

Source: See Table 2, this chapter.

Table 4. Percentage of state spending to nonfederal public spending by regions, 1871 and 1899

Year	New England	Middle Atlantic	East-North Central	West-North Central	South Atlantic
1871	34	26	23	21	37
1899	42	22	20	20	37

Year	East-South Central	West-South Central	Mountain	Pacific
1871	35	50	95	38
1899	35	40	20	27

Source: See Table 2, this chapter.

government, it probably was growing no faster than national income as the Davis-Legler regional data tend to indicate. Thus, Studenski and Kroos would seem to be totally wrong about the spending patterns of state and local governments in the period in question. All of this would seem to indicate three significant facts worth repeating:

1. The growth of government in the last third of the nineteenth century was relatively slow (3% or so) compared to the GNP (over 5%). Hence the share of government in total economic activity was at least unchanged or, more likely, actually declining.

2. The federal government's position vis à vis the nonfederal sector was diminishing and so was its share of national income. Government growth was at the periphery, not the center.

3. Although state and local spending was increasing faster than total government spending, it is not clear that it was growing much faster

Table 5. Percentage of state government spending to all government spending by regions, 1871 and 1899

Year	New England	Middle Atlantic	East-North Central	West-North Central	South Atlantic
1871	19	13	15	13	9
1899	35	12	11	12	9

Year	East-South Central	West-South Central	Mountain	Pacific
1871	33	33	15	12
1899	20	25	13	17

Source: See Table 2, this chapter.

Table 6. Percentage of local spending to total spending by regions, 1871 and 1899

Year	New England	Middle Atlantic	East-North Central	West-North Central	South Atlantic
1871	38	41	53	48	16
1899	41	44	48	49	16

Year	East-South Central	West-South Central	Mountain	Pacific
1871	51	37	Negligible	20
1899	36	40	52	46

Source: See Table 2, this chapter.

than the general economy, if at all. Local public spending was undoubtedly rising relative to that of state governments, though perhaps not faster than the GNP.

These patterns of the last century were not to be maintained, however, but were to be inverted in the next seventy years. That our public sector would change its character markedly in the twentieth century is shown in the next section.

Public Spending in This Century

Table 7 shows the figures for public spending for several periods from 1902 to 1970. These data indicate several dramatic changes from the late nineteenth-century experience. For one, this century has been characterized by a growing public share of the economy. Another difference is the increased centralization of spending (see Table 8), though when transfers are considered to be spent at the level received (see Table 9) this centralization is less pronounced. Still, intergovernmental transfers (Table 10) should not be overlooked, since they surely are accompanied by some political preconditions set by the donor government. Thus emerges a public sector increasing its claims on the economy from less than one-eighth of the GNP at the beginning of the century to about one-third today; a public sector budget that was about two-thirds state and local in 1902, but only slightly more than one-third (pre-transfer) nonfederal in 1970 or slightly less than one-half (post-transfer) state-local by 1970; and finally a nonfederal sector that spent seven-eighths of its budget at the local level in 1902 but only two-thirds of this budget by 1970. The impression is that of a rapidly expanding, centralizing government—just the opposite of nineteenth-century fiscal history.

Table 7. Federal, state and local expenditures in constant dollars (1929), 1902 to 1970

Year	Billions of spending			Per capita spending			Percentage of GNP		
	Total	Federal	Nonfederal	Total	Federal	Nonfederal	Total	Federal	Nonfederal
1902	3.2	1.1	2.1	41	14	27	6.8	2.4	4.4
1913	5.0	1.5	3.5	52	16	36	8.0	2.4	5.6
1922	9.5	3.7	5.7	87	35	52	12.6	5.1	7.5
1932	15.4	5.5	10.8	140	44	86	21.3	7.3	14.0
1940	24.0	11.8	13.2	190	90	100	20.3	10.0	10.3
1950	46.5	28.7	17.9	307	189	118	24.7	15.7	9.0
1960	79.6	48.9	30.6	439	270	169	30.1	19.4	10.7
1970	135.5	79.8	56.7	667	389	278	34.1	21.3	12.8

Source: Price index for 1902–22 from U.S. Bureau of the Census, *Historical Statistics of the United States: Colonial Times to 1957* (Washington, D.C.: U.S. Government Printing Office, 1961); 1932–50 from Office of Business Economics (OBE), *U.S. Income and Output* (Washington, D.C.: U.S. Government Printing Office, 1958); 1960 from OBE, *Survey of Current Business* (Washington, D.C.: U.S. Government Printing Office, July, 1964); 1970 from Office of the President, *Economic Report of the President, 1972* (Washington, D.C.: U.S. Government Printing Office, 1972); population data taken from Bureau of the Census, *Statistical Abstract of the United States: 1971* (Washington, D.C.: U.S. Government Printing Office, 1971); government spending to 1950 from Bureau of the Census, *Historical Statistics; 1960* from Bureau of the Census, *Historical Statistics of the United States Colonial Times to 1951; Continuations to 1962 and Revisions* (Washington, D.C.: U.S. Government Printing Office, 1965); 1970 from Bureau of the Census, *Governmental Finances in 1969–70* (Washington, D.C.: U.S. Government Printing Office, 1971); GNP data to 1960 from Bureau of the Census, *Historical Statistics . . . Continuations;* for 1970 from Bureau of the Census, *Statistical Abstract . . . 1971.*

Table 8. Percentage distribution of public expenditures by levels of government, 1902–1970 (Transfers allocated to donor level)

Year	Federal	Non-Federal	State	Local
1902	34.5	65.5	10.8	54.8
1913	30.2	69.8	11.6	58.3
1922	40.5	59.5	13.6	46.0
1932	34.3	65.7	20.6	45.1
1940	49.3	50.7	22.3	28.5
1950	63.7	36.3	18.2	18.1
1960	64.3	35.7	16.5	19.1
1970	62.5	37.5	19.4	18.1

Source: Tax Foundation, *Facts and Figures on Government Finances* (New York: The Foundation, 1971).

Table 15 is instructive here, too. Over the approximately seventy years since 1902, government spending has been rising at the rate of 5.3% per year, while incomes rose at only 3.0%, just the reverse of these rates for the previous thirty years. Breaking the periods into the first 30 years (1902–1932) and last thirty-eight years (1932–1970) it appears that the acceleration has largely taken place in the last four decades: 5.4% versus 7.0% per annum. Removal of defense does seem to change matters slightly. Removing just Department of Defense-type spending, the rate of growth is 5.2% per annum for the 68-year period, with the increase of 5.6% before 1932 and 5.3% after. In other words, defense spending has accelerated in the last forty years, bringing up the total rate in the process. However, using Buchanan's wider definition of defense, the yearly rate over the entire period is 5.5% with the early period at 5.4% but the latter period at 7.2%. Clearly, using this measure, it has been "ci-

Table 9. Percentage distribution of direct public expenditure by levels of government, 1902–1970 (Transfers allocated to recipient level)

Year	Federal	Nonfederal	State	Local
1902	34.1	66.0	8.2	57.7
1913	30.0	69.9	9.0	61.0
1922	39.4	60.7	10.3	50.3
1932	32.5	67.6	16.6	51.0
1940	45.0	55.0	17.4	37.6
1950	60.2	39.9	16.8	24.2
1960	59.8	40.3	14.5	25.6
1970	54.5	45.5	16.5	29.2

Source: See Table 7, this chapter.

Table 10. Intergovernmental transfers in constant 1929 dollars (billions), 1902–1970

Year	Federal to state & local	State to local	Federal grant as % nonfederal spending	State grant as % local spending
1902	.01	.10	.6	5.7
1913	.02	.14	.5	4.8
1922	.12	.32	2.1	7.3
1932	.30	1.03	2.8	14.3
1940	1.04	1.95	7.8	28.4
1950	1.52	2.70	8.5	32.4
1960	3.52	4.74	11.5	32.6
1970	8.91	11.07	15.7	48.2

Source: See Table 7, this chapter.

vilian" expenditures which have risen most rapidly in the last 40 years. Table 11 looks at "civilian" spending (total spending minus Buchanan's war and war-related sum). It is clear that as a share of government "civilian" activities have declined, but as a share of the GNP they still direct one-fourth of the economy's purchasing power as against only one-twentieth at the turn of the century. Another way to put this is that war and war-related expenditures explain about one-twelfth of the growth of government since 1902.

It is also interesting to look at the changes in the composition of government spending since 1902. In Table 12, I have broken spending into five categories following a convention developed by Stubble-bine [25]. The first, "big debate," represents those activities which are controversial according to the so-called social imbalance hypotheses. By the latter is meant those activities which are alleged to produce benefits over and above those which would be captured by private sellers

Table 11. "Civilian" spending in the public sector

Year	As % of all government spending	As % of GNP
1902	78.2	5.4
1913	80.8	6.5
1922	70.1	8.9
1932	76.1	16.5
1940	82.2	17.6
1950	63.5	16.2
1960	62.5	19.4
1970	70.0	25.4

Source: See Table 7, this chapter.

Table 12. Government spending by Stubblebine's categorization as a % of total public spending and GNP, 1902–1970 (as % of GNP in parentheses)

Year	"Big Debate"	Government housekeeping	Transfer excluding interest	Interest	National security	Total
1902	40.9(2.8)	36.3(2.5)	4.5(0.3)	4.5(0.3)	13.6(1.0)	100(6.8)
1913	40.2(3.3)	40.2(3.3)	6.1(0.5)	6.1(0.5)	9.1(0.8)	100(8.0)
1922	41.2(5.2)	28.2(3.5)	7.1(0.9)	15.6(1.9)	9.4(1.2)	100(12.8)
1932	46.5(9.8)	27.3(5.8)	9.1(1.9)	10.1(2.1)	6.1(1.3)	100(21.2)
1940	47.5(9.6)	26.0(5.2)	5.9(1.1)	12.8(2.6)	12.8(2.6)	100(21.0)
1950	33.0(8.2)	15.8(3.9)	18.3(4.5)	7.0(1.7)	26.2(6.5)	100(24.8)
1960	30.2(9.1)	14.4(4.3)	17.4(5.2)	6.2(1.8)	30.8(9.3)	100(30.0)
1970	34.7(11.8)	17.4(5.9)	18.0(6.1)	5.6(1.9)	25.5(8.6)	100(33.8)

Source: See Table 7, this chapter.

and purchasers and hence are publicly provided. The extent of this spill-over is the subject of some disagreement; hence the term, "big debate." Activities in this category are education, highways, welfare, hospitals and health care, local sanitation, parks and recreation, natural resources, housing and community development. The second category, "government housekeeping," is less controversial perhaps and covers the more traditional kinds of spending: general control (courts, etc.), canals and navigation, postal services, fire and police, local utilities and liquor stores. "Transfers" refer to farm stabilization payments, veterans' benefits, and social insurance trusts. "Interest" represents payment of interest for the national and nonfederal debt. "National security" is the narrowly defined notion of defense. The patterns of this classification over time are unfortunately not entirely clear. "Big debate" appears to have fallen slightly and "government housekeeping" by quite a bit since 1902. "Transfers" have increased markedly, as has "national security." "Interest" has remained fairly constant.

Tables 13 and 14 represent two alternative classifications suggested by Abramovitz and Eliasberg [1]. In the first, expenditures are broken up into four classifications: "Protective services" (police and fire, general control and financial administration, national defense and international relations, veterans, and interest); "environmental services" (highways, other transportation, sanitation, natural resources, parks and recreation); "personal services" (education, welfare, health and hospitals, housing and community redevelopment, farm subsidies); and "trading" (post office and utilities). In the second classification there are only two: "traditional" (all protective and trading, environmental minus parks, and education) and "modern" (personal services minus education but plus parks). On the basis of the first classification it would appear that the protective services' share of government has remained the same; environmental has declined, as has trading, but personal services has increased its relative size of the budget. Using the second classification it appears there has been a marked switch favoring the modern services since 1932, which some believe to be the beginning of the welfare state [12].

Table 15 summarizes the growth rates for various levels of government and spending categories for the period 1870 to 1970 and for several subperiods. Since the table is self-explanatory I will do no more than point out a few interesting trends for just the last decade. First of all it appears that the nonfederal sector is beginning to grow faster than the federal sector (but not when the latter excludes defense and war-related activities). Second, educational growth in this period was faster than in any other period. Third, welfare also grew at an unprecedented rate, a fact causing not some little debate during the last several years. Finally, the

Table 13. Abramovitz and Eliasberg's four-category classification of spending as a % of all government expenditures, 1902–1970

Year	Protective services	Environmental services	Personal services	Trading services
1902	43.6	19.2	23.6	13.6
1913	34.8	24.1	25.6	15.5
1922	40.9	23.2	25.3	10.5
1932	36.1	23.2	29.3	11.4
1940	27.9	27.7	32.5	11.9
1950	48.2	13.1	30.5	8.2
1960	51.9	13.8	27.4	6.9
1970	46.3	12.4	34.9	6.4

Source: See Table 7, this chapter.

total growth of 5.1% per year was less than for the 1900–1972 period and, when coupled with a 3.8% yearly growth for the GNP, meant that the public sector's share of the nation's income (or claims thereon) rose only by 1.3% per year, whereas for the period 1902–1970 it rose an annual average of 2.3%. Of course, 1960–1970 is too short a period to extrapolate safely, but one wonders if it signifies a permanent reduction in the relative growth of the public sector. (At the time of publication the answer to this last question appears to be negative.)

Two other measures of government activity over time are given in Tables 16 and 17. In Table 16 exhaustive spending is examined over time as a percentage of all public spending and of the GNP. Exhaustive expenditure is defined as actual payments for the scarce resources used in the production of public services and it excludes all transfer payments such as

Table 14. Abramovitz and Eliasberg's two-category classification of spending as a % of all public expenditures, 1902–1970

Year	Traditional	Modern
1902	91.3	8.7
1913	92.3	7.7
1922	93.5	6.5
1932	89.8	10.2
1940	82.3	17.7
1950	84.8	15.2
1960	87.1	12.9
1970	85.0	15.0

Source: See Table 7, this chapter.

Table 15. Annual rates of various expenditures (in 1929 constant dollars) and other items

Category	1870–1902	1870–1970	1902–1970	1902–1932	1932–1970	1960–1970
Population	2.3	1.6	1.4	1.5	1.3	1.2
GNP	5.5	3.7	3.0	1.1	4.2	3.8
All government spending	3 to 4	4 to 5	5.3	5.4	7.0	5.1
All non-defense spending	–	–	5.2	5.6	5.3	6.0
All "civilian" spending	–	–	5.5	5.4	7.2	6.6
Federal spending	3.3	5.3	6.1	5.3	7.1	4.8
Defense spending	3.3	5.6	6.6	3.4	9.5	3.9
War and war-related spending	2.3	4.8	5.8	4.6	6.2	3.9
Federal nondefense spending	3.5	4.7	5.9	5.9	6.1	6.4
Federal "civilian"	4.0	5.7	6.6	4.7	8.3	8.4
Post Office spending	–	–	3.6	4.8	2.8	4.6
All state and local spending	3 to 4	4 to 5	4.7	5.4	4.4	6.2
Nonfederal education	–	–	5.4	5.1	5.0	7.6
"Big debate"	–	–	6.1	4.2	4.7	6.4
"Government housekeeping"	–	–	4.3	2.8	4.2	7.0
Education	–	–	5.5	5.1	5.2	7.7
Welfare	–	–	6.4	6.9	6.4	11.3
"Protective"	–	–	5.3	4.8	5.9	3.6
"Environmental"	–	–	4.5	6.0	3.4	3.9
"Personal"	–	–	5.8	6.0	5.7	7.2
"Trading"	–	–	4.1	4.7	3.6	4.0
"Traditional"	–	–	5.1	13.0	5.0	4.2
"Modern"	–	–	6.2	5.6	6.4	6.3

Source: See Table 7, this chapter.

Table 16. Exhaustive spending as % of public spending and GNP

Year	Government outlays for payrolls and purchases as % total public spending	Exhaustive spending as % of GNP
1903	86	5.8
1929	82	17.5
1939	67	13.5
1949	73	18.0
1959	73	22.0
1969	74	25.1

Source: 1903 to 1949: "Government outlays" column from Solomon Fabricant, assisted by Robert E. Lipsey, *The Trend of Government Activity in the United States Since 1900* (New York: National Bureau of Economic Research, Inc., 1952); "Exhaustive spending" column produced by multiplying figures in "Government outlays" column by "Percentage of GNP, Total" column of Table 7, this chapter. 1959 and 1969: See Table 7.

welfare, social security, and interest on the public debt. It is, in fact, the sum of public payrolls and direct government purchases. Using this definition, public spending has grown by 5.1% per year as opposed to 5.3% per annum for all government spending reflecting the increasing role over time of transfers, welfare, etc. Viewed in absolute terms, the 0.2% per annum differential between exhaustive and total spending may appear negligible. Its effect is not, however, as the second column of Table 16 indicates: in 1969 exhaustive spending made direct claims of one-quarter of GNP whereas all spending was slightly over one-third. Put another way, increased transfers, welfare payments and other nonresource-using expenditures explain about 20% of the increase in total government spending over the last seven decades.

Table 17 gives yet another widely employed measure of the direct resource usage by governments, public employment. Since the latter is a fairly good proxy for direct spending (at a given point of time) its breakdown in terms of percentage of the labor force employment gives an accurate notion in relative terms of the direct claims by government on the economy taken as a whole.[3] This measure suggests that the public sector's direct employment of real resources has risen from 6% of real income in 1900 to almost 20% in 1970, a more than trebling of its importance in resource usage.

Thus a pattern completely contrary to the nineteenth-century experience emerges for this century: an expansion of the public sector relative to the private sector; a relative increase in spending at the federal as compared to the nonfederal level; and to a lesser extent, an increase in state

3. Borcherding [4] also establishes that there is a close correlation between public employment and public expenditures.

Table 17. Public employment by levels and categories as a % of the labor force

	1900	1910	1920	1930	1940	1950	1960	1970
Federal	1.8	1.9	3.2	2.6	4.3	7.5	8.3	8.3
Defense	.9	.6	1.8	1.1	2.2	5.1	6.2	5.6
Post Office and enterprise	.6	.8	.8	.9	1.1	1.1	1.0	1.1
Other	.3	.4	.6	.6	1.0	1.4	1.1	1.6
Nonfederal	4.2	4.5	5.0	7.2	7.9	7.6	9.6	11.9
Education	2.4	2.3	2.5	3.3	3.4	3.2	4.3	5.9
Enterprises	.2	.2	.2	.3	.4	.5	.6	.7
Other	1.6	2.0	2.3	3.6	1.6	4.0	4.7	5.3
All government	6.0	6.4	8.2	9.8	12.2	15.2	17.9	20.1
Total labor force (millions in full-time equivalent units)	18.9	25.7	31.5	33.8	36.5	48.7	57.6	71.6

Source: 1900 to 1930 from multitudinous sources and primary data cited in Thomas E. Borcherding, "The Growth of Non-Federal Public Employment in the United States, 1900 to 1963," Ph.D. dissertation, Duke University, 1965; for 1930–1970 from OBE, Survey of Current Business, July, 1964; and Bureau of the Census, Historical Statistics, 1961.

spending relative to that of local government. Traditional activities as a share of the public sector declined and growth was significant in many activities that were of little importance (in terms of dollar spending) at the beginning of the century. Defense was an important contributor to this growth, but nondefense and "civilian" activities were of even greater consequence. Only in the last decade does it appear that some changes may be occurring: a reduction in the rate of growth and a slight decrease in the degree of centralization. All spending levels and categories, however, still remained at an extremely high level.

One question comes to mind after surveying this growth: can it continue? Of course, no economist can with much certainty make such a prediction since a myriad of factors are involved, most of which we do not yet well understand. I can, however, discuss what has happened in other countries very briefly and comment on a couple of the available long-term public spending forecasts of the past. By so doing the reader can (1) form a notion of where we stand in public-private spending vis à vis some other wealthy countries, and (2) see how accurately in the past economists understood where the public sector was actually going.

Table 18 compares spending in the United States with five other relatively wealthy and industrialized countries. In terms of direct resource absorption by government, the United States was second only to Sweden. In terms of all spending, exhaustive and transfers, it was next to Japan, the lowest. The difference is in the transfer category. The United States transfers less of its national income among its citizens than any of the other countries excepting Japan. If one believes that the fiscal behavior of other developed countries is relevant to the American experience, it could be that in the future we will be expanding the public sector still

Table 18. Taxes and public spending as a % of GNP in various countries for 1967 (nondefense in parentheses)

Country	Exhaustive spending[a]	Transfers	Total[b]
France	14 (12)	23	39 (37)
Great Britain	17 (14)	10	31 (28)
Japan	9 (8)	6	20 (19)
Sweden	21 (17)	12	41 (37)
West Germany	17 (13)	19	35 (31)
United States	20 (16)	7	28 (24)

Source: Organization for Economic Cooperation and Development, *National Accounts Statistics, 1958–67* (Washington D.C.: U.S. Government Printing Office, 1968); defense ratios from Arthur S. Banks, *Cross-Polity Time Series Data* (Cambridge, Mass.: M.I.T. Press, 1971).

a. Excludes capital expenditures.

b. Includes Social Security taxes.

further, though largely in the direction of providing income redistribution. Pressures for this in the form of various "welfare reform" packages and guaranteed income plans are rapidly developing.

As to past long-term predictions, I could locate only two. In 1959 the Committee for Economic Development commissioned two studies: *Trends in Public Expenditures in the Next Decade,* and *Paying for Better Public Schools.* Both studies projected public spending to 1968 on the assumption that "[t]he political attitudes toward expenditures will not undergo a revolution" (*Trends*). Herbert Stein said that Professor Otto Eckstein's study was a "[c]areful, comprehensive and sophisticated appraisal of the quantitative implications of various possible policies and developments [that] provide[d] valuable new assistance for thinking about expenditure and tax decisions that lie ahead" (*Trends*). It was, unfortunately, a very poor forecast.

Eckstein estimated (and I have adjusted for his slight underestimation of inflation) that in 1968 the federal budget would most likely be $121.3 billion, $139.8 billion at the highest; state and local spending was estimated to be $55.3 billion; so the total would most likely be $176.4 billion, $185.1 billion on the high side. In fact, the budget in 1968 was $166.4 billion for the federal government, $116.2 billion for state and local governments and $282.6 billion in total. This means that Eckstein underestimated by 50 to 70%. Even allowing for the Vietnam buildup, which he could not have foreseen, he was still off by almost the same range in nondefense public spending.

In the education study the authors (not mentioned) argued that by the school year 1969–1970 we would be spending about $29 billion on schools. In fact, outlays on education were $56 billion, a 95% underestimate! Clearly, for economists the past is not always a clear guide to the future. Could it be, therefore, that public spending will continue to grow yearly at 5.3% as it has done in the past or even higher, although for the last decade it has increased only 5.1% per annum? Given our state-of-the-art forecasts of the past, one cannot honestly say no. Should the long term 5.3% annual rate persist, however, 40% of our society's income will be channelled through government, excluding Social Security, by the end of this decade.

Fiscal Perversity and the Displacement-Concentration Hypothesis

What happens to government spending during the business cycle? According to the conventional wisdom known as the Fiscal Perversity hypothesis, state and local governments exacerbate the business cycle by procyclical spending while the federal government's spending is contra-cyclical, hence, stabilizing.[4] But is this really true?

Instead of observing spending over the cycle to test this proposition I will use public employment as a proxy. I do so for two good reasons: First, employment is available as monthly data since World War 2, whereas spending is only available quarterly. Second, and more important, I want an index of exhaustive spending, but quarterly spending figures do not permit segregating out only exhaustive expenditures. The reason for excluding transfers is simply that there is no evidence to sug-gest that they have any effects whatsoever on aggregate demand. This follows, since savings rates do not appear to differ significantly among various income groups [16], Keynes's hypothesis of Diminishing Mar-ginal Propensity to Consume notwithstanding [20]. Thus, if one dollar is taxed away from A, a rich person, and given to B, a poor individual, the net effect on aggregate spending is not significantly different from zero. Since public employment is a good short-run indicator of exhaustive spending, I feel secure in using it as its proxy.

Table 19 indicates behavior for downswings in economic activity only, since there is no apparent pattern for the upswings. It appears the Fiscal Perversity hypothesis is falsified in practically every period of economic decline: state and local activity always moved against the cycle and in all but one period, the 1923–1924 recession, federal activity has been either procyclical or of negligible consequence.

Another interesting but also insubstantial hypothesis is that offered by two British economists, Alan Peacock and Jack Wiseman [22]. They believe that under normal conditions of peace and economic stability, public expenditure changes are extremely limited, bounded by what individuals consider to be the "tolerable" limits of taxation.[5] When a major crisis threatens the community, however, people do not object at all to supporting measures specifically designed to eliminate or alleviate the calamity. During this crisis period people's thresholds of tax tolerance permanently rise. After the crisis ends, however, the level of expenditure does not recede to precrisis levels, but instead noncrisis activities are

4. Hansen and Perloff [18] are "classic" here. They state that "state and local govern-mental units have usually followed the swings of the business cycle, from crest to trough, spending and building in prosperity periods and contracting their activities during depres-sion. . . ." They cite no firm evidence to support their hypothesis.

5. The hypothesis of tolerable limits to taxation is quite widespread in the literature of public finance, though its bases are more metaphysical than behavioral. Perhaps the best known discussion of "toleration" limits is found in Clark [9]. The tolerance hypothesis had its origins well before Peacock and Wiseman's [22] or Clark's discussions, however. Bastable [2] discusses and severely criticizes it. It is, to be sure, part-and-parcel of the whole fiscal illusion argument which Charles Goetz analyzes in "Fiscal Illusion in State-Local Finance," in this volume.

Table 19. Relative change in public employments during business cycle downswing (% on yearly basis)

National Bureau of Economic Research reference cycle period	All employment	Private	Public	Federal	Nonfederal
1920–1921[a]	−10.5	−11.6	+0.3	−10.8	+7.0
1923–1924[a]	− 2.2	− 2.9	+4.5	+ 2.3	+5.3
1926–1927[a]	− 0.4	− 0.8	+3.1	0.0	+4.1
1929–1932[a]	−24.6	−27.6	+2.7	− 1.3	+3.6
1937–1938[a]	− 6.6	− 7.1	+3.4	− 0.5	+2.8
Nov. 1948–Sept. 1949	− 3.8	− 4.8	+2.6	− 2.5	+5.1
July 1953–Aug. 1954	− 3.1	− 4.1	+2.8	− 4.8	+6.7
July 1957–Apr. 1958	− 5.5	− 6.8	+2.7	− 2.9	+4.9
Apr. 1960–Feb. 1961	− 2.6	− 3.8	+1.5	− 7.0	+5.1
Nov. 1969–Dec. 1970	− 0.2	− 0.9	+3.6	− 0.4	+4.7

Source: Cycles: National Bureau of Economic Research Cycles – 1920–1938, Wesley C. Mitchell, *What Happens During Business Cycles* (New York: National Bureau of Economic Research, Inc., 1951); 1948–1954, Geoffrey H. Moore, *Business Cycle Indicators,* 2 vols. (New York: National Bureau of Economic Research, Inc., 1961); 1957–58 and 1960–61 privately estimated; 1969–70, Federal Reserve Bank of St. Louis, *National Economic Trends* (St. Louis, Mo.: The Bank, November 22, 1972); employment: U.S. Bureau of Labor Statistics (BLS), *Employment and Earnings: 1902–1962* (Washington, D.C.: U.S. Government Printing Office, 1963); BLS, *Employment and Earnings* (Washington, D.C.: U.S. Government Printing Office, Jan., Feb., and March, 1971).

a. Monthly data unavailable.

enlarged in scope by expansion-minded politicians and bureaucrats. This is known as the Displacement Effect. For similar reasons, they argue that activities are centralized during the crises since the top level of government is best able to cope with a society-wide cataclysm. This is called the Concentration Effect. Using British data their hypothesis is not rejected. However, Davies [10] has recently tested the hypothesis for several other Western countries and finds no evidence to support this theory. Using government employment data I found none for the period 1900–1963 [4]. This is easily explained. It appears that the expansionary and centralizing trends in nondefense activities were present well before either World War 2 or the Great Depression. After these crises the spending returned to the long-term growth path as did the centralizing tendency that one might have predicted had these calamities not ever taken place. World War 1, the Korean conflict and the height of the Vietnam action seemed to have had no effect either. Thus, over the long run, growth rates of nondefense, nonrecession type activities are fairly stable as has been the rate of centralization.

The Public Sector and the Growth of the Service Industry

It has often been argued that as an economy grows it goes through three stages of development. At the initial stage it appears that most of the activity is concentrated in agriculture, fisheries, and natural resource extraction. This follows, since with limited human and physical capital relative to an abundance of "land," the returns to these primary activities are fairly high as compared to more capital-intensive activities. Later on manufacturing, the secondary sector, develops as markets broaden, facilitating a more sophisticated division of labor. Finally, at a still more advanced stage of economic development, services become important since they represent supplies of intermediate factors used by the primary and secondary levels of the economy as well as final consumer goods.[6]

Colin Clark [8] presents massive evidence which suggests the plausibility of this hypothesis, though because of foreign trade there are plenty of exceptions to this rule of development, for instance, countries with high per capita incomes that have skipped the second stage such as Denmark, Holland and New Zealand. Given a large enough trading area, however, the proposition seems fairly secure.

Fuchs [17] has suggested three specific reasons to explain the growth of the service sector for the United States. First, there has been a growth in demand for service because of the steady rise of real incomes. Second, as the demand for goods grows, the demand for services necessarily increases as well since the latter are integral factors in the production and distribution of the former (education, banking and insurance, retail trade, etc.). And finally, the fact that productivity has grown more slowly in the services (1.25% per year) than in the goods (3% per annum) means that the price of services rises over time. Since service demands seem to be price inelastic, the use of real resources to produce them will necessarily increase.[7]

Stigler [24] argues that government should be classified as a service so it too should be expected to increase along with private services. Table 20 shows the Census' classification of government employment for 1940, 1950, and 1960 by industrial classification (unfortunately, data for 1970 had not been released at the time of the writing of this essay). It appears that Stigler is correct since the bulk of these employment classifications are services by Census' definitions and seem to be becoming more so over time. It is instructive, therefore, to compare the growth of public and private services against that of the entire economy. Unfortunately, spending data by sectors before 1929 are totally lacking. Employment statistics are available, however, and as I said before, they

6. The hypothesis is really quite ancient. Sir William Petty is its first known expositor and stated the proposition as a "law" or regularity in his *Political Arithmetic* (1671) fully over a century before Adam Smith made more or less the same argument in *The Wealth of Nations* (1776).

7. Baumol [3] has a detailed discussion of this hypothesis. It can be shown that if a demand function is price inelastic, a rise in price will lead to a larger total amount of spending on the commodity, other effects held constant.

Table 20. Percentage distribution of public employment by industries: 1940, 1950 and 1960

Industry group	1940	1950	1960
Goods producing			
Agriculture	.5	.3	.2
Forestry and fisheries	.6	.4	.4
Mining	.1	–	–
Construction	11.0	5.1	4.7
Manufacturing	2.9	2.0	2.2
Transportation	4.1	5.4	4.3
Total	20.0	13.0	12.0
Service producing			
Trade	.3	.5	.5
Banking and finance	.5	.8	.7
Personal and business services	.4	.6	.6
Professional and related	35.6	31.1	34.1
Public administration	43.0	53.6	52.0
Total	80.0	87.0	88.0

Source: 1940: U.S. Bureau of the Census, *Reports of the 16th Census of Population, Vol. III: The Labor Force* (Washington, D.C.: U.S. Government Printing Office, 1943); 1950: Bureau of the Census, *Reports of the 17th Census of Population, Vol. II: Characteristics of the Population* (Washington, D.C.: U.S. Government Printing Office, 1953); 1960: Bureau of the Census, *Reports of the 18th Census of Population, 1960, Vol. I: Characteristics of the Population* (Washington, D.C.: U.S. Government Printing Office, 1964).

provide a reasonably good first-approximation to the level of exhaustive activities. Table 21 indicates employment data for public and private services and the entire labor force for the last seventy years. In 1900 (using full- and part-time measures of employment) only 1 worker in 25 was employed by government and 1 in 4 by the private services sector. By 1970 1 in 7 workers were employed by government and 2 in 5 by the private services sector. Clearly both sectors grew, but the annual growth of government was at a much faster annual rate (3.5% for government as opposed to 2.2% for private services). This is indicated in the increase in the share of government employees in all service employment from 16% in 1900 to 29% in 1970.

It is evident, therefore, that Petty, Smith, Clark, Stigler, and others are correct that development is associated with the growth of the services industry, since the economy devoted 30% of its labor resources in 1900 to service production and by 1970 it had risen to 50%. What is at issue is why over the last seventy years the ratio of public to total service activity has almost doubled.

Table 21. Service employment in the United States 1900–1970 (millions of persons in full and part-time terms)

Year	Total labor force	Private services	Public services	Public share of all service employment (%)
1900	27.0	6.9	1.1	16.0
1910	35.6	9.8	1.7	17.8
1920	40.2	11.4	2.5	22.3
1930	45.0	17.2	3.2	18.7
1940	48.0	20.1	3.6	18.1
1950	61.6	25.6	6.6	25.8
1960	73.1	31.2	11.0	28.4
1970	85.9	32.1	12.3	29.0

Source: Service employment, government employment, and total labor force for 1900 to 1950 from George J. Stigler, *Trends in Employment in the Service Industries* (Princeton, N.J.: Princeton University Press for the National Bureau of Economic Research, Inc., 1956); service employment, 1960 and 1970, OBE, *Survey of Current Business,* July, 1972; labor force and public employment from Bureau of the Census, *Statistical Abstract of the United States: 1971.*

Bureaucracy and "Do-It-Yourself"

In an important new book William A. Niskanen [21] claims, among other things, that public activities are becoming more bureaucratized. By this he means that civil servants are becoming increasingly more important in the production of government services. Far from being passive, Niskanen argues, bureaucrats wish to have a larger control over public spending and want to reduce competition among each other and, a fortiori, from private supply sources. It is the latter source on which I have some data.

There is, of course, little intrinsic reason why most publicly financed activities should be produced by the government. Letting bids to the private sector is a real (and often efficient) alternative. Of course, difficulty in writing contracts and enforcing their terms may make private supply of public services too costly, but some proportion of activities could, no doubt, be privately supplied. Is there any reason to believe that this proportion should change over time? Do bureaucracies have a comparative advantage in supplying services that are increasingly "modern" (to use Abramovitz and Eliasberg's terminology) but involve transfers? Perhaps so, and this deserves further research.

Table 22 suggests that with the exception of the defense sector, which relies heavily on private contractors, there has been a slight tendency to produce goods "in house." It is also interesting to note that this effect is extremely small at the nondefense federal level, whereas at the state and

Table 22. Percentage of exhaustive government expenditures provided by the private sector

		Total excluding defense		
Year	All governments	All	Federal	Nonfederal
1903	51	50	48	52
1913	52	52	39	57
1963	54	55	50	43
1970	48	45	47	44

Source: 1903 and 1913, from Solomon Fabricant, assisted by Robert E. Lipsey, *The Trend of Government Activity in the United States Since 1900* (New York: National Bureau of Economic Research, Inc., 1952); 1963 and 1970, U.S. Department of Labor, *Manpower Reports: Resources, Utilization, and Training* (Washington, D.C.: U.S. Government Printing Office, 1964 and 1971).

local level it is more pronounced. Perhaps this is explained by the fact that civil service was already well entrenched at the federal level by the early part of this century, whereas it was exceedingly weak among state and local governments. In any case, for the most recent period it appears that federal spending may have moved very slightly toward self-supply, whereas the state and local ratio has remained fairly stable. All this is only suggestive since this factor is only one of many affecting the efficiency of production of public services.[8]

Concluding Comments

A number of disjointed, but I hope not uninteresting, facts concerning American fiscal history have been cited in this essay. In addition, a few ad hoc historical interpretations have been questioned. Although plausible hypotheses for the growth of public expenditures for this century are offered in my companion paper and in some others in this volume, other phenomena have not been explained. For instance, why, if my facts are correct, was the public sector's relative size contracting and decentralization occurring in the last third of the nineteenth century while the opposite seems to be the case since 1900? Further, what explains the change in the patterns of spending if one uses the kinds of categories suggested by Stubblebine or Abramovitz and Eliasberg? If, in fact, the public sector is becoming more "bureaucratic," what factors explain the division of labor between private contractors and self-supply of government services? I believe that these questions merit inquiry. I hope to answer some of them

8. Robert M. Spann, in "Public versus Private Provision of Governmental Services," in this volume, discusses some other important factors that affect efficiency of public agencies.

at a later date and I invite other interested scholars to join me in this search for a better understanding of these issues.

References

1. Abramovitz, Moses, and Vera F. Eliasberg. *The Growth of Public Employ-ment in Great Britain.* Princeton, N.J.: Princeton University Press for the National Bureau of Economic Research, 1957.
2. Bastable, C. F. *Public Finance,* 3rd ed. New York: Macmillan and Co., 1903.
3. Baumol, William J. "The Macroeconomics of Unbalanced Growth: The Anat-omy of the Urban Crisis." *American Economic Review* (June, 1967).
4. Borcherding, Thomas E. "The Growth of Non-Federal Public Employment in the United States, 1900 to 1963." Ph.D. dissertation, Duke University, 1965.
5. _____, and Robert T. Deacon. "The Demand for the Services of Non-Fed-eral Governments." *American Economic Review* (Dec., 1972).
6. Buchanan, James M. *The Public Finances,* 3rd ed. Homewood, Ill.: Rich-ard D. Irwin, 1970.
7. Carson, Daniel. "Changes in the Industrial Composition of Manpower Since the Civil War." In National Bureau of Economic Research, *Studies in In-come and Wealth.* Vol. 9. New York: National Bureau of Economic Re-search, Inc., 1949.
8. Clark, Colin. *The Conditions of Economic Progress.* London: Macmillan and Co., 1940.
9. _____. "Public Finance and Changes in the Value of Money." *Economic Journal* (Dec., 1945).
10. Davies, David G. "The Concentration Process and the Growing Importance of Non-Central Governments in Federal States." *Public Policy* (fall, 1970).
11. Davis, Lance E., and John Legler. "Government in the American Economy, 1815–1902: A Quantitative Study." *Journal of Economic History* (Dec., 1966).
12. _____, and Douglass C. North. *Institutional Change and American Eco-nomic Growth.* Cambridge: Cambridge University Press, 1971.
13. Edwards, Abba P., for the U.S. Bureau of the Census. *Comparative Occupa-tion Statistics for the United States, 1870 to 1940; Sixteenth Dicennial Cen-sus of the United States: 1940, Population.* Washington, D.C.: U.S. Gov-ernment Printing Office, 1943.
14. Fabricant, Solomon. "The Changing Industrial Distribution of Gainful Work-ers: Comments on the Decennial Statistics, 1820–1940." In National Bu-reau of Educational Research, *Studies in Income and Wealth,* Vol. 9. New York: National Bureau of Economic Research, Inc., 1949.
15. _____, assisted by Robert E. Lipsey. *The Trend of Government Activity in the United States Since 1900.* New York: National Bureau of Economic Research, Inc., 1952.
16. Friedman, Milton. *A Theory of the Consumption Function.* Princeton, N.J.: Princeton University Press for the National Bureau of Economic Research, 1957.
17. Fuchs, Victor. *The Service Economy.* New York: Columbia University Press for the National Bureau of Economic Research, Inc., 1968.
18. Hansen, Alvin H., and Harvey S. Perloff. *State and Local Finance and the National Economy.* New York: W. W. Norton and Co., 1944.

19. Kendrick, John W., assisted by Maude R. Peck. *Productivity Trends in the United States*. New York: National Bureau of Economic Research, Inc., 1961.
20. Keynes, John Maynard. *The General Theory of Employment, Interest and Money*. New York: Harcourt, Brace, 1936.
21. Niskanen, William A. *Bureaucracy and Representative Government*. Chicago: Aldine-Atherton, 1971.
22. Peacock, Alan T., and Jack Wiseman. *The Growth of Public Expenditure in the United Kingdom*. Princeton, N.J.: Princeton University Press for the National Bureau of Economic Research, 1961.
23. Rees, Albert. *Real Wages in Manufacturing, 1890–1914*. Princeton, N.J.: Princeton University Press for the National Bureau of Economic Research, Inc., 1961.
24. Stigler, George J. *Trends in Employment in the Service*. Princeton, N.J.: Princeton University Press for the National Bureau of Economic Research, 1956.
25. Stubblebine, William Craig. "The Social Imbalance Hypothesis." Ph.D. dissertation, University of Virginia, 1963.
26. Studenski, Paul, and Hermann E. Kroos. *Financial History of the United States*. New York: McGraw-Hill Book Co., 1952.

3. The Sources of Growth of Public Expenditures in the United States, 1902–1970   *Thomas E. Borcherding*

Since the turn of the century, at least, the public sector in the United States has assumed an increasingly important role in the conduct of the economy and society. One important index of this incursion is the growth of public spending. It is the goal of this paper to draw conclusions from the empirical literature on this topic[1] and to determine the contribution that each of the relevant factors has made to this growth over the past seven decades. These estimates, though at best crude approximations, are nonetheless useful since they suggest questions that need to be pursued if we are to understand better the process that brought about this growth.

The growth with which we are concerned is nothing short of phenomenal. In 1902 total government spending was about $1.7 billion; by 1970 this total had risen to $333 billion, an increase by a factor of almost 200 (19,500 percent), or by 7.8 percent per year. This estimate is a gross overstatement, however, since inflation is responsible for two-thirds of the change. To correct for this, an adjustment by a price index is required. Using constant 1929 dollars (and I will continue to do so for the rest of the paper), the real rise in public spending was from $3.2 billion in 1902 to $112.6 billion in 1970, an increase of about 4300 percent or an annual growth rate of 5.3 percent.

My purpose is to explain as much of this increase as possible, based upon our current understanding of the determinants of public expenditures. As we will see, these determinants can be analyzed using economic

Source note: I would like to thank my former colleagues in the Non-Market Bureaucracy Seminar at the Center for Study of Public Choice at Virginia Tech who read this and whose own works are presented in this volume. I was financially assisted in my work by the Earhart Foundation of Ann Arbor and the Foundation for Research in Economics and Education of Los Angeles.

1. See the bibliography at the end of the paper for a fairly complete listing of the available research on the subject. In the discussion that follows I have attempted to be selective. Hence, a hypothesis is not discussed if it appears to be lacking in evidence. An example of such a hypothesis is the so-called concentration-displacement theory of Peacock and Wiseman [30], which Davies [10] has shown to be without foundation. Also, changes in "tastes" are not discussed since no means of operationalizing a test to detect such perturbations in preferences or in measuring their effects on spending can be accomplished with the current tools at our disposal, social psychology notwithstanding.

theory, just as is commonly done for private goods and services where industry studies revolve around factors which alter supply and demand.

The answers to five questions will be sought in this study. First, has the supply price of government services become cheaper or dearer over time, and how has this affected total spending? Second, how has the rise in the incomes of the decision-making units affected output demand and spending in the public sector? Third, how has the increase in population size of each unit affected the level of spending? Fourth, to what extent has increased economic interdependency associated with economic development caused private markets to "fail," and in turn, led to an increased demand for public activity? Finally, to what extent have the change in the fiscal constitution, the rise in the power of special interests, and increased monopoly power of the governmental bureaucracies added to public spending?

I hope to answer these questions attributing to each factor its quantitative contribution to the change in government spending whenever the theory and data permit. The reader is forewarned, however, that both the theory and data are sufficiently crude that the numerical estimates offered are best interpreted as rough indicators rather than precise imputations.

Price and the Demand for Public Services

When an economist talks of price changes he is always careful to differentiate between the changes in the level of all prices from changes in relative (the ratio of) prices. Changes in the level of all prices caused by purely monetary phenomenon need not alter the basic underlying decision functions in real terms, given sufficient time for all participants in the economic "game" to apprise themselves of this change. Thus, a rational individual with a nominal income of $100, facing prices for X and Y, the only goods he purchases, of $5 and $10 respectively will not behave differently when his nominal income rises to $200 but the unit prices of X and Y are twice as high. In short, people are assumed to be interested only in the real (relative) prices, i.e., what their incomes will actually buy.

Now it may be true that inflation can "fool all of the people, some of the time," but probably not indefinitely.[2] Thus it seems unlikely that the real cost of government finance can long be hidden or understated by

2. Recent evidence on the instability of the so-called Phillips Curve seems to bear out the fact that people's "money illusions" are not permanent. Recent unpublished and independent work on the so-called debt illusion by Galen D. Burghardt, University of Massachusetts, and Levis Cochin, University of Washington, suggests that even future tax liabilities of government expenditure financed by bonds sold to the public are discounted in a remarkably short time. People, it appears, do learn though supporters of the notion of fiscal illusion are numerous and the hypothesis is far from disproven. See, for example, the paper by Charles J. Goetz, "Fiscal Illusion and Public Spending," in this volume.

resorting to inflationary finance.[3] It seems prudent to say, therefore, that real government expenditures have not, over the long run, been influenced by the purely monetary phenomenon of inflation.[4] Nonetheless, this is hardly the last word on this topic. Research into the long-run consequences of inflation on the real spending of government is certainly to be encouraged.[5]

Changes in the ratio of prices of government services relative to private goods and services are another matter. Such changes will be subject to the Law of Demand which says that when the ratio of the price of X to the price of Y rises, the consumer will attempt to substitute away from X and in favor of Y. The inverse is true when that ratio falls. Thus, the Law of Demand is depicted as describing a negative correlation between the real price of X (how much Y must be given up per unit of X) and the quantity of X desired.

Exactly who the chooser(s) is (are) when it comes to the public sector is a matter of some scholarly conjecture. But many economists, assuming that our system is reasonably representative of citizen interest, believe it reflects the preferences of the so-called median or average voter as transmitted to his elected representative. Actually, this is not crucial in this section, since whomever the system serves can be safely assumed to behave according to the Law of Demand. Empirical evidence for this proposition at the nonfederal level has been offered by Barr and Davis [3],

3. Technically this is not quite true. If the government persisted in financing deficits by monetizing its debt and did so at rates faster than anticipated by private parties, the amount of resources it could appropriate to itself by purchasing resources with soon-to-be-devalued fiat money from uninformed sellers might be large. This would, however, require a galloping rate of inflation of the South American variety completely unknown in the United States in this century. Thus, it is a curiosity of little relevance for the last seventy years of U.S. fiscal history.

4. This is not to say that in the short run governments are not tempted to inflate in order to finance budgets that would otherwise be unacceptably high to taxpayers. My point is that in the long run people learn of this strategy and take appropriate precautions. It can be shown, however, that even with perfect anticipation some revenues will accrue to the state, an equivalent to a tax on so-called high-powered money balances. This revenue can be shown to be rather small for the kind of steady state inflations we have experienced in this century. In any case, once realized, this tax is no different than any other, and its continuance depends on the assent of the electorate. It should be clear that state and local governments in no way affect inflation, though as is pointed out in n. 5, it may have the effect of raising the effective marginal tax rates. Inflation, therefore, is largely a federal issue and one which I do not believe affects the long-term growth of the public sector, federal or nonfederal.

5. As Goetz and Weber [18] show, given that federal progressive income tax schedules are written in nominal terms, inflation is equivalent to an income tax increase or surcharge. Also see Buchanan [8]. To the extent that some state income taxes also have a progressive feature the effect is similar but empirically can be shown to be smaller in terms of the tax yields. My contention is that such increases may well be appreciated by the taxpaying public in a reasonably short time. Part of the recent so-called taxpayers' revolution may reflect such desire for adjustment. The evidence is lacking so no effort is made to measure this.

Borcherding and Deacon [7], and Bergstrom and Goodman [5]. Although the time and data bases differ for each study, the parameters found are sufficiently similar to suggest some stability of the underlying relationships and are, therefore, assumed to obtain for the federal level as well.[6]

The latter two studies look at the representative voter as having a demand for government services, q, measured empirically by the function $q = Ap^\eta m^\phi$ which can be transformed into

$$(1) \qquad Npq = E = AP^{\eta+1}Nm^\phi$$

where p is the real price of q, A is some constant, N is population, m represents a shorthand term for all other variables, and E is total government expenditure in 1929 constant dollars. One is tempted to use differentials on (1) to derive an approximation for the effect of a change of relative price on total spending of the form

$$\% \text{ change in spending} = (\eta + 1) \times \% \text{ change in } p$$

where $\times$ is the multiplication operator and the effects of other variables are held constant. Unfortunately, this will not do as the use of this technique holds only for very small changes in price.[7] Since over this century the change in p can be shown to be very large, the following alternative method will be employed:

Let E_o, p_o, N_o and m_o be the initial (1902) values. Assuming that the underlying parameters η and ϕ are stable over time, (1) can be rewritten

$$(1') \qquad E_t = E_o e^{rt} = A \ (p_o e^{r_p t})^{\eta+1} \ (N_o e^{r_N t}) \ (m_o e^{r_m t})^\phi$$

where t is the number of years since 1902 and the subscripted r's represent the annual growth of each of the independent variables p, N and m, yields the relationships

$$(1a) \qquad e^r = e^{r_p(\eta+1)} \times e^{r_N} \times e^{r_m \phi}$$

so

6. Defense services are much akin to police and fire services; federal health, education, and welfare have their direct nonfederal counterparts; the Post Office may not be all that different from publicly owned utilities, etc. Unfortunately, federal studies are lacking except over time when other factors appear to be shifting. On this see Weber [45]. He looks only at the effects of incomes and "time" on spending in various countries.

7. As is well known, the approximation for the partial change $\dfrac{\frac{\partial Z}{\partial x_i}\Delta x_i}{\Delta Z}$ $\left\{ \text{where } \Delta Z_i = \dfrac{\partial Z}{\partial x_i}\Delta x_i \right\}$ is accurate only if Z is linear in the x_i's or if all Δx_i's are small. If, as in the cases to be examined, the changes are large and the form of the function nonlinear, second order effects are nonnegligible. The impracticality of measuring and incorporating these second-order terms is well known. For one, *all* contributing factors must be included in these interaction terms, a presumptuous undertaking at this time as the reader will soon see.

(1b) $r = r_p (\eta + 1) + r_N + r_m \phi$

It follows that the percentage contribution of change in relative price, p, to the total growth of government spending, r, is $\dfrac{(\eta + 1)r_p}{r} \times 100$. (The contribution of N and m can be similarly measured.)

It appears that η, the elasticity of demand for public services, is estimated to be around -0.5, taking Borcherding and Deacon's and Bergstrom and Goodman's nonfederal studies as rough indicators for the total for all governments. A measure or indication of the change of p over this century will then provide us with the information necessary to determine its impact on total growth. Fortunately, such a measure is available.

Baumol [4] has hypothesized that, because the government sector is labor intensive, its rate of productivity increase is small compared to the capital-intensive private goods producing sector. This may be correct, since empirical evidence shows the productivity increase in the private services sector to be only 1.25 percent per year, less than half the rate of the goods sector.[8]

On the basis of this information it can be shown (with some further assumptions) that the price of services has also been rising relative to goods at a rate of 1.25 percent per annum.[9] Since it is unlikely that productivity is increasing any faster in government than for private services (the evidence to be presented later suggests it is less), the implication is that unit costs of government output have been rising by at least 1.25 percent yearly. Using 1.25 percent as the lower bound on the annual rise in p, it appears that slightly more than one-tenth of the increase in government budgets can be explained by rising costs facing price inelastic demands for government services.[10]

Income Changes

It can also be shown that for most goods an increase in income will, other things being equal, lead to an increase in their demand. It is this effect on which almost every empirical study of the determinants of public spending has concentrated, and as a result a great deal is known about this relationship. Now contrary to the widely stated position known as

8. Fuchs [16]. Kendrick assisted by Pech [22] finds the aggregate growth rate to be 2.5% per year. This means that annual growth in the private goods sector is around 3.0%.

9. Assuming that in the relevant range the rates of transformation between goods and services are approximately constant, change in relative price is equal to the difference in their productivity growths. See Baumol [4].

10. The reader is reminded of the technique used to obtain this imputation from the text immediately below equation (1b). Since $\eta = -\frac{1}{2}$, $r_p = 1.25$ and $r = 5.3$, the contribution of relative price rise to the growth of spending is $\dfrac{(\eta + 1) r_p}{r} \times 100$ percent or about 12% of the total rate.

Wagner's Law, it does not appear that the elasticity of public expenditures is greater than 1.0, but a great deal less.[11] My own "guesstimate," based on a survey of the literature and my own research, places it around 0.75. Thus if all other factors affecting the demand for public services are held constant, a 10 percent increase in income of the decision making unit should lead to an increase in spending of 7.5 percent. Given the estimation function:

(2) $E = Ap^{\eta+1} Ny^{\delta}m^{\phi}$

where y is per capita income and δ is the income elasticity of the average citizen yields

$$\% \text{ of public spending due to income growth} = \delta \times \frac{r_y}{r} \times 100$$

again holding the effects of all other factors constant. Given the rise in real per capita income from \$588 in 1902 to \$1825 in 1970 (1.6 percent per annum), increased affluence accounts for slightly more than one-fourth of the increase in public spending.

Spann's Method of Accounting for Relative Price and Income Effects

Although it is true that my method of calculation is fairly accurate for small price and income changes, it has an upward bias when the increase in p becomes large. Let me attempt an explanation. Given a nominal income of \$100 and prices of X and Y of \$5 and \$10 each, a rise in the price of X to \$10 is equivalent to a decrease in real income because the cost of X went up and Y's price remained unchanged. To adjust for this, nominal income would have to be raised by the amount of the price increase times the original quantity of X purchased, if the consumer was to be in the same apparent real income position. Thus, initially if $X = 6$ and $Y = 10$, the price increase of X from \$5 to \$10 would require an increase in money income of \$30 in order that 6 and 10 units of X and Y respectively still could be purchased. Given the new relative price of X the chooser would then purchase less X and more Y, but the measured "cost-of-living" would not have been altered in the process.

However, the official measure of income change from 1902 until 1970 has some upward bias since no attempt was made to incorporate the rise in the price of government services in the price or cost-of-living indices. Spann [33] has a method for taking account of this fact. He shows that the combined effect of the increase in y and p to be one-third of public

11. See Weber [45]. An income elasticity greater than one would be consistent with a growing government sector. Wagner [44] was simply trying to rationalize what he observed in a few Western European countries around the turn of the century without engaging in any serious theoretical or statistical analysis. That the myth of Wagner's Law persists is a wonder left to the historians of science.

sector growth over the period. This would appear only trivially different from my combined total of 38 percent given the roughness of our respective methods and measures.[12]

Population Increase

Population increase can be assumed to affect the demand for the services of government too. If the goods are what economists call private (holding their quantity constant, an additional unit for one person means one less unit for all the rest), a change in the population should lead to a change in spending by an identical percentage. On the other hand, if the goods have some public aspect to them (adding an additional person to the group sharing the service does not diminish consumption by the others by as much as that person gets), there exist economies in joint consumption which effectively lower the real price of the good to the decision-making unit and more will be purchased. The exact effect on total real spending in this latter case depends on the economies realized and the elasticity of demand. All of this has been statistically explored by Borcherding-Deacon and Bergstrom-Goodman according to the equation:

(3) $\qquad E = Ap^{\eta+1} y^{\delta} N^{\theta+1} m^{\phi}$

where θ equals $(\alpha - 1)(\eta + 1)$ and α, the coefficient of publicness in consumption, ranges between 0 when the good is capable of perfect joint consumption (a purely public good) and 1 when there are no economies of sharing in consumption (a purely private good). Now Borcherding-Deacon and Bergstrom-Goodman generally find that α is not significantly different from 1. Thus it follows that

% of public spending due to population increase
$$= (\theta + 1) \times \frac{r_N}{r} \times 100$$

other things held constant. Now because $\alpha \approx 1$, θ is zero, meaning spending changes should be proportional to population increases. Since between 1902 and 1970 population rose from 79 to 205 million persons ($r = 1.4\%$), population increase explains a little more than a quarter of the total increase in public spending.

12. The appropriate percentage adjustment of income for rising governmental costs can be shown to be $(-1)\left(\frac{\Delta p}{p}\right)$ (public sector's share in national income) (real per capita income). Using 1902 weights for the shares and 1970 income, the adjusted or apparent real per capita income for 1970 is $122 less than the official figure. Using the 1970 share, this rises to $345. Since both figures have the familiar index number problem, averaging the two seemed wise, giving an adjusted or apparent real income for 1970 of $1600 and lowering per capita annual income growth to 1.4%. The result is that price and income, using these corrected figures, now explain about 34%, very nearly Spann's estimated 35%.

Of course, the assumption of purely private but publicly supplied goods may appear to be highly questionable considering the aggregate nature of the data and the possibility of misspecification of the relationship. Further, this possibility seems difficult to accept since it implies that there is no justification for public provision of these services. Indeed, if there is no publicness to these services, why do free people put up with their continued collectivization?[13] Recently, however, unpublished work of Deacon [12] for the city of Seattle shows that careful specification yields an α of between 0.50 to 0.75. Assuming that this is approximately correct, and using the most "public" estimate, $\alpha = 0.50$, the effect of population on the change in spending explains only one-eight of the growth. Given this as the lower-bound estimate, the actual contribution of population increase to the rise of government spending can perhaps be taken as explaining no more than one-fifth of the total.

Interdependencies

It has long been argued that as an economy develops and its population becomes larger, more densely settled, and more urbanized, types of interdependencies develop that are not well handled by private markets. Examples of such are problems of public health, environment, fire, public safety, congestion, and sanitation that seem to accompany an urbanized, industrially developing economy. Since individuals acting in their private capacities take into account only the benefits they receive from a service and its direct costs to them, an excess cost (or sometimes a benefit) spills over to outsiders (often and aptly called a spillover, an externality, or a neighborhood effect) can result from some social interactions. Recognizing that the full consequences of behavior are not always properly accounted for in private interaction, individuals may find it advantageous to "club" together to correct the allocational error due to this so-called market failure. However, because the number of persons affected is large, a completely cooperative or voluntary organization is often not feasible or efficient. Under these conditions governmental solutions may become appealing.[14] Of course, the cost of "polity failure" associated with growing governments relatively insensitive to general interests may

13. However, it might be argued that some of these goods, though private, are less expensive to supply publicly because of scale economies (Social Security) or because the cost of excluding users, i.e., the costs of transacting between buyers and sellers, is higher in market contexts than through governments (city streets and sidewalks). Alternatively, for some services at least (colleges, fire, police, recreation) Borcherding and Deacon [7] have argued that the median group, the middle class, may find it privately profitable to publicly finance private services because they pay less than their share of the taxes. In other words, they use their political power to get other groups to subsidize them. This point is discussed in the last section of this paper.

14. This position is clearly stated by Hirschman [20] and Kapp [21], but the argument is at least as old as Wagner.

diminish some of the benefits from collectivization.[15] The net effect is somewhat conjectoral so a look at factors associated with interdependence seems warranted.

Indices which have been used as empirical proxies of interdependence are population size and density, per capita income, and urbanization. Population size and income have already been discussed and their contribution to spending noted. On the other hand, the evidence concerning density and urbanization appears to suggest little or no relationship to public spending. In fact, their respective effects do not appear to be statistically different from zero, though the signs of the coefficients and their magnitudes differ from one another among the many studies perused. Such instability in parameter values when coupled with statistical insignificance suggests that these factors are of small consequence. Perhaps other indicators of interdependence might be developed which would have explanatory value. To date no such series has been offered.

One type of interdependency, the so-called intergovernmental fiscal externality, has been studied in some detail and its suggested means of political internalization, the grant-in-aid, has been the subject of much empirical scrutiny. The argument justifying grants is developed as follows: Because of demographic mobility and geographical contiguity some or many of the benefits of a unit of a government's services spill out and are captured by nonresidents in other jurisdictions. In such cases, the full valuation of the output will not enter into the political decision process of the unit, hence too little will be locally produced. To correct for this, subsidies are given by a higher level of government to a lower level to encourage additional spending. Thus, the political process supposedly internalizes these intergovernmental externalities.

However, the facts do not wholly support this explanation. In the United States direct intergovernmental grants are for the most part not made on a matching basis. In those few cases where grants are matching they are limited in the total amount available, that is, they are not open-ended. Thus, grants for the most part are not tied directly to the amount of local or state spending effort in a particular activity. Since "money mixes," the possibility of substitution of the grant for some or a great deal of local tax effort is a distinct possibility, and the evidence suggests that such a substitution regularly takes place.

Renshaw [32] shows for education that $1 in per capita aid increases spending by only 16¢. Recent evidence by Wilensky [47] suggests a similarly small effect. Denzau [13] estimates that the elasticity for federal and state per capita aid to local education is really not significantly different from zero. Borcherding and Deacon found the same for each of

15. McKean [24 and 25] provides excellent catalogs of these collective action externalities.

the nonfederal functions they studied.[16] Some researchers have found an elasticity as high as 0.2, but the statistical significance of these estimates is questionable.[17] Prudence in the face of this evidence of little positive relationship suggests that the elasticity is probably very low if not zero. Using 0.1 as an arbitrary but probably generous estimate, the effect of aid on the level of spending can be given an upper-bound estimate as follows:

In 1902 real federal grants to state and local governments were in the neighborhood of $13 million, while the states gave $100 million to local governments. By 1970 this had risen to $8.9 and $110.7 billion, respectively, a rise of 9 percent per year. Using the estimation equation

$$(4) \qquad E = A p^{\eta+1} y^{\delta} N^{\theta+1} g^{\psi} m^{\phi}$$

where g represents per capita aid and ψ its elasticity

$$\% \text{ change in } E \text{ due to grants} = \psi \times \frac{r_g}{r} \times 100$$

other factors held constant. Since $r_g \approx .09$, $\frac{\psi r_g}{r} \times 100 = 17\%$. However, since there are no grants from the nonfederal to the federal level and a negligible amount from local to state governments, this figure should be more than halved when applied to the rise in all government spending. Given that the lower bound is zero, the contribution of aid is still rather small; perhaps 4 or 5 percent is still too generous.

However, even this small figure may overstate the contribution grants from higher to lower governments made to the public budget's growth. This follows because the taxes levied to supply these subsidies are also borne by their recipients. What matters then is the distribution of these grants *net* of taxes.

For instance, if δ, the income elasticity, is less than one and is stable across jurisdictions, a net transfer of income from rich to poor units via grants and taxes will lead to a net expansion of state and local public spending. This follows since that transfer will decrease relatively the wealthier unit's income less than it increase's the poor. Although empirically it is observed, as was earlier mentioned, that δ is less than 1, grants appear to be only very weakly redistributive in favor of the poorer units.[18] Thus, though in principle aid could be nonfederal expenditure enlarging, in actual fact it is of little explanatory value.

16. Unpublished results not included in [7].
17. This was the highest figure I came across. Often it was more like 0.05 or sometimes even slightly negative. Usually it was insignificant in that the hypothesis could not be rejected since it differed from zero at the usual levels of statistical confidence.
18. At the federal level, because of the progressive income tax and redistributive formulae, aid is probably channeled from the wealthier to the poorer parts of the national community. At the state level, however, the effect may be just the opposite. The net result may be only a small interstate wealth redistribution.

Last in this section I will consider one sort of fiscal interdependence or externality discussed by Goetz and McLure [17]. They point out that the deductability of certain local and state taxes from taxable income to higher (state and federal) levels of government effectively reduces the cost of the lower unit's public services to its citizenry. Thus the federal income tax makes all the taxpayers of the U.S. share in providing public services to New York State, San Francisco, Peoria and Denton, Texas. McLure [26] recognizes this and the fact that the incidence or burden of a tax is often not fully borne by a jurisdiction's nominal citizen-taxpayers, but is shifted to outsiders via market adjustments. Thus, a good deal of the gambling tax in Nevada is probably borne by Californians and other tourists not enjoying much political power over Nevada's public choices. In both these cases of fiscal externalities the anticipated costs to the unit's citizenry falls below budgetary spendings encouraging larger outputs and, hence, budgets.

Using McLure's estimates Goetz found that all these kinds of tax exportations lowered the "private" costs to nonfederal jurisdictions by as much as 15 to 40 percent, a sizeable subsidy. Presumably shifting can be neglected at the federal level as such a small share of GNP involves trade with the rest of the world. Besides, all levels of U.S. governments have great difficulties in shifting their taxes and tariffs to foreigners. The demand for U.S. commodities and services by foreigners is highly elastic while the rest of the world's supply of goods to the U.S. is also very elastic. Thus, tax exportation is, for all practical purposes, a domestic and nonfederal phenomenon.

Now at the beginning of the period the income tax was not used at any level of government. Further, the economies of the various political units were only partially integrated as compared with today's. Thus, the amount of nonfederal implicit grants from tax exportations must have been negligible in 1902. Using McLure's estimates for 1962 then suggests that over the period the subsidy to state and local governments could not have risen by more than .7% per annum, but probably not less than .2%. Since the price elasticity is taken as $-\frac{1}{2}$, this implicit subsidy increased nonfederal outputs, hence state and local budgets (assuming, of course, constant costs at the margins), by .1 to .7 percent annually. Because this subsidy affects only the nonfederal public sector, it can be said to account for between 1 and 3% of the total growth of the entire public sector.[19]

Given the effects of both direct grants and the implicit subsidies from

19. A 15 to 40% subsidy for 1970 (which was not available in 1902) implies an annual price decrease of .2 to .7%. Given that $\eta = -\frac{1}{2}$ and $r = 5.3$, such a rate of subsidy implies an effect on spending of 1.8 to 6.6% of the total. Since federal spending for the period averaged about half the public sector's total, the effect of implicit grants on the growth of government spending is 1 to 3%.

tax exportations, it seems safe to conclude that their combined effect, while absolutely significant, explains probably no more than one-twentieth of the public sector's expansion over the century.

The Total Effect of "Economic" Changes

It appears then that the rise in relative price of public services, increased affluence and a larger population probably explain little more than one-half of the increase in public sector's real spending over the last seventy years. Thus, I can explain why government spending would be about $375 per capita in 1970 but not $622. Put differently, all these factors explain why almost one-fifth of our GNP is spent through the public sector, but not a third. Such an explanation is perhaps less than I would like to offer, but I think it is reasonably accurate given our current and imperfect understanding of the process.

To test the reasonableness of my estimates, one has only to look at changes in the private services sector over time. Given the character of the output of the latter, might one not expect that government services should behave in about the same way? If this were the case, government spending should bear a more-or-less constant ratio to spending on private services.[20] Unfortunately, income data for the service sector is unavailable for 1902, so census data on employment is substituted. For 1900 Stigler estimated that about 5.8 million persons were employed by the private services sector and 1.1 million in government, a ratio of a little less than 1 to 5. Assuming productivities in both service sectors were about equal and capital-labor ratios were not terribly different, government spending was in the neighborhood of 20 percent of that of private service industries. In 1970 private service employment had risen to 31.2 million persons. Assuming again the same productivities and identical forces working on both sectors, government employment should have been about 7.2 million. Instead it was 16.1 million. This technique explains only two-fifths of the increase in public activity, somewhat less than the lower-bound estimate of my "sophisticated" explanation.[21]

Given the possible range of error associated with both measures, it seems fairly safe to say that "other" factors explain more than one-third, and possibly one-half of the growth of government spending. What these "other" factors might be is the subject of the next and last section of the paper.

20. Stigler [38] suggests this approach.

21. Blank and Stigler [6] find evidence suggesting that over time public services have been steadily substituted for private services. If this had not taken place, the 1970 private service employment would have been larger and, hence, assuming no substitution, the public employment would have been smaller. Given this, perhaps the difference between Stigler's technique of n. 20 and the lower bound of my more sophisticated approach is even larger.

The Political Side of Public Spending

In this section of the paper I will cite "noneconomic" or political arguments used to explain the growth of government spending. Unfortunately, almost all have one thing in common—they are purely qualitative and do not permit imputing even in the roughest numerical terms their impact on government spending over the period in question. I hope, however, they are suggestive and scholars will soon remedy our ignorance.

It was implicitly assumed earlier by equation (1) that the average or median voter paid either an aliquot share of taxes over the whole period or, more realistically, the ratio of his taxes to his benefits was a constant. But, what if this were not true? Suppose instead that over time the median voter was able to pay a smaller and smaller share of the total cost of government. Likewise, what if over time expenditures were more and more specialized, more private in nature, and favored the median group? Either would be equivalent to a fall in price of q and more government services would be desired. In fact, it can be shown that if π represents the median voter's share of taxes then

(5) $$E = A\pi^{\eta}p^{\eta+1}y^{\delta}N^{\theta+1} g^{\psi}m^{\theta}$$

and

% of public spending due to political discrimination
$$= \eta \times \frac{r_{\pi}}{r} \times 100$$

other things held constant. Since η is negative, a fall in π over time (a negative r_{π}) would necessarily lead to an increase in public spending. The question whether or not π has fallen since 1902 is then of prime importance.

Stigler [36] definitely thinks it has. In a paper in which he announced Director's Law of Public Expenditures (after its putative discoverer, Aaron Director), he states the premise for his argument: "Public expenditures are made for the benefit primarily of the middle classes, and financed by taxes which are borne in considerable part by the poor and the rich." He argues that the power of the state is exercised in behalf of the majority coalition, though subject to certain fiscal and political constraints.[22] He states that over the last century (and this holds until at least World War 1) the sources of taxes were, for the most part, not closely tied to incomes nor were the attendant benefits of public spending. At the federal level there were various tariffs and excises, but only

22. Tullock [40] makes the point that almost all redistributions appear to be from the poorer and wealthier segments of society to the middle class. Hansen and Weisbrod [19] give empirical evidence to show that this is true in the case of higher education in California.

in 1909 was the Corporate Tax introduced (and then only at 1 percent!).
Not until 1913 after a constitutional amendment was the Federal Personal Income Tax levied and its effective rate was proportional and low
(also 1 percent). At the state and local levels taxes on land and real
property existed and these were (and still are) not closely correlated with
income. It was not until much later that state sales, income, and corporation taxes were introduced. On the other hand, the activities of these
governments were mostly in the areas of protection, adjudication of com-
mercial conflicts, some roads and utilities, and provision of a minimal
amount of education, categories that are rather general in their benefits.
There simply was little incentive on the part of the middle class, the
dominant political grouping, to expand government for purposes of income redistribution towards itself. Taxes and benefits were not class
structured to permit such fiscal discrimination.

Today, Stigler believes, this is no longer true. Expenditures are quite
narrow, particularized as to beneficiary group, and taxes are closely
connected to incomes. Unfortunately, I do not know how to translate
this into the quantitative terms of the π coefficient. If, for instance, I
could show that the ratio of taxes to benefits to the median voter has

fallen by r_π over the century, I could say, given $-\eta$ is one-half, that $\dfrac{-r_\pi}{2r}$

of the increase in government spending is explained by Director's Law.
To give another example, if it could be shown that the median citizen has
received a 30 percent "subsidy" over the last seven decades as a result
of the operation of Director's Law, 5 percent of the total growth of public
spending would be accounted for. Unfortunately, no empirical evidence
for r_π is yet available.

Fiscal illusion is perhaps another source of budget expansion. As
Goetz indicates, the public's perception of taxes may be very imperfect
and subject to gross understatement.[23] Their ignorance may derive from
rational political apathy first discussed by Downs.[24] In any case, it would
not seem that fiscal illusion is sufficient to explain much of the growth of
government over the century, since there is no evidence to suggest that
tax prices were more correctly perceived in the 1900s than they are
today. In fact, if Stigler is correct and there has been a shift of taxes to
more well defined economic groups, perhaps just the opposite is the case.

The growth and proliferation of special interest groups is yet another
possible reason for an expanding government sector. Downs shows that
even though the benefits to a small group of a certain government policy
may be dwarfed by the damages done to a larger one, there is no com-

23. "Fiscal Illusion," in this volume.
24. Downs [14] shows that given the low probability that a citizen will be able to influence political choice, he will choose to inform himself very poorly on the issues.

pelling reason that the political process will reverse that decision as long as the former group is very cohesive and the latter group is diffuse. Thus, if a coalition consisting of 100 persons stands to make a net gain of $3000 each from a policy, they may successfully push it through the legislature even though the attendant net damage is $1 each to 500,000 people. (This principle was summed up long ago by Mark Twain who noted that although the free traders always won the debates, the protectionists always seemed to win the votes.) Thus, the payoff to special interests of political action is high compared to the general or so-called public interest.[25] In support of this Spengler has argued and evidenced that in a society that is growing in numbers and becoming more specialized in its division of labor the power of special interest grows at an even faster rate.[26] Buchanan and Tullock [9] show theoretically that by clever gerrymandering a coalition consisting of slightly over 25 percent of the voters in a multi-districted constituency can control a political unit. Given third parties and plurality rules this fraction can fall to as low as one-sixth of the voting population. Given the political apathy which Downs shows to be expected as the individual voter feels less and less important, the relative size of the group necessary to dominate the larger group may be getting relatively smaller over time. Unfortunately, how much change in the power of special interests has occurred since 1902 and its equivalent effects on π is a matter of speculation and no hard evidence. A casual reading of the legislative report of any political unit indicates, however, that a good deal of special interests legislation and spending is annually or biannually authorized.[27] It also appears that this fraction is increasing.[28]

It is interesting to note that one study by Glen W. Fisher has attempted to relate the degree of political competition to the level of spending. Fisher [15] argues that the more vigorous the level of competition for office, the more likely that the general interest will be considered. He found that political competition is inversely related to spending, i.e., the more competition, the less spending on a per capita basis. Unfortunately, the coefficient of competition was not statistically significant. This may come, of course, from the extremely crude nature of his index of competition based on the division by party of the legislature and state houses in the recent past. Since party division is only one element in the whole question of political competition, it would not be surprising to find

25. Ibid. Also see Stigler [37], who has an excellent discussion of this and offers empirical evidence in its support.

26. Spengler [34]. He also cites L. S. Penrose [31].

27. Tuerck [39] shows, however, that the courts have limited the ability of government to impose completely arbitrary taxation. This perhaps has been an important constraint on the growth of public spending.

28. Clyde Reed of Simon Fraser University is currently researching this topic and his early results are consistent with this hypothesis.

the forementioned hypothesis bolstered when a better index is designed.

Ease of entry is one important factor to consider in this index too. Tullock [41] has argued that barriers exist to political entrepreneurs seeking elected offices because of high costs of entry. Campaigns are becoming more expensive and incumbents have a great advantage because they are able to appropriate to themselves at state expense all types of resources that insure that they maintain their tenure in office: travel allowances, staff salaries paid at state expense, newsletters and mailing, control of patronage positions, favors in return for campaign contributions, and so on. Money cannot be easily borrowed by office seekers since the returns to the office are largely in-kind and do not normally (legally, at least) permit market distribution. Tullock suggests that over time these barriers have gotten higher.

It would appear that he is correct, too, as over the last few decades the success of incumbents at all levels of government in retaining office has improved markedly. Now chief executives in many states and the president of the United States have constitutional limits imposed on how often they may succeed themselves. For some reason, however, legislators, who generally initiated these constitutional restrictions, have not seen fit to limit their own tenures. The current interest in limiting campaign contributions among members of the Congress (and also in certain state legislatures) may be interpreted as an attempt to reduce competition still further, since no provision is made for the reduction of the various aforementioned subsidies to incumbents.[29]

Finally, the effect of the bureaucracy on its own growth is possibly an important factor that has all but been overlooked except in a recent and provocative book by William N. Niskanen, *Bureaucracy and Representative Government* [27]. Niskanen's hypothesis is that bureaucrats desire as large a budget as they can possibly get the legislature and executive to approve. This follows, he says, since their pay, power and prestige is positively related, a hypothesis which Staaf has found empirical evidence to substantiate.[30]

No doubt this motivation has always driven career civil servants, but Niskanen [28] argues that only in the last few decades has it caused the budget to grow. At the turn of the century civil service was still a rather new institution and almost totally absent at the nonfederal level. On the

29. Niskanen [28] argues that at the federal level, and inferentially at the nonfederal level too, the fiscal constitution over time has been altered, making it easier to pass special interest legislation. This has taken place for a number of reasons, but the increased seniority and power of certain incumbents, particularly committee chairmen, is a major factor. Elongation of the legislative session is also cited as causal—a political change he partially explains by the advent of air-conditioning!

30. Robert J. Staaf, "The Growth of the Educational Bureaucracy: Do Teachers Make a Difference?" and "The Public School System in Transition: Consolidation and Parental Choice," both in this volume.

contrary, competition for positions was keen and tenure of appointed office depended on the whim of office holders elected in fairly competitive (though possibly corrupt) contests. Besides this, competition among the various bureaus for the custom of the legislature was brisk as well, since duplication of function was widespread and letting bids to private firms was common. It would appear then that no bureau had very much power. During the Progressive Movement which began right before the First World War, attacks on the so-called spoils system and on "duplication of function" began. "Rationalization" of government structure took precedence over competition, just as "honesty" in government became more highly prized than its efficiency. Civil service tenured positions and centralization of administration began in earnest. "Do-it-yourself" bureaucracy supply began to replace competitive bidding, though not in all areas. This suggests that the end result of the Progressive Movement was to effectively cartelize the labor market through civil service and to reduce competition facing the legislature as buyers of government services.[31] This increase in monopoly power also manifested itself in bureaus demanding larger budgets than legislatures would otherwise approve. (No doubt, they are often aided in this process by special interests groups which the bureau itself may have organized.)[32]

Using an extreme model where the bureaus are perfectly (first degree) discriminating monopolists and the legislature is a completely passive buyer, Niskanen shows that outputs will be exactly twice that forthcoming under competitive conditions. This is an exaggeration, no doubt, but it would seem some excess is likely, since there is a constant pressure to expansion, given that the bureaucrats' self-interests are so served. Given the development of the latter's monopoly supply privilege, only a brisker competition over time for office among political entrepreneurs would offset (some of) these expansionist tendencies. As was earlier stated, however, it appears that this competition may have declined over the period.

Niskanen's model unfortunately does not allow for waste, but it can be easily incorporated into the analysis by assuming that the bureaucrat is interested both in larger budgets and in appropriating some of the budget to himself, if only to secure the proverbially quiet and secure life. Results

31. This position is taken by William Turn [42] and more recently by James Q. Wilson [48]. Borcherding, Bush, and Spann, in "The Effects on Public Spending of the Divisibility of Public Outputs in Consumption, Bureaucratic Power, and the Size of the Tax-Sharing Group," in this volume, present evidence consistent with the view that civil service is not passive in budgetary process.

32. Cf. Borcherding, Bush, and Spann's paper, "The Effects on Public Spending." Also see Bush and Arthur Denzau in "Voting Behavior and the Public Sector's Growth" and Bush and Robert Mackay, "Private vs. Public Sector Growth," both in this volume. They give excellent reasons why office holders may now be less watchful over the bureaucracy than in the past.

of recent studies by Davies [11], Ahlbrandt [1], Spann,[33] and the Urban Institute [43] suggest that waste is an inverse function of the competition facing a bureau from other suppliers, a prediction made by Alchian and Kessel [2] a decade ago. In their paper Alchian and Kessel hypothesized that firms with some monopoly power but seriously constrained in their ability to earn profits would instead take them in nonpecuniary forms such as soft carpets, pretty but incompetent secretaries, long lunch hours, sloppy supervision, etc. Since profits are correlated with monopoly power, it would seem logical that as a bureau's competition diminished, the level of "wasteful" activity would rise too.

It appears that there is confirmatory evidence for this hypothesis. Ahlbrandt [1] found that the costs of fire services provided through the government, supplied almost always under monopoly conditions, are 50 percent higher than the competitive minimum; Davies [11] found that in a "duopolistic" situation a government airline had at least 15 percent higher costs than its private, though partially profit-constrained, counterpart even though routes, service, and prices were virtually identical. Spann found that where competition was really keen the cost differentials between private and publicly owned power firms were very small.[34] Thus, it appears that waste is directly related to a bureau's monopoly power.

The exact effect on costs of the gradual monopoly-bureaucratization over the century is difficult to assess. Earlier I assumed that government services were as productively rendered as services in the private sector. As I have shown, however, the evidence does not suggest this, but instead the Bureaucratic Rule of Two seems the more appropriate description: to wit, removal of an activity from the private to the public sector will double its unit costs of production. If because of competition among suppliers this phenomenon was absent in 1902, p rose yet another 1.25 percent per annum over the period.[35] This increase would then explain another one-eighth of the total budget's growth over the period, a not insignificant portion. More detailed cost studies, especially over time, are needed to raise this proposition above the level of an interesting and perhaps exaggerated conjecture.

Evidence on "budgetary push" suggested by Niskanen's model is rather meager too. Staaf's research suggests that for local education, at least, supervisory salaries are correlated by law with the number of teachers in the district.[36] Such relationship is part-and-parcel of almost

33. Spann, "Public vs. Private Provision of Governmental Services," in this volume.
34. Spann, "Rates of Productivity Change and the Growth of State and Local Spending," in this volume.
35. Spann, "Public vs. Private," suggests that productivity rise has been zero in recent times at least.
36. Staaf, "The Growth of the Educational Bureaucracy: Do Teachers Make a Difference?" in this volume, shows that it appears that bureaucrats do, in fact, have monopoly

all civil service codes, a point noted by Parkinson [29]. This may, of course, reflect only the higher opportunity cost of efficient supervisors as the number of subordinates grow, but it could also reflect the ability of bureaucrats to appropriate profits to themselves via administrative procedures. Unfortunately, discrimination between these two explanations is not immediately obvious. In fact, they might not be inconsistent with one another if the market supply price of potential bureaucrats elsewhere employed rises as more are demanded by a public agency. Since salary discrimination is patently difficult, if not obviously illegal, bureau expansion leads to higher incomes for the inframarginal (existing) bureaucrats. Of course, all this is sufficient to establish the plausibility of incentive to bureaucrats to expand their budgets. Whether they are able to do so is the crucial point.

Borcherding, Bush, and Spann have attempted to test this proposition empirically.[37] They argue that bureaucrats coalesce through the agency of civil service rules and regulation. If this is true, then there should be a positive relationship between the existence of the latter and size of budgets. The evidence does, in fact, bear this out, the presence of civil service explaining anywhere from 2 percent to 80 percent of spending in nonfederal governments. These authors point out that the special interests of public bureaucracies may be articulated by their unions and by the exercise of the voting franchise. The general position of public employee unions towards budget increases and cuts is well known and seems consistent with that predicted. Less well known, however, is the fact that civil servants are twice as likely to vote as their nonbureaucrat fellow citizens.[38] Orzechowski presents further evidence of the political potency of the bureaucracy in his study of factor propositions in colleges and universities. He finds that public institutions of higher learning use considerably more labor intensive techniques than do their not-for-profit, private counterparts.[39] The "political" productivity of labor is the hypothesized cause of this bias.

All this evidence supporting Niskanen's hypothesis is still only suggestive. More work certainly needs to be done to ascertain whether the private interests of public employees are served by expanding agencies; whether they can, indeed, affect budgets through their monopoly

---

power in the educational sector of the government; use it to extract higher budgets than would otherwise be forthcoming; and produce their output rather inefficiently. Perhaps that is why they are the most vociferous opponents of the voucher system. For more on the self-interested behavior of public school bureaucrats, see West [46].

37. "The Effects on Public Spending," in this volume.

38. See the several studies cited in Lipset [23] and Bush and Denzau, "Voting Behavior of Bureaucrats," in this volume.

39. William P. Orzechowski, "Economic Models of Bureaucracy: Survey, Extensions, and Evidence," in this volume.

supply and their own political powers; and by how much this has contributed to the growth of the public sector. For instance, if it can be established that at the turn of the century the power of bureaucrats was feeble (see Stahl [35]), but today their power increases demand for their services by 11 percent, considerably less than the 100 percent figure Niskanen suggests, then "budget push" would explain about one-tenth the growth of public spending. When coupled with the "waste" that has also accompanied this growth, public bureaucracies would account for about one-fourth of the growth of public government expenditures. Such a potentially important explanator surely deserves the scrutiny that economists have so far been unwilling to devote to it.

Some Final Thoughts

Although a massive amount has been written describing the growth of government, little attempt has been made to explain this growth using a model that is consistent with the modern theory of collective choice. It is hoped that this paper is an exception and will be among the first of many to grapple with the social dynamics of Leviathan.

The evidence suggests that the growth of government has been 40 to 50 percent faster than would be predicted just on the basis of changes in relative prices, incomes, population, and indices of interdependence. It also seems likely that the development of political forces such as the sales tax, corporation and personal income tax, the growth of special interests, the ability to channel taxes and expenditures in a discriminatory fashion and the growth of bureaucracy enter into the picture with significant force. Economists have too long ignored these latter issues on the grounds that they were "noneconomic" or difficult to measure. Neither excuse is acceptable since a major fraction of national income is at issue. Besides, economists, because of their special familiarity with the world of self-interested choosing individuals, have a comparative advantage in exploring the economics and politics of the budgetary decision. It is hoped that many will take up this challenge and dispassionately dissect public budgetary choices as they have so admirably analyzed the private sector over the last two hundred years.

References

1. Ahlbrandt, Roger, "Efficiency in the Provision of Fire Services." *Public Choice* (fall, 1973).
2. Alchian, Armen A., and Reuben A. Kessel. "Competition, Monopoly, and the Pursuit of Money." In *Aspects of Labor Economics,* National Bureau of Economic Research (NBER) Special Conference Series, No. 14. Princeton, N.J.: Princeton University Press, 1962.

3. Barr, James, and Otto A. Davis. "An Elementary Political and Economic Theory of the Expenditures of Local Governments." *Southern Economic Journal* (Oct., 1966).
4. Baumol, William J. "Macroeconomics of Unbalanced Growth: The Anatomy of the Urban Crisis." *American Economic Review* (June, 1967).
5. Bergstrom, Theodore C., and Robert Goodman. "The Price and Income Elasticities of Demand for Public Goods." *American Economic Review* (June, 1973).
6. Blank, David M., and George J. Stigler. *The Demand and Supply of Scientific Personnel*, NBER General Series No. 62. New York: National Bureau of Economic Research, Inc., 1957.
7. Borcherding, Thomas E., and Robert T. Deacon. "The Demand for the Services of Non-Federal Governments." *American Economic Review* (Dec., 1972).
8. Buchanan, James M. "Inflation, Progression and Politics." Research Paper No. 808231-1-11, Center for Study of Public Choice, Virginia Polytechnic Institute and State University (June, 1973).
9. _____, and Gordon Tullock. *The Calculus of Consent.* Ann Arbor, Mich.: University of Michigan Press, 1962.
10. Davies, David G. "The Concentration Process and the Growing Importance of Non-Central Governments in Federal States." *Public Policy* (fall, 1970).
11. _____. "The Efficiency of Public and Private Firms: The Case of Australia's Two Airlines." *Journal of Law and Economics* (April, 1972).
12. Deacon, Robert T. "The Demand for Services of Local Governments: Theory and Evidence." Ph.D. dissertation, University of Washington, 1972.
13. Denzau, Arthur. "A Median-Voter Model of Public Education: Some Preliminary Results, Virginia, 1969–1970." Report on Ph.D. dissertation in progress at Washington University presented at the Bureaucracy Seminar, Virginia Polytechnic Institute and State University (Nov., 1972).
14. Downs, Anthony. *An Economic Theory of Democracy.* New York: Harper & Row, 1957.
15. Fisher, Glenn W. "Interstate Variations in State and Local Government Expenditure." *National Tax Journal* (March, 1964).
16. Fuchs, Victor R. *Productivity Trends in the Goods and Services, 1929–61.* NBER Occasional Paper No. 81. New York: Columbia University Press, 1962.
17. Goetz, Charles J., and Charles McClure, Jr. *What Is Revenue Sharing?* Washington, D.C.: The Urban Institute, 1972.
18. _____, and Warren L. Weber. "Intertemporal Changes in Federal Income Tax Rates, 1954–1970." *National Tax Journal* (March, 1971).
19. Hansen, H. Lee, and Burton A. Weisbrod. *Benefits, Costs, and Finance of Public Higher Education.* Chicago: Markham Press, 1969.
20. Hirschman, Albert O. *The Strategy of Economic Development.* New Haven, Conn.: Yale University Press, 1958.
21. Kapp, K. William. *The Social Costs and Private Enterprise.* Cambridge, Mass.: Harvard University Press, 1950.
22. Kendrick, John W., assisted by Maude R. Pech. *Productivity Trends in the United States,* NBER General Series No. 71. Princeton, N.J.: Princeton University Press, 1961.
23. Lipset, Seymour M. *Political Man: The Social Bases of Politics.* New York: Doubleday, 1960.

24. McKean, Ronald. "Government and the Consumer." *Southern Economic Journal* (April, 1973).
25. _____. "The Unseen Hand in Government." *American Economic Review* (June, 1965).
26. McLure, Charles, Jr. "The Interstate Exploiting of State and Local Taxes: Estimates for 1962." *National Tax Journal* (March, 1967).
27. Niskanen, William N. *Bureaucracy and Representative Government.* Chicago: Aldine-Atherton Press, 1971.
28. _____. "The Pathology of Politics." Presented at the Conference on Capitalism and Freedom in honor of Milton Friedman, Charlottesville, Virginia (Oct., 1972).
29. Parkinson, C. Northcote. *Parkinson's Law and Other Studies in Administration.* Boston: Houghton Mifflin Co., 1957.
30. Peacock, Alan T., and Jack Wiseman. *The Growth of Public Expenditures in the United Kingdom,* NBER General Series No. 72. Princeton, N.J.: Princeton University Press, 1961.
31. Penrose, L. S. "Elementary Statistics of Majority Voting." *Journal of the Royal Statistics Society* (April, 1946).
32. Renshaw, E. F. "A Note on the Expenditure Effect of State Aid to Education." *Journal of Political Economy* (April, 1960).
33. Spann, Robert M. "The Macroeconomics of Unbalanced Growth and the Increase in Government Spending." Unpublished paper, Department of Economics, Virginia Polytechnic Institute and State University (Nov., 1972).
34. Spengler, Joseph J. "The Economist and the Population Question." *American Economic Review* (March, 1966).
35. Stahl, O. Glenn. *Public Personnel Administration,* 6th ed. New York: Harper & Row, 1972.
36. Stigler, George J. "Director's Law of Public Income Distribution." *Journal of Law and Economics* (April, 1970).
37. _____. "The Theory of Regulation." *The Bell Journal of Economics and Management Science* (spring, 1971).
38. _____. *Trends in Employment in the Service Industries.* NBER General Series No. 59. Princeton, N.J.: Princeton University Press, 1956.
39. Tuerck, David G. "Constitutional Asymmetry." *Public Choice* (1967).
40. Tullock, Gordon. "The Charity of the Uncharitable." *Western Economic Journal* (Dec., 1971).
41. _____. "Entry Barriers in Politics." *American Economic Review: Supplement* (May, 1965).
42. Turn, William. "In Defense of Patronage." *Annals of the American Academy of Political and Social Science* (Jan., 1937).
43. Urban Institute. *Improving Productivity Measures: An Evaluation in Local Government.* Washington, D.C.: The Institute, 1972.
44. Wagner, Adolph. *Grundlegung der politschen Ökonomie,* 3rd ed. Leipzig: C. F. Winter, 1893.
45. Weber, Warren E. "Wagner's Law of Public Expenditure." Unpublished paper, Department of Economics, Virginia Polytechnic Institute and State University (Nov., 1972).
46. West, E. G. "The Political Economy of American Public School Legislation." *Journal of Law and Economics* (Oct., 1967).
47. Wilensky, Gail R. *State Aid and Educational Opportunity.* Beverley Hills, Calif.: Sage Publications, 1970.

48. Wilson, James Q. "The Economy of Patronage." *Journal of Political Economy* (Aug., 1961).

Bibliography on the Growth of Government Spending

Abramovitz, Moses, and Vera Eliasberg. *The Growth of Public Employment in Great Britain.* National Bureau of Economic Research (NBER) General Series No. 60. Princeton, N.J.: Princeton University Press, 1957.

————. "The Trend of Public Employment in Great Britain and the United States." *American Economic Review: Supplement* (May, 1953).

Adams, Robert F. "The Fiscal Response to Intergovernmental Transfers in Less Developed Areas of the United States." *Review of Economics and Statistics* (Aug., 1966).

Bahl, Roy W., Jr., and Robert J. Saunders. "Determinants of Changes in State and Local Government Expenditures." *National Tax Journal* (March, 1965).

————. "Factors Associated with Variations in State and Local Spending." *Journal of Finance* (Sept., 1966).

Barr, James, and Otto A. Davis. "An Elementary Political and Economic Theory of the Expenditures of Local Governments." *Southern Economic Journal* (Oct., 1966).

Bator, Francis M. *The Question of Government Spending: Public Needs and Private Wants.* New York: Harper & Row, 1960.

Benson, Charles S. *The Economics of Public Education.* Boston: Houghton Mifflin, 1968.

Bergstrom, Theodore C., and Robert Goodman. "The Price and Income Elasticities of Demand for Public Goods." *American Economic Review* (June, 1973).

Berlozheimer, Josef. "Influences Shaping Expenditures for Operation of State and Local Governments." *Bulletin of the National Tax Association* (March, 1947).

Bishop, George A. "Stimulative Versus Substitutive Effects of State School Aid in New England." *National Tax Journal* (June, 1964).

Booms, Bernard H. "City Governmental Form and Public Expenditure Levels." *National Tax Journal* (June, 1966).

Borcherding, Thomas E. "The Growth of Non-Federal Public Employment in the United States, 1900 to 1963." Ph.D. dissertation, Duke University, 1965.

————, and Robert T. Deacon. "The Demand for the Services of Non-Federal Governments." *American Economic Review* (Dec., 1972).

Brainerd, Carol P. "Non-Federal Governments and Their Growth 1909–1948: A Study of Employment and Pay Rolls of State and Local Governments." Ph.D. dissertation, University of Pennsylvania, 1950.

Brazer, Harvey. *City Expenditures in the United States.* NBER Occasional Paper No. 66. New York: NBER Inc., 1959.

Brecht, Arnold. "Three Topics in Comparative Administration – Organization of Government Departments, Government Corporations, Expenditures in Relation to Population." In Carl J. Friedrich and Edward S. Mason (eds.), *Public Policy.* Cambridge, Mass.: Harvard University Press, 1941.

Burkhead, Jesse. *State and Local Taxes for Public Education.* Syracuse, N.Y.: University of Syracuse Press, 1963.

Clark, Colin. "Public Finance and Changes in the Value of Money." *Economic Journal* (Dec., 1945).

Coase, Ronald et al. "Government Economic Activities: Discussion." *American Economic Review Supplement* (May, 1953).

Committee for Economic Development. *Paying for Better Public Schools.* New York: Committee for Economic Development, n.d. (ca. 1960).

———. *Trends in Public Expenditure in the Next Decade.* New York: Committee for Economic Development, 1959.

Davies, David G. "The Concentration Process and the Growing Importance of Noncentral Governments in Federal States." *Public Policy* (fall, 1970).

———. "Financing Urban Functions and Services." *Law and Contemporary Problems* (winter, 1965).

Deacon, Robert T. "The Demand for Services of Local governments: Theory and Evidence." Ph.D. dissertation, University of Washington, 1972.

Downs, Anthony. "Why the Government Budget is too Small in a Democracy." *World Politics* (June, 1960).

Dress, W., Jr. *On the Level of Government Expenditure in the Netherlands after the War.* Aspecten der Economische Politik, 3. Leiden: H. E. Stenfert Kroese, 1955.

Ecker-Racz, L. L. *The Politics and Economics of State-Local Finance.* Englewood Cliffs, N.J.: Prentice-Hall, 1970.

Edleberg, Lucy, et al. "Public Expenditures and Economic Structure in the United States." *Social Forces* (February, 1936).

Elsner, Gary H., and Stephen Sosnick. *Municipal Expenditures in California: Statistical Correlates.* University of California Institute of Government Affairs Occasional Paper No. 2. Davis, Calf.: The Institute, July, 1964.

Fabricant, Solomon. *The Rising Trend of Government Employment.* NBER Occasional Paper No. 29. New York: NBER Inc., 1949.

———, assisted by Robert E. Lipsey. *The Trend of Government Activity in the United States since 1900.* NBER General Series No. 56. New York: NBER, Inc., 1952.

Fenton, John H. "Two-Party Competition and Governmental Expenditures." Mimeographed, Sept., 1962.

Fisher, Glen W. "Interstate Variation in State and Local Government Expenditure." *National Tax Journal* (March, 1964).

Gates, Thomas V., and Philip G. Hudson. "The Patterns of Public Expenditure." In The Committee on Public Finance, *Public Finance.* New York: Pittman Publishing Corporation, 1959.

Gupta, Shibshankar P. "Public Expenditures and Economic Growth: A Time Series Analysis." *Public Finance* 4 (1967).

Hansen, Alvin, and Harvey S. Perloff. *State and Local Finance and the National Economy.* New York: W. W. Norton & Co., 1944.

Hanson, Nels W. "Economy of Scale as a Cost Factor in Financing Public Schools." *National Tax Journal* (March, 1964).

Haskell, Mark A. "Federal Grants-in-Aid: Their Influence on State and Local Expenditures." *Canadian Journal of Economics and Political Science* (Nov., 1964).

Hirsch, Werner Z. "Cost Functions of an Urban Government Service: Refuse Collection." *Review of Economics and Statistics* (Feb., 1965).

———. "Determinants of Public Education Expenditure." *National Tax Journal* (March, 1960).

_____. "Expenditure Implications of Metropolitan Growth." *Review of Economics and Statistics* (Aug., 1959).

Hook, Erik. *Den Offentliga Sektorns Expansion.* Stockholm: Almqvist and Wiksell, 1962.

Johnson, S. R., and Paul E. Junk. "Source of Tax Revenues and Expenditures in Large U.S. Cities." *Quarterly Review of Economics and Business* (winter, 1970).

Kee, Woo Sik. "Central City Expenditures and Metropolitan Areas." *National Tax Journal* (Dec., 1965).

Kendrick, John W. "Exploring Productivity Measurement in Government." *Public Administration Review* (June, 1963).

King, Wilfred, assisted by Lillian Epstein. *The National Income and Its Purchasing Power.* NBER General Series No. 15. New York: NBER Inc., 1954.

Kurnow, Ernest. "Determinants of State and Local Expenditure." *National Tax Journal* (Sept., 1963).

Kuznets, Simon. *National Income and Its Composition, 1919–1938.* NBER General Series No. 40. New York: NBER Inc., 1954.

Lytton, Henry D. "Recent Productivity Trends in the Federal Government: An Exploratory Study." *Review of Economics and Statistics* (Nov., 1959).

Maxwell, James A. *Financing State and Local Governments.* Rev. ed. Washington, D. C.: The Brookings Institution, 1970.

Morss, Eliott R. "Some Thoughts on the Determinants of State and Local Expenditures." *National Tax Journal* (March, 1965).

_____, J. Eric Fredland, and Saul H. Hymans. "Fluctuations in State Expenditures: An Econometric Analysis." *Southern Economic Journal* (April, 1967).

Osman, Jack W. "The Dual Impact of Federal Aid on State and Local Government Expenditures." *National Tax Journal* (Dec., 1966).

Peacock, Alan T., and Jack Wiseman. *The Growth of Public Expenditures in the United Kingdom.* NBER General Series No. 72. Princeton, N.J.: Princeton University Press, 1961.

Pidot, George B., Jr. "A Principal Component Analysis of the Determinants of Local Government Fiscal Patterns." *Review of Economics and Statistics* (May, 1969).

Pogue, Thomas F., and L. G. Sgontz. "The Effect of Grants-in-Aid on State-Local Spending." *National Tax Journal* (June, 1968).

Poland, Orville F. *Public Employment in California.* Berkeley, Calif.: Institute of Government Studies, University of California, 1964.

Ratchford, B. U. *Public Expenditure in Australia.* Durham, N.C.: Duke University Press, 1959.

Russet, Bruce M., et al. *World Handbook of Political and Social Indicators.* New Haven, Conn.: Yale University Press, 1964.

Sacks, Seymour. "Metropolitan Fiscal Disparities: Their Nature and Determinants." *Journal of Finance* (May, 1968).

_____, and Robert Harris. "The Determinants of State and Local Government Expenditures and Intergovernmental Flows and Funds." *National Tax Journal* (March, 1964).

_____, and William F. Hellmuth, Jr. *Financing Government in a Metropolitan Area.* New York: The Free Press of Glencoe, 1961.

Schmandt, Henry J., and G. Ross Stephens. "Local Government Expenditure Patterns." *Land Economics* (Nov., 1963).

Schultze, Charles L. *The Politics and Economics of Public Spending.* Washington, D.C.: The Brookings Institution, 1969.

Scott, Stanley, and Edward L. Feder. *Factors Associated with Variations in Municipal Expenditure Levels.* Berkeley, Calif.: Bureau of Public Administration, University of California, 1957.

Sharkansky, Ira. "Some More Thoughts About the Determinants of Governmental Expenditures." *National Tax Journal* (June, 1967).

Smith, David L. "The Response of State and Local Governments to Federal Grants." *National Tax Journal* (Sept., 1968).

Stubblebine, W. Craig. *The Social Imbalance Hypothesis.* Ph.D. dissertation, University of Virginia, 1963.

Studenski, Paul, and Herman E. Krooss. *Financial History of the United States.* New York: McGraw-Hill, 1952.

Tax Foundation. *Facts and Figures on Government Finance; 16th Biennial Edition.* New York: The Foundation, 1971.

_____. *Growth Trends of New Federal Programs: 1955–1968.* New York: The Foundation, 1967.

U.S. Bureau of the Census. *Governmental Finances in 1970.* Washington, D.C.: U.S. Government Printing Office, 1971.

_____. *Historical Statistics of the United States: Colonial Times to 1957.* Washington, D.C.: U.S. Government Printing Office, 1961.

_____. *Statistical Abstract of the United States.* Washington, D.C.: U.S. Government Printing Office, 1960, 1963, 1965, 1966, 1968, 1969, and 1970.

Weicher, John F. "Determinants of Central City Expenditures: Some Overlooked Factors and Problems." *National Tax Journal,* 3 (Dec., 1970).

Wilensky, Gail R. *State Aid and Educational Opportunity.* Beverly Hills, Calif.: Sage Publications, 1970.

4. Public versus Private Provision of Governmental Services   *Robert M. Spann*

Introduction

Society chooses to consume many goods and services on a collective basis. Examples of such goods and services include garbage collection, education, police protection, fire protection, and in some areas, the provision of electric power. The fact that such goods and services are financed by tax revenues (in whole or in part) and consumed in some type of collective fashion does not mean that such goods must be produced by the government. Many cities, instead of having their own sanitation and fire departments, contract private firms, via competitive bidding, to provide such services. Some hospitals are privately owned, some are publicly owned. Electric utilities may be either publicly or privately owned.

An important question is, does the substitution of a private firm for a government producer lower the costs of providing such services? There are reasons to suspect that private ownership of supplying units may reduce the costs of providing local government services. As Professor A. A. Alchian [2] notes, the rewards and costs of an activity are more directly concentrated on each individual responsible for decisions in private enterprise. An individual will take more care in making decisions when his own wealth is at stake than when the wealth of others is at stake. Private firms must meet the pressure of the market place. Inefficient firms can be underpriced and driven out of business by more efficient firms.

The case of public firms is somewhat different. Government decision makers (especially tenured civil servants) have much less of their own wealth at stake in decisions made in governmental agencies.

The average stockholder can monitor the activities of any firm in which he owns an interest by examining the firm's profit and loss statement. The owners of government enterprises (the electorate) are not provided with any such balance sheet. The individual voter can scan newspapers, city budgets, and legislative hearings in order to determine the efficiency of governmental endeavors. However, this information is costly to obtain (if only in terms of the time involved), and the reduction in one's tax bill due to discerning such information may be small.

Source note: This paper benefited from helpful comments and criticisms of participants in the bureaucracy seminar at Virginia Polytechnic Institute and State University.

The stockholder in a private firm has another advantage over the owners of government enterprises (the voters). If a stockholder in a private firm is dissatisfied with management's performance, he can sell his stock in the enterprise. The only way in which a voter can "sell his stock" in a public enterprise is by moving outside the boundaries of that political jurisdiction. While this might be an effective long-run constraint on state and local governments, it is expensive for the average voter to express his dissatisfaction in this manner in the short run. With regard to federal governments, this option is virtually unfeasible for the average voter.

On the grounds of the direct incentives inherent in private enterprise but lacking in governmental enterprise, and on the basis the differences in options open to the "stockholders" of the two enterprises, one would expect private firms to be more efficient than governmental enterprises.

There may, of course, be some incentives within the political structure which act to counterbalance these effects. Different candidates and different political parties compete for government office. One way in which these candidates or parties may compete for voter support is by offering to provide the same services at lower cost (in terms of taxes).[1] In some areas of government enterprise, the output of the government is sold at a price and any "profits" can be used to reduce local taxes. One example is municipal utilities. In other areas government suppliers might compete directly with private suppliers of the same services. An example of this type of competition is hospitals.

In what follows, I shall discuss the conditions under which government supply of goods and services may be efficient or inefficient relative to private suppliers. Then some examples will be presented which illustrate these points and serve as base points for estimates to the efficiency of public versus private supply of government services. These examples will be in the areas of Australian airlines, fire protection, electricity, hospitals, and garbage collection. In all of these cases, private firms are more efficient or at least no less efficient than publicly owned enterprises.

Factors Affecting the Efficiency of Governmental Provision of Services

In this section, four factors[2] that might affect the efficiency of government provision of goods and services are discussed. They are:

1. Competition between political parties may not lead to increased efficiency because of factors inherent in the democratic process. Voters are faced with numerous complex issues, and the returns to any one voter of becoming informed on these issues may be small. See Tullock [11].

2. One factor that is omitted in this discussion is competition between political parties as a source of governmental efficiency or inefficiency. Empirical estimates of the degree of

1. Whether the output is sold at a positive price;

2. The size of the political unit versus the optimum scale of operation for governmental services;

3. How much competition there is from alternative sources of supply; and,

4. The mobility of citizens between alternative governmental units.

Each will be discussed individually.

Pricing of Governmental Outputs

Governments at all levels provide a variety of services under various "terms of sale." Police protection is provided to all members of the community. The amount an individual pays for police services is dependent on his tax bill, not on the amount of police services he consumes.[3] Municipal electric companies sell electricity at a price. The amount one pays for electricity is dependent on the amount of electricity he uses. When an output is sold at a price that must cover costs, a limit on governmental inefficiency is automatically determined. In addition, consumers can directly compare the price they pay for such a service to the prices charged in other localities. The easier it is for voters to compare costs, the easier it is for them to press, at election time, for efficient operation of such services.

That an output is sold at a positive price also means that consumers can choose to consume less of that output if the price is too high or the quality of service is too low. This subjects governmental enterprise to at least some of the same pressures that the market place imposes on private firms. Most nonpriced outputs are sold on an all-or-nothing basis. A person either receives police protection or he doesn't. One's children either receive an education or they don't. The average voter can change the quantity of police protection or education he (or his children) receive only at election time. A voter cannot continuously decide how much police services he desires based on the cost to him of alternative levels of police protection. A voter can continuously decide on the amount of

competition between political parties are hard to come by. Even in states with only one political party (such as in the South before the rise of Republicanism in that area) there may be substantial political competition. The primaries in such states may offer as many, if not more, contrasting philosophies and methods of running the government than the general elections in two-party states.

3. If police protection is a pure public good, each citizen's level of consumption is the same. For some estimates of the degree of "publicness" of many state and local services, see Borcherding and Deacon [4]. That paper argues that many of the services provided by state and local governments may be much closer to private goods than public goods.

electricity he will consume based on the costs of alternative levels of consumption.

It is true that many of these market forces can be circumvented by tax subsidization. In many municipal water systems, the revenue collected via water bills does not cover the costs of providing water. This might reduce some of the market forces operating to increase efficiency in government enterprise. But, by the same token, excess revenues (i.e., revenues which exceed costs) from government enterprise can be used to subsidize other governmental activities. Thus, opportunities for subsidization work two ways, and it is still possible that the pricing of government-produced goods and services, with the opportunities for citizens to quantity adjust, will lead to more efficient production of these outputs.

Size of Political Unit versus Optimum Scale of Operation

For any particular product, there is some scale of operation (or level of output) at which the unit cost of producing that output is minimized. In some production processes, the cost minimizing size of plant may be fairly small. For others, the optimum size of plant or operation may be very large. This is true of government-produced goods and services also.

In competitive markets, firms and plants generally operate at the optimum scale for that particular output. Profit maximization requires that one minimize the costs of producing any given output. This does not occur in the case of goods and services provided by governments. The scale of operation for most government-produced goods and services is identical to the size of the political unit corresponding to that government. There is no reason to believe that political units are set up so as to minimize the costs of government provided goods and services. Even if political units were set up in such a fashion, it still does not follow (except by chance) that all the goods and services provided by a particular governmental unit have the same optimum scale of operation.

One good example of this problem is municipal electric systems.[4] The optimum scale of operation for both electrical generating plants and electrical companies as a whole is fairly large. Municipal electrical systems are generally restricted to one municipality plus some surrounding areas. If this area or size of operation is small, the costs of electricity produced by small municipalities may be fairly high even if there are no inefficiencies in operation because of bureaucratic behavior and so on. The high cost of producing electricity in this system would be due to the fact that the size of the system is controlled by political boundaries, not by the forces of the market place.

4. For more on municipal electric systems, see the section on electric utilities below.

The optimum scale of operation for other government-produced goods and services may be much smaller than the political unit. In many local governments the optimum size school may be smaller than the total number of children in the community. In this case, it is true that several schools, each of optimum size, can be built. However, there may be diseconomies of scale in the management and administration of many schools. The optimum number of schools per school board (optimum in the sense of minimizing per unit administrative and managerial costs) may be fewer than the number of schools in the community. In this case, cost inefficiencies will be introduced due to an administrative system that exceeds the optimum size.

Competition from Alternative Sources of Supply

In some areas government enterprises compete directly or indirectly with private suppliers. Hospitals may be privately or publicly owned. In many areas of the country, doctors and patients have a choice of using either a public or private hospital. Many universities run on-campus hotels that compete, at least indirectly, with privately owned hotels and motels. Some areas of the country are served by municipal electric companies and privately owned gas companies. These two firms, one government, one private, compete directly for heating customers.

One would expect competition to exert some market pressure on government enterprises to hold down costs (since customers can always opt for the privately produced output if they desire) and to eliminate some of the opportunities for discretionary behavior on the part of bureaucracies.[5]

Competition from private firms may also lead to a higher quality of government services. A government enterprise cannot survive long if its customers can get a product more to their liking from a privately owned firm in the market place. Privately owned firms must produce what consumers desire or they go out of business. Thus, privately owned firms have a strong incentive to produce the type of output the public desires (measured by the fact that the public is willing to pay for it). Government enterprises, when in competition with private firms, must be able to produce a product of similar quality or they will have no customers.[6]

5. That competition from private, profit-maximizing firms eliminates some of the opportunities for discretionary behavior on the part of bureaucracies may explain why professional educators are the most vocal opponents of voucher systems in local education.

6. This is the reverse of the often cited argument in the public press that government producers set quality standards which must be followed by private firms in order for those firms to stay in business. This argument reverses the causation in the text. It is also erroneous. A private firm can stay in business only if the public is willing to buy its product. As noted in the introduction, the reward structure in private enterprise is such that the costs and benefits of decision are borne by those who make decisions. This is not always

Mobility of the Citizenry

One way citizens can exert an important restraining force on governmental inefficiency is by "voting with their feet." If citizens are dissatisfied with the performance of the government, the level of services or the level of taxes, they always have the option of moving. People moving into a new locality often have the choice of living in any one of several communities. Suburban areas, in which there are numerous political units, offer a good illustration. An individual moving to the New York City area has the option of living in any one of several communities in three states (New Jersey, Connecticut, or New York) all with similar commuting distances to New York City. The individual can "shop around" for the community with the level of services, degree of taxation, and general atmosphere most to his liking. The opportunity for citizens to "vote with their feet" places many governments in a position similar to firms in a competitive market. These governmental units must be at least as efficient as neighboring units or they will lose residents (customers).[7]

Since citizens are more mobile between local governments than between states we would expect local government services to be provided more efficiently than state government services. The costs of moving from one nation to another are extremely high, so we would not expect citizen mobility to exert much pressure on efficiency in the federal government.[8]

Empirical Evidence on the Efficiency of Public versus Private Provision of Goods and Services

In this section several empirical studies of the relative costs of government enterprises versus private enterprises are summarized. These studies are in the areas of Australian airlines, electric utilities, fire protection, hospitals, and garbage collection.

---

true in the public sector. Therefore, there are much stronger incentives for private firms to be "in tune" with what the public desires. This proposition is difficult, if not impossible, to test empirically. Some casual empiricism seems to confirm it, however. Ralph Nader to the contrary, we observe far more complaints about the quality of service in local education, garbage pickup, and police services than the quality of American automobiles. We observe families willing to pay substantial sums of money to send their children to private instead of public colleges. At the height of complaints about phone service in New York City, no one suggested that the situation could be improved by allowing New York City to take over the operation of the New York Telephone Company.

7. It is true that the reward structure in public enterprise, even with this mobility, is not as keyed to the actual costs and benefits of decisions as the reward structure in private enterprise. However, this mobility will increase the efficiency of local governments per se.

8. Tullock, in some as yet unpublished work [11], has argued that local governments show fewer signs of bureaucratic behavior than do other governmental units.

Australian Airlines

Australia[9] has two trunk airlines (equivalent to interstate airlines in the U.S.A.): TransAustralian Airways (TAA), a government firm, and Ansett Australian National Airways (Ansett ANA), a private firm. Government policy is purposely designed to make these airlines similar in many important aspects. The government requires that the airlines fly similar routes, make similar ports of call, be treated equally with respect to airport facilities, charge equal prices, and use similar aircraft.

D. G. Davies has compared the efficiency of these two airlines using three productivity measures: tons of freight and mail carried per employee, passengers carried per employee, and revenue earned per employee. These three productivity measures for the two airlines are listed in Table 1. In order to determine the relative efficiency of the two airlines, Davies divides the productivity measure for Ansett ANA (the privately owned firm) by the productivity measure for TAA (the government airline). These figures are listed in Table 2 in percentage terms.

The data clearly indicate that the private airline is more efficient than the public airline. In terms of freight and mail, the private airline is twice as efficient as the public airline; in terms of passengers, the private airline is 22 percent more efficient than the public airline; and, in terms of revenue per employee, the private airline is 13 percent more efficient than the public airline.

Davies's study would probably indicate an even stronger indictment of public ownership if Australian law did not require the two airlines to be similar in every respect. The pricing, routing, and service levels required by the government are not necessarily the most efficient pricing, routing, and service levels. If the private airline were allowed to determine its own routing and service levels, it is possible that the measured inefficiency of public ownership relative to private ownership would be even greater.

In any event, Davies's study is strong evidence that private ownership and production is more efficient than public ownership. According to Davies's study, substitution of private production for public production would reduce costs by at least 13 percent.

Electric Utilities

Electricity is produced and sold by both publicly owned and privately owned firms. In this section, two studies of electric utility costs by mode of ownership are presented.

Wallace and Junk [12] have examined the costs of electrical gen-

9. This section is based on Davies [6].

Robert M. Spann

Table 1. Productivity of Australian trunk airlines

Year	Tons of freight and mail carried per employee	Passengers carried per employee	Revenue earned per employee
	TAA		
1958–59	4.42	217	$ 6104
1959–60	4.57	259	7016
1960–61	4.52	228	7052
1961–62	4.64	246	7367
1962–63	4.69	255	7726
1963–64	4.83	274	8093
1964–65	5.02	287	8553
1965–66	4.88	294	9072
1966–67	5.11	316	9954
1967–68	5.41	337	11033
1968–69	5.34	356	11734
Mean	4.86	279	8428
	Ansett Transport Industries, Air Group		
1958–59	10.69	282	$ 7172
1959–60	10.77	309	7758
1960–61	10.96	337	8679
1961–62	10.84	331	8425
1962–63	11.09	316	8510
1963–64	11.06	324	9071
1964–65	12.14	352	9705
1965–66	11.08	354	10479
1966–67	10.34	348	10829
1967–68	9.57	363	12080
1968–69	9.54	392	13185
Mean	10.73	337	9627

Source: D. G. Davies, "The Efficiency of Public versus Private Firms, The Case of Australia's Two Airlines," *Journal of Law and Economics* (April, 1971).

erating systems by mode of ownership. They computed both operating costs on a per kilowatt hour basis and capacity costs on a kilowatt basis for eight regions of the country for municipal and investor owned utilities.[10] The results of that study are listed in Table 3.

10. State lines were followed in setting up the regions. Region I includes Maine, Vermont, New Hampshire, Massachusetts, Connecticut, Rhode Island, New Jersey, Delaware, New York, Maryland, Pennsylvania, and the District of Columbia. Region II includes Michigan, Indiana, Ohio, West Virginia, and Kentucky. Region III includes Virginia, North Carolina, South Carolina, Georgia, Florida, Alabama, Mississippi, and Tennessee. Region IV includes Wisconsin, Minnesota, Iowa, Missouri, and Illinois. Region V includes Kansas, Oklahoma, Arkansas, Louisiana, Texas, and New Mexico. Region VI includes North Dakota, South Dakota, Nebraska, Wyoming, and Colorado. Region VII includes

Table 2. Ansett productivity measures as a percentage of TAA productivity measures

Year	Freight and mail	Passengers	Revenue
1958–59	242	130	117
1959–60	236	119	111
1960–61	242	148	123
1961–62	234	135	114
1962–63	236	124	110
1963–64	229	118	112
1964–65	242	123	113
1965–66	227	120	116
1966–67	202	110	109
1967–68	177	108	109
1968–69	179	110	112
Mean	204	122	113

Source: Davies, "The Efficiency of Public versus Private Firms."

As can be readily seen, municipal generating systems have both higher operating costs and higher investment costs than do private firms. Unfortunately, the Wallace and Junk study confounds two effects in its measurement of the relative costs of municipal versus investor owned utilities. The municipal utilities could have higher costs because they are smaller than the investor-owned utilities or they could have higher costs because they are publicly owned (or both).[11] The optimum scale of operation for an electric company is fairly large. Therefore, the Wallace and Junk results could indicate that municipal electric systems are costly because of their small size alone. Alternatively, their results could indicate not only inefficiencies because of small size, but additional inefficiencies in the operation of municipal electric systems because of public ownership.

In order to eliminate the effect of size on cost comparisons between municipal and privately owned electric companies, I examined two large municipal electric companies, one in Los Angeles and one in San Antonio, and compared them to two similar privately owned companies,

---

Washington, Oregon, Idaho, Montana, and Utah. Region VIII includes California, Nevada, and Arizona. The averages were also computed for states and a finer regional breakdown based on the 16 National Power Survey study areas. The results were similar to those presented in Table 1 and hence were excluded from this paper.

11. Wallace and Junk explicitly recognize this in their paper. They state that their primary purpose is to derive estimates of the inefficiency of municipal generating systems due to their small size. As such they eliminated seven municipal generating systems with KWH sales in excess of 200,000 KWH annually.

Table 3. Steam generating investment and operating cost comparisons: Selected municipal and private electric systems

Region	Operating cost per KWH (mills)		Investment per KWH ($)	
	1. Municipal	2. Private	3. Municipal	4. Private
I	8.61	4.30	209	145
II	5.88	2.96	166	126
III	6.67	3.31	202	104
IV	6.21	3.79	179	137
V	4.82	2.65	157	94
VI	4.87	3.99	156	151
VII	–	2.79	–	145
VIII	5.25	3.75	129	116
All systems	6.09	3.49	172	124

Source: Based on data reported in Federal Power Commission, *Statistics of Electric Utilities in the United States: Publicly Owned* (Washington, D.C.: U.S. Government Printing Office, 1964 and 1965).

San Diego Gas and Electric Company and Dallas Power and Light.[12] For each company, I calculated the operating costs (net of taxes) and net electric plant per 1000 KWH for both 1969 and 1965. These results are listed in Tables 4 and 5.

In 1965, the privately owned companies (San Diego and Dallas) had lower operating costs and smaller amounts of investment per 1000 KWH than did their publicly owned counterparts (Los Angeles and San Antonio, respectively). In 1969, Los Angeles appears to have lower costs than San Diego. San Antonio had higher investment costs but lower operating costs than did Dallas. In order to obtain a direct cost comparison for the two Texas utilities, average costs were computed for each company. Average costs were defined to be investment costs per 1000 KWH times the cost of raising funds plus operating costs per 1000 KWH. Average costs estimates were made using interest rates or cost of funds estimates of 4, 6, and 8 percent. These cost estimates are listed in

12. The private companies chosen for comparison (Dallas Power and Light in the case of San Antonio and San Diego Gas and Electric in the case of Los Angeles) were chosen on the following grounds: Fuel costs and capacity costs are the major components of electrical generating costs; by comparing companies in similar areas of the country I am able to hold these factors constant. Second, the cost of transmitting and distributing electric power is generally higher in rural areas than in urban areas. Urban-rural cost differences are recognized in the rate structure of many investor owned companies. One large municipal system, Jacksonville, Florida, was not used because of the lack of a comparable urban privately owned system in Florida. Preliminary work indicated that Jacksonville has lower operating costs than the two large investor owned companies in Florida, but it could not be determined whether this was due to actual efficiency or urban-rural cost differences.

Table 4. Cost comparisons for private and publicly owned electric utilities — 1965

	Los Angeles	San Diego	San Antonio	Dallas
Net electric plant per 1000 KWH	$77.25	$65.49	$68.62	$53.91
Operating costs per 1000 KWH	10.65	10.64	8.17	7.50

Table 6. As can be seen, Dallas Power and Light (the private firm) has lower average costs at every interest rate.

In Table 7 costs per kilowatt (KW) of capacity for each of the four firms are listed. In both years the privately owned firms, Dallas Power and Light and San Diego Gas and Electric, have smaller investment costs per KW of installed capacity. The fact that San Diego's cost per KW of installed capacity is much less than that of Los Angeles is due to differences in capacity utilization between the two firms. One measure of capacity utilization is the system load factor. The system load factor is the amount of KWH actually generated divided by the number of KWH that could have been generated had the system operated at full capacity all year long. The maximum KWH that could have been generated if the system always operated at full capacity is computed by taking the kilowatt capacity of the firm and multiplying it by 8760, the number of hours in a year. Load factors for each of these four firms are listed in Table 8.

As can be seen Los Angeles has a much higher load factor than San Diego. This load factor difference could be because of differences in the characteristics of the customers served by the two systems or the fact that Los Angeles is able to use its existing plant more efficiently than is San Diego.

The data do allow us to draw some tentative conclusions concerning the efficiency of public versus private supply of electric power. The high cost of many municipal electric systems (as indicated by the data in Table 3) is due partly to their small size. When systems of similar size are com-

Table 5. Cost comparisons for private and publicly owned electric utilities — 1969

	Los Angeles	San Diego	San Antonio	Dallas
Net electric plant per 1000 KWH	$74.60	$77.67	$60.65	$50.05
Operating costs per 1000 KWH	9.98	10.27	6.86	7.20

Table 6. 1965 Average cost comparisons at various interest rates – Dallas and San Antonio

Interest rate or cost of funds (%)	Cost per 1000 KWH ($)	
	San Antonio	Dallas
4	9.46	9.20
6	10.76	10.21
8	12.07	11.21

pared, private firms may still be less expensive to operate. There are too few observations for valid statistical inferences, however. San Antonio's municipal power company has higher costs than Dallas Power and Light. Depending on how one treats the problem of capacity utilization, the Los Angeles Municipal electric company may or may not be less efficient than San Diego Gas and Electric, a privately owned firm. Los Angeles and San Diego have similar costs per KWH but Los Angeles has much higher costs per KW of installed capacity.

The weakest conclusion allowed by the data is that the costs of government services would be no more if private producers were substituted for public firms of equal size in this sector.[13] It is possible, however, that private firms are more efficient.

Fire Protection

Fire protection is provided by almost every local government via publicly owned fire departments. One city, Scottsdale, Arizona, has elected not to have a public fire department but to contract with the Rural-Metropolitan Fire Protection Company for the provision of fire services.

Table 7. Net electric plant per KW of capacity: 1965 and 1969

	1965	1969
Los Angeles	$342.48	$352.08
San Diego	205.47	214.18
San Antonio	172.17	161.93
Dallas	153.44	160.79

13. That the privately owned utilities pay federal income taxes presents no problem. Suppose the sole difference in rates between a private and a publicly owned firm is federal income tax. Then taxpayers in other sections of the country are subsidizing the customers of the municipal electric system. If this subsidization is what the electorate actually desires, it could be accomplished through a direct transfer of income.

Table 8. Load factors: 1965 and 1969

Los Angeles	.5212	.5212
San Diego	.3953	.4187
San Antonio	.3065	.3065
Dallas	.3468	.3508

The city's contract with the firm is for four years. If the city is not satisfied with the service it receives, it can always form its own fire protection company or seek out an alternative supplier of fire protection services. The difference between the amount Scottsdale pays for fire protection presently and what it would cost to operate an equivalent public fire department has been examined in a recent paper by Ahlbrandt [1].

In order to determine the costs of publicly owned fire departments, Ahlbrandt estimated cost relationships for 44 publicly owned fire departments in the state of Washington. Cost equations were estimated in which costs per capita was dependent on population, area served, assessed value, percentage of housing units lacking plumbing, a wage index, fire insurance rating, number of aid cars, number of volunteers, number of fire stations, number of full-time personnel and a set of variables to distinguish volunteer from paid fire departments.[14]

Ahlbrandt then used the cost function to predict costs for some Arizona cities with public fire departments. It predicted these costs accurately. He then made cost predictions for Scottsdale, Arizona. Predicted fire protection costs per capita (assuming a public fire department) were $7.10, whereas the cost of the services of the Rural-Metropolitan Fire Protection Company were $3.78.[15] In other words, were Scottsdale to establish its own fire department, and operate it at the same level of efficiency as other public fire departments, the costs of fire protection to the residents would double. Thus, in this sector, private firms appear to be much more efficient than public firms.

Garbage Collection

Garbage collection services are provided both by public sanitation departments and by private contractors. Some cities use their own sanitation departments whereas others contract private firms to provide garbage collection services. In this section, several studies of the costs of solid waste disposal are presented and reviewed.

14. For a more detailed discussion of this cost function and why each variable was included, see Ahlbrandt [1].

15. Some of Rural-Metropolitan's overhead is allocated to other cities it serves. Even if one allocates all this overhead to Scottsdale, that city's fire protection charges would increase only to $5.12. This is still less than the estimated costs of a public fire department.

The Planning Board in Monmouth County, New Jersey conducted a survey of garbage collection costs in the communities in that county [10]. The results of that study are reproduced in Table 9.[16] As can be seen communities using private contractors have significantly lower costs than communities with public sanitation departments. The average per capita cost of garbage collection is $8.33 for cities with municipal sanitation departments and $5.84 for cities using private contractors.

W. Hirsch, in a paper published in the *Review of Economics and Statistics* [7] examined the costs of garbage collection in 24 St. Louis suburbs. Hirsch found that costs were lower in communities that used private contractors (see Table 10).[17] This effect is not statistically significant.

One explanation of the fact that Hirsch found private collection less costly but not significantly so, is the small size and relative proximity of the cities in his sample. All the observations are from neighboring suburban communities. One might expect a high degree of mobility between communities. Residents of the entire St. Louis area are able to choose among different communities based on the attributes of those communities and the level of services provided by the governments in those communities.

This competition between communities forces public firms to behave more like private firms and should reduce the costs of publicly provided services to somewhere near the costs of private provision of those services.

Table 9. 1965 average per capita cost of refuse collection and disposal — Monmouth County

	Services provided by	
	Municipality	Contractor
Average per capita cost	$ 8.33	$5.84
Residential communities with a small business district		
Two residential collections/week	6.06	5.29
Three residential collections/week	(None)	6.84
Residential community with a large business district		
Two residential collections/week	9.61	5.76
Three residential collections/week	(None)	4.67
Residential community with a large summer population influx		
Three summer residential collections/week	10.40	8.49

16. No tests of statistical significance were reported in the Monmouth County study.

17. Hirsch finds that user cost pricing raises costs, contrary to our expectations. However, he notes that this may be due to the small number of cities with such pricing.

Table 10. Cost function for garbage collection[a]

$X_1 = 6.16 + 0.000\ 0890\ X_2$
           $(0.000\ 195)$
  $-\ 0.000\ 000\ 000\ 436\ X_2^2 + 3.61\ X_3$
       $(0.000\ 000\ 000\ 832)$ (1.14)
  $+\ 3.97\ X_4 - 0.000\ 611\ X_5 - 1.87\ X_6$
       (1.50) $(0.000\ 442)$ (2.40)
  $+\ 3.43\ X_7$
       (1.10)

where,

X_1 = 1960 average annual residential refuse collection and disposal cost per
      pickup in dollars,
X_2 = number of pickup units,
X_3 = weekly collection frequency,
X_4 = pickup location, where curb pickup is 0 and rear of house pickup is 1,
X_5 = pickup density, i.e., number of residential pickups per square mile,
X_6 = nature of contractual arrangements, where municipal collection is 0 and
      private collection is 1, and
X_7 = type of financing, where general revenue financing is 0 and user charge
      financing is 1.

a. Standard errors of estimate are in parenthesis.

Health Care

Cost considerations may not be the only relevant variable in comparison between public and private provision of goods and services. One might also be concerned with the quality of services provided. This is especially true in areas that involve human life[18] and in areas in which consumers may have difficulty in making accurate a priori quality comparisons. A good example of such a good or service is health care. In this section cost and quality differences[19] between public, nonprofit, and profit hospitals and nursing homes are examined.

Accurate cost and quality comparisons in the health care sector are difficult to obtain. Several studies have been conducted which attempt to make such comparisons. Unfortunately, it is impossible to hold all the important variables constant in such studies, and, as a result, these studies must be interpreted with care.

A study of 118 Minnesota nursing homes [3] attempted to discern quality differences by mode of ownership. Four categories of nursing

18. Much of this section is based on "Proprietary and Non-Proprietary Health Care" [9].
19. Comparing cost and quality independently is not quite correct. Under competitive conditions, one would expect differences in quality to be compensated for by price differences.

homes were examined: corporate taxables, noncorporate taxables, non-government nontaxable, and government.

Only four quality variables (out of a possible 96) were found to differ significantly between the four modes of ownership. They were:

1. Nongovernment nontaxables have more registered nurses per licensed practical nurse than do all taxables;

2. Corporate taxables have a greater variety of physician specialities than do all nontaxables;

3. Corporate taxables have more therapeutic services than do non-taxables; and,

4. All nontaxables have fewer patients per room than do corporate taxables.

The study also found that nonprofit hospitals have somewhat more physician hours per patient than do profit hospitals. However, no other quality indicators were found to differ by mode by ownership.

A study by Schuyler Kohl [8] examined cases of perinatal mortality in New York City hospitals for the period 1950–1951 by mode of ownership. Once the relevant adjustments are made to the data, there was little difference in the percentage of preventable deaths (one index of quality) between proprietary (profit) and nonproprietary hospitals.[20] Both these studies would indicate that the quality of health care, as measured by various variables, differs little among ownership modes.

Another, quasi-quality characteristic of health care might be participation in state and local health care programs and the willingness of various hospitals to take high-risk, expensive patients who might not be able to pay their bills. A recent Ph.D. thesis by Lloyd L. Cannedy [5] found that investor owned hospitals and nonprofit hospitals participated equally in local, state, and county health insurance programs. This implies that profit hospitals are not more likely to exclude high-risk patients who are typically sponsored by the local, county, state, and federal government.

Another way of comparing health care facilities is to ask potential customers to rate various institutions. Such a study of New York nursing homes was conducted using potential nursing home customers. Both proprietary and other nursing homes were found in the group of highly rated nursing homes. Similarly, the group of homes rated lower by potential customers included both proprietary and nonproprietary hospitals.[21] Thus, potential consumers feel that there are some good hospitals in both types of ownership and some bad hospitals in both types of owner-

20. For a more detailed discussion of the Kohl study, see [9].
21. See [9], p. 20.

Table 11. Construction costs for nursing homes

	Average cost per bed	
Size in beds	Voluntary[a]	Proprietary[b]
300 and over	24,959.00	11,811.00
200–299	19,350.00	9,181.00
1–199	18,230.00	8,888.00

Source: "Planned Capital Formation in Nursing Homes in New York City," *Inquiry* (Dec., 1969).
  a. Does not include land costs
  b. Includes land costs

ship. No general inferences about quality can be drawn based on mode of ownership alone.

Cost and price comparisons by mode of ownership are shown in Tables 11 and 12. Average construction costs per bed from a 1969 nursing home study are shown in Table 11. The data indicates construction costs are much higher in voluntary hospitals than in profit hospitals. This study did not adjust for quality differences so exact cost inferences may not be appropriate. In Table 12 mean charges and costs per patient day from the Minnesota nursing home study indicates that profit hospitals have slightly higher prices but slightly lower costs. In Table 13 costs per in-patient day for various size hospitals are compared by mode of ownership. It appears that nonprofits are cheaper in the small size categories while profit hospitals are cheaper in the larger size classes.

The data in Tables 11–13 might be construed to imply that profit hospitals have lower costs than nonprofits. Even though evidence was presented earlier to the effect that there are no quality differences systematically related to ownership, the costs in Tables 11–13 are not quality adjusted. Thus, one cannot be sure that the cost comparisons are completely accurate.

The overall picture generated by the results cited in this section is important. Quality differences in health care institutions are not systematically related to mode of ownership. We observe both good and bad profit hospitals and both good and bad nonprofit hospitals. Although there

Table 12. Mean charges per month and estimated costs per patient day by nursing home type – 1967

	Proprietary	Non-proprietary
Charge per month	$298.60	$270.84
Cost per day	7.47	7.91

Source: Nursing Home Care, ibid.

Table 13. Mean expense per inpatient day for community hospitals in 1968

Number of beds	Non-profit	For-profit chain	For-profit non-chain
under 50	$44.73	$60.78	$51.55
50–99	47.64	67.73	52.42
100–199	55.23	66.20	46.77
200 and over	67.44	58.72	56.33

Source: "Study of For-Profit Hospitals Chains," mimeographed, May 22, 1970.

is some indication that profit hospitals may have lower costs than non-profits, any such conclusion is tenuous at best due to quality adjustment problems. The implications of this study is that the substitution of private provision of health care for the public provision of health care will not lower health care quality but might lower health care costs slightly.

Conclusion

The costs of public versus private provision of goods and services have been compared for five activities: airlines, garbage collection, hospitals, fire protection, and electric utilities. For the majority of activities, private producers can provide the same services at the same, or lower costs than can public producers. In some cases, the costs of private firms are half that of governmental agencies for producing the same good or service.

In the case of electricity, a major portion of the cost differences between publicly owned and privately owned utilities is due to size differences. Most municipal electric systems are simply too small to be efficient. Even for similar sized electric firms, there is some evidence that private producers may be more efficient than public firms. In the case of hospitals and nursing homes, there are little cost or quality differences between profit, nonprofit, and government hospitals.

These results also indicate that market forces are an important means of encouraging efficiency. The two services for which private and public production has similar costs, at similar sized scales of operation, electricity and health care, are both services in which governmental suppliers must compete (indirectly or directly) with private firms. In addition, the output of these sectors are sold on a per unit basis and consumers can quantity adjust.

Size of community and competition between communities appears to effect costs also. Hirsch in his refuse collection cost study, found that suburban communities close to each other have costs similar to those of private firms, probably resulting from competition between communities for new residents which leads to a more efficient provision of public services.

The results also indicate that a number of governmental functions can be taken over by private producers with an attendent reduction in the costs of government (or at least no increase). Public provision or consumption of a good or service does not imply public production of that good or service. As indicated in this study, garbage and fire services may be provided more cheaply by contracting with private firms rather than by using city run sanitation or fire departments. There is no reason why similar results would not be true of education, police, and other services. Even in areas where quality may be very important, such as health care, there is no reason to prefer government producers over private producers.

The savings due to the use of private contractors as opposed to public firms can be imputed to two factors: (1) private profit-maximizing firms have an incentive to minimize costs whereas public firms or agencies do not (except under the circumstances noted above); and (2) the size of private firms is not restricted by political boundaries as is the size of governmental producers; private firms are able to reach the maximum efficient size, an opportunity necessarily not allowed public firms.

References

1. Ahlbrandt, Roger. "Efficiency in the Provision of Fire Services." *Public Choice* (fall, 1973).
2. Alchian, A. A. "Some Economics of Property Rights." Paper delivered at the 15th General Meeting of the Mont Pelerin Society, Stresa, Italy. (Mimeographed, Sept., 1965).
3. American Rehabilitation Foundation. *Nursing Home Care: A Minnesota Analysis.* Minneapolis, Minn.: The Foundation, summer, 1968.
4. Borcherding, T. E., and R. T. Deacon. "The Demand for the Services of Non-Federal Governments: An Econometric Approach to Collective Choice." *American Economic Review* (Dec., 1973).
5. Cannedy, Lloyd L. "A Heuristic Inquiry Into the Variability of Investor Owned For-Profit Hospital Chains: An Exploratory Consideration of Social Impact and Public Policy." Unpublished Ph.D. thesis, University of Iowa, 1971.
6. Davies, D. G. "The Efficiency of Public versus Private Firms: The Case of Australia's Two Airlines." *Journal of Law and Economics* (April, 1971).
7. Hirsch, W. "Cost Functions of Government Service: Refuse Collection." *Review of Economics and Statistics* (Feb., 1965).
8. Kohl, Schuyler G. *Perinatal Mortality in New York City.* Cambridge, Mass.: Harvard University Press, 1955.
9. *Proprietary and Non-Proprietary Health Care.* Washington, D.C.: ICF, Inc., 1970.
10. *Study and Plan of Refuse Collection and Disposal — Monmouth County.* Monmouth County, N.J.: Monmouth County Planning Board, June, 1966 (reprinted May, 1971).
11. Tullock, Gordon. "On the Social Costs of Eliminating Social Costs." Unpublished paper, Virginia Polytechnic Institute and State University, 1972.
12. Wallace, R. L., and P. E. Junk. "Economic Inefficiency of Small Municipal Electrical Generating Systems." *Land Economics* (Nov., 1970).

5. The Voting Behavior of Bureaucrats and Public Sector Growth   *Winston C. Bush and Arthur T. Denzau*

Introduction

It has long been recognized that minority groups who have intense preferences concerning certain public policies have a disproportionate influence on the outcomes of elections. The influence of one growing minority group, government employees, on the growth of the public sector will be the subject of this paper. We have made a search of the literature and, with the exception of Tullock [18, 19], no social scientist has analyzed this question directly. Niskanen [14] does indirectly examine some of the problems discussed here.

Although it may be argued that everyone is affected by government policies, some groups are more affected than others. These groups might be expected to show a higher turnout at the polls than the public at large. Data from national and local elections in both the United States and European countries show that government employees have the highest turnout of any occupational group (see Martin [13], Tingsten [17] and Dupeaux [10]). Although this result suggests that bureaucratic involvement in government is greater than that of any other, the relevant question is in what direction do bureaucrats influence government spending and how important is this influence? Before data are brought to bear on this problem, a theoretical model must be developed to determine some hypotheses to be tested that would confirm our suspicions about bureaucratic influence and which suggest the needed data. In the following pages such a theoretical model is developed.

Two questions are investigated concerning the influence of the voting behavior of bureaucrats on public sector growth. First, the relationship between the income of bureaucrats and the growth of the public sector good they produce is analyzed. The application of traditional economic theory suggests that a positive relationship exists. This positive relationship would motivate a bureaucrat to demand a greater quantity of the public good he produces than he would if he were not a bureaucrat. The second question analyzed is, given this motivation on the part of bureaucrats, can they as a group through voting influence the rate of growth of the public sector?

Since rule by the majority is the predominant mechanism for determining the output of public goods in this country, the problem is investigated in this framework. It is shown that since the voting behavior of individuals changes toward a higher demand for public goods as they become bureaucrats, excess public sector growth may be created. Take an initial situation in which the output of the public good is zero. By majority voting it is decided to produce some of the good. This means that bureaucrats are created who will favor a larger quantity of the good in the next election than they did when they were not bureaucrats. A larger quantity of the public good means more bureaucrats who favor larger quantities. This process creates excessive public sector growth.

The Relationship between Wages and Output in a Firm

One can establish a positive relationship between the value of life-time wages of an individual employee of a firm (whether the firm is producing public or private goods) and the growth of the firm. When an individual is hired by a firm, he brings to the firm his general capacities to produce. These general abilities may have been acquired through formal education, through past experience on similar jobs, or in a variety of other ways. But it is not likely that the general training that new employees have acquired will enable them to perform as efficiently at the time they are hired as they will perform after more on-the-job training related to their specific duties with this particular firm is acquired. That is, as an employee obtains more specific, on-the-job training, he can perform more efficiently (more output per hours worked).

The wages per time period (hours, week, month, etc.) that are paid to a wage earner are closely tied to the contribution that he makes to additional value of the output of the firm. Wages of an individual are the productivity attributed to that individual. Therefore, the longer an individual is employed by a firm the more efficient he becomes and the higher are his wages.[1] The reason for the increase in wages is the specific training that an individual obtains from working at his job and not from general training he obtained elsewhere.

With competition among firms for employees, the wages an individual with a certain level of general training can earn with different firms should be about the same. By definition, the specific training an employee obtains from a firm will not increase his productivity with other firms by the same amount. Between firms, only general training is related to productivity and wages. Therefore, if an individual works with one firm for a

---

1. Note that we assume everyone is paid his marginal product. For a more detailed analysis in which gaming between workers and managers is allowed see Becker [1]. Becker demonstrates that workers may not obtain all the returns from specific training when gaming takes place.

number of years, he is usually earning more than he could if he quit his job and went to work for another firm.

As long as the output of the firm in which an employee sells his labor services does not decrease, the employee will continue to hold his job and earn a return on both his general and specific training. But, if the demand for the firm's product decreases, the firm's output will decrease and there is a possibility that the individual will be laid off. In such a case, the lifetime earnings are reduced by the probability of layoff multiplied by the difference in wages earned due to the effect of specific training. (Note that we will not consider the complication introduced by the beliefs of nonbureaucrats that they may become bureaucrats after the budget increases. In certain simple formulations of this idea, our result still holds.)

This establishes a positive relationship between a decrease in the output of a firm and a decrease in the lifetime wages of an employee of that firm. The argument for a positive relationship between an increase in the output of a firm and the lifetime wages of an individual employee is more subtle.

There are usually different types of jobs in one firm. The productivity of an individual and, therefore, the returns to both general and specific training will be different on different jobs. When a job is vacated or newly created the managers of a firm will, of course, select the most productive person for the job. All other things the same, the most productive person would be one who is already employed by the firm. He would have picked up some specific training for the job by just working for the firm. Therefore as a firm grows and new jobs are created, the likelihood of a person moving to another job in which his productivity and wages are higher increases. This establishes a positive relationship between the growth of firms and the lifetime wages of workers.

This positive relationship between growth and wages has an effect on the quantity an individual demands for the product of the firm in which he is employed. When he increases his purchase of output from this firm he benefits from the fact that output increases. In effect, the price per unit of output is lowered when an individual buys the product that his firm produces. In the private sector this effect is not a problem and not a significant effect. But as we will show below, it may be an important effect when the public sector is considered.[2]

2. With some validity, a static version of the above argument can be made, comparing two bureaus, one larger than the other. In the larger, the value of specific training is greater, particularly in decision-making areas, as each decision becomes more valuable. To the extent that a worker captures part of the increased value of his specific training, his wage is greater.

A second argument, based on inefficiency, can also be made: bureaucrats are paid more than their marginal products, and larger budgets allow them to increase this differential. Our purpose in this paper is to derive similar results without resorting to such an argument.

An Example of an Ideal Tax and Benefit System[3]

Ranchers have always faced the problem of predators destroying parts of their herd. When a rancher kills a predator, he experiences a net gain of the difference between the value to him of the stock the predator would have destroyed and the cost to him of killing the predator. Although neighboring ranchers do not bear any of the cost of killing the predator, they do gain by the value of their stock the predator would have killed. This means that dead predators are a public good.[4] In this situation, the private net benefit to the rancher who killed the predator is less than the sum of the net benefits to all the ranchers in the community.

For this example let us assume that only a few ranchers are more efficient at destroying predators relative to raising livestock to make private net benefit. Since the community's net benefits of killing predators are greater than private net benefits, further gains are possible to the ranchers from collective action. All ranchers, including the hunting ranchers, could benefit by paying the more efficient hunters to increase their hunting activity. After some point, the net benefits to any one rancher of a dead predator will decrease as more predators are destroyed. If this were not so, a rancher would be making a net benefit from dead predators even after he had paid hunters an amount that was greater than the value of his herd. An efficient, or optimal, quantity of hunting for the community of ranchers would be where the net benefit of an additional dollar paid out to kill predators is zero to each rancher.[5] If any rancher paid less he would lose an opportunity for a net gain. If he paid out more he would incur a net loss at the margin. This holds true for both hunting and nonhunting ranchers. The hunting ranchers must also pay each other up to the point where their net benefits are zero.

Note that in this example, the quantity of the public good, predators killed, is the same for all ranchers, but they may not pay the same amount toward killing predators. This could come about for several reasons: (1) the value of the different ranchers' livestock could be different; (2) some ranchers could be located in an area where predators are less

3. For a more detailed analysis, see Buchanan [7].

4. A public good is one for which the consumption of the good by one individual does not diminish the quantity available for consumption by any other individual (see Samuelson [16]). A public good can also be considered an external effect on individuals of a special sort: only the total production of the good is important. The assignment of the rights to consume a public good are not important. In the case considered, it is quite obvious that dead predators are the matter for rejoicing, not an irrelevant distribution of rights to the carcasses. For a more rigorous statement concerning public goods, see Buchanan [7], Evans [11], or Oakland [15].

5. In more technical terms, the marginal rate of substitution (MRS) between the public good and each private good is equal to the ratio of the marginal cost share of the public good to the price of each private good for all individuals. This is the Lindahl [11] voluntary exchange decision rule.

likely to go; or (3) different ranchers may have different tastes as to risk. In an ideal tax and benefit system in which the quantity of the public good is the same for everyone, each individual is taxed at a rate that will make the net benefits of the last tax dollar paid out zero. But the benefits of a dead predator may not be the same to all; therefore, different ranchers may contribute different amounts of money toward hunting activity.

Bureaucrats and an Ideal Tax and Benefit System

In the above example, the hunting ranchers are the bureaucrats. They devote some or all of their labor services to hunting predators because the wages they earn from the time devoted to hunting is greater than the wages they could earn from time devoted to raising livestock. By organizing their resources as any other firm, the hunters can increase their efficiency, and therefore, their wages. Organization will increase efficiency by eliminating such things as overhunting some areas and underhunting in others. As was discovered above, the wages of the bureaucrats (hunters) are positively related to the growth of output of the public good (hunting and destroying predators).

Since the hunter's wages are related to the quantity of hunting, they receive an additional benefit from increases in hunting activity that they would not receive if they were not bureaucrats. All ranchers benefit from more dead predators since smaller amounts of their herd will be destroyed, but the hunting ranchers' wages also increase. A hunting rancher will, all other things the same, receive a greater net benefit from a dollar spent on hunting activity than he would if he were not a hunting rancher. Because of this additional benefit, a hunting rancher will desire a greater quantity of hunting activity when he becomes a bureaucrat. Although wages and growth of output are positively related in this example, that relationship causes no problem in the ideal tax and benefit system. All ranchers receive the optimal quantity of hunting services.

Since, all other things the same, a hunting rancher receives a higher net benefit from a dollar spent on hunting activity he also pays more per unit of output of hunting services. A higher net benefit for each dollar contributed toward hunting activity means that more dollars must be contributed by a bureaucrat before net benefits are zero than if he were not a bureaucrat.[6]

Bureaucrats in a Democracy

The ideal benefit and tax system described in the last two sections is very difficult to implement when a large number of people are involved.

6. See Borcherding, Bush, and Spann's paper in this volume, chap. 12, Figures 1 and 2 and accompanying text for a more rigorous treatment.

Any one individual in a large group will feel that nonpayment of his taxes will not change the output of the public good significantly. Since he feels that the benefits he receives are not dependent on his tax share, it will be rational for him not to pay. If most people act similarly, the actual quantity of the public good produced will be less than the ideal quantity. Economist refer to this behavior as the "free rider" problem.

A rule prescribing the ideal benefit and tax system will be of little use in solving the "free rider" problem. The net benefits a person receives from a public good is subjective and known only to that person. Since the net benefit to a person is not known by others, there is no obvious way to know whether a person is honestly revealing his preferences.

More sensible as a positive model is a theory of majority rule. In such a model, the citizens vote on changes in the public sector budget, with any proposed change that receives a majority of votes becoming the public policy. Within certain institutional assumptions the equilibrium budget is a well-defined quantity.[7]

If the indifference curves of individuals are concave from above, a majority voting Bowen solution is implied. A Bowen solution is an outcome in which the quantity of the public good supplied is the median of the distribution of the preferred quantities. An individual who demands the median quantity is labeled a median voter.

With a majority voting rule, the rational voting behavior of bureaucrats creates excessive growth of the output of public goods. Let us take an initial situation in which there is no collectively organized hunting activity. The ranchers recognize that hunting activity is a public good and hold a meeting to determine collectively how much will be produced. They decide to use the majority rule in determining the quantity of hunting activity. With respect to the present problem, how or why they choose this rule need not concern us. Tax rates for each individual are also decided upon. Again, how or why these rates are determined need not concern us.

Until the quantity of the hunting activity is decided upon and an agency is set up to carry out the hunting activity, no rancher knows who will be the bureaucrats (hunting ranchers). Therefore, I will assume that, until a rancher is hired to be a bureaucrat, he votes as if he will continue to raise livestock only. He does not take into account that, if hired, his income will increase with increases in the output of the public good (hunting activity). The initial quantity of the public good will be the quantity

7. These institutional assumptions are (1) any individual can submit a proposal for a particular quantity of the public good to be supplied; (2) this proposal is paired against the status quo; (3) voting is instantaneous, costless, and all individuals participate; (4) the majority rules; and (5) logrolling and all other types of gaming are absent. For early analyses of this model, see Bowen [6] or Black [3]. See Bergstrom and Goodman [2], Borcherding and Deacon [5], and Denzau [9] for their applications of the Bowen model.

desired by the rancher who is the median voter. But once the agency is set up to produce hunting activity, the initial situation may be a disequilibrium situation.

As shown above, when a rancher becomes a hunter the optimal quantity of the public good he demands increases. This change in the optimal quantity of hunting activity for hunters will change the distribution of preferred quantities described above. If at least one hunter's optimal quantity before he becomes a bureaucrat was the same as or less than the quantity preferred by the median voters in the initial voting, new median voters may emerge. The reason is that becoming a bureaucrat increases a hunter's optimal quantity of hunting activity and they shift forward in the distribution of preferred quantities of the public good. Therefore, if new median voters emerge, the quantity of the public good they prefer will be greater than that of the initial median voters. In this case, when another meeting is held to determine the level of hunting activity, a larger quantity will be selected since the new median voter's optimal quantity is greater than the initial quantity. This means that more hunters will be hired by the public agency and a possibility that the ordered distribution of optimal quantities is changed such that the median optimal quantity is greater. Another change in the median optimal quantity may set off another round of increases in the number of hunters and a greater optimal quantity. Such a process could cause excessive growth of the public sector.

This growth, however, will not continue forever, even in a converging sequence. Rather, it is more likely that as the public sector budget rises, the wages paid to an individual bureaucrat rise more and more rapidly. A greater proportion of any further increase in the budget will go toward raising the wages of those already employed. An equilibrium position can then occur when an increased budget no longer means a larger employment of bureaucrats. The growth, caused by the switching of individuals from citizens to bureaucrats, will then cease.

The example of excessive growth of hunting activity for the community of ranchers can be applied to the production of public sector goods, in general. This growth process may be called excessive since no changes in underlying conditions are needed to start this process except the change in the quantity demanded of the public good by new bureaucrats. As output of the public good is increased, new bureaucrats are hired. This changes the optimal quantity of the public good desired by the new bureaucrats and the ordered distribution of the optimal quantities for all voters. At this point the possibility of a disequilibrium situation exists in which the median optimal quantity has increased. If so, the outcome of a new vote will be to increase the quantity of the public good until the equilibrium suggested above results.

The likelihood and the extent of excessive public sector growth depends on several things. If for all new bureaucrats hired, their optimal quantity is greater than that of the median voter, no shift in the position of the median voter will take place. Some new bureaucrats' optimal quantity must be the same as or less than the optimal quantity of the median voter for excessive public sector growth to take place. If new bureaucrats are hired at random, there exists a high probability that some will have optimal quantities less than the median voter's. The more closely the bureaucrat's income is tied to the output of the public good the greater the shift in the optimal quantity desired by the new bureaucrat. The greater this shift the greater the change in the ordered distribution and the more likely the optimal median quantity of the public good will increase.

Some Evidence of the Voting Behavior of Bureaucrats

Although we are not able to offer any direct evidence on the influence of bureaucrats on the output of public goods, a study by Martin [13] on voter participation by occupation groups is suggestive. Martin's data are taken from local elections in Austin, Texas, during 1933. Martin found that overall voter participation was 58.1 percent whereas city employees' was 87.6. He concluded that "if all elements comprising Austin's population were as election-minded as municipal employees this city would have no serious problems . . . !" If Martin's findings are general over time and political geography the influence of bureaucrats on election outcomes might be substantial. For instance, if the ratio of bureaucrats and their families to the number of eligible voters is 0.1, a reasonable estimate, and Martin's figures are correct, bureaucrats make up 16 percent of those voting. Of course, 16 percent may be a minimum estimate of their effect when it is recalled that these individuals can also be relied on to contribute in other ways to the success of candidates taking congenial platform positions on their preferred programs.

Assuming Martin is correct on the voting habits of bureaucrats and non-bureaucrats, a power-index of bureaucrats in affecting outcomes is easily computed according to the formula[8]

$$\pi = \frac{V_b}{V_b + V_{nb}(1 - g)/g}$$

where the V's are the voting participation rates of bureaucrats and non-bureaucrats (and their families) and g is the percent of bureaucrats in the labor force. Given that $V_{nb} = .50$ and $V_b = .90$, the following table is computed.

---

8. Developed by Borcherding and Bush in an unpublished paper [4]. The final version of this paper is found in this volume with the additional authorship of Robert M. Spann (see chap. 12).

g	π
0.05	0.08
0.10	0.16
0.20	0.30
0.30	0.44
0.38	0.51
0.40	0.51
.	.
.	.
.	.
1.00	1.00

It is clear now why at one time bureaucrats were not permitted to vote in the political unit where they worked. Consider those employed in education by state and local governments. Though they compose only 5 percent of the work force, by the power-index they effectively hold almost one-tenth of the votes. It seems plausible that such a group may have some effect on public education budgets. Further, with the creation of unions which represent diverse groups of government employees the actual power index of state and local employees may not be much less than their aggregate percentage in the labor force would suggest. In any case, given recent court interpretations collusion among and consolidation of various diverse government unions may be predicted. Perhaps this index also explains why the Hatch Act and state and local variants of this legislation prohibiting overt political activity on the part of civil servants have been so general. They act as a check in one dimension of the budget expanding tendencies of bureaucrats. It appears, however, that this check too may soon be overruled by judicial decision.

Two more institutional facts might be added to the analysis. Many cities and most counties and states require that an individual must reside in the unit if he is to be an employee of that government. The orthodox interpretation is that the individual bureaucrat is expected to be more "sensitive" to local preferences if he is a fellow citizen. Our interpretation would be different since the regulations are almost always civil service rules, not statute or common law. Another point to recall is the low cost of voting to bureaucrats. Most governments give anywhere from one hour to all day off with pay on election day, even though polling hours now extend considerably outside of the ordinary working hours. Private firms are required by law in most localities to give time off but not with pay. What role bureaucrats had in instituting these rules can only be conjectural, but their influence on voting behavior should nonetheless be noted.

References

1. Becker, G. *Human Capital*. New York: National Bureau of Economic Research, 1964.
2. Bergstrom, T., and Robert Goodman. "Private Demands for Public Goods." *American Economic Review* 26 (1973): 280–296.
3. Black, D. *The Theory of Committees and Elections*. Cambridge: Cambridge University Press, 1958.
4. Borcherding, Thomas E., and Winston C. Bush. "The Effects of Divisibility of Public Outputs in Consumption, Bureaucratic Power and the Size of the Tax-Sharing Group on Public Spending." Unpublished paper presented at the Econometric Society meetings, Dec. 27, 1972, Toronto.
5. Borcherding, Thomas E., and Robert T. Deacon. "The Demand for the Services of Non-Federal Governments: An Econometric Approach to Collective Choice." *American Economic Review* 62 (1972): 891–906.
6. Bowen, H. "The Interpretation of Voting in the Allocation of Economic Resources." *Quarterly Journal of Economics* 58 (1943). Reprinted in American Economic Association, *Readings in Welfare Economics*, K. Arrow and T. Scitovsky (eds.). Homewood, Ill., Irwin, 1969.
7. Buchanan, James M. *The Demand and Supply of Public Goods*. Chicago: Rand McNally, 1968.
8. _____. "Joint Supply, Externality and Optimality." *Economica* 33 (1966): 404–415.
9. Denzau, Arthur. "Majority Voting, Residential Migration and the Local Public Sector." Mimeographed. St. Louis: Washington University, 1972.
10. Dupeaux, G. "Le Probleme des abstentions dans le département du Loir-et-Cher au début de la troisième république." *Revue francaise de science politique* 2 (1952): 71–95.
11. Evans, A. W. "Private Goods, Externality, Public Goods." *Scottish Journal of Political Economy* (1970): 79–89.
12. Lindahl, Erik. "Just Taxation—A Positive Solution." In *Classics in the Theory of Public Finance*, R. Musgrave and A. Peacock (eds.). London: Macmillan Co., 1958.
13. Martin, Rosco C. "The Municipal Electorate: A Case Study." *Southwestern Social Science Quarterly* (Dec., 1933).
14. Niskanen, William A., Jr. *Bureaucracy and Representative Government*. Chicago: Aldine-Atherton, 1971.
15. Oakland, William H. "Joint Goods." *Economica* 36 (1969): 253–268.
16. Samuelson, P. "The Pure Theory of Public Expenditure." *Review of Economics and Statistics* 36 (1954): 387–389.
17. Tingsten, Herbert. *Political Behavior: Studies in Election Statistics*. London: P. S. King and Son, 1937.
18. Tullock, Gordon. *Private Wants, Public Means*. New York: Basic Books, 1970.
19. _____. Book review of Niskanen [14]. *Public Choice* 12 (1972): 119–124.

6. Rates of Productivity Change and the Growth of State and Local Governmental Expenditures
Robert M. Spann

Introduction

Government expenditures have risen at a rapid rate in recent years. Numerous models have been proposed to explain this phenomenon. Existing explanations include governmental ineptitude, increased demand for public services, bureaucratic behavior, and lagging productivity in the public sector. This paper is concerned with the fourth explanation.

The hypothesis that government expenditure growth may be due to low productivity growth in that sector was first advanced by Baumol [1]. In what follows productivity estimates for six state and local services are made. Those estimates indicate that, on average, productivity gains were zero or negative in state and local services during the period 1962–1967. In addition, data on price and income elasticities for select state and local functions plus the hypothesis of low rates and productivity in the public sector can explain the intrasectorial pattern of expenditure growth.

There is considerable variability in productivity gains among states. Econometric analysis of the pattern of productivity gains and losses indicates that productivity gains were least in smaller governmental units.

Estimates of the effects of zero productivity gains on the government expenditure increase are presented in this paper. Approximately 20 to 25% of the growth in state and local expenditures during the period 1962–1967 was due to low productivity gains in the public sector.

In the final section of the paper, the causes of low or zero productivity changes in the public sector are investigated. The data presented in that section indicate that service and retailing industries exhibit positive productivity trends (but less than the economy as a whole). This would seem to imply that the low or zero rates of productivity change in the public sector are due partially to the nature of the services provided by state and local governments but not completely. Some of this low rate of productivity must be due to behavioral differences between public and private firms.

Source note: The author is indebted to James M. Buchanan, who suggested this investigation, and to Thomas E. Borcherding, Gordon Tullock, David Warner, and William Orzechowski for helpful comments and criticisms on an earlier draft. Responsibility for all errors and opinions rests with the author.

Alternative Models of the Growth in Governmental Expenditures

For several decades, governmental expenditures have risen both absolutely and relative to private expenditures. In 1950 government purchases of goods and services (federal, state, and local) accounted for 13% of the Gross National Product. In 1970, they accounted for 23% of the GNP. During this same period, the number of people employed by local governments increased by more than 120% and federal government employment increased by more than 35% [14].

Estimates of future governmental growth suggests that these trends will continue [16]. The overall annual rate of growth of local expenditures is expected to be 5.5 percent (in constant dollars). This compares with projected rates of growth of federal expenditures of 2.5% and a projected annual increase in the GNP of 4.3%.

To a certain extent, these increases in governmental expenditures might represent an increase demand for governmental services due to a shift in the electorate's tastes towards more publicly produced goods and fewer privately produced goods. Alternatively, government produced goods and services could be more income elastic than privately produced goods and services. This would imply that the rapid increase in government expenditure is due to rising per cápita incomes.

Neither of these explanations is completely satisfactory. Recent studies of the demand for government services indicate a wide range of income elasticities, but there is no tendency for these elasticities to be uniformly high.[1] Changing tastes could explain the expansion of the government sector, but this argument is inherently circular. If one argues that tastes do explain government growth, one must be able to develop some testable model that explains such a change in tastes.

It is possible that some of this increase in governmental expenditures represents changes in environmental variables beyond the control of the individual voter. For example, the output of local police departments is measurable not by merely so many blocks patrolled each hour or a number of squad cars on the streets, but by protection of the citizenry against crime. If the propensity to commit crime rises over time, or if an increasing population leads to more interaction and opportunities for violence, the cost of providing a given amount of protection will increase. In the case of the courts and regulatory bodies, increases in population and an increasingly complex society might lead one to expect increases in both the number of cases per capita and complexity of cases before such bodies.

There is some evidence that such a phenomenon exists. In Table 1,

1. For example, see Borcherding and Deacon [2].

Table 1. Police and fire employment per capita and city size

Full-time equivalent employment per 10,000 population by function	over 1,000,000	500,000 to 999,999	300,000 to 499,999	200,000 to 299,999	100,000 to 199,999
Police	32.3	25.9	19.6	19.5	18.7
Fire	15.1	17.4	15.4	15.4	17.5

Source: D. F. Bradford, R. A. Malt, and W. E. Oates, "The Rising Cost of Local Public Services: Some Evidence and Reflections," *National Tax Journal* (June, 1969).

police and fire employment per capita for various city sizes is listed. In the case of police services, it appears that more police per capita are required in larger cities than in smaller cities. There appears to be no relationship between fire employment and city size. Other researchers have found that many classes of governmental expenditures are higher in urbanized areas.[2] Some previous studies have shown that governmental expenditures are directly proportional to population, all other things held constant. The magnitudes of the parameters in the studies are not such that one can explain a major portion of the growth of governmental expenditures by environmental factors alone.

Finally, it is possible that such expenditure increases are inherent in the nature of governments. For example, Whalen [18] has stated:

> The plain fact is that municipal spending is out of control and the world's richest city lives in a state of chronic bankruptcy.
>
> . . . In spite of the opaque language, the Mayor's budget message expresses a tragedy as poignant as any dramatist might contrive. We are told, in effect, that certain fantastic expenditures will grow more fantastic; that they simply cannot be controlled nor can alternatives be devised.

Niskanen, in a recent book [10], has argued that not only will more of a good be produced when it is governmentally instead of privately produced, but the output of service will grow faster under public management. Other authors have argued that there are behavioral differences between the public and private sector. Migue and Belanger [8] have argued that one should not expect government bureaus to behave as cost-minimizers. Rather, they argue that bureaus maximize utility functions which consist of output and "slack" of nonpecuniary gains to the managers. Orzechowski has argued that bureaus desire to be labor intensive so as to maximize the number of individuals (and hence voters) dependent on the bureau for income.[3]

2. Ibid.
3. William Orzechowski, "Economic Models of Bureaucracy," chap. 13 in this volume.

The forces of changing environmental conditions, changes in tastes and preferences, ineptness, and bureaucratic behavior certainly have contributed to increasing governmental expenditures, but they are not the only forces at work. This paper is concerned with an additional, built-in source of governmental expenditure growth, namely changes in the relative costs of governmental and privately produced services due to differing rates of productivity change in the two sectors.

This hypothesis was first advanced by W. J. Baumol [1]. Baumol hypothesized that governmental services were highly labor intensive, and would exhibit much lower rates of productivity increase than outputs produced in the private sector. Over time, the costs of producing a unit of governmental services will increase relative to the costs of producing a unit of privately produced goods.

In the remainder of this paper, I shall examine Baumol's hypothesis in detail, use existing data to test its validity for state and local government expenditures, and attempt to determine the extent to which the increase in these expenditures has been the result of productivity gains smaller in the public sector than in the private.

The Effects of Differing Rates of Productivity Change on Governmental Expenditures

In order to illustrate the effects of differing rates of productivity change on the composition of national expenditures, I shall begin with a simple example. Assume that only two goods are produced in the economy, a privately produced product and a governmental service. Gross National Product in this simple model is the price of the privately produced product times the volume of output of that product plus the cost of producing a unit of governmental services times the volume of such services produced.

Suppose that at some point in time it takes two man-hours to produce a unit of governmental services (measured in some real output sense such as protection from crime, education received, etc.) and two man-hours to produce a unit of private goods.

The output of the many government sectors may be primarily labor intensive services. Thus, there might not be many opportunities for technological advancement in this sector. Protection from crime is and always has been provided by policemen patrolling or being on the scene of possible sources of violence. Fire protection is provided by firemen waiting at a station until a fire breaks out and then rushing to the scene and trying to minimize the losses due to the fire. Similar arguments apply to other governmental services. In the private sector, there might be many opportunities for technological advancement. The entire history of U.S.

economic growth has been one of technological advancement allowing more units of output to be produced at the same input levels.

Suppose that these arguments are valid and, that over a period of time, technological advances reduce the number of man-hours it takes to produce a unit of private output from two to one. Over the same period of time, there are no technological advances in the public sector, and it still takes two man-hours to produce a unit of public output.

This implies that the real price to the consumer of privately produced goods has been cut in half, while the cost of government services (represented by the taxes needed to pay for producing those services) has remained constant. If all that had occurred was a change in the relative prices of public versus privately produced commodities, one might expect consumers to vote for smaller levels of governmental services and a reduction in the share of national income devoted to the public sector.

The productivity increase in the private sector has increased income per capita however. Since both income and relative prices have changed, the change in governmental output and expenditures desired by consumers will depend on both the price elasticity and income elasticity of governmental services demanded by citizens. An increase in the price of governmental services (relative to other commodities) reduces the demand for these services. At higher per capita incomes, consumers demand increased amounts of almost every commodity. Governmental services are no exception to this rule. If the demand on the part of citizens for governmental services is not very sensitive to price changes, but is increased greatly as income increases, the real output of the governmental sector will rise. If this condition is not met, the real output of governmental services will fall. Government expenditures as a fraction of the GNP will increase if the price elasticity of governmental services is less than the income elasticity of those goods and services.[4]

Previous Work on Productivity in the Public Sector

Productivity measurement in the public sector is a relatively new research topic for economists; there are not many studies in this area currently available. One of the first attempts to examine productivity in state and local governments was made by Bradford, Malt, and Oates [3]. These authors attempt to measure the rate of productivity change in four local government services, education, police, fire and hospitals. Each sector will be discussed individually.

4. For more on this point, see Spann [12].

Education

In calculating productivity trends in education, Bradford, Malt, and Oates examined the trends in teachers' salaries and in cost per pupil day. Their results are reproduced here in Tables 2 and 3.

Costs per pupil day rose at a rate of 6.7% per year during the period 1947–1967. Teacher's salaries rose at a rate of 4.8% per year during this period. One way to interpret this data is to note that the wholesale price index rose at a rate of 1.4% per year during the period 1947–1966. Thus the cost of a unit of education rose relative to the cost of other goods and services at a rate of 5.3% per year (the 6.7% annual increase in costs per pupil day less the 1.4% increase in the wholesale price index). If one assumes that the rate of increase in the quality of education was approximately the same as the rate of increase in the quality of the goods and services represented in the wholesale price index, the difference in the rate of productivity change between education and privately produced goods was around 5.3%.

The quality of education may have increased both absolutely and relative to other goods and services over the periods covered by the Bradford, Malt, and Oates data. But, the authors argue, it is doubtful that these quality increases are of the same order or greater than the increases in costs relative to other goods and services. Therefore, it appears that the low rate of productivity hypothesis is confirmed in the educational sector at least.[5]

Table 2. Index of average annual salaries of city public school teachers (1957–1959 $= 100$)

1925	37	1947	55	
1927	38	1949	67	
1929	40	1951	71	
1931	41	1953	81	Annual rate of increase:
1933	38	1955	87	(compounded)
1935	37	1957	96	1925–1965 3.2%
1937	39	1959	104	1947–1965 4.8%
1939	41	1961	113	
1941	42	1963	121	
1943	44	1965	128	
1945	48			

Source: City Public School Teachers, 1925–65, Bulletin No. 1504 (Washington, D.C.: U.S. Department of Labor Statistics, May, 1966), pp. 24, 35.

5. In fact, the data indicate that the rate of productivity growth in education may have been negative during this period.

Table 3. Current costs per pupil-day in U.S. public schools (in dollars)

1900	.12	1955	1.51	
1910	.18	1956	1.67	
1920	.33	1957	1.69	
1930	.50	1958	1.85	
1940	.50	1959	1.94	
1946	.77	1960	2.13	Annual rate of increase:
1947	.86	1961	2.20	(compounded)
1948	1.02	1962	2.37	1900–1967 5.0%
1949	1.11	1963	2.42	1947–1967 6.7%
1950	1.18	1964	2.57	
1951	1.26	1965	2.70	
1952	1.39	1966	2.93	
1953	1.35	1967	3.15	
1954	1.48			

Source: These figures were calculated by multiplying average daily school attendance for each year by the average number of days in the school year to give a number of pupil-days figure. This last number was then divided into the annual current expenditure on public elementary and secondary education to give the current cost per pupil day. The sources of the data for these calculations are: Research Division, National Education Association, *Status and Trends: Vital Statistics, Education, and Public Finance,* Report R13; *Estimates of School Statistics, 1966–67,* Report R20 (Washington, D.C.: The Association, Aug., 1959; 1966), pp. 11, 22; 10, 20; and U.S. Department of Health, Education, and Welfare, *Statistics of State School Systems, 1963–64* (Washington, D.C.: U.S. Government Printing Office, 1967), p. 21. There were a few gaps in the data for the average length of the school term. For these years, see D. F. Bradford, R. A. Malt, and W. E. Oates, "The Rising Cost of Local Public Services: Some Evidence and Reflections," *National Tax Journal* (June, 1969), for interpolations of the available data.

Health and Hospitals

Measuring productivity gains in hospitals and health care is exceedingly difficult. Costs have increased but so has the quality of services offered by hospitals. The current level of health care in the United States is superior to the health care of past decades. This does not destroy the usefulness of examining data on hospital costs. In Tables 4 and 5, data on hospital costs and characteristics of hospital costs are reproduced from the Bradford, Malt, and Oates study. The data indicate that hospital costs have risen at a rapid rate and that hospital employees per 100 patients have almost doubled in the 19 years between 1946 and 1965. Surely some of these cost increases represent quality increases, but it is doubtful that these quality increases are of the same order of magnitude as the cost increases.

This view is also reflected in a study of hospital costs in New York City conducted by Klarman [7]. That study concluded that "medical advances, insofar as they are reflected in the ancillary services of the hospital, account for less than one-fourth of the dollar increase in patient-day cost in the 1950's." That study concludes that the most important cause of cost increases is the "lag in productivity gains."

Table 4. Index of hospital daily service charge (1957–1959 = 100)

1935	23.8	1951	64.1	
1939	25.3	1952	70.4	
1940	25.4	1953	74.8	
1941	25.9	1954	79.2	
1942	28.0	1955	83.0	Annual rate of increase:
1943	30.2	1956	87.5	(compounded)
1944	31.5	1957	94.5	1935–1963 6.5%
1945	32.5	1958	99.9	1947–1963 7.4%
1946	37.0	1959	105.5	
1947	44.1	1960	112.7	
1948	51.5	1961	121.3	
1949	55.7	1962	129.8	
1950	57.8	1963	138.0	

Source: U.S. Department of Health, Education, and Welfare, *Health, Education and Welfare Trends,* 1964 ed. (Washington, D.C.: U.S. Government Printing Office, 1964), Part 1, p. 22.

Police and Fire

The output of police and fire departments is difficult to measure in a quantitative fashion. One possible assumption is that the level of protection provided on a per capita basis has been constant over time. Then, one can ascertain the changes in productivity in this sector by looking at movements in the ratio of policemen or firemen to population. If per capita protection is falling over time, this measure will overstate

Table 5. Employment, expenses, and average length of stay in state and local government short-term general and other special hospitals, 1946–1965.

Year-end	Personnel per 100 patients[a]	Payroll per patient day ($)	Total expense per patient day ($)	Average length of stay in days
1946	129	4.58	7.39	11.4
1948	136	6.20	10.27	11.0
1950	149	7.80	12.56	10.7
1952	153	9.63	15.37	10.7
1954	175	12.66	19.34	9.9
1956	195	14.46	22.08	9.4
1958	206	16.51	25.82	9.0
1960	215	19.47	29.43	8.8
1961	227	20.75	32.27	8.8
1962	232	22.69	34.45	8.5
1963	237	23.57	36.19	8.5
1964	236	25.05	38.57	8.5
1965	234	27.17	41.84	8.5

Source: Hospitals, Guide Issue 40, Part 2 (August 1, 1966): 439.

a. Personnel data for 1954 and thereafter include full-time personnel plus full-time equivalents of part-time personnel; previously, the figures were for full-time personnel only. From 1952 onward, residents, interns, and students are excluded.

any productivity gains. If per capita protection has increased, the opposite is true. In examining both per capita expenditures on police and fire services and employment per capita, Bradford, Malt, and Oates found that costs per capita rose faster than the wholesale price index and that police and fire employment per capita was constant, or rose slightly between 1954 and 1963. This is consistent both with the other services examined by the authors and with the hypothesis that the rate of growth of productivity in the public sector is much less than productivity gains in the private sector.

Other Studies of Productivity in the Public Sector

The only studies on productivity in the public sector other than the Bradford, Malt, and Oates paper are a study conducted by the Urban Institute and a study of productivity in the federal government conducted by the Civil Service Commission General Accounting Office and the Office of Management and Budget. The Urban Institute has examined trends in tons of garbage collected per man-day for the cities of New York and Washington [6]. The results of the Urban Institute's studies are shown in Figures 1 and 2. Although there have been some upward move-

Figure 1. Tons of solid waste collected per man-day in New York City.

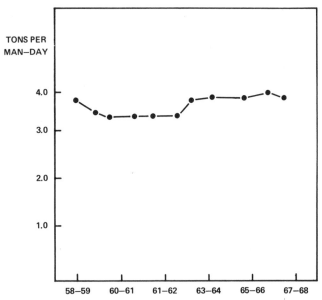

Source. H. P. Hatry and D. M. Fisk, *Improving Productivity and Productivity Measurement in Local Governments* (Washington, D.C.: The Urban Institute, 1971).

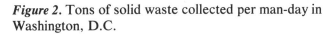

Figure 2. Tons of solid waste collected per man-day in Washington, D.C.

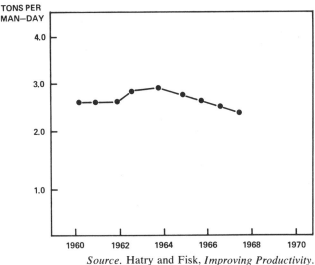

Source. Hatry and Fisk, *Improving Productivity.*

ments in output per man-day, the general trend of output per man-day for refuse collection in both cities is flat. This indicates that productivity growth in garbage collection has been nil (in these cities at least). This is consistent with the Bradford, Malt, and Oates study of other governmental services.

The Civil Service Commission General Accounting Office and the Office of Management and Budget have examined productivity gains in the federal government [4]. This study estimated productivity in the federal government by computing indexes of inputs and outputs that covered 56% of the civilian personnel employed by 17 executive agencies. The results of this study are listed in Table 6. The results indicate that there have been some productivity gains in the federal sector but that these productivity gains are still slightly less than productivity gains in the private sector.

In some ways, it is not surprising that there have been productivity gains in the federal sector. Some of the functions of the federal government (particularly in the executive agencies) are administrative in nature, and there may be opportunities for productivity gains via improved data processing, etc. Therefore, these results do not necessarily destroy the validity of the low productivity gain in state and local governments hypothesis.

Table 6. Productivity indices for select federal government functions

	Fiscal year				
	1967	1968	1969	1970	1971
Weighted output	100.0	105.0	107.6	109.4	110.1
Input	100.0	103.0	104.2	102.9	101.3
Compensation	100.0	107.4	116.7	128.6	141.2
Productivity (output/manyear)	100.0	101.8	103.4	106.4	108.8
Unit labor cost (current $)	100.0	102.5	108.5	117.2	127.2
Unit labor cost (constant $)	100.0	97.5	96.0	91.3	91.3

Source: Civil Service Commission General Accounting Office and Office of Management and Budget, *Measuring and Enhancing Productivity in the Federal Sector,* prepared for the Joint Economic Committee of the Congress of the United States (Washington, D.C.: U.S. Government Printing Office, 1972).

Measuring Productivity Gains in State and Local Governments

The studies cited previously lend some support to the argument that low rates of productivity gains might be a substantial contributory factor to the rising cost of government. These studies do not provide complete support for this hypothesis. The Bradford, Malt, and Oates study uses highly aggregated data and does not allow one to examine exactly which governmental units have the lowest rates of productivity gains and which have the highest productivity gains. The Urban Institute data is for one specific function in two large cities. The federal government study is not applicable to state and local governments. In what follows, I shall propose a method of examining productivity gains in state and local governments on a state by state basis. This methodology is then applied to data from the 1962 and 1967 *Census of Governments* [13].

Six specific state and local government functions are examined in this study: police, fire, highways, general control, financial and administration, and public welfare. The major problem in any such productivity study is defining the output of state and local government[6]; unfortunately, no precise definitions or measures are available. I use a series of proxy measures for the output of state and local governments and discuss each function individually.

6. For a good discussion of the problem inherent in measuring productivity in state and local governments, see Hatry and Fisk [6].

Police

The output of police departments is maintenance of the public safety. One possible measure of police output then is some index of public safety, say the inverse of the crime rate. Movements in this variable are not solely under the control of the police department. The crime rate can increase because of factors completely independent of the productivity of the police department. An increase in the propensity to commit crime will raise the crime rate. Thus, we could end up measuring not productivity losses or gains, but merely changes in the environment within which the policeman serves.

In order to have a working definition of the output of the police department, I assume that the average citizen was no safer in 1967 than in 1962.[7] Then the output of the police department is proportional to the size of the population. This proportionality constant is assumed to be the same in both 1962 and 1967 for any one state but may vary across states without destroying the validity of my method.

Fire

The output of the fire department is assumed to be proportional to population. There is no reason to suspect that the expected fire losses perceived by an average citizen changed dramatically between 1962 and 1967. Therefore, population is as good a proxy as any other that could be devised to measure the output of fire departments.

General Control

General control expenditures refer to expenditures for the courts and other control bodies. Ideally, the measure of output for this governmental function should be some index of the number and complexity of cases before these bodies. Unfortunately, no such index exists. In this study I assume the output of this sector is proportional to population. This will bias the productivity index toward an understatement of any productivity gains in this sector.[8] As will be seen below, this will not present too great a problem in the interpretation of the results.

Highways

The output of the highway department is the maintenance and design of passable roads for the motoring public. Therefore, one should use an

7. In fact, the average citizen was probably less safe in 1967. This will bias my output measure for 1967 upward and tend to overstate any productivity gain in police services.
8. Productivity gains will be understated since the complexity of cases before control bodies probably increased during this period.

output proxy that measures road usage. In this study, I assume that the
output of the highway department is proportional to the number of registered vehicles in the state.

Financial and Administrative

The output of financial and administrative employees is managerial and
administrative services. Therefore, the output represented by this sector
is proportional to the total size of the budget. The larger the size of state
and local budgets, the greater the responsibilities placed on financial and
administrative employees. An alternative proxy for the output of financial
and administrative departments is the total number of state and local
employees.

Public Welfare

Two proxies are developed for the output of state and local public
welfare departments. The first is total cash assistance payments made by
the state. An alternative measure is total recipients of state and local
welfare services. The first measure is probably more appropriate as higher
assistance payments might also be a proxy for higher levels of other
welfare services given to the recipient. Both measures lead to similar
results.

Measuring Productivity Changes in State and Local Governments, 1962–1967

In order to estimate productivity changes in state and local governments, I compute the ratio of full-time equivalent employees in October
to the output proxy for each of the six functions for each state in both
1962 and 1967.[9] This yields a proxy for the labor-output ratio for each
function. I then divide the labor-output ratio for 1967 by the labor-output
ratio for 1962. Since my output proxy is proportional to actual output,
and since output is in both the numerator and denominator of the computed labor-output ratios, this proportionality constant cancels out. Thus,
I have an unbiased estimate of the percent growth or decline in the labor-
output ratio for each function between 1962 and 1967. The only assumption necessary for this result to hold is that the ratio between my output
proxy and actual output is the same in both 1962 and 1967. The ratio can
vary from state to state without destroying the validity of my results.

If the labor-output ratio is increasing, productivity is falling over time.
If the labor-output ratio is falling, productivity is rising over time. In

9. Four states were omitted in this analysis. Alaska and Hawaii were omitted since they
are relatively new to statehood. Florida and Utah were omitted because of data deficiencies.

other words, I am measuring the change in the labor input required to produce a unit of governmental output.[10]

Productivity Changes in State and Local Services

In this study, productivity changes are measured by changes in the labor-output ratios for specific services. Increases in labor-output ratios indicate decreases in productivity while decreases in labor-output ratios indicate productivity gains. In Table 7 average percent changes in labor-output ratios for six state and local government functions are listed. In four of the categories (police, fire, general control, and public welfare), labor-output ratios increased on average. This indicates the absence of any productivity gains in these sectors and raises the possibility of actual productivity declines in these functions. In two sectors (financial administration and highways), labor-output ratios fell between 1962 and 1967.

As noted in the previous section, these measures are not perfect measures of the actual levels of productivity gains and losses. They are indicative of trends in productivity, gains which in state and local governments are on the average very small or negative. This implies that lagging productivity may be an important factor contributing to the rise in the cost of state and local governments. Each measure is discussed in turn below.

Table 7. Changes in labor-output ratios in the public sector, 1962–1967

Sector	Average % change in employees per unit of output, 1962–1967	Measures of output
Police	14.36	Population
Fire	11.13	Population
Financial administrative	−28.21	Total expenditures[b]
General control	29.15	Population
Highway employees	−10.87	Number of motor vehicles
Public welfare[a]	28.56	Value of cash assistance payments[c]

a. Alabama, Idaho, Indiana, Kentucky, and Nebraska are not included due to data deficiencies.
b. Similar results were obtained when total employment was used.
c. Similar results were obtained using total welfare recipients.

10. Labor-output ratios are not the best measures of productivity. Ideally one should use a measure of total factor productivity such as one of the measures discussed in an article by Nadiri [9]. Unfortunately, data on capital in the public sector are not readily available.

Police

Police per capita increased, on average, 14.4% during this period. Not all of this increase represents productivity losses. There was an increase in the propensity to commit crime during this period. The crime rate rose by 50 to 60% between 1962 and 1967. Police per capita rose in response to increased demands for protection. The safety of the average citizen fell however. These two effects probably cancel each other out so, on net, the rate of productivity change in this sector may have been close to zero.

Another measure of the output of police might be automobiles in the state, since a large part of police work involves traffic control, etc. Automobiles per capita during this period rose by roughly 14 percent, a rise almost identical to that rise in police per capita. Thus, if automobiles were used as an output proxy, the productivity gain estimate in police would be zero.

Fire

The labor-output ratio for fire protection increased by 11.13 percent on average between 1962 and 1967. It is possible that some of this increase in firemen per capita is due to increased fire protection provided in urban areas due to urban strife during this period. It is also possible that increases in population in areas with volunteer fire departments led to the formation of professional fire departments. Thus, not all of the increase in firemen per capita represents net declines in productivity. It is doubtful that these two factors can account for all of the increase in firemen per capita. As a result, it seems safe to conclude that productivity gains in fire services were nonexistent during this period.

Financial and Administration

This sector is one of two that seemed to experience productivity gains during the period 1962–1967. Financial and administrative employees per dollar of state and local expenditures fell by 28.21% on average during this period. Part of this apparent productivity gain is illusionary. The output of financial and administrative employees depends on the constant dollar, not the undeflated budget. The consumer price index rose by 10.3% during this period. An index of the cost of inputs used in municipal services rose by 21.2% during this period.[11] Correcting the productivity index for inflation leads to an estimate of the true fall in the labor-output ratio in this sector of 7 to 18%. The lower range of this estimate is similar

11. This index is from Walzer [17]. This price index is also discussed in the final section of this paper.

to the estimates of federal executive agency productivity gains for the period 1967–1971 (see Table 6). Even this rate of productivity increase is not enough to offset negative or zero rates of productivity gain in other governmental services.

General Control

General control employees per capita rose by 29.2% during this period. Some of this increase was the result of increased caseloads due to rising crime rates during the period. Exactly how much was due to this factor and how much was due to productivity changes cannot be determined. It is probably safest to conclude that the rate of productivity was near zero in this sector.

Highway Employees

Highway departments appear to have achieved productivity gains during the period 1962–1967. Highway employees per registered automobile fell by an average of 10.87%. Part of this productivity gain may be due to measurement errors. The average change in population per state was 5.72% during this period. The number of registered automobiles per state increased by 19.29% on average. Since automobiles per capita was rising at a substantial rate, it is reasonable to suppose that miles driven per auto declined (or at least did not increase too rapidly). This implies that I have overestimated the change in the output of highway departments and any productivity gains in that sector. In all probability, there was a small gain in productivity in this sector, but it was not as large as that indicated by the data in Table 7.

Public Welfare

This sector appears to have experienced a large drop in productivity during the 1962–1967 period. The number of welfare department employees per dollar of cash assistance rose by more than 29% in five years. Similar results are obtained when total recipients were used as a measure of output.

It is true, of course, that there may have been changes in both the quality and magnitude of services provided by state and local public welfare departments.[12] It is doubtful that any such changes in the quality

12. Although the 1962–67 period represented the years of the "Great Society" programs, the data used here are for state and local welfare department employees and state and local welfare recipients. Even if federal programs had some effects on the level of state welfare departments, such an increase in welfare output should be reflected in the level of cash assistance payments.

of output were in excess of 28%. Thus, productivity change in state and local welfare departments was negative or zero during this period.

An Overview of the Results

The results presented so far provide direct evidence that lagging productivity is a factor contributory to the rising costs of state and local government. Although the results vary from sector to sector and must be subject to numerous qualifications, an overall pattern is discernable. That pattern is one of little or no productivity gains in the production of services provided by state and local governments. It may even be that productivity deteriorated over this period. The growth rate of output per man hour in the private sector was positive for almost all industries [15]. Productivity gains of as great as 8.2 percent per year were realized in some industries for the period 1957–1969. Therefore, it is not surprising that the relative cost of government, at least at the state and local level, is increasing.

In the next section, the distribution of gains and losses in productivity for individual states is discussed. A model is proposed and estimated which yields some interesting clues into the behavior of bureaucracies. The following section contains an alternative test of the lagging productivity hypothesis and uses this hypothesis to explain the pattern of expenditure increases in state and local governments. Finally, I present some estimates of the amount of state and local government expenditure increase that is due solely to lagging productivity in the public sector and examine some of the possible causes of low productivity in the public sector.

The Distribution of Productivity Changes Across States

In the previous section average productivity changes for six state and local government functions were estimated. In this section the distribution of those productivity changes across states is discussed. This distribution of changes leads to some interesting insights into the behavior of governmental units.

In Tables 8 through 13, the five states with the largest percent change in employees per unit of output (the states with the smallest productivity gains or the greatest productivity losses) are listed along with the five states with the smallest changes in employees per unit of output (the states with the largest productivity gains or smallest productivity losses) for each of the six functions. As a standard of comparison, the average percent change in employees per unit of output plus the percent change in this variable for California and New York are shown.

Table 8. Percentage change in employees per unit of output: Police

Highest five	% change	Lowest five	% change		% change
Arkansas	46.7	Massachusetts	3.4	Average	14.4
South Dakota	32.9	Georgia	3.5	California	14.6
New Mexico	29.7	New Jersey	4.6	New York	14.4
Mississippi	29.1	South Carolina	5.0		
Nevada	24.6	Illinois	5.3		

Several striking conclusions emerge from examining these tables. In each of the six services, the productivity gains in New York and California are equal to, or in excess of, the national average (in the sense that the labor-output ratio increase was less than average). With the exception of "general control," at least one large state (in the sense of government expenditures) is always among the group of states with the smallest increases in the labor-output ratio for specific services. The states with the greatest increases in employees per unit of output for specific services almost invariably have small populations and small governments.

These results imply that, all other things held constant, it was not the large states which one might classify as having large bureaucratic governments that experienced the greatest increase in the cost of governmental services between 1962 and 1967. The states which faced the largest increase in the unit costs of providing specific government services were the smaller, less populated states.[13] The increase in the unit cost of government services was greatest in these smaller states due to the fact that they experienced the largest increases in the ratio of inputs to outputs in governmental services.

Table 9. Percentage change in employees per unit of output: Fire

Highest five	% change	Lowest five	% change		% change
Arkansas	59.6	Delaware	−11.1	Average	11.1
South Dakota	39.4	Pennsylvania	− 2.7	California	2.2
Nevada	38.5	Connecticut	− 1.5	New York	2.4
Oklahoma	29.7	Georgia	− .8		
Alabama	28.6	New Jersey	− .1		

13. Assuming the same rate of wage increase in all states, the larger the increase in the labor-output ratio, the greater the increase in the number of man-hours needed to produce a unit of governmental services. As the number of man-hours needed to produce a unit of output increases, the unit costs of that output increase (or smallest falls) in the labor-output ratio for governmental services experienced the greatest increases in the costs of governmental services.

Table 10. Percentage change in employees per unit of output: Financial and administrative

Highest five	% change	Lowest five	% change		% change
Nebraska	−10.7	Ohio	−40.0	Average	−28.2
Wyoming	−13.4	Rhode Island	−36.9	California	−31.1
South Dakota	−18.9	Alabama	−36.5	New York	−30.5
Arkansas	−21.9	West Virginia	−36.5		
Vermont	−22.0	Maine	−36.0		

Table 11. Percentage change in employees per unit of output: General control

Highest five	% change	Lowest five	% change		% change
Vermont	105.3	Louisiana	3.2	Average	29.2
Arizona	53.6	Nebraska	4.1	California	17.7
Rhode Island	49.8	Missouri	7.5	New York	29.7
New Hampshire	46.8	Virginia	7.7		
Delaware	43.4	Kentucky	9.1		

Table 12. Percentage change in employees per unit of output: Highways

Highest five	% change	Lowest five	% change		% change
Wyoming	16.7	Missouri	−22.4	Average	−10.9
Nevada	6.1	Tennessee	−17.7	California	−10.4
South Dakota	5.7	Oregon	−17.7	New York	−13.8
Arizona	2.8	Mississippi	−17.6		
West Virginia	− .6	Connecticut	−17.0		

Table 13. Percentage change in employees per unit of output: Public welfare

Highest five	% change	Lowest five	% change		% change
Missouri	93.6	Arkansas	−17.9	Average	28.6
South Carolina	84.4	New York	−10.9	California	.1
Wisconsin	81.1	Ohio	− 8.3		
Montana	62.6	Massachusetts	− 5.3		
Nevada	72.9	New Jersey	− 4.8		

Explaining the Variation in Productivity Changes Across States

In this section, I attempt to explain the variation in employee per unit of output changes across states by the use of several variables in a multiple regression analysis. These variables are listed and discussed below. In this section it is assumed that productivity changes are not simply given by nature. They are determined within some logical system of behavioral patterns that describe bureaucratic and governmental behavior.[14]

Per Capita Bureau Employment

The first variable used to explain changes in employees per unit of output is employment in that function relative to the state's population in 1962. This variable can affect the growth path of bureaus and productivity changes over time in two ways. The size of the government is decided by the tastes and preferences of the electorate. Given that government employees have the right to vote, they have incentives to lobby for changes in both the size of government and the nature of public output. One such change government employees might lobby for is changes in work rules, procedures, or the nature of public output that will permit an expansion of the bureau along with a reduction in the actual workload per employee. This model would predict a positive relationship between initial size of the bureau (relative to population) and the percent change in the bureau's labor-output ratio over time.

Alternatively, it is possible that bureaus exhibit S-shaped growth curves over time. Neglecting extremely small bureaus, small- and medium-size bureaus grow faster than large ones. There are several arguments that would generate such a conclusion. States with a low level of government employees per capita have lower taxes. Therefore, they have a "price" advantage in attracting new residents and industry. State and local employees might attempt to capture some of the returns to this price advantage by lowering the workload per employee or by decreasing the effort required to generate a unit of output.

There might be threshold effects in the public scrutiny of governmental budgets. If the governmental unit is small, the investment required to oppose budget or tax increases may exceed the gains to such opposition. If the budget is fairly large, this threshold might be passed and public scrutiny of the budget and tax levels might provide an incentive for governmental agencies to improve their productivity.

14. For more on models of the behavioral patterns of bureaucracies, see Niskanen [10] and the papers in this volume by Borcherding and Bush and their co-authors, Spann and Denzau, as well as the essay by Orzechowski.

The second set of arguments would predict a negative relationship between government employees per capita and changes in the labor-output ratio in government.

The Growth Rate of Population

Has the change in governmental efficiency been greatest in states that are growing rapidly or in those states with small population growth rates? In states with rapid population growth, changes in environmental factors may lead to increased measured inefficiency. For example, rapid population growth might lead to greater opportunities for crime and hence more police per capita are required to maintain the same level of public safety. A rapidly growing budget might require more than proportional increases in financial personnel to cope with the change in the size of the government.

Alternatively, rapid population growth may lead to increased governmental efficiency in the short run. Bureaus adjust to changing conditions slowly. The legislative and budgeting process is often slow. The optimum short-run response of governmental units might be to increase efficiency while lobbying for increase in bureau or governmental size.

Population per Square Mile in 1962

Population density is included in order to further quantify the types of states in which governmental efficiency is changing the most.

Local Governments per Capita in 1962

If small bureaus tend to grow more rapidly than large bureaus, one would expect states with the largest number of local governments per capita to exhibit the largest increases in governmental employees per unit of output. If the reverse is true (large bureaus grow faster than small ones), the relationship between this variable and the change in employees per unit of output will be negative.

Percent Change in Employees' Wages: 1962–1967

Are the governmental employees getting the largest wage increases the ones with the greatest increases in efficiency? To what extent do salary wage increases in governmental bodies represent improved productivity? Finally, to what extent do wage increases in the public sector lead to greater demands for a more efficient provision of governmental services (or a lower level of output)?

Affirmative answers to these questions imply a negative relationship between the change in wages and the change in employees per unit of output.[15]

Estimating the Effects of Select Variable on Changes in Employees per Unit of Output

The effects of various variables on changes in employees per unit of output was estimated by multiple regression analysis. In each sector the percentage change in employees per unit of output was regressed on employees per 1000 population in 1962, the percentage change in population between 1962 and 1967, population density in 1962, local governments per 1000 population in 1962, and the percent change in wages in that sector from 1962 to 1967. The results of that analysis are summarized in Table 14. Each column of Table 14 reports the regression results for a particular sector. In all cases the dependent variable is the percentage change in employees per unit of output between 1962 and 1967.

The majority of the "t" statistics are not significant. The R^2's are uniformly low and are not impressive. The pattern of signs on the individual coefficients is consistent, both across equations and within individual equations. This information is worth something, and I shall base the inferences drawn below on this consistent pattern of coefficients.[16]

The increase in the number of employees per unit of output was greater in states with low rates of population increase. For the majority of bureaus, the percent change in employees per unit of output is negatively related to population growth. The effects of population density are small and present no clear-cut pattern.

The results of this analysis generate a consistent overall pattern. It is the states with small governments (measured by low levels of governmental employees per capita and a large number of local governments per capita) that appear to be experiencing the largest declines (or smallest increases) in governmental efficiency and the largest increases in the size of government (at least for the six functions examined). It is possible that some of the measured increases in employees per unit of output represent a catching-up process on the part of states with a low level of governmental services per capita instead of a pure deterioration (or lack of increase) in productivity. This may be true and the data used in this study do not allow one to separate out these two effects. This does not destroy the central conclusion of this section, namely that the cost of

15. More formally, as wages increase in the public sector, one should expect substitution of capital for labor and a reduced demand for the service.

16. A consistent pattern of signs and magnitudes may be more important than formal significance. For more on this point, see Fisher [5].

Table 14. Effects of select variables on percent change in employees per unit of output[a]

Independent variables	Sector[b]					
	Police	Fire	Financial administration	General control	Highways	Public welfare
Employees per 1000 population in 1962	-.0217 (.5336)	-.0380 (.432)	-.00639 (.1731)	-.277 (1.907)	.01444 (1.283)	-.1250 (.6763)
Percent change in population	-.0409 (.1590)	.1477 (.3705)	-.11422	-.3205 (.6044)	-.3585 (2.144)	.1978 (.2349)
Population density in 1962	-.000166 (2.062)	-.000196 (1.41)	.000008 (.1842)	-.00002 (.1485)	.000004 (.08477)	-.000055 (2.503)
Local governments per 1000 population in 1962	.000181 (.015)	.0257 (1.350)	.01338 (1.51)	-.0110 (.3488)	.0225 (2.546)	-.0188 (.449)
Percent change in wages	-.07368 (.611)	.3681 (1.114)	-.09571 (.8397)	.286 (2.023)	-.4866 (5.9921)	-.3773 (.88971)
R^2	.25	.20	.14	.18	.54	.20

a. Change in ratio of employees per unit of output in 1967 divided by employees per unit of output in 1962.
b. "t" statistics in parentheses.

government appears to be growing most in those states with relatively small governments in 1962.[17]

Lagging Productivity and the Changing Distribution of State and Local Expenditures

In an earlier section of this paper, it was asserted that if governmental productivity lags behind productivity gains in the private sector, governmental expenditures will grow the most in the sectors in which the demand for governmental services is the least price elastic. Expenditures will grow more rapidly in those sectors in which the demand for government services is the most income elastic. This is because a positive rate of productivity gain in the private sector raises the costs of governmental services relative to privately produced goods and increases per capita income. The increase in the cost of publicly produced goods decreases the demand for those goods. The increase in per capita income raises the demands for publicly produced goods. If the public's demand for a particular government service is more sensitive to the price of that service (represented by the taxes citizens must pay to cover the cost of providing that service) than to the level of income, expenditures will fall (or grow at a slow rate) and vice versa.

Some estimates of the price and income elasticities of demand for specific state and local services are contained in a paper by T. E. Borcherding and R. T. Deacon [2]. These elasticity estimates for five local government functions are listed in Table 15. The average annual rate of increase in expenditures (in 1958 dollars) between 1957 and 1965 for each function is also listed. During this period, the annual growth rate of total local expenditures was 5.3%.

For the three sectors (local education, health-hospitals, and sanitation) for which the absolute value of the price elasticity of demand exceeds the income elasticity of demand, the growth rate of expenditures was equal to, or less than, the overall rate of expenditure increase (5.3%). In two sectors (higher education and parks) the price elasticity is less than the income elasticity and the growth rate of expenditures exceeded the overall growth rate. This pattern of expenditure increase is exactly what one would predict from a zero rate of productivity gain in the public sector and a positive productivity gain in the private sector.

There are other models that might lead to the same conclusions. This does not mean that the validity of the lagging productivity explanation

17. It is also possible that these results represent the early signs of the taxpayers' revolt. One would expect such a revolt to occur first in states with a high level of governmental services.

Table 15. Income and price elasticities and rates of growth in local expenditures: 1957–1965

Sector	Price elasticity	Income elasticity	Annual rate of expenditure growth (%)[a]
Local education	−1.1596	.8093	5.3
Higher education	− .1671	.2948	9.8
Health-hospitals	−1.1283	.4970	1.9–3.9
Sanitation	−1.4945	.7326	2.8
Parks	− .4958	2.7359	6.6
Police	− .9001	1.2136	N.A.
Fire	− .3203	1.6156	N.A.

a. *Source:* U.S. Department of Labor, *Patterns of Economic Growth,* Bulletin 1672 (Washington, D.C.: U.S. Government Printing Office, 1970).

of governmental expenditure is not strengthened by the results of this section. Predictive ability is one way to test the validity of any model. The lagging productivity hypothesis passes this test.

Table 15 also provides another insight into the taxpayers' revolt. The price elasticity of local education is larger in absolute value than the price elasticity of most governmental services. The first signs of tax-payers' revolt were the defeats of local school bond issues in the late 1960s. One would expect that the first sectors to feel a taxpayers' revolt would be those most sensitive to prices.

Lagging Productivity and the Growth of Governmental Expenditures

A zero rate of growth of productivity in the public sector means that the price of governmental services (represented by the taxes citizens pay to support a specific level of service) will increase over time relative to the price of privately produced commodities. One measure of the price of privately produced commodities is the Consumer Price Index. The price of governmental services is proportional to an index of input prices since the rate of productivity growth is zero in that sector.[18]

The values of the Municipal Price Deflator and the Consumer Price Index are listed in Table 16. Between 1962 and 1968, the price of munici-pal services (measured by input prices) increased 29.5% whereas the

18. In general, the difference between the rate of change in prices and the rate of change in input prices is equal to the rate of productivity growth. If productivity is increasing (productivity growth is positive), input prices can rise at a higher rate than output prices. If productivity increases are zero, all input price increases will lead to output price increases according to the formula: % price increase = % input price increase × share of input in total cost of output.

price of the goods represented by the CPI only increased by 14.9%. The third column of Table 16 is column one divided by column two. Thus, it measures changes in the price of governmental output relative to the price of goods produced in the public sector. The price of public output rose 12.7% relative to the price of privately produced output during this period.

One can also use the Municipal Price Index and the Consumer Price Index to estimate the growth in governmental expenditures that would have occurred in the absence of any changes in the demand for governmental services. State and local expenditures per capita were $287.62 in 1962 and $503.24 in 1968. Out of this increase in per capita expenditures $42.86 was due to the 14.9% increase in the Consumer Price Index (.149 times $287.62). This still leaves an increase of $172.76 to be explained. Part of this increase is due to the 12.7% increase in the Municipal Price Index relative to the Consumer Price Index. This source of expenditure growth was responsible for $36.53 (.127 times $287.62) out of the $171.86 increase in per capita expenditures that cannot be explained by changes in the Consumer Price Index. This is the change in governmental expenditures solely due to lagging productivity in the governmental sector. One way to interpret these figures is that even if there had been no change in the consumer price index during the period 1962–1968 or no change in the level of governmental services, state and local government expenditures would have increased by 12.7% ($36.53 divided by $287.62). Alternatively, out of the increase in per capita state and local government expenditures of $171.86 that was not due to increases in the CPI, $36.53, or about 22%, was due to the fact that the cost of providing a constant level of governmental services increased by 12.7% during this period.

Table 16. Governmental output price, consumer prices and the relative price of governmental services

Year	Municipal Price Deflator	Consumer Price Index	Relative price of public output index
1962	100.0	100.0	100.0
1963	102.5	101.2	101.3
1964	105.6	102.5	103.0
1965	108.8	104.2	104.1
1966	113.5	107.3	105.8
1967	121.4	110.3	110.1
1968	129.5	114.9	112.7

Source: Norman Walzer, "A Price Index for Municipal Purchases," *National Tax Journal* (Dec., 1970).

Sources of Low Productivity Gains in the Public Sector

The data presented in the previous section indicate that productivity gains in state and local services have been, on average, about zero. The data do not tell us the source of these low productivity increases. The low observed rates of productivity could be due to either or both of two factors. The first is the nature of the services provided. It is conceivable that the type of service provided by state and local governments is simply not susceptible to productivity increases. Alternatively, it is possible that the data indicate fundamental differences in the behavior of public and private enterprises.

Baumol argued that one would predict low rates of productivity in the public sector since this is primarily a service sector. He argued that this sector would be labor intensive and subject to little opportunity for productivity gains.

Models of bureaucratic behavior would predict similar low productivity gains but for different reasons. Models of bureaucratic behavior would argue that the low rate of productivity in the public sector is due to the differences in the incentives facing public and private suppliers.[19]

There are methods which allow one to discriminate between these two alternative explanations of the data. In Table 17 the percent of total expenditures accounted for by wages and salaries in various local services are listed. These estimates of labor's share range from .21 to .79. For the total U.S. economy, wages and salaries account for about 70% of the GNP. Thus, on balance, labor's share is not larger in the non-

Table 17. Labor's share in various nonfederal government activities

Sector	Labor's share
Local education	.7899
Higher education	.6449
Highways	.2647
Health-hospitals	.5677
Police	.7947
Fire	.7487
Sewers-sanitation	.4175
Parks-recreation	.4485

Source: T. E. Borcherding and R. T. Deacon, "The Demand for the Services of Non-Federal Governments: A Public Choice Approach," *American Economic Review* (Dec., 1972).

19. For more on this point, see Niskanen [10] or R. M. Spann in this volume.

federal public sector than in the private sector.[20] Given the data in Table 17, low rates of productivity in the public sector cannot be due to labor intensity alone.

The low rates of productivity in the public sector do not appear to be due solely to the nature of the services provided in that sector either. In Table 18, productivity estimates for eight service industries and ten retail trades are listed. While these productivity estimates are lower than those for the economy as a whole, they are positive. The estimates of productivity gains for the public sector were zero or negative in the paper.

To the extent that the output of state and local governments represent services which are somehow similar to the services and retail trades listed in Table 18, the low rates of productivity in the public sector cannot be attributed to the nature of the services provided alone. Rates of productivity gain have been positive in the private services sector whereas they are zero or negative in the public sector. At least some of

Table 18. Average annual % rates of change, output per man and related variables, 18 selected service industries, 1939–1963

Industry	Real output per man	Real output	Employment	Compensation per man
Services				
Auto repair	3.32	7.14	3.82	5.06
Barber shops	.60	.60	.00	5.67
Beauty shops	1.69	4.08	2.39	5.37
Dry cleaning	2.47	4.41	1.94	4.75
Hotels and motels	.49	2.20	1.71	5.35
Laundries	1.42	2.36	.94	4.78
Motion picture theaters	−2.83	−3.28	−.45	2.98
Shoe repair	1.16	−2.07	−3.23	4.77
Retail trades				
Apparel stores	.99	2.86	1.87	4.17
Automobile dealers	2.09	4.82	2.73	5.19
Drug stores	2.68	4.71	2.03	5.29
Eating and drinking places	− .18	2.30	2.48	5.31
Food stores	2.44	3.62	1.18	5.32
Furniture and appliances	2.88	5.37	2.49	4.88
Gasoline stations	3.25	5.25	2.00	5.08
General merchandise	1.40	3.53	2.13	4.38
Lumber dealers	1.21	3.07	1.86	4.99
Other	2.09	4.11	2.02	4.63

Source: Victor Fuchs, *Productivity Differences Within the Service Sector* (New York: National Bureau of Economic Research, 1967).

20. Similar results for the federal sector may be found in an article by Orzechowski [11].

the low rate of productivity in the public sector must then be due to be-havioral differences between public and private firms.[21]

Summary and Conclusions

This paper began by segmenting the sources of government expendi-ture growth into four categories: increased demands for public services, ineptitude, bureaucratic behavior, and lagging productivity in the public sector. The fourth explanation was examined in detail. It was found that productivity gains in six state and local services were, on average, zero or negative. The pattern of government expenditure increase is also consistent with a low rate of productivity in the public sector (given the pattern of recent price and income elasticity estimates for various ex-penditure categories).

Analysis of the interstate variation in productivity gains indicates that smaller governmental units have the lowest (or in some cases most nega-tive) productivity changes. Several explanations of this result were presented, including the fact that citizens have higher returns to moni-toring the activity of the public sector, the larger that sector is.

Estimates of the fraction of state and local governmental expenditure growth due to productivity differentials between the public and private sectors were presented. For the period 1962–1967, only about 20 to 25 percent of the growth of these expenditures could be attributed to productivity differentials alone.

Finally, the sources of low productivity gains in the public sector were examined. The observed low rate of productivity change in the public sector could be due to the nature of the services provided or due to behavioral differences between the public and private sectors. It was argued that productivity gains in the public sector have been less than those in the private service and retail trades sectors. Thus, at least some of the low or zero rates of productivity change in the public sector must be due to behavioral differences between the public and private sectors.

Thus one must conclude that the separation between various explana-tions of government expenditure increase discussed at the beginning of this paper is somewhat invalid. It is true that lagging productivity is one explanation of the rise in government expenditures. However, this lagging productivity is itself partially due to the behavioral charac-teristics of bureaus.

21. This is not surprising. The incentives faced by public and private firms are in fact different. For more on this point, see Spann, in this volume, and Niskanen [10].

References

1. Baumol, William J. "Macroeconomics of Unbalanced Growth: The Anatomy of the Urban Crisis." *American Economic Review* (June, 1967).
2. Borcherding, T. E., and R. T. Deacon. "The Demand for the Services of Non-Federal Governments: A Public Choice Approach." *American Economic Review* (Dec., 1972).
3. Bradford, D. F., R. A. Malt, and W. E. Oates. "The Rising Cost of Local Public Services: Some Evidence and Reflections." *National Tax Journal* (June, 1969).
4. Civil Service Commission, General Accounting Office, and Office of Management and Budget. *Measuring and Enhancing Productivity in the Federal Sector.* Prepared for the Joint Economic Committee of the Congress of the United States. Washington, D.C.: U.S. Government Printing Office, 1972.
5. Fisher, F. M. *A Priori Information and Times Series Analysis.* Amsterdam: North Holland Publishing Company, 1966.
6. Hatry, H. P., and D. M. Fisk. *Improving Productivity and Productivity Measurement in Local Governments.* Washington, D.C.: The Urban Institute, 1971.
7. Klarman, H. *The Economics of Health and Medical Care.* Ann Arbor, Mich.: University of Michigan Press, 1964.
8. Migue, Jean-Luc, and Gerard Belanger. "Toward a General Theory of Managerial Discretion." *Public Choice* (spring, 1974).
9. Nadiri, M. Ishaq. "Some Approaches to the Theory and Measurement of Total Factor Productivity: A Survey." *Journal of Economic Literature* (Dec., 1970).
10. Niskanen, W. A. *Bureaucracy and Representative Government.* Chicago: Aldine-Atherton, 1971.
11. Orzechowski, William. "Labor Intensity, Productivity, and the Growth of the Federal Sector." *Public Choice* (fall, 1974).
12. Spann, R. M. "The Macro-Economics of Unbalanced Growth and the Expansion of Governmental Expenditures." Unpublished manuscript, Virginia Polytechnic Institute and State University, 1973.
13. U.S. Bureau of the Census. *Census of Governments.* Washington, D.C.: U.S. Government Printing Office, 1962 and 1967.
14. _____. *Public Employment in 1970.* Washington, D.C.: U.S. Government Printing Office, 1971.
15. U.S. Department of Labor. *Indexes of Output Per Man-Hour: Selected Industries 1939 and 1947–69,* Bulletin 1680. Washington, D.C.: U.S. Government Printing Office, 1970.
16. _____. *Patterns of U.S. Economic Growth,* Bulletin 1672. Washington, D.C.: U.S. Government Printing Office, 1970.
17. Walzer, Norman. "A Price Index for Municipal Purchases." *National Tax Journal* (Dec., 1970).
18. Whalen, R. A. *A City Destroying Itself.* New York: Morrow, 1965.

7. The Public School System in Transition: Consolidation and Parental Choice   *Robert J. Staaf*

The number of public school districts in the United States has had a precipitous decline in the last three decades: from 117,108 districts in 1939–1940 to 17,995 in 1970–1971. In the last ten years alone the number of districts decreased by over 100% (40,520 to 17,995), while at the same time total public school enrollment has been increasing (over 30%). In 1966–1967, 42% of all elementary and secondary students in the United States were enrolled in a district in excess of 12,000 students, and 29% were enrolled in districts of 25,000 students or more. School consolidation is further reflected in the percent of total enrollment that is transported at public expense, 16.3% in 1939–1940 which increased to 43.0% by 1969–1970. The number of districts varies dramatically among states. Hawaii and the District of Columbia have only one district, while California has 1,070 and Nebraska 1,665.

A school district is defined as a governmental unit within a geographical area. Revenue sources for local school districts are from federal, state, and local governments. Since federal funding is a relatively small percentage of total funding it will not be discussed. State funding is usually on a per student basis with relatively little variation among districts except for special formulas to account for variations in the tax base or fiscal effort of local governments. The largest variation in revenue sources and thus per student expenditures among districts within a state is the result of local fiscal decisions.[1] Therefore, local collective choice decisions on public education have a significant impact on local residents as well as potential migrants. The bundle of educational services and their associated tax prices offered by various communities is an extremely important item of fiscal choice since education accounts for over 40% of all state and local expenditures.[2]

Conceptually we can define a unit of education in constant quality terms. Similarly, we can conceptualize a tax-price (or share) for each unit of education. Each citizen in the district has a desired optimal amount of educational units given his marginal tax-price/unit of education. Citizens are assumed to have different tastes, income, and tax-prices that in-

1. *Local* is used as a synonym for community or school district. A school district can be a state (e.g., Hawaii), county, city, town, or special district.
2. Chap. 8, table 2, in this volume.

fluence their optimal desired quantity of education. For example, in terms of tastes, a childless couple may be assumed to have a lower demand for education than a couple with children. Therefore, we can visualize a whole array (distribution) of optimal educational levels demanded by individual citizens within a district. However, the nature of the political and judicial process permits only one level of education (e.g., constant per pupil expenditure) be provided by the school bureaucracy such that each child within a district receives an equal quantity of educational units and each district receives an offer of an equal quantity of educational units (e.g., equal student/teacher ratios, equal allocation of time on subjects, equal access to facilities, etc.). We shall assume that the level of education supplied is determined by the median voter.[3] Through referendums or various platforms of school board members, an amount is approved or appropriated which reflects the preferences of the median voter. The level of education expenditures as a result of the political process, therefore, satisfies those voters whose preferences are close to the median voter but is considered to be an oversupply for those voters to the left of the median (e.g., childless couples) and an undersupply for those voters to the right of the median (e.g., parents who feel very intensely about education for their children). Note that institutional arrangements prohibit individual parents to *quantity adjust*. For example, an alternative institutional arrangement could give educational vouchers to parents. Instead of public monies going directly to school districts resulting in equal expenditures per student, the public monies could be channeled to parents in the form of vouchers to be spent on any approved school. Thus, if a parent feels intensely about education, the voucher could be supplemented by personal income. The fundamental distinction between the two arrangements is that the voucher system allows for public *provision* but not necessarily public *supply* of education. (The G.I. Bill is an example of the voucher system). However, present institutional arrangements allow for individual adjustment in the quantity of education offered only through voting *or* opting out of the public system and turning to private supply, a costly alternative. Voting is a viable alternative only if the individual parent feels that there is some probability of being the median voter, that is that his vote will count.

Median voter analysis brings us to our first implication of school district consolidation. Downs [10] and Tullock [18] have shown that the larger the number of voters, the lower the probability of any single voter being the median voter. This can be expressed as a simple equation:

$$B_i = A_i \cdot P_i \cdot D_i - C_{v_i} - C_{I_i},$$

3. See Black [2] and Bush [8] for further discussion of median voter analysis.

where B_i is the net benefit (cost) of voting to any individual (i); A_i is an estimate of the accuracy of an individual's (i) judgment; P_i is the probability of any one individual (i) being the median voter; D_i is the net differential benefit (cost) any individual (i) receives by having his candidate win (lose) *or* his preferred alternative win (lose), e.g., acceptance or rejection of bond referendum; C_{v_i} is the cost of voting; and C_{I_i} is the cost of information. For our purposes we are interested in P_i, the probability of being the median voter. P_i can be viewed as $\frac{1}{N}$ for the large numbers case and no cooperation.[4] Therefore, the larger the district, the larger the number (N) of potential voters, the lower the probability $\left(\frac{1}{N}\right)$ of any one individual being the median voter. The consequence of large districts is voter apathy and a low participation rate in the political process. More importantly, however, there is little incentive to gain information (C_I) about school district behavior resulting from a lack of power of any single individual to change the system through political action.

A hypothetical example will illustrate that the payoffs are not significant to an individual to obtain information on the school system according to the formula:

$$B_i = A_i \cdot P_i \cdot D_i - C_{v_i} - C_{I_i}.$$

Assume that a hypothetical individual feels the accuracy of his judgment to be 50% correct given his current state of information on school system behavior. Assume he lives in a school district of 25,000 students and that the number of voters is 25,000, a very conservative figure. Assume that he feels an increase in per pupil expenditure by 50% would result in a *net* increase in the present value of his child's education of $10,000. Assume it costs him $2.00 to vote in terms of opportunity and transportation costs. Further, assume he does not invest any resources to gather information. These assumptions yield a negative net payoff of $-$1.80$. $\left(-\$1.80 = .50 \cdot \frac{1}{25,000} \cdot \$10,000 - \$2.00\right)$. It clearly does not pay voters to gather information of the school system since each dollar expended on information yields a further net loss. Gathering information only affects A_i (accuracy of his judgment) and thus even if he were certain that his

---

4. The expression $\left(\frac{1}{N}\right)$ is not entirely accurate since p_i also depends on an individual's perception of how contested the election is going to be and the information of the preferences of other voters. For example, an unopposed candidate, or an election which the public opinion polls show to be very one-sided may also lower p_i.

judgment was correct, there would still be a negative net payoff. Furthermore, since school bureaucracies are the "gatekeepers" of information, the cost of accurate information acquisition may be very high.

As another example, in 1939–1940 there were 113,600 *one teacher* elementary schools in the United States (by contrast, there were only 2,143 in 1970). Individual parents clearly have a significant influence on the outcomes and behavior of single teacher district as opposed to districts of 25,000 or more (these districts comprise at least 28% of total enrollment in 1967) or the District of Columbia (one district of 145,704 students). The red tape of a bureaucracy this size and the bargaining power of teacher unions raise the cost of parent influence significantly in this case.

It follows then that as school district size increases through consolidation, the individual parent or voter has less influence on educational outcomes. Given this impotency, the rational citizen will choose in favor of ignorance and apathy.[5] Of course, this allows the educational bureaucracy more freedom in its decisions.

A major premise required for the voter apathy argument is the absence of political entrepreneurial competition (see chapter 8). While there may be little incentive for a single individual voter to expend resources on gathering information, there would appear to be a strong incentive for a political entrepreneur to gather and release information to citizens in order to defeat other candidates. More research is necessary on this topic and for the purposes of this paper we will assume that political entrepreneurial competition is not brisk.

As developed in a later section, it appears that economies of scale are not realized by school districts beyond a relatively small size (e.g., 2,000 students). At the same time we observe a trend towards larger and larger school districts (see Table 1). This in turn reduces the options of parents as well as the competition among school bureaucracies. School board members may sense the costs of school consolidation imposed on their constituents very slightly. However, they may sense the benefits of school consolidation from highly articulate and influential groups very keenly. As Bush and Denzau [8] point out, bureaucrats (e.g., school teachers and administrators) vote and have a high voter participation rate relative to nonbureaucrats. The point stressed here is that the school board members as well as school bureaucrats need not be acting in any malevolent or anomalous fashion. They are simply acting rationally and behave in a manner similar to any individual faced with the same costs and rewards.

5. Local demands for neighborhood schools is of course a reaction to consolidation and large district size. Objections to bussing of students may also in part be interpreted as a reaction to a form of consolidation.

Table 1. Number of public school districts and pupil/supervisor–pupil/principal ratios

School year	Number of public school districts	Pupils/ supervisors ratio[a]	Pupils/principals & asst. principals ratio
1939–40	117,108		
1941–42	115,493		
1943–44	111,383		
1945–46	101,382		
1947–48	94,926		
1949–50	83,718	2,790	643
1951–52	71,904		
1953–54	63,057		
1955–56	54,859		
1957–58	47,594		
1959–60	40,520	2,513	549
1961–62	35,676		
1963–64	31,705		
1965–66	26,983	1,916	547
1967–68	22,010	1,513	510
1970–71	17,995		

Source: National Center for Educational Statistics, U.S. Office of Education, *Digest of Educational Statistics* (Washington, D.C.: U.S. Government Printing Office, 1972).

a. Does not include psychologists. Data for ratios available for only selected years.

Bureaucracy Gains from Consolidation

While median voter analysis raises some difficulty in interpreting the net benefits the median or average voter may receive, we assume that the demand for educational services (q) is still subject to the law of demand. The law of demand essentially says a consumer will substitute away from q when the price of q (education) increases towards other goods, services or alternatives. The law of demand states that there is an inverse relationship between price and quantity. In fact, there are several empirical studies as cited by Borcherding [3] and Borcherding and Deacon [5] which offer evidence of the law of demand for public education. Following Borcherding's methodology [3] q is written $q = Ap^\eta y^\delta m$, which can be transformed into

(1) $$Npq = Ap^{\eta+1}y^\delta N^{\theta+1}m^\phi$$

where p is the tax price of q, A is a constant, y is per capita income, m represents all other variables, and N is the population in the school district. Using differentials on (1) as an extremely crude approximation for the effect of a change of p on Npq (total educational expenditures), can be estimated according to the form:

(1')   percent change in district educational expenditures = $(\eta + 1)$ times the percent change in p, holding the effects of other variables constant.

Assume p is represented by the wage rate (salaries of teachers and administrators).[6] The estimated parameter n is the elasticity of demand and measures the sensitivity of the change in quantity to a change in price. Borcherding's and Deacon's [5] estimate of n indicates that it is inelastic. Thus an increase in price (salaries) will increase total educational expenditures. For example, a salary increase, all other things equal, means fewer teachers hired and higher student/teacher ratios, thus resulting in lower quantity of educational units (in constant quality terms) demanded.[7] Table 2 illustrates that in 1950 the average classroom expenditure and student/teacher ratio increase as the size of the district increase.

Salary schedules of administrators are directly related to some size variable such as the number of students or number of teachers within the administrator's control. In fact, actual salaries of teachers, supervisors, and administrators increase as the size of the district increases. Data on the salary differentials according to district size is presented in part 4. Higher salary schedules and higher salaries may simply reflect a decrease in competition as the school district size increases. One of the factors that affect price elasticity (η) is the number of substitutes available. Consolidation of districts decreases the number of alternatives (substitutes) available and thus price elasticity becomes more inelastic.

Bureaucrats who are income maximizers should behave rationally to increase school district size through school district consolidation in order to increase their income. In spite of the rapid decline in school districts, the student/principal and student/supervisor ratio (see Table 1) has been increasing. Thus, consolidation does not necessarily mean the elimination of administrative positions but simply the addition of more vice principals, etc. School consolidation results in an increased price to the taxpayer-

6. The price the taxpayer confronts is the property tax. We assume here that when salaries increase, property taxes increase proportionately. This is, of course, a gross oversimplification of price since other costs besides salaries must be met by the property tax (i.e. capital costs, supplies, etc.). However, salaries do constitute 70% to 90% of total operating costs.

7. Larger student/teacher ratios are evident in larger school districts. Thus, as it will be demonstrated, their salaries are a function of size, so as consolidation to larger districts increases, we should expect fewer teachers hired (higher student/teacher ratios) because of the law of demand. Note that if price elasticity (η) is highly elastic (increase in p, decreases total educational expenditures, Npq), the increase in the student/teacher ratio may lead to the firing of a significant number of teachers. Thus if the price elasticity (η) was elastic you might expect little consolidation because of the pressures exerted by teachers on administrators and school board members. Consolidation, assuming price to be inelastic, may simply mean not hiring (or hiring fewer) new teachers to accommodate student enrollment growth.

Table 2. Expenditures among districts of various sizes, 1949–1950

District enrollment size	Avg. expend./ classroom unit ($)	Avg. daily attendance/ classroom unit	Avg. expenditure per pupil in ave. daily attendance ($)
40,000 and up	6,161	25.7	239
16,000–39,999	5,122	25.4	201
7,000–15,999	4,599	25.1	183
3,000–6,999	4,053	24.6	164
1,500–2,999	4,164	24.7	168
800–1,499	4,313	24.7	174
400–799	4,174	24.1	173
200–399	4,020	23.1	174
100–199	3,993	22.3	179
50–99	3,670	20.3	181
20–49	3,154	18.8	168
1–19	2,516	11.2	225

Source: U.S. Office of Education, Department of Health, Education, and Welfare, *Expenditures for Education at the Midcentury,* Misc. No. 18 (Washington, D.C.: U.S. Government Printing Office, 1953).

voter through an increase in the level of salaries. Note again that we do not have an explanation of how this is possible or why the political process permits consolidation other than to say that political entrepreneurial competition is absent. There is some evidence to support the assumption that there are no significant savings in nonsalary costs (e.g., capital costs) to offset the increased salary costs. The empirical studies on economies of scale of various district sizes are limited, but several studies that will be presented in part 3 find no significant scale economies.

It can be shown that for most goods and services an increase in income will, all other things equal, lead to an increase in their demand. Borcherding and Deacon [4] have estimated the income elasticity, the sensitivity of quality demand to income changes, to be around .75 for public education. Restating equation (1) we take into account income effects of consolidation.

(2) $\quad Npq = Ap^{\eta+1}y^{\delta}Nm^{\phi},$

where y is per capita income and δ is the income elasticity of the average voter, yields

(2′) $\quad$ percentage change in district educational expenditures = δ times the percentage change in per capita income, again holding the effects of all other factors constant.

Assume two districts have identical demand functions and identical price and income elasticities, η and δ. However, assume district one has a per capital income y_1 that is higher than district two, y_2, such that $y_1 > y_2$. Under the assumptions of the median preference voter model, all other things equal, a merger of the two districts affects the median or average voter resulting in increased educational expenditures (Npq_1) for what would have been district one and a decrease in educational expenditures (Npq_2) for district two prior to the merger. This argument may be expressed in the following way. Assume a single district of N individuals having a demand for education expressed as $q_j = Apq^\eta y^\delta m$, $j = \{1, \ldots N\}$ where there is a constraint imposed by the political process such that the median or average voter demand is satisfied, i.e., $q_{m_1} = Ap^\eta y^\delta m$ subject further to the constraint that $q_{m_1} =$ for all q_j; $j = \{1, \ldots N - 1\}$. The latter condition simply means that the quantity of education supplied to the median voter must be equal to the amount supplied for all other voters 1 through N (e.g., equal per student expenditures).

Now, assume that a second district has a median voter who demands q_{m_2}; and $q_{m_2} < q_{m_1}$ because $Y_2 < Y_1$. A merger of these voters should result in a new median voter whose demand is $q_{m_{12}}$ such that $q_{m_1} > q_{m_{12}} > q_{m_2}$. To determine whether Npq, total school expenditures, increase or decrease after consolidation it is necessary to consider the aforementioned price effects and the relative sizes of the two districts. For example, if a large low per capita income district merged with a relatively small high income per capita district, we should expect total educational expenditures to increase from consolidation (Npq_{12}) relative to the summation of the two separate districts ($Npq_1 + Npq_2$) such that $Npq_{12} > Npq_1 + Npq_2$. This conclusion follows from the nature of the collective decision process which is similar to a tie-in-sale.[8] The high per capita income residents who demand a higher quantity of education must also purchase additional units of education for the low per capita income residents, since the collective choice process requires an equal quantity available to all students and does not allow discriminatory practices which offer less education to some and more to other students within the same district. This effect will increase the *implicit* price to high per capita income residents since every unit of education demanded for their children must be equally provided for low income children. This implicit price effect may offset the income effect of the merger.

In summary, the effect on total educational expenditures is indeterminate. If the demand for education is price inelastic, and there is some evidence to suggest it is, then consolidation will increase total expenditures relative to a decentralized system as a result of the cost effect alone. Depending on the weights of population in the two districts, the income effect of consolidation may increase or decrease total expenditures. Finally, the implicit price effect of consolidation may increase or decrease total expenditures depending on the tax structure and income weighting after consolidation. All of these effects are empirically testable. Table 2

8. See Thomas E. Borcherding [4] for a more formal development of this model as it relates to school bussing.

suggests that these effects combined lead to an increase in expenditures as the district size increases.

Our major focus has been on why bureaucrats may rationally behave to move towards consolidation of districts. The price effect of consolidation clearly works in the favor of existing bureaucrats by raising their salaries.[9] The effect on total educational expenditures is indeterminate theoretically. However, it is interesting to note that even if total expenditures decrease or remain constant either through cost savings, income effects, or implicit price effects, the consolidated bureaucracy is able to increase their salaries. This case is contrary to the standard bureaucracy behavior postulate of maximizing the size of the budget. This does not imply that increases in bureaucrats' income and increases in the total budget of the bureaucracy are necessarily inconsistent by means of consolidation.

Some may argue on egalitarian lines that consolidation provides equality of opportunity for students of various family income backgrounds. The discussion thus far has been concerned with expenditures and salaries. If these expenditures are related to student output performance, then there is an equity argument. However, if there is no relationship, or an inverse relationship, then the equity argument based on equality of inputs seems to be a rather strong argument based more on the equality of income for teachers rather than equality of output for students and an argument for raising the income of teachers and administrators.

The next section presents a brief discussion of the Tiebout model as it relates to decreased competition and increased salary levels; following that we will examine several studies that relate to economies of scale of increasing the size of the school district.

The Tiebout Model and Competition

The Tiebout model [17] attempts to demonstrate that despite the "publicness" of goods provided by local governments, there are behavioral processes at work that lead to efficiency in public goods provision. This paper is not concerned with the "publicness" or "privateness" of education.[10] We take as a given that education is financed and supplied

9. Note that this argument is similar to union behavior of trading off increased membership (teachers) and lower wages for higher wages and lower membership.

10. A "public good" is defined as a good which has the characteristic that one individual's consumption of that good does not diminish the consumption of that good for other individuals. A "private good" is a good where my consumption diminishes the amount available for others. In the case of education, as well as other goods, an important distinction is that of public *provision* versus public *supply*. Thus there may be argument for the public provision of education due to spillover effects to other individuals; however, public provision does not necessarily entail public supply. Some writers have argued that education is a

by the public sector. The assumptions in the Tiebout model are the following:

1. Consumer-voters are fully mobile and will move to that community where their preference patterns, which are set, are best satisfied.

2. Consumer-voters are assumed to have full knowledge of differences among revenue and expenditure patterns and to react to these differences.

3. There are a large number of communities in which the consumer-voter may choose to live.

4. Restrictions due to employment opportunities are not considered. It may be assumed that all persons are living on dividend income.

5. The public services supplied exhibit no external economies or diseconomies between communities.

6. For every pattern of community services set by, say, the city manager who follows the preferences of the older residents of the community there is an optimal community size. This optimum is defined in terms of the number of residents for which this bundle of services can be produced at the lowest average cost.

7. The last assumption is that communities below the optimum size seek to attract new residents to lower average costs. Those above optimum size do just the opposite.

For the purposes of this paper, we will add an additional assumption.[11] Assume goods and services other than education are provided by the private sector and that education is the sole activity of government.[12]

Under these assumptions, individuals dissatisfied with their districts' supply of educational services would simply "vote with their feet." Various communities would offer different bundles of educational services with associated tax prices. Individuals would shop around and choose that community which best satisfied their preferences given the tax

---

private good [1] or is a private good at the margin [19] with possible infra-marginal social benefits. We shall ignore the important distinction concerning whether education is a "public good" or a "private good" to focus on the distinction of public provision versus public supply. Tiebout does consider a purely private good case where the allocation of resources would be the same as if normal market forces were operating. This case is simply a lumping together of all similar tastes for the purpose of making joint purchases where the city manager is substituted for the broker or middleman. However, the analogy crucially depends on several of his assumptions.

11. See Tiebout [17] for a more detailed explanation of assumptions 6 and 7.

12. This assumption is for expository reasons; however, there may be some important interdependencies between functions of government that modify the analysis.

prices they confront and their income. This case is similar to individuals shopping at Sears and Roebuck, Wards, and Spiegel. Under Tiebout's assumptions, all goods and services are provided efficiently in each community and individuals would locate in communities (school districts) which were homogeneous in tastes.

Let us examine Tiebout's assumptions. Assumption one is simply the self interest behavioral postulate. Assumption four allows full mobility except for transportation costs which we will also assume to be zero. Relaxing this assumption simply means there may be less competition among communities to attain an optimum size.[13] Assumption three (a large number of communities) and assumption six (there is an optimum size) are interrelated. If there are large economies of scale for school services then by definition there will be few communities. Alternatively, if there are no significant economies and significant diseconomies beyond a certain size, which available evidence seems to suggest, then there should be a large number of communities (school districts) *if* according to assumption six and seven the city manager (school bureaucracy) chooses or is constrained to operate at the optimum size.[14] Assumptions six and seven relating to optimum size of communities (school districts) implicitly assume bureaucracies are efficient and behave to achieve the lowest average cost and that there is brisk political entrepreneurial competition to keep bureaucracies efficient. Consider the three cases of district size.

Below Optimum Size. This case is not inconsistent with bureaucracy behavior since both the community and the bureaucrats could be made better off. Taxes could be lower and/or bureaucracy salaries increased, depending on the bargaining power of citizens and bureaucrats.

Optimum Size. There is here no incentive structure in existing salary schedules to maintain an efficient size district. In fact for administrators, salary schedules provide incentives to increase the size of the school

13. See Buchanan and Goetz [7] for a critical analysis of this assumption in terms of locational rents.

14. Assumption five of no external economies or diseconomies between communities will be accounted for by assuming that state appropriations provide sufficient funding to local districts to internalize these externalities. These externalities may be termed consumption externalities. Thus individuals other than parents may receive external benefits of having universal education in the three R's. This assumption avoids the case where children receive no schooling because of a parent's (communities) preferences or income constraint. Therefore, some minimum level of education is guaranteed to localities such that local revenue sources devoted to education at the margin generate strictly private returns to residents of the school district. This assumes that the social benefits from education are infra-marginal and the marginal benefits beyond state expenditures are private. This argument provides a rationale for state appropriations other than for merely income redistribution. State compulsory attendance laws, accreditation, and standards are a means of enforcing some minimum (social) standard. See West [19] for a further development of this argument.

district and the size of schools. Actual salaries for teachers are higher for larger districts. Thus there is opportunity cost to maintain an optimum size district from the bureaucracy viewpoint.

Above Optimum Size. As in the previous case there is a real cost incurred by administrators for the breaking up of one district into a number of smaller districts. Tiebout recognized the problems associated with this case. "No alderman in his right political mind would ever admit that the city is too big. Nevertheless, economic forces are at work to push people out of it. Every resident who moves to the suburbs to find better schools, more parks, and so forth, is reacting, in part, against the pattern the city has to offer" [17]. The same can be argued for school districts. However, if the number of alternatives continue to decline, there is a lesser chance of registering a dislike. More consolidation increases the monopoly power of each district and increases the cost to parents of opting for a preferred alternative supply, since there is a lower probability of finding a district that best satisfies the preferences of parents. It is rational for individual suppliers (districts) to favor a monopoly position rather than a highly competitive position. Monopolists are able to charge higher prices than competitive suppliers. In addition, a large local teacher's union resulting from consolidating districts increases its bargaining power to raise salaries if the only alternative to parents is to move a considerable distance (for example, out of the state in the case of Hawaii) to avoid the increase in the price of education. As I show in chapter 8 of this volume, the incentive structure (salary schedules) of bureaucrats is in conflict with outcomes we might expect in the market or under alternative institutional arrangements such as a voucher system.

The Tiebout model is an attempt to deal with difficulties of the political process.[15] Clearly, if the political process in each district worked in such a way to satisfy all voters, then there would be no need to discuss voting with your feet since optimal outcomes could be attained by voting at the ballot box. Note the critical difference between voting at the ballot box and voting with your feet in terms of our previous model. Parents voting at the ballot box are faced with a probability $\left(\frac{1}{N}\right)$ of affecting educational decisions. However, voting with your feet allows certainty (probability equals one) in the choice of attaining the desired bundle of educational services providing there are a large number of alternatives (districts)

---

15. More accurately, the model is an attempt to deal with problems associated with "public goods." Because of the so-called market failure of public goods provision, most writers have assumed that these goods should be provided by the public sector to meet the efficiency criteria as developed by Wicksell and Samuelson. However, other writers have noted the difficulties of the political process in providing public goods at the ballot box.

to choose among. Therefore, we should expect mobile parents to expend resources to gather information on alternatives since their location decision is determining and not affected by the collective decisions of others. Of course, the incentive to invest in information decreases as the number of viable alternatives (districts) decreases.

We now turn to a brief survey of the literature on economies of scale in education. If there are economies of scale, they may be sufficient to allow gains to be achieved by both bureaucracies and voters through consolidation. The preceding analysis has suggested that there are diseconomies of scale of school consolidation from the standpoint of taxpayers which fall out mainly in the ability of bureaucrats to increase their salaries with no significant change in either other costs or school outputs.

Economies or Diseconomies of Scale

There is a paucity of data and studies on economies of scale in public education. Table 2 illustrates that in 1949–1950 the average expenditure per classroom and the average expenditure per pupil increase dramatically as the size of the district increases. Hirsh [11, 12], who found no significant economies of scale in the St. Louis City-County area, remarks, "This study cannot find significant economies of scale and suggests that consolidation is unlikely to solve the fiscal problems of schools in urban America" [12, p. 39]. It should be pointed out that Hirsch's study is not related to changes in achievement levels, but rather examines per pupil expenditure as a function of district size. Katzman [13] found in Boston schools that the size of the attendance district appeared to provide some economies of scale when judged on the output criteria of reading scores and holding power (e.g., rates of higher attendance and fewer dropouts). However, significant diseconomies of scale were found in terms of a smaller proportion of students who sat for and passed the Latin High School's entrance examination. The Latin High School is Boston's elite high school. This suggests that large districts converge the distribution of achievement towards the mean. Finally, Brown [6] in analyzing over 500 Michigan school districts found that the relationship between school district size and achievement was significant and negative.

Several studies have dealt with school enrollment size. One district may have more than one school. Cohn [9] found that high schools with enrollments between approximately 1,250 and 1,650 students to be the most cost effective. Riew [15] found scale economies in school sizes of up to 1,675 pupils. Osburn's [14] analysis indicates that economies of scale in high schools are negligible with only $47.00 per pupil annual savings on increasing school size from 200 to 2,244 pupils.

The evidence, then, is far from conclusive that significant economies of scale exist. It is difficult to conceptualize why there should be economies of scale. It is conceivable that voluntary cooperation among districts could jointly hire factors that are highly indivisible such as a guidance counselor, coach, football stadium. The following data is perhaps the most conclusive evidence to date that costs increase significantly as school district size increases.

Administrative and Teaching Salaries

Since salaries constitute 70 to 90% of the operating costs of public education, a relationship of salaries to school district size should suggest diseconomies of scale if our models hold. Table 3 illustrates the frequency of relating principal's salaries to size. Note the higher propensity of larger school districts (over 25,000) to relate principal's salaries with size.

Table 4 illustrates the *actual* national mean salary paid for various positions in 1968–1969.

With the one exception in the case of librarians, salaries (including those of teachers) are an increasing function of district size. These figures lend support to the Tiebout model discussed earlier. In addition, the number of pupils per administrator has been decreasing over the years (see Table 1). In spite of consolidation, the rate of increase in administrators is greater than the rate of increase in students. Finally, Table 5 presents historical trend data on consolidation.

Most of the studies surveyed indicated no significant economies of scale beyond 2,000 students. Taking 3,000 students as a breaking point, we can see that in 1945–1950 only 52% of the total student enrollment in

Table 3. Methods used for establishing varying salary classes for supervising principals, 1969–1970

	Enrollment in district			
	100,000 or more	50,000– 99,999	25,000– 49,999	12,000– 24,999
Percent of classroom teachers supervised	25.0	31.9	32.1	21.3
Percent of pupils in building assigned to principal	37.5	34.0	23.8	18.3
Other methods, e.g., number of classrooms (%)		2.1	4.8	2.1
None specified (%)	37.5	31.9	39.3	58.3

Source: National Education Association, *Salary Schedules for Principals, 1969–70*, R5 (Washington, D.C.: The Association, 1970).

Table 4. Salaries of school personnel by district size 1969–1970

	25,000 or more	3,000– 24,000	300– 2,999	Under 300
Teachers	$ 8,069	$ 7,850	$ 7,696	$ 7,093
Superintendents	28,798	20,112	14,538	10,424
Senior high principals	15,515	13,116	11,539	9,335
Junior high principals	14,485	13,825	11,021	10,249
Elementary principals	14,072	12,261	10,561	8,242
Counselors	10,584	10,511	9,273	8,199
School nurses	8,319	7,441	6,470	5,158

Source: Research Division, National Education Association, *24th Biennial Salary Survey of Public School Professional Personnel,* 1969, R7 (Washington, D.C.: The Association, 1969).

the United States was in districts that could be considered beyond the least cost district. This percentage increase to 74.8% by 1966–1967. The trend in the sixties is likely to persist into the seventies.

Conclusion

No doubt there are other reasons for consolidation that have not been discussed in this paper. Much of the consolidation of districts has occurred in the Midwest where many districts were only one-teacher schools. On the other hand, there is a definite trend towards large district sizes above 3,000 students. Unless incentive structures or institutional arrangements change in the future, we should expect a continual increase in the monopoly powers of public school districts.[16]

This chapter, as well as the next chapter, attempts to demonstrate that more so-called inputs (e.g., education) or higher priced inputs (salary increases through consolidation) do not seem to matter in terms of output. At the same time, we have had the landmark decision of *Serrano* vs. *Priest* in the California Supreme Court in 1971. That decision held that expenditures per pupil in public schools must be equal for all students within the state or may not differ in amounts clearly associated with the differing per capita wealth of different school districts. These two papers have identified three dimensions on which teachers and administrators are generally paid: experience, education, and district size. There is no conclusive evidence that any one or combination of these dimensions increase output levels. Therefore, if per pupil expenditures are equalized within states, and this results in higher total expenditures, who are the

16. Annexation is similar to school consolidation. The model of bureaucracy gains could equally apply to annexation.

Table 5. Percent of public school systems and percent of pupils enrolled by size of district for selected years

Enrollment size (number of pupils)	Number of districts				Pupils enrolled			
	1949–50	1961–62	1964–65	1966–67	1949–50	1961–62	1964–65	1966–67
25,000 or more	⎫ 1.9	.4	.5	.7	⎫ 51.8	26.3	27.5	⎫ 28.7
12,000–24,999	⎪	.7	1.0	1.5	⎪	11.4	12.4	⎪ 13.1 ⎫
6,000–11,999	⎬	1.8	2.6	3.8	⎬	14.7	15.7	⎬ 16.6 } 74.8
3,000–5,999	⎭	4.0	5.5	7.4	⎭	16.6	16.5	⎭ 16.4
1,800–2,999	⎫ 98.1	4.6	⎱ 12.1	7.8	⎫ 48.2	10.3	⎱ 16.5	⎫ 9.6
1,200–1,799	⎪	4.3	⎰	7.0	⎪	6.2	⎰	⎪ 5.5 ⎫
600–1,199	⎪	8.5	10.8	12.2	⎪	7.1	6.4	⎬ 5.6 } 25.2
300–599	⎬	9.4	⎱ 9.0	11.6	⎬	4.0	⎱ 2.6	⎭ 2.7
150–299	⎪	8.3	⎰	8.9	⎪	1.8	⎰	1.0
50–149	⎪	11.4	⎱ 58.5	9.5	⎪	1.0	⎱ 2.4	.5
15–49	⎪	17.8	⎪	11.4	⎪	0.5	⎰	.2
1–14	⎭	12.5	⎰	10.2	⎭	0.1		.1
None		16.3		8.0				
Total	100.0	100.0	100.0	100.0	100.0	100.0	100.0	100.0

Source: U.S. Office of Education, *Digest of Educational Statistics* (Washington, D.C.: U.S. Government Printing Office, 1967).
Note: Annual data were not always available by various enrollment categories. The arrows indicate that the percentages include all categories in that range.

net gainers? Equal per pupil expenditures are likely to increase the standard of living of teachers and administrators but we should expect little in the way of increased output levels. The *Serrano* decision seems to be a decision to transfer income to the school bureaucracy. The revenue sources of the transfer will depend critically on the means of taxation used and it is by no means clear that the poor will come out as net gainers.

If the California Supreme Court's intent was to move towards equality of output, then such alternative institutional arrangements as performance contracting or a variant of the voucher system should be considered.

References

1. Barzel, Yoram. "Private Schools and Public School Finance." *Journal of Political Economy* (1973).
2. Black, Duncan. *The Theory of Committees and Elections*. Cambridge: Cambridge University Press, 1958.
3. Borcherding, Thomas E. "The Sources of Growth of Public Expenditures, 1902–1970." Chap. 3 in this volume.
4. _____. "The Economics of School Busing." Unpublished paper (Nov., 1972).
5. _____, and Robert A. Deacon. "The Demand for the Services of Non-Federal Governments." *American Economic Review* (Dec., 1972).
6. Brown, Byron W. "Achievement, Costs, and the Demand for Public Education." *Western Economic Journal* 10 (June, 1972).
7. Buchanan, James M., and Charles J. Goetz. "Efficiency Limits of Fiscal Mobility: An Assessment of the Tiebout Model." *Journal of Public Economics* 1 (April 1972).
8. Bush, Winston C., and Denzau, Arthur. "The Voting Behavior of Bureaucrats and Public Sector Growth." Chap. 5 in this volume.
9. Cohn, Elchanan. "Economies of Scale in High School Operation." *Journal of Human Resources* 3 (fall, 1968).
10. Downs, Anthony. *An Economic Theory of Democracy*. New York: Harper & Row, 1957.
11. Hirsch, Werner Z. "Expenditure Implications of Metropolitan Growth and Consolidation." *Review of Economics and Statistics* 41 (Aug., 1959): 239–240.
12. _____. "Determinants of Public Education Expenditures." *National Tax Journal* 12 (March, 1960): 29–40.
13. Katzman, Theodore M. "Distribution and Production in a Big City Elementary School System." *Yale Economic Essays* 8 (spring, 1968).
14. Osburn, Donald D. "Economies of Size Associated with Public High Schools." *Review of Economics and Statistics* (1967).
15. Riew, John. "Economies of Scale in High School Operation." *Review of Economics and Statistics*. (August, 1966): 280–287.
16. Spann, Robert M. "Rates of Productivity Change and the Growth of State and Local Government Expenditures." Unpublished paper (Dec., 1972).
17. Tiebout, Charles M. "A Pure Theory of Local Expenditure." *Journal of Political Economy* 64 (Oct., 1956).

18. Tullock, Gordon. *Towards a Mathematics of Politics*. Ann Arbor, Mich.: University of Michigan Press, 1967.
19. West, Edward G. "The Political Economy of American Public School Legislation." *Journal of Law and Economics* 10 (1967).

8. The Growth of the Educational Bureaucracy: Do Teachers Make a Difference?   *Robert J. Staaf*

This chapter, like the previous one, is exclusively devoted to public school bureaucratic behavior. At the outset, it should be pointed out that this analysis emphasizes the supply side of educational services with little attention paid to the demand side. This methodological bias is based on Niskanen's model of bureaucracy [16]. If political competition is absent, and most decisions are made in the absence of popular referendums, then this approach is somewhat justified.[1] An example of the lack of political competition is the payment of salary differentials to teachers who hold higher degrees, while most studies indicate that the teacher's educational level is inconclusive proof that student achievement scores or any other outcomes will be significantly changed by hiring these costly inputs. A second example is the rapid consolidation of school districts with no apparent effect on student achievement or the realization of scale economies. In fact, data on salaries suggest diseconomies. A candidate for the local school board or a candidate for the state assembly should be able to defeat other candidates or incumbents (who have a platform of maintaining the status quo) by running on a platform to eliminate bureaucracy waste in the presence of political competition.

A possible explanation for the absence of competition is that constituents are uninformed or ignorant of the workings of the public school system. Under present institutional arrangements of having monopoly school districts, there are negligible benefits to parents of gathering information. The typical parent is faced with a situation where he (she) is not allowed to make a choice among school districts, nor schools within a district, nor teachers within a school, nor subject matter. If parents are not allowed to choose among alternatives, then it is not rational to gain information about alternatives.[2] Moreover, the school bureaucracies are the gatekeepers of information, making reliable information costly to obtain. The companion paper has discussed the difficulties of adjustments by voting at the ballot box and the increasing costs to individuals of a "vote with their feet."

This paper is organized in five parts. Part 1 will present a statistical summary of the relative magnitude of educational expenditures and his-

1. See Winston C. Bush and Arthur Denzau, chap. 5 in this volume, for a more detailed account of bureaucracy and political competition.
2. See chap. 7 in this volume for a more formal model of the benefits and costs of voters obtaining information.

torical trends; Part 2 will survey the empirical literature on factors affecting school outputs defined as student achievement. Parts 3 and 4 will interpret these findings in terms of a model of teacher and administrator behavior, given the current structure of salary schedules, and part 5 will end with a summary, policy alternatives, and suggested further research.

Statistical Trends

Public employees in education outnumber any other function of government by a wide margin, including national defense. In 1967 there were 3,675,000 public employees in education at all levels. (Figure 1). In terms of public finance, educational expenditures accounted for 40.6% of the total state and local expenditures in 1967, a 5% increase over 1957 (Table 1).

Figure 1. Functions of distribution of public employment, October, 1967 (employees in full-time equivalents, in thousands)

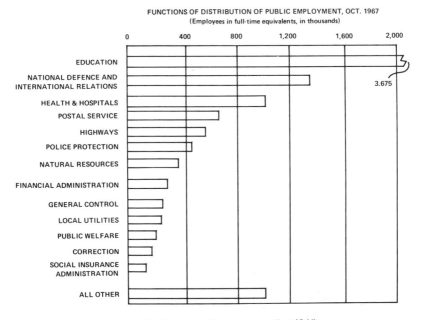

FUNCTIONS OF DISTRIBUTION OF PUBLIC EMPLOYMENT, OCT. 1967
(Employees in full-time equivalents, in thousands)

SOURCE: 1967 Census of Governments, Compedium of Public Employments, Vol. 3, No. 2, U.S. Department of Commerce. Bureau of the Census, p. 13.

Source. Bureau of the Census, U.S. Department of Commerce, *1967 Census of Governments, Compendium of Public Employments,* Vol. 3, No. 2. (Washington, D.C.: U.S. Government Printing Office, 1967).

Table 1. Data reflecting trends between 1957 and 1966–1967 on general expenditure of state and local governments by function

| Functions | Percent distribution | | Average annual % increase 1957–67 |
	1966–67	1957	
Total	100.0	100.0	8.7
Education	40.6	35.0	10.4
Highways	14.9	19.4	6.0
Public welfare	8.8	8.6	9.1
Health & hospitals	7.1	7.7	7.7
Public protection	3.3	3.7	7.6
Local fire protection	1.6	2.0	6.3
Sanitation	2.7	3.6	5.7
Natural resources	2.5	2.3	8.6
Financial administration & general control	3.5	4.3	6.8
Interest on general debt	3.2	2.7	10.6
All other	11.7	10.8	10.0

Source: Bureau of the Census, U.S. Department of Commerce, *1967 Census of Government No. 5: Compendium of Government Finances,* Vol 4 (Washington, D.C.: U.S. Government Printing Office, 1968), p. 7.

Educational expenditures as a percentage of the GNP have increased from 3.4% in 1951–1952 to 8% in 1970–1971 (Table 2). Clearly, by almost any criterion – employment, expenditures, and revenue – the educational bureaucracy is one of the most important factors that influence the magnitude and growth of government.

Table 2 illustrates several trends occurring in public education. From 1959 to 1970, per pupil total expenditures increased 113% in unadjusted dollars. Per pupil expenditures adjusted for inflation increased 57% for this same period. Current operating expenditures per pupil (excludes capital expenditures) increased 69% in real terms, a greater increase than per pupil capital costs. The average salary per member of the instructional staff increased 36% in this eleven year period. The student/teacher ratio has decreased from 28.4 in 1959 to 24.4 in 1970 for elementary schools and 21.5 to 20.0 for secondary schools. The decrease in student/teacher ratio is reflected by a 51% increase in the number of school teachers while total enrollment increased only 30%. The percentage distribution of total revenues for public schools between federal, state, and local levels has

Table 2. Public education trends

School year	Total & current expenditures per pupil in A.D.A. in public elementary & secondary schools.				Salary per member of instructional staff		Elementary student/teacher ratio	Secondary student/teacher ratio	Public enrollment K-12 (000's)	Public school teachers K-12 (000's)	Percentage distribution of total revenues for public elem. & sec. ed.			Total educ. expend. as % of GNP	Pupils/supervisors (psych. not included)	Pupils/principals & asst. principals	Number of public school districts
	Unadjusted dollars		Adjusted dollars (1970–71)		Unadjd. dol.	Adjusted dol. (71)					Fed.	Stat.	Lcl				
	Totl.	Crnt	Totl.	Crnt													
1939–40	$ 106	$ 88	$ 301	250	1,441	4,093			25,434	875	1.8	30.3	68.0	3.5			117,108
1941–42	110	98	280	250	1,507	3,840					1.4	31.5	67.1	2.6			115,493
1943–44	125	117	285	267	1,728	3,940					1.4	33.0	65.6	1.8			111,383
1945–46	145	136	316	296	1,995	4,344					1.4	34.7	63.8	2.0			101,382
1947–48	203	179	346	305	2,639	4,494					2.8	38.9	58.3	2.8			94,926
1949–50	259	209	434	350	3,010	5,046			25,111	914	2.9	39.8	57.3	3.4	2,790	643	83,718
1951–52	313	244	473	368	3,450	5,209					3.5	38.6	57.8	3.4			71,904
1953–54	351	265	518	391	3,825	5,644					4.5	37.4	58.1	3.8			63,057
1955–56	338	294	573	434	4,165	6,137					4.6	39.5	55.9	4.2			54,859
1957–58	449	341	624	474	4,702	6,530					4.0	39.4	56.6	4.8			47,594
1959–60	472	375	638	507	5,174	6,991	28.4	21.5	35,182	1,355	4.4	39.1	56.5	5.1	2,513	549	40,520
1961–62	530	419	700	553	5,700	7,525	28.3	21.7	37,464	1,461	4.3	38.7	56.9	5.6			35,676
1963–64	559	460	719	592	6,240	8,027	28.4	21.5	40,187	1,578	4.4	39.3	56.3	6.1			31,705
1965–66	654	537	813	668	6,935	8,621	27.6	20.8	42,173	1,710	7.9	39.1	53.0	6.6	1,916	547	26,983
1967–68	786	658	917	768	7,885	9,201	26.3	20.3	43,891	1,855	8.8	38.5	52.7	7.2	1,513	510	22,010
1969–70	926	783	973	873	8,840	9,291	24.8	20.0	45,619	2,014	7.9	38.5	53.2	7.6			
1970–71	1008	858	1008	858	9,570	9,570	24.5	20.0	46,000	2,050	7.9	38.9	53.2	8.0			17,995
Ratio change from 1959 to 1970	2.13	2.28	1.57	1.69	1.84	1.36	.86	.93	1.30	1.50				1.56	.60	.92	.22

Source: National Center for Educational Statistics, U.S. Office of Education, Digest of Educational Statistics (Washington, D.C.: U.S. Government Printing Office, 1971).

Note: The ratio change from 1959 to 1970 would equal 1 if no change; a value greater than 1 indicates an increase; a value of less than 1 indicates a decrease.

not changed drastically. The local share has remained constant at about 38 to 39%, while the federal share is increasing from 4 to 8%, offsetting the decreased state share from 57% to 53% in this eleven-year period. The increased federal share represents the passage of the Elementary and Secondary Education Act of 1965. Perhaps the most important trend is that of total educational expenditures (including higher education) as a percentage of the GNP. In 1959–1960, this percentage was 5.1 and increased to 8.0 in 1970, a 50% increase.

Finally, the number of school districts has continued to decline. The number of school districts in 1970 (17,995) was only 44% of the number of districts in 1956–1960 (40,520). At the same time, the students/supervisors ratio has decreased to 60% of 1959–1960 levels, and the students/ principals ratio is also decreasing, 92% of 1959–1960 levels. That the number of districts has experienced a rapid decline while the number of principals and supervisors has increased suggests that there are no administrative cost savings resulting from consolidation. Table 2, then, is a summary of trends in inputs or factors of production. The following section will examine some of these factors as they relate to output measures.

A Survey on the Relationships of School Inputs to Outputs

In February 1970 the U.S. Office of Education held a conference by a group of educational researchers. Out of this conference came a publication entitled *Do Teachers Make a Difference?* The conference participants agreed that the available data convinced them that "teacher performance indicators are more relevant for judging teaching effectiveness than certification, education, and experience" [23, p. 3]. Many of the studies surveyed used data gathered by the U.S. Office of Education in its 1965 Equality of Educational Opportunity Survey of the U.S. public schools. This data was used for the Coleman report, named after the principal investigator, James Coleman. The Coleman study found, as did others, that socioeconomic status of students and a brief self-administered test on verbal facility taken by teachers are the two most significant factors affecting student cognitive achievement levels. The following is a brief but rather comprehensive survey of empirical studies on factors affecting student output usually measured in terms of student achievement levels or gains. It should be noted from the outset that the methodological and statistical approaches and techniques are not always comparable, and thus results are often inconsistent across studies. In addition, different data sets are often used.

Teacher Salaries

Teacher salaries are usually determined solely on the basis of the teacher's educational and experience level. Brown found that "pay-inputs such as lower class sizes and more qualified teachers have no effect on achievement. . . . The percent of teachers with masters' degrees and the years of staff experience have insignificant regression coefficients in all but one case and have the wrong sign in two cases" [4, pp. 215–17]. Kiesling [13, p. 24] states in a summary of over one dozen studies: "It is striking to note that such pay-parameter variables (as teacher experience and training) were seldom found to be related to pupil performance. . . ." The Coleman study found that teachers' age, sex, race, socioeconomic status, education, experience, certification, salary, and professional activity were not particularly powerful discriminators for predicting student achievement [7, p. 2]. Hanushek [9] found two teacher characteristics that were favorably related to the verbal scores of sixth graders: the number of years of teacher experience and teacher's verbal score. It is also interesting to note that Hanushek found no significant relationship associated with a teacher's degree level and student achievement. These results suggest, as does Coleman's study, that a teacher's verbal score is not strongly correlated with the teacher's educational level.

Guthrie [24, p. 47] surveyed 19 studies and summarizes the factors that appear to be significant in effecting student achievement. A total of 12 studies out of 19 found some pay characteristics to be significant (teacher salary, experience, or degree level). However, of these 19 studies, only two found the teacher's educational level significant: the Powden report and the Bowles study.[3] Guthrie's survey is clearly inconsistent in terms of teacher effectiveness with Kiesling's survey. The issue of whether teachers make a difference on some dimensions is not completely settled.

An important question to ask is how much of a difference various teacher characteristics make. Levin found that with regard to the two teacher characteristics Hanushek found important, verbal ability and experience, obtaining more teachers with higher verbal scores is about one-fifth as costly as obtaining more teacher experience [14, p. 31].

Hanushek states that "the strongest conclusion from the models is that school systems now operate quite inefficiently. They are buying the wrong attributes of teachers, i.e., attributes which lead to little or no achievement gains" [9, p. 95].[4]

3. Bowles's study of teacher preparation was not significant at the .05 level [3], p. 43.
4. Levin also notes that graduates of teachers colleges were receiving less than graduates of other institutions [14, p. 30].

Pupil/Teacher Ratio

Of the 19 studies surveyed by Guthrie [24], only three indicated that the pupil/teacher ratio was significant.[5] Brown's study [4] indicates that the ratio of pupil per professional personnel is not significant and has the wrong sign (positively related to achievement) in two out of five cases. Coleman's study suggests no significant relationship between student achievement and the pupil/teacher ratio. Finally, Otto and Bergersrocle [81], after reviewing a large number of class size studies, conclude that mere class size has little significance in terms of achievement in academic studies.

Socioeconomic Status

Most of the above studies have examined the effects of various inputs on achievement while controlling for the socioeconomic status of students. Students from well-educated and well-to-do families tend to make higher achievement scores as do students who go to schools which have higher per pupil expenditures. Higher per pupil expenditures, however, tend to be highly correlated with neighborhoods or school districts which have families that are well off either educationally or financially. The only significant factor that affected student achievement (other than the teacher's verbal score) in the Coleman study as well as numerous other studies, is the socioeconomic status of students. Many have concluded from the Coleman study that little can be done in terms of changing student achievement levels through public policy (e.g., increasing school expenditures) since the students' home environments are largely beyond the control of school administrators. A major exception to this viewpoint was that expressed by the justices of the California Supreme Court in handing down the decision of *Serrano vs. Priest* in 1971.

In conclusion, this section has surveyed the literature on several input dimensions (characteristics of teachers, student/teacher ratio, class size). The evidence is by no means conclusive that these inputs significantly affect student performance once the student's socioeconomic status is taken into account. This survey is by no means exhaustive. Several important studies [24, p. 9] indicate that a teacher's verbal score on a rather simple self-administered test makes a significant difference in terms of student achievement. On the other hand, this variable is not a pay parameter of salary schedules, nor does it appear to be significantly correlated with pay parameters such as educational level. Most of the above studies have implicitly assumed a model of teacher behavior that relates pay parameters with output. A notable exception to this is a paper by Levin

5. Some of these studies may not have included the pupil/teacher ratio. However, this seems unlikely since it is a factor that a priori should affect costs.

[15]. The next two sections will interpret the empirical results surveyed in terms of a model of school bureaucratic behavior.

Teacher Behavior

The previously cited studies implicitly used a theory of the firm model in which the educational bureaucracy is assumed to maximize student achievement. In light of the weak, if any, relationships between school inputs that are related to pay parameters and outputs, one writer has concluded that "we must look beyond the three R's for what makes a good school good or what might make a poor one better" [4, p. 219]. This section offers an alternative explanation.[6] It is assumed that teachers and administrators are utility maximizers that respond to rewards and constraints within a bureaucratic framework. It is also assumed that parents receive a higher level of satisfaction by increased achievement levels of their children and view the school system as an institution that *should* attempt to maximize achievement levels.[7]

A bureaucracy is defined by William Niskanen [16], as having the following characteristics:[8]

1. The employees of a bureau do not appropriate any part of the difference between revenue and costs as personal income.

2. Some part, or all, of the recurring revenues of the organization derive from other than the sale of output at a per-unit rate.

The first characteristic essentially means that there are no pecuniary payoffs to teachers or administrators for being efficient. Suppose there is a move that will result in a cost savings to the school district. Under present institutional arrangements an individual teacher or administrator does not receive a salary increase, bonus, or reward for cost savings suggestions. Many states and localities require that unexpended appropriations at the end of the fiscal year revert back to the respective government. In addition, many school budgets are of the line item type. Thus, any savings in one area (e.g., salaries) that may generate a surplus (appropriations minus expenditures) cannot be transferred to another area (e.g., supplies) or another fiscal year.[9] Therefore, there is no financial incentive

6. Much of this section borrows from a paper by Bush, Freiden, and Staaf. See [5].

7. There may, of course, be other outputs that parents expect from schools, such as child care services, which presumably are complementary to achievement.

8. The terms *bureaucrat* or *bureaucracy* are not intended to have any pejorative meaning. The term *bureaucracy* is used to distinguish organizational behavior from other types of behavior (e.g., profit maximizing).

9. Procedural rules such as line item budgets can be viewed as a restriction on internal consumption by bureaucrats as suggested by Alchian and Kessel [1].

to introduce cost saving techniques or practices since teachers or administrators are not able to appropriate any portion of the gains. In fact, there may be disincentives to reducing expenditures since next year's budget may be at least partially based on last year's expenditures.

The second characteristic relates to salary schedules. The funding of the bureaucracy is usually made annually in lump sums appropriated by a legislature or council. This lump sum appropriation is usually based on the number of students enrolled which in turn determines the number of teachers through some student/teacher ratio formula. The portion of the appropriation going to salaries (usually 65% to 85% of the budget) is determined by number of students and the educational and experience level of teachers and administrators. Neither the size of the budget nor revenue received by the bureaucracy is based on what might be defined as output measures such as achievement scores or percentage of students reaching certain achievement levels.[10] The public school bureaucracy under present institutional arrangements may be defined as monopolistic. First of all, the law requires compulsory education for children within certain age ranges. Second, judicial decisions have prevented parents from choosing districts other than the district of residence. Furthermore, parents do not necessarily have rights to choose either schools or teachers within a district. These decisions are usually made by administrative fiat. Finally, state and local school boards and judicial decisions have limited entry into the education industry through accreditation procedures of teachers as well as private schools. A major barrier to entry is the recent decision of the United States Supreme Court regarding the constitutionality of vouchers.

Within the above definition of bureaucracy we seek to explain why the educational and experience level of teachers does not seem to significantly influence student output as measured by various achievement test scores. An implicit assumption underlying the previous studies is that increased educational and experience levels of teachers increase their ability to teach. That is, for any given effort (e.g., twenty hours in the classroom) it is assumed that the teacher with the higher level of education is more successful in transforming his or her effort into more student achievement relative to a less educated teacher who expends the same effort. This assumption does not appear to be valid. In fact Hanushek's findings suggest that a teacher's verbal score is not strongly correlated with the teacher's educational level.

Another factor that should influence student achievement levels, after

10. Some districts are experimenting with what is termed "performance contracting" in which bonuses or losses are incurred based on the level of output. One of the first experiments of this sort was the Texarkansas School District, funded by HEW. Performance contracting does not fall under the previous definition of bureaucracy.

controlling for various factors such as the students' socioeconomic status, is the amount of effort devoted to teaching. We are now considering effort or time expenditures beyond the time the teacher spends in class. Bowles [3] found that the average amount of time a teacher spends in guidance activities and the number of days the school stays in session during a school year to be significantly related to student's scores on tests of verbal ability. By assuming that student achievement is directly related to a teacher's time expenditure we are assuming that teachers *can* make a difference rather than that they *do* make a difference. However, there is no monetary incentive for a teacher to make a difference since her or his salary is not based on achievement levels but rather on her or his educational and experience level. Additional effort or time expenditure on the part of teachers above some minimally accepted level (e.g., showing up in class) can be classified as charitable behavior since leisure is foregone without additional monetary compensation. We can, of course, simply rely on the charitable behavior of teachers to achieve desired output levels. But what is important is that we should not expect significant changes in charitable behavior brought about by increasing a teacher's salary because of more experience or more education.[11] In fact, if leisure is a normal good, in the sense that as incomes rise individuals prefer more leisure, then salary increases could have detrimental effects on achievement.[12]

If teacher salaries were directly related to student achievement performance levels, leisure would become more costly to teachers. The higher the wage rate paid for each increment in student achievement, the more costly it is for the teacher to consume leisure. Under an incentive system, based on outputs (e.g., student achievement) rather than one based on inputs, we should expect regression models that attempt to empirically relate salaries and achievement to be positive and significant. In the absence of a positive wage rate for achievement output, it is difficult to determine which teachers are charitable and which are not.[13] Salaries based on student performance would reward those teachers who are presently charitable and penalize those who are not so charitable. Re-

11. One might argue that teachers with more education or experience are more efficient given a certain time expenditure, that is, teachers with these characteristics can increase student achievement for any given time expenditure more than teachers without these characteristics. With respect to educational levels, this does not seem to be the case since there appears to be a low correlation between a teacher's verbal ability, which does count, and the level of education. The evidence with respect to experience is still not conclusive. The point stressed here is that there is a quality-quantity tradeoff: a teacher with greater efficiency than average can decrease his (her) time effort to compensate or vice versa.

12. Of course, charity may also be a normal good which is offsetting.

13. There is some evidence that students in Catholic schools are similar to public school students in terms of performance even though salaries are significantly lower in Catholic schools. This may suggest that nuns are more charitable than laymen.

cent experiments with "performance contracting" in several school districts is a movement towards rewarding teachers and administrators on the basis of outputs rather than inputs. Performance contracting simply is a contract between the school district and a firm. The firm is rewarded if it goes beyond the terms of the contract in the form of bonuses. It is punished (fined) if its performance falls below the terms of the contract. Performance criteria are usually based on achievement such as 90% of the third grade class attaining fourth grade reading levels in nine months. The National Education Association, a teachers' union, has generally been opposed to performance contracting.

A teacher's charity may take on several dimensions. A teacher may concentrate her (his) effort on select students in the class at the expense of other students or concentrate on nonacademic efforts (e.g., discipline, socialization, ethics) at the expense of academic subjects like the three R's. A teacher is relatively unconstrained in a classroom so that he (she) is able to follow his (her) own preferences. Thus when achievement scores of individual students are averaged within a class, the averages may indicate that teachers do not make a difference, even though at the margin within a class, teacher effects may be significant for some students or for other definitions of outputs.

Finally, the nature of the educational production process limits the amount of charitable behavior in which teachers are willing to engage. Usually, a student or class cohort will be assigned no fewer than twelve different teachers from first grade to high school graduation. Each of these teachers will regard their output as relatively insignificant in the total process. Furthermore, each teacher's productivity is one of the major determinants of the next teacher's input. A teacher in the first grade who is extremely charitable (expends a lot of effort) may transfer this charity to the second grade teacher rather than her students if the second grade teacher simply views this as a gift thereby leading her to reduce her effort level. The first teacher will, therefore, learn that her intended charitable behavior towards students is, in fact, charity to succeeding teachers.

In light of the evidence in part 2 and the model developed in part 3, we now inquire into the utility maximizing behavior of administrators (e.g., superintendents and principals).

Administrators' Behavior

The number of master's degrees in the field of education awarded in 1969–1970 amounted to 79,841, compared to 33,512 awarded in 1959–1960. The rate of production increased 2.4 times within this ten year period (Table 3).[14] Over this ten year period, 547,094 master's degrees were produced. The rate of increase in the educational levels of teachers far exceeded total student enrollment growth of only 30% during 1959–1970 and exceeded the 51% rate of growth in the number of public school teachers during this same period. In 1970–1971 there were 254,473 full- and part-time students enrolled for advanced degrees in the field of education. This represents one out of eight teachers for this one year.

Table 3. Masters and Ph.D. production in the field of education: 1949–1971.

Year	Master's			Doctorate			Students enrolled[a] for advanced degrees
	Male	Female	Total	Male	Female	Total	
1949–50	10,588	7,723	18,311	719	142	861	
1950–51	13,055	9,154	22,209	783	150	933	
1951–52	15,194	11,184	26,382	884	177	1,061	
1952–53	15,168	11,659	26,827	1,111	246	1,357	
1953–54	15,423	12,362	27,785	1,237	261	1,498	
1954–55	15,108	12,512	27,620	1,221	249	1,470	
1955–56	16,005	14,133	30,138	1,301	282	1,583	
1956–57	16,455	14,517	30,972	1,241	292	1,533	
1957–58	16,479	14,633	31,112	1,291	341	1,638	
1958–59	N/A	N/A	31,569	N/A	N/A	1,614	
1959–60	18,126	15,386	33,512	1,281	309	1,590	
1960–61	18,915	15,495	34,410	1,384	359	1,743	
1961–62	19,838	16,094	35,932	1,537	363	1,900	102,967
1962–63	20,439	17,083	37,522	1,672	403	2,075	114,641
1963–64	21,869	18,841	40,710	1,892	456	2,348	123,241
1964–65	22,976	20,765	43,741	2,179	529	2,708	133,478
1965–66	25,837	24,641	50,478	2,461	602	3,063	150,300
1966–67	27,943	27,918	55,861	2,807	722	3,529	156,434
1967–68	30,891	32,773	63,664	3,249	830	4,079	189,809
1968–69	33,430	37,993	71,423	3,859	970	4,829	215,131
1969–70	35,696	44,145	79,841	4,698	1,196	5,894	234,042
1970–71							254,473
1949–59	Total		272,925			13,548	
1959–70	Total		547,094			33,758	
1949–70	Total		820,019			47,306	

Source: National Center for Educational Statistics, U.S. Office of Education, *Earned Degrees* and *Students Enrolled for Advanced Degrees* (Washington, D.C.: U.S. Government Printing Office, 1949–1971).

a. Includes part-time and full-time students enrolled.

14. Note that these teachers should be fairly young, since the rate of return to human capital is higher the greater the number of years remaining in the labor force.

Table 4 is a crude estimate of the cost of hiring and/or employing teachers with a master's degree as opposed to a bachelor's degree. In 1969–1970, it is estimated using very rough figures that the salary differential paid for master's degrees is between one half and one billion dollars annually. For the period 1965–1966 to 1969–1970, the total cost to U.S. taxpayers is between 1.4 billion dollars to 3.0 billion dollars. These costs do not include differentials paid to doctorates nor salary increments paid for earning credit hours without a degree (e.g., bachelor's degree plus 30 semester hours). Assume that each student enrolled for an advanced degree in 1970 (254,000) will earn on the average an additional $100 per year. This represents a marginal cost for 1970 of an additional 25 million dollars.

The above calculations are very crude and at an aggregate level. Table 5 is a more accurate figure for school districts which have enrollments of 12,000 or more students. The data represents only 425 districts which is less than 40% of the total U.S. public school enrollment. The net annual expenditure for paying differential salaries beyond four years of college education is estimated at 530 million dollars for these 425 large school districts in 1968–1969. Thus an estimate of one billion dollars for 1971–1972 which includes all teachers would seem to be conservative.

Levin [14] and Hanushek [9] have argued that school administrators seem to be hiring the wrong inputs in terms of cost minimization for any given level of output. The cost of hiring higher educational levels is quite significant at the national level. Why is it rational for administrators to hire costly inputs or accede to demands in collective bargaining to pay salary differentials for additional education? Some states and districts formally and informally require a teacher to complete a certain number of graduate credits or attain a higher degree within a certain time constraint in order to maintain his (her) position. In some cases this is necessary to maintain accreditation status.[15]

As discussed previously, administrators are not able to appropriate any savings that are possible by hiring more efficient input combinations given a certain output level. In addition, there are constraints on school administrators to transfer budget appropriations from salaries to non-salary items. Thus it may appear at first glance that an administrator is indifferent with regard to hiring various teacher combinations of experience and educational levels.

However, assume school administrative positions such as superintendents, principals, and supervisors are rationed on the basis of higher

15. Note that if the rate of return for additional education is sufficiently high, there is no reason for mandating such requirements since teachers would voluntarily invest in education. Alternatively, if it is not high enough, then we can assume that salary schedules which pay differentials for education do not benefit teachers, students, or taxpayers. See paper delivered at the American Educational Research Association, Chicago, 1972 [22].

Table 4. Average annual cost of paying differential salaries for master's degree.

Year	Stock of master's degree by year[a]	Average salary differential between bachelor's & master's[c]		Estimated annual cost of teachers having a master's degree	
		Minimum	Maximum	Minimum	Maximum
1965–66[b]	374,490	$421	$889	157,660,000	332,922,000
1966–67	430,351	$457	$987	196,670,000	424,756,000
1967–68	494,015	$521	$1,115	257,382,000	550,827,000
1968–69	565,438	$605	$1,291	342,090,000	729,980,000
1969–70	645,279	$675	$1,440	435,563,000	929,202,000
1965–69 Total				1,389,365,000	2,967,696,000
Percentage change 1965–69		160%	161%	276%	279%

a. Calculated by adding earned degree production for each year (from Table 2); does not take into account retirements and deaths.
b. Of the 1,710,000 teachers in 1965–1966, an estimated 374,490 or 21.9% held master's degrees. National Center for Educational Statistics, U.S. Office of Education, *Digest of Educational Statistics,* 1971, p. 41.
c. This is admittedly a rough approximation. Source: Research Division, National Education Association, *Salary Schedules for Teachers* (Washington, D.C.: The Association, 1966–1970). Includes only schedules for enrollment districts that exceed 6,000 students.

Table 5. Distribution of classroom teachers by preparation level with enrollments of 12,000 or more 1968–1969.

	Enrollment stratum of districts							
	100,000 or more		50,000– 99,000		25,000– 49,999		12,000– 24,999	
	%	Index[a]	%	Index[a]	%	Index[a]	%	Index[a]
Number of districts reporting	22		40		85		274	
Less than bachelor's	1.7	85.0	1.8	93.2	1.7	103.2	2.2	91.9
Bachelor's (4 yrs)	60.8	100.0	63.2	100.0	61.3	100.0	61.5	100.0
Master's (less than 6 yrs)	24.0	120.3	26.9	126.6	27.7	128.4	28.2	128.7
6 years of college	7.3	134.6	7.4	151.4	7.6	152.7	6.7	153.1
Doctoral degree or 7 yrs	6.1	145.2	7	161.5	1.7	160.8	1.4	160.0
Percent with master's or above	37.4		35.0		37.0		36.3	
Number of master's (or 5 yrs)		41,349		31,344		32,961		55,177
Mean salary diff. (M.A–B.A)		$1,666		$1,925		$2,056		$2,104
Dollar cost		$68,887,000		$60,337,000		$67,768,000		$116,092,000
Number with 6 years		12,570		8,605		9,000		13,200
Mean salary diff. (6 yrs–B.A.)		$2,833		$3,719		$3,813		$3,892
Dollar cost		$35,611,000		$32,002,000		$34,317,000		$51,374,000
Number with doctoral (or 7 yrs)		10,531		873		1,973		2,709
Mean salary diff. (7 yrs–B.A.)		$3,707		$4,451		$4,399		$4,401
Dollar cost		$39,038,000		$ 3,854,000		$ 8,679,000		$11,922,000

Source: Research Division, National Education Association, *24th Biennial Salary Survey of Public School Professional Personnel, 1969* (Washington, D.C.: The Association, 1969), Table 20, p. 28.

Note: Total number of teachers reported with at least five years of education: 220,286. Total number of school districts for the above data: 425. Total net cost of hiring teachers beyond four years of education: $530 million.

a. Index relationship of mean salaries: bachelor's degree = 100.0.

degree levels. We are assuming that at least a master's degree is a necessary credential to be considered for and employed in administrative positions.[16] In 1969–1970 between 50% to 78% of administrative salary schedules were some function of salary schedules for classroom teachers on either a ratio basis or a dollar differential.[17] The National Education Association reports that "in recent years the practice of relating the ad-

16. This is a reasonable assumption since many of the administrative schedules start with a master's degree.

17. The percentage distribution varied according to the size of the school district. See Table 10 of [19]. There is a third relationship called "independent" in addition to the "ratio" and "dollar differential." These schedules are classified as having "no apparent relationship." There may be informal procedures rather than formal ratios or dollar differentials.

ministrative schedule to that of classroom teachers has continued to expand" [19, p. 7]. Among those salary schedules for administrators which are derived as an index or ratio of the schedule for classroom teachers, the most common base of reference is the salary the administrator would earn if he or she were on the teacher's schedule (teacher's schedule = 100.0). The dollar differential refers to administrators receiving fixed sums of money above the salary they would receive as teachers. Table 6 is an example of the salary schedule differences between teachers (base 100.0) and administrators.

Salary schedules are usually determined through collective bargaining. Teacher demands for salary increases brought before the bargaining table reflect some coalition of at least a majority of teachers. The schedule can be viewed as a set of *relative* prices for various combinations of experience and education. The coalition that would most likely form is that group of teachers with common experience and educational levels. Therefore, a teaching staff in a district with little experience and all bachelors degrees is likely to bargain much harder for beginning salaries and bachelor's degree *relative* to salary increases for more experience and higher degree levels.[18] Alternatively, a teaching staff with a large per-

Table 6. Mean maximum schedule salaries for classroom teachers and supervisors, administrative personnel of districts with enrollments of 25,000 or more 1969–1970.

	Salary	Ratio
Classroom teachers	$12,274	100.0
Elementary principals	16,657	135.7
Junior high principals	17,521	142.7
Senior high principals	18,735	152.6
Elementary asst. principals	14,742	120.1
Junior high asst. principals	14,988	122.1
Senior high asst. principals	15,806	128.8
Counselors	13,484	109.9
Deans	14,596	118.9
Supervisors	16,684	135.9
Consultants and coordinators	17,523	142.8
Directors	19,581	159.5
Asst. superintendents	22,929	186.8
Superintendents	30,398	247.7

Source: National Education Association, *Maximum Salaries for School Administrators,* Research Report 1970–72 (Washington, D.C.: The Association, 1972).

18. There may still be pressure for bargaining for experience since this represents future payoffs. However, assuming the personal discount rates are positive, there is a stronger incentive to bargain for present income over future income.

centage of master's degrees and above is likely to stress increasing the *relative* differential of educational levels. If administrators are income maximizers and have master's degrees, then they should clearly prefer a teaching staff with more master's degrees since they can expect this group to represent their interest more so than a staff comprised mostly of bachelor's degrees and no experience. In addition, administrators may argue that it is necessary to increase the salary differential to higher degrees in order to induce the existing teaching staff to invest in further education.

Administrative salary schedules based on a ratio or salary differential of teachers' salaries clearly indicate a certain degree of mutual gain to both administrators and teachers at the bargaining table rather than a conflict of interest.

The constraints imposed on salary increases may rest primarily with the local school board which is either elected or appointed. Assume that school board members are primarily interested in minimizing the lump sum total of a salary schedule increase and not the distributional effects among educational and experience levels. Under these circumstances, intense bargaining between *relative* increases for different experience and educational levels is likely to occur. Again administrators would benefit by having a teaching staff whose educational levels coincided with their own. For example, assume a schedule which pays $8,000 to a bachelor's degree and $10,000 to a master's degree prior to bargaining. Assume administrators have master's degrees and their salary is based on a ratio of 1.5 which yields a current salary of $15,000. Further, assume that after collective bargaining the salary for bachelor's increases to $9,000 and masters remained at $10,000. Under these assumptions, the administrators would not receive any salary increase. Alternatively, assume the dominant coalition is comprised on master's degrees. After bargaining, assume teachers with bachelor's receive no increase (maintain $8,000) and master's degrees receive an increase of $2,000, raising their salary to $12,000. In this case, administrators would receive an automatic increase of $3,000 ($1.5 \times 12,000 = \$18,000$). Again, it is advantageous for administrators to hire higher degree levels to form dominant coalitions that have educational levels similar to their own. This incentive arises because of the automatic linking of teacher salaries to administrative salaries. A similar argument can be developed for experience levels.

Now assume administrators' salaries are related to student output levels (e.g., student achievement) rather than input levels (e.g., education and experience). Under these circumstances, administrators would hire teachers or teacher characteristics which seem to improve student achievement, such as verbal ability or the school where the degree is earned. In addition, administrators would probably hire an efficient mix of these various characteristics where a dollar spent on verbal ability yields the same marginal output as a dollar spent on some other characteristic such as experience. Under these circumstances, colleges and universities that train teachers are likely to respond to these price signals by producing graduates with training that affects student output levels. As it stands now, colleges and universities simply have to produce earned credit hours or degrees for teachers to be rewarded.

Under present institutional arrangements, there is little incentive for teachers or administrators to determine "what makes a difference." Teachers are rewarded for "living" and "earning college credits." Administrators are also rewarded on the basis of these same characteristics. It should be stressed that it is rational behavior for both teachers and administrators to behave in a manner that leads to higher and higher educational levels. Teachers and administrators can appropriate (have a right to) income from the school system by achieving higher degree levels. They do not have a right to appropriate income from the school system by achieving higher output levels of students or attaining other efficiency moves. If educational levels of teachers are not related to student achievement levels, then each marginal dollar expended on educational training of teachers beyond some threshold can be considered as wasted from the parents' viewpoint. Moreover, given the design of administrative and teaching salary schedules we should expect the educational bureaucracy to increasingly expand in this dimension over time. Table 3 clearly illustrates this trend. The growth rate in the last ten years of earned master's degrees, doctorates, and students enrolled for advanced degrees in the field of education has far exceeded the growth rate of any other dimension in education such as students, teachers, per pupil expenditures, and educational expenditures as a percentage of GNP.

Summary and Policy Implications

William Niskanen [16] offers a different perspective than that commonly held on why democracy and bureaucracy work as they do. Following Niskanen it is assumed the political process is passive. A crucial question remains concerning how the educational bureaucracy has been able to behave in the manner it has without more severe constraints placed upon it by representatives or voters. Simply stated, why don't school board members constrain the behavior of school bureaucracies to be efficient from the standpoint of the taxpayers? One reason may be that of "fiscal illusion" on the part of taxpayers.[19] Fiscal illusion assumes taxpayers are not informed or have illusions with respect to the benefits

19. This is the subject of chap. 10 in this volume by Charles Goetz.

and/or costs (taxes) of the educational process. Fiscal illusion seems to be inconsistent with political entrepreneurial competition. While it may not pay one voter to gather information on the educational process, it should always pay a political entrepreneur to gather information to beat a rival candidate. The fact of negative price elasticities for educational services as well as other government services (shown by Borcherding and Spann) seems to weaken the argument of taxpayers' fiscal illusion.[20] The answer to the above question is, however, beyond the scope of this paper. Hopefully, more research will be directed towards political entrepreneurial competition.

An argument that may be raised against the conclusion that the educational bureaucracy is inefficient from a taxpayer's standpoint is that the term output has been misspecified. Output in this paper has been defined strictly in terms of student scholastic achievement levels (e.g., the three R's). Outputs perceived by voters may be more inclusive than simply scholastic achievement. To date, these outputs other than achievement levels have not been operationally defined. Teachers and administrators speak of the socialization process and instilling good citizenship; however, these "other" outputs are still abstractions with no operational meaning. If an output is not defined operationally then it is not possible to design an incentive structure to optimize these "other" outputs. Furthermore, there is no reason to believe that higher degree levels or experience are more productive of these other outputs.[21]

This paper has emphasized the role that salary schedules play in explaining bureaucratic behavior. Many bureaucracy models assume that bureaucrats simply maximize the size of their budget. If bureaucrats are not able to appropriate any of the budget increases, it may not be rational to maximize the size of the budget.[22] Other models assume that the lack of appropriability leads to internal consumption with the bureau such as plush offices, attractive and less efficient secretaries, nepotism, and so on. The decrease in student/teacher ratios, the increase in administrators, and the increase of educational levels may be a form of this behavior leading to a more pleasant atmosphere. However, the salary schedules, if they are as general as they are in education, provide us with an institutional measure to examine and predict the behavior of bureaucrats by simply assuming income maximizing behavior.

20. See Thomas E. Borcherding, "The Sources of Growth of Public Expenditures 1902–1970," and Robert M. Spann, "Rates of Productivity Change and the Growth of State and Local Government Expenditures," both in this volume.

21. Child care or—more crudely put—babysitting service is often defined as one of the spillover benefits of public education. There is no reason to believe that a master's degree is an input that has a positive marginal product in producing child care services.

22. Many assume that the size of the budget is a proxy for power, increased probability of promotion, etc.

The analysis suggests that pay schedules should be examined more closely for bureaus at all levels of government. For example, U.S. postmasters were paid by how many employees they had, how many branch offices they had, and how many trucks were under their control [20]. A case similar to education may be the practice of requiring master's degrees as an entry requirement to become a social worker which may not yield any productivity gain.[23] A recent article by Weiss [22] showed that the coefficient of variation in income for those with bachelor and Ph.D. degrees who were employed in educational institutions and government was much smaller relative to private industry. Employment in private industry has a higher risk associated with it than education or government. A salary schedule based on education rather than output performance should indeed be less risky. Weiss's [24] analysis also suggests that the average income for these various occupation groups should not be equalized if individuals are generally risk adverse. Therefore, arguments to equalize government pay scales with that of the private sector should be reexamined.

There are a number of policy moves that could be initiated which could change bureaucratic behavior. One policy is to pay teachers and administrators on the basis of outputs rather than characteristics. This policy is similar to performance contracting which is currently being experimented with in several districts. A second policy is that of giving educational vouchers to parents and allowing them to choose among schools, as suggested by Professor Friedman [8]. This too, is being experimented with. A voucher system would induce competition among bureaus (schools) which would considerably weaken the monopolistic power of bureaucracies. Although the political realities of full scale implementation of these policies beyond the experimental stage is a matter of conjecture, in closing, the following quote from de Tocqueville seems appropriate:

> . . . and how far indeed, those which we call necessary institutions are simply no more than institutions to which we have become accustomed.

References

1. Alchian, A., and R. Kessel. "Competition, Monopoly, and the Pursuit of Money." In *Aspects of Labor Economics,* NBER Special Conference Series No. 14. Princeton, N.J.: Princeton University Press, 1962.
2. Bailey, D., and C. Schotta. "Private and Social Rates of Return to Education of Academicians." *American Economic Review* (March, 1972): 20.
3. Bowles, Samuel S. "Towards an Educational Production Function." Mimeographed. Presented at the Conference on Research in Income and Wealth (Nov., 1968).

23. Approximately one out of four Ph.D's in the social sciences were employed in government in the period 1958–1966 [19].

4. Brown, Byron W. "Achievement, Costs, and the Demand for Public Education." *Western Economic Journal* 10, no. 2 (June, 1972).
5. Bush, Winston C., Alan Freiden, and Robert J. Staaf. "Of the Expense of the Institutions for the Education of Youth: Adam Smith Revisited." Research paper, Center for Public Choice, Virginia Polytechnic Institute and State University, 1972.
6. Cohn, Elchanan. "Economies of Scale in Iowa High School Operation." *Journal of Human Resources* 3, no. 4 (fall, 1968).
7. Coleman, James S., et al. *Equality of Educational Opportunity.* Washington, D.C.: U.S. Government Printing Office, 1966.
8. Friedman, Milton. *Capitalism and Freedom.* Chicago: University of Chicago Press, 1964.
9. Hanushek, Eric. "The Education of Negros and Whites." Ph.D. dissertation, Department of Economics, Massachusetts Institute of Technology, 1968.
10. Hirsch, Werner Z. "Expenditure Implications of Metropolitan Growth and Consolidation." *Review of Economics and Statistics* 41 (August, 1959): 239–240.
11. _____. "Determinants of Public Education Expenditures." *National Tax Journal* 13 (March, 1960): 29–40.
12. Katzman, Theodore M. "Distribution and Production in a Big City Elementary School System." *Yale Economic Essays* 8, no. 1 (spring, 1968).
13. Kiesling, H. *Multivariate Analysis of Schools and Educational Policy.* Santa Monica, Calif.: The Rand Corporation, 1971.
14. Levin, Henry M. "A Cost-Effectiveness Analysis of Teacher Selection." *The Journal of Human Resources* 5, no. 1 (winter, 1970).
15. _____. "Concepts of Economic Efficiency and Educational Production." Conference on Education as an Industry, National Bureau of Economic Research, New York, 1971.
16. Niskanen, William. *Bureaucracy and Representative Government,* Chicago: Aldine Press, 1971.
17. Osburn, Donald D. "Economies of Size Associated with Public High Schools." *Review of Economics and Statistics* (1967).
18. Otto, Henry J., and Fred von Bergersrode. "Class Size." In Walter S. Monroe (ed.), *Encyclopedia of Educational Research.* New York: MacMillan, 1950.
19. Research Division, National Education Association. *Maximum Salaries Scheduled for School Administrators,* Research Report 1970–72. Washington, D.C.: The Association, 1970.
20. Riew, John. "Economies of Scale in High School Operation." *Review of Economics and Statistics* (Aug., 1966): pp. 280–287.
21. Samuelson, Robert J. "Why the Mail is a Mess." *Washington Post* (Nov. 26, 1972).
22. Staaf, Robert, Francis Tannian, and Edward Ratledge. "A Human Capital Approach to Designing Salary Schedules: A Case Study of Wilmington." Paper presented to American Educational Research Association, April, 1972.
23. U.S. Office of Education. *Do Teachers Make a Difference? A Report on Recent Research on Pupil Achievement.* Bureau of Educational Personnel Development, OE-58042. Washington, D.C.: U.S. Government Printing Office, 1970.
24. Weiss, Yoram. "The Risk Element in Occupational and Educational Choices." *Journal of Political Economy* 80 (Nov./Dec., 1972).

9. Federal Propensities To Spend and To Tax
Dennis J. Jacobe

Two digit inflation during the first quarter of 1974 stimulated renewed interest among economic observers in the topic of federal government spending. At issue of course is the question of whether stimulative fiscal policies are a root cause of the rampant inflation experienced by the United States in 1974.

So that this question can be answered and understood, and corrective proposals suggested, it is necessary to develop an information base. The objective of this paper is to aid in the construction of this information base. It is hoped this project will answer such questions as what are the results of projecting current trends, can current spending patterns be maintained, and will government spending soon absorb all of the GNP? In order to answer these questions and to provide a data base for the discussion of other similar questions, it is necessary to develop a set of projections for total federal revenues, total federal expenditures, and their major components. The projection technique employed involves the calculation of federal propensities to spend and to tax.

Projection Procedure

The first step in the estimating procedure is to obtain the average yearly change in both federal receipts and outlays. This requires that a decision be made as to the base period employed in this calculation.[1] Four were considered in this paper: the Nixon period of 1969 to 1971, the Short period of 1964 to 1971, the Medium period of 1959 to 1971, and the Long period of 1952 to 1971. Calculations as to average yearly change in federal receipts ranged from a low of 0.075 per year to a high of 0.085 per year, a difference in base period estimates totaling 0.010. Similar computations for federal outlays ranged between 0.057 and 0.100 per year.[2] These estimates permit projections of future federal receipts and outlays to be made, assuming the trend exhibited during the base period continues.

The next step involves projecting the major sources and expenditure areas of future federal budgets. The technique employed involves the

1. The term *base period* refers to the years analyzed in order to obtain some trend measure, such as an average yearly change.
2. These calculations are available upon request.

calculation of "federal propensities."[3] Once again, the assumption is made that the federal government will follow the same pattern in acquiring and spending its funds among the various areas that it followed during the base period. For example, if total federal government expenditures expanded by $2 billion over the Nixon period (1969–1971), and its expenditure on national defense expanded by $1 billion, it is assumed that the federal government has a propensity to spend 50 percent of its new outlays on national defense. Such "federal propensities" were computed for several of the major functional areas of federal government expenditures. Similar federal propensities were calculated, once appropriate adjustments were made, for various major tax sources of the federal government.[4]

Once these estimates are made, projections for each federal government source and expenditure area can be derived. Since this paper is only an attempt to obtain ballpark estimates, four sets of projections are superfluous. Sufficient accuracy for analysis can be achieved if a bracketing process is employed. Thus, for each variable involved, a high and low estimate is obtained. These are compiled into a series of estimates labeled *A Series* for high estimates, and *B Series* for low estimates. Although the probabilities of either series resulting in a large number of highly accurate projections is relatively low, there is reasonable assurance that future receipts or expenditures will be in the area bracketed by these projections.[5] In a number of cases adjustments were necessary before an estimate was entered in either *A Series* or *B Series*. These consisted of reducing the bracketed projection area by common sense elimination or alternation of some estimating variables. For a number of variables data restrictions required that only two bases be used. These entries complete *A Series* and *B Series* estimates.

Edie Approach

Many methods can be used in making projections of the sort attempted in this study. One such different procedure was employed by the Lionel D. Edie Company while projecting federal outlays for the National Dividend Foundation.[6] This approach involved a look at expenditures in the 1960 to 1971 period, a review of legislation proposed during the Nixon period of 1969–1971, consideration of prevailing attitudes during the

3. This technique stems directly from two articles dealing with revenue sharing. For more information see U.S. Congress, Joint Economic Committee [4], pp. 659–660, and Plummer [2], pp. 122–124.

4. These expenditures are also assumed to remain at the zero level once they reach that point. It seems reasonable to assume that no large quantity of federal receipts will be obtained from this expenditure area.

5. Projection results from this section are available upon request.

6. See Edie and Company [1].

Nixon period toward the country's future needs, and anticipation of the future costs of governmental provision of goods, taking inflation into account.[7] Once these factors were evaluated, average annual rates of growth were inferred.[8] Total federal expenditures were forecast to increase at an average yearly rate of 9.5 percent.[9] Subgroup rates range from a low of 2 percent per year for commerce and transportation to a high of 22 percent for health.[10] In addition to health outlays, two other areas were expected to have relatively large growth rates. These were housing and community development expenditures at 13.1 percent per year, and education and manpower expenditures at 12.1 percent per year.

Comparative Results

Data for the years 1980 and 1991 show that total federal expenditures as projected using the Edie approach are in the range established by the *A Series* and *B Series* results. The low estimate for national defense expenditures (*B Series*) in 1980 is $132 billion, while the Edie estimate is $104 billion, a difference of $28 billion. For 1991, the difference in estimates is $126 billion, which, considered with the 1980 difference, reveals the lack of emphasis the Edie approach predicts in this area. In the area of international affairs and finance outlays, the Edie projections for both of these years are $2 billion over the *A Series* (high estimates). Expenditures on space research and technology, and on commerce and transportation, are projected low by the Edie estimates as compared to the *B Series* (low) estimates. These differences ranged from $1 billion in space research outlays in 1980 to approximately $37 billion in commerce and transportation outlays in 1991. A number of Edie-based projections for federal government expenditures by function were within the high-low estimate range. These functions included housing and community development, education and manpower, veterans' benefits, and general government. Finally, health outlays as projected by the Edie approach far exceeded the *A Series* estimates. For 1980 the Edie-based projection was $79 billion, $21 billion in excess of the $58 billion *A Series* projection, while for 1991 these estimates differed by $576 billion with the Edie-based projection totaling $772 billion.

7. These procedures are not explicitly stated in the Edie report. It appears, however, when one reads this report that this was the Edie Company's approach.

8. It should be noted that the Edie report used these rates only to project outlays for the year 1980. In this section they are used to project for the two decades of 1971–1991, so they would be comparable to the *A* and *B Series* projections made earlier.

9. Those subgroups included that are treated in this paper are not the only such estimates made in the Edie report. They were selected because they were comparable in composition to the *A* and *B Series* estimates made earlier.

10. Although subgroups not treated in this paper were considered in the Edie report, only those comparable in terms of expenditure area were treated in this section.

"Real" Terms

The *A series, B Series,* and Edie estimates of federal government revenues by source and outlays by function are calculated using current price terms. The results all indicate expansive trends, but this might not be the case if inflation and population growth were taken into account. These factors can be accounted for if federal budget trends are examined in constant January, 1971 dollars per capita; that is, "real" terms.[11] The results are similar to those derived in current dollars, but with a lesser rate of yearly expansion. Total federal outlays per capita increase at a real yearly rate of between 0.5, *B Series,* and 4.9, *A Series.* These rates of expansion yield an increase of total federal outlays, *A Series,* from $1,038 per capita in 1971 to $2,682 in 1991, and an increase of total federal outlays, *B Series,* from the same $1,038 per capita in 1971 to $1,119 in 1991. Total federal revenues per capita change at a real yearly rate of between −4.8 and +3.4. The result is a change from a 1971 level of $947 per capita to between $360 per capita (low series) and $1,834 (high series) in 1991. These estimates indicate that the federal budget trends derived previously in current dollars do exist in "real" constant terms. As one might expect, the rate of expansion is less in "real" terms than in current dollars; thus, the current dollar projections indicate a actual trend.

Constraint[12]

Only the most meager of claims have been made with respect to the projections produced. Even so, the projections made are, to say the least, of surprising magnitude. The Edie-based estimates, although they point to different areas of emphasis, also indicate tremendously high federal expenditure levels between 1971 and 1991. The alarming nature of these estimates becomes abundantly clear when GNP figures are examined.

Over the period 1960–1969 the GNP expanded at an average yearly rate of 7.3 percent. When compared to the 6.5 percent high and 5.5 percent low, growth rates sometimes used to make GNP projections, 7.3 percent appears to be a relatively high estimate.[13] If it is assumed that GNP increases at this rate (7.3 percent per year), then the 1991 GNP is projected to be $4,388 billion, better than 4 times the 1969 level of $999

11. Figures and tables for the "real" GNP and constraint sections of this paper are available upon request.

12. Money GNP and federal budget data are treated while real values are not. The result in each case is the same.

13. These percentages were used by the U.S. Congress, Joint Economic Committee [5] and illustrated in U.S. Bureau of the Census [3], Table 457, p. 314.

billion. The $2 trillion mark is reached by 1985, and the $4 trillion mark is estimated for 1989. Combination of this projection date with the historical data available permits an examination of federal budget receipts and outlays as a portion of the GNP over the time period 1930–1991.

In 1930 total federal revenues were 3 percent of GNP, and increased to 5 percent by 1940. The 21 percent level was reached during World War 2 (1945), but went down to 14 percent in 1950. In 1960 federal revenues were 18 percent of the GNP, 17 percent in 1965, and 19 percent in 1970. Over the period 1970–1991, total federal receipts decreased to 18 percent of GNP when *B Series* projections were used, but increased to 22 percent when *A Series* projections were considered. The portion of GNP that federal receipts represents increased from 3 percent to 19 percent over the period from 1930 to 1970. *A Series* estimates are shown to implicity assume that this expansion continues with this ratio reaching 22 percent in 1991. Conversely, *B Series* estimates show federal receipts as being 18 percent of the GNP in 1991. To find collecting receipts amounting to 19 percent of the GNP in 1970 may surprise many citizens. For this to be reduced to 18 percent of the GNP by 1991 may not be sufficient to satisfy some citizens, but an increase to 22 percent should be more disturbing.

If this seems like a large slice of the GNP for the federal government to collect in receipts, the percentage of the GNP it purchases (expenditures) is even larger. From 1930 to 1940 total federal expenditures as a portion of GNP increased from 3 percent to 9 percent. During the World War 2 year of 1945 this portion expanded to 46 percent of GNP. These percentages ranged from 14 percent in 1950 to 20 percent in 1970. *B Series* estimates show federal outlays as a percentage of GNP increasing to 22 percent in 1991. Using Edie-based estimates this same portion expands to 30 percent in 1991. This value is 32 percent if *A Series* projections are considered. Regardless of the set of estimates used in calculating the federal government consumption in 1991 as a portion of the GNP, it is clearly relatively large. Each set of projections implicitly assumes that total federal outlays will continue to increase as a part of GNP. Such expansion is shocking even when compared to federal receipts/GNP ratios.

The extraordinary nature of these projections becomes even more evident if one projects the trend onward in time past 1991. By the year 2000 the percentage of GNP consumed by total federal outlays (*A Series*) expands to 40 percent, 50 percent in 2010, 66 percent in 2020, 86 percent in 2030, and 100 percent in 2036. Thus, if the *A Series* trend continues, total federal outlays would consume better than one-half of the nation's GNP in less than 40 years from 1972, and all of the GNP in less than

65 years from 1972.[14] A similar trend is indicated by *B Series* data, but at a somewhat slower rate.

The growth of total federal receipts and total federal outlays as portions of GNP implies that federal government propensities to tax and to consume changed over the time period considered. As the period considered shortens from 1952–1969 and 1959–1969, to 1964–1968, the marginal propensity to consume federally provided goods increases from 0.205 to 0.221. Similarly, as the period considered shortens, the marginal propensity to tax of the federal government expands from 0.211 to 0.251.[15] If these propensities are examined it is clear that as the time period progresses toward 1990, the MPT_t^a and the MPC_t^a increase; the MPT_t^a expands from 0.158 to 0.245 and the MPC_t^a expands from 0.267 to 0.403.[16] Using *A Series* projections, these estimates indicate that the federal government is implicitly assumed to consume 35 percent of the expansion in GNP over the period 1970–1990 and to tax 22 percent of this growth during the same time interval. Even if *B Series* data are used the results show that the same trends are revealed and that the federal government is presumed to consume 23 percent of the growth in GNP during the 1970–1990 time period, and to tax 18 percent of this same expansion over this period. These results indicate that the *A Series*, *B Series*, and Edie-based projections implicitly assume that the U.S. society's marginal propensities to tax and to consume will continue to increase from 1970 to 1991, as they did during the 1950s and 1960s.

These assumptions may not be warranted. At some point, the society may not wish to follow this presumed pattern. If the assumption that the U.S. society's marginal propensities to consume federally provided goods and/or to tax of the federal government are held constant or presumed to increase at a lesser rate, is substituted for the implicit assumption previously discussed, new projections can be made. The 20 percent *MPT* assumption yield a set of projections between those of the *A Series* and *B Series* made earlier, and a 15 percent *MPT* yields a set of projections lower than either the *A Series* or the *B Series*. Assumption of a 30 percent *MPC* results in projections ranging between the *A Series* and *B Series*, while the presumption of a 20 percent *MPC* yields results lower than those of the other two sets (*A and B Series*).

14. Of course the trend line continues past the GNP line once it intersects it, but this required some type of capital consumption or foreign borrowing.

15. The *MPC*'s and *MPT*'s of the U.S. society increased during the 1950s and 1960s. Yearly and/or 5-year calculations of these propensities reveal the same trend.

16. The MPT_t^a is the marginal propensity to tax of the federal government in time period t, calculated using *A Series* projections. The MPC_t^a is the marginal propensity to consume federally provided goods in the time period t, calculated using *B Series* projections.

Summary and Conclusions

A propensity variant to simple trend analysis was employed to project federal revenues and outlays over the period of 1971–1991, and once this procedure was established an alternative (Edie) approach was discussed and the results of both approaches compared. They were related to federal budget projections in "real" terms and to GNP. Finally the implicit assumptions about federal propensities to spend and to tax made by a simple trend projection approach were discussed.

The results of this study are, to say the least, shocking in what they imply about the size and future of the federal government revenues, expenditures, and deficits. When one sees the way that federal government activities absorb more and more of the country's GNP, one seems justified in assuming that something will halt this expansion at some point. Projections developed in this paper, however, simply point out the speed of a runaway horse (the federal budget). Whether the horse can be slowed, halted, or turned around is subject to further analysis.

References

1. Edie, Lionel, and Company. "Federal Spending and Revenues in the 1970's," prepared for the National Dividend Foundation (Jan., 1972).
2. Plummer, James L. "Federal-State Revenue Sharing." *Southern Economic Journal* (July, 1966), pp. 122–124.
3. U.S. Bureau of the Census. *Statistical Abstract of the United States: 1968.* Washington, D.C.: U.S. Government Printing Office, 1968.
4. U.S. Congress, Joint Economic Committee, 90th Congress, 1st session. *Revenue Sharing and Its Alternatives: What Future for Fiscal Federalism?* Washington, D.C.: U.S. Government Printing Office, 1967.
5. U.S. Congress, Joint Economic Committee. *U.S. Economic Growth to 1975: Potentials and Problems.* Washington, D.C.: U.S. Government Printing Office, 1971.

10. Fiscal Illusion in State and Local Finance
Charles J. Goetz

Introduction

At one time, political economists widely agreed that the best tax for raising any given sum is the tax which causes the least inconvenience and subjective cost to the taxpayer. Recently, however, it has been recognized that, where applied to the context of democratic societies, this seemingly plausible burden-minimization theorem is seriously defective because it neglects the unavoidable influence of perceived tax burden on the determination of an optimal total level of public expenditure.

One of the major distinguishing features of the "new public finance" which has emerged in the past twenty years is its conception of taxes as prices for public products and of taxpayers as consumers who register their demands for these public products through the political process. Since the cost-benefit calculus of the individual taxpayer-voter occupies such a central place in recent "public choice" models of the democratic process, it seems logical to be attentive to potential sources of systematic bias or illusion in the cost-benefit calculus of individual citizens. To the extent that "fiscal illusion" affects voter behavior, the tax and expenditure decisions of democratic governments will tend to be characterized by a certain degree of inefficiency, if not even outright irrationality.

Fiscal illusion may, of course, occur with respect to both taxes and expenditures. Expenditure illusion is similar to the private sector phenomenon of over- or underevaluating the quality or quantity of services flowing from a product. Tax illusion's private sector analogues include certain types of "easy down-payment" installment contracts, hidden service charges, etc. Whether the purchase be in the public sector or the private sector, the principle is the same: a misinformed consumer will make poor purchases.

Anthony Downs [4] was among the first to provide a simple but compelling economic rationale for the poor quality of information which characterizes the average citizen's assessments of the costs and benefits from government activity. Although the individual citizen has influence on his private purchases, he has negligible influence on the size and composition of the public goods bundle that his taxes purchase. Investment in better public sector cost and product-quality information therefore cannot be expected to result in any perceptible improvement of the individual's consumption pattern. Should there be any surprise, then, if the decision making environment of public goods purchases is beclouded by suspicions of widespread and systematic fiscal illusion?

In surveying the possible impact of fiscal illusion on the recent history of state-local finance in the U.S., this paper purposefully, albeit regretfully, neglects the expenditure side. It is not that the issue of over- or underevaluation of the benefits of public goods is not a trenchant one. Quite the contrary. In the last analysis, however, assessments of the relative values of goods are intrinsically subjective and highly personal. Just as there can be no "scientific" or objective answer to whether Chryslers are underrated relative to Fords, there is little hope for establishing either the truth or falsity of J. K. Galbraith's contention that the preference of Americans for automobiles over public parks is symptomatic of illusion.

With respect to taxes and other forms of government finance, the possibility of dispassionate analysis seems more hopeful. The cost of government to any taxpayer is, after all, to a large extent objectively identifiable. If the taxpayer's perception of his costs can be reasonably determined, then any difference is attributable to fiscal illusion.

Potential Illusion in Major Tax Forms

In a turn-of-the-century work which recalls the tradition of Machiavelli's advice to rulers in the classic *The Prince,* Italian scholar Amilcare Puviani described methods of encouraging "optimistic'" illusion wherein citizens underestimate their tax burdens.[1] Although Puviani's hypotheses emerged out of a dramatically different environment, they are remarkably relevant to American political economy in the 1970s.

Taxes Incorporated in Prices

Puviani pointed out that taxes which are levied at other than the retail level have important advantages from the standpoint of felt cost. Such taxes tend to become incorporated into the price of the product so that the taxpayer may be largely unaware of their existence or quantitative importance. Even when excise taxes are levied at the retail level, consumers may become unable to distinguish between the tax element and the "resource cost" element in the sum they actually pay for a product.

Some empirical evidence exists to support Puviani's notions about the awareness of excise taxes. A study by Ferber [7] indicated that only

1. Puviani's work is summarized in [13], but has unfortunately never been published in English translation. A short English summary by Buchanan is available [3], pp. 59–64.

30 percent of the people surveyed were aware of the substantial 1954 reduction in U.S. excise tax rates. Also, many consumers were unable to distinguish between taxed and untaxed products. These findings are corroborated in a 1958 study by Schmölders [14]. This latter analysis of German taxpayers uncovered extreme ignorance of the individual tax rates while, with regard to total excise tax burden, low-income families systematically seemed to overestimate their burdens while upper-income families tended to commit the opposite error of *under*estimation.

Business taxation in general raises the issue of "forward shifting" of taxes onto consumers via tax-induced price increases. For instance, the ultimate economic incidence of the national tax on corporate profits is an unsettled issue. For the "open economy" context of state and local governments, however, the ability to tax ownership or equity capital must surely be greatly curtailed by interstate and intercommunity mobility which sets a minimum lower bound on the required return to capital. Hence, at least a substantial proportion of business taxation is probably, if the truth were known, unknowingly borne by the local consumer.

The relative importance of specific excise taxes at the state-local level has consistently declined during the postwar period, falling from about 15 percent to roughly 11 percent in recent years. Estimates of the proportion of state-local taxes initially imposed on business (see [1]) also show a modest decline from about 37 percent in 1957 to just under 33 percent in 1967. Nonetheless, in absolute terms the "incorporation in product price" illusion may have an impact on over 40 percent of the revenues generated by state and local governments.

The General Sales Tax

In terms of tax consciousness, the general sales tax ought to rank above the taxes described in the previous section. The tax is levied at the retail level and the effective rate is likely to be well known. General sales taxes have about doubled in relative importance since the mid-forties, presently accounting for just over 12 percent of state-local general revenues. A total of 21 states which had no sales tax have enacted general sales levies during this period, leaving only 5 states which do not employ this major tax form.

Two reservations may be cited about the possible illusory effects of the general sales tax. One relates to the increasingly popular "piggyback" feature now used in 25 states. Under this arrangement, the state permits an optional local sales tax to be collected in tandem with the state levy. Even if the total tax is accurately perceived, this raises questions about the taxpayer's ability to impute the appropriate portions of the tax to two different governments. Is this tax predominantly associated in the taxpayer's mind with state rather than local government? To the extent that this occurs, the subjective cost of state government is overemphasized relative to that of local government.

The second reservation to note is simply that knowledge of the correct tax rate is not necessarily to be equated with a correct conception of the total tax payment. To say I know that the sales tax rate is 4 percent in my state does not imply that I know how much I pay in sales taxes each year. Although there is no direct empirical evidence on either of these reservations, the evidence cited below about income tax payments can perhaps be taken as suggestive that sales tax payments are probably widely misevaluated.

The value-added tax (VAT) has never been adopted in the U.S. at the state level, although it has been considered in several states.[2] Current discussion of the VAT at the federal level has suggested that a VAT is "like an equivalent-rate sales tax." It is perhaps worth pointing out that the VAT, which is levied at every production stage, might be predicted to differ in important respects from an allegedly equivalent general sales tax. Since the nominal payment at the retail level would be much smaller than under an equal-yield sales tax, the public perception of costs under this tax form might well be considerably lower. This factor should be borne in mind if the VAT comes under consideration as a replacement for existing state sales taxes.

Income Taxation

A major move toward personal income taxation has been perhaps the most important institutional change in state-local fiscal structure during the post-war era. By 1971, only six states had no personal income tax levy, with 11 states having adopted personal income taxation since 1961. As a percent of total state-local revenues, income taxes have risen from about 3 percent in the mid-forties to approximately 9 percent in the early seventies. How does this increasingly important tax form rank in tax awareness terms? The only empirical studies of income tax awareness deal with the federal tax, but the results seem reasonably extendable to state levies.

Two studies by Enrick [5, 6] in the early sixties showed that only slightly more than one-half of the respondents were able to estimate their true income tax payments within a plus or minus 10 percent range. Over one-fourth of the taxpayers surveyed either over- or underestimated their liabilities by more than 20 percent. On the average, slight under-

---

2. The closest approach to an exception is the business activities tax adopted by Michigan in 1953. An interesting description of the experience with this tax is provided by Papke [12].

estimation was indicated, although the dispersion around the mean was enormous. Enrick's findings about the low level of awareness of total income tax payment are complemented by the work of a group of Michigan researchers into awareness of marginal income tax *rates* [8]. About 30 percent of taxpayers in the above-average $10,000+ category were found to be under misapprehensions concerning their marginal tax rates.

One hypothesis about the low level of income tax awareness places the blame upon the "withholding" provision. The taxpayer never actually pays out the tax money because he never receives it in the first place. Also, the tax liability is spread out over a period of time rather than being concentrated in a more obvious single payment. Puviani specifically mentioned the fractionalization of a tax as being conducive to minimizing felt burden. (The "spreading out" factor is, of course, equally applicable to the general sales and excise tax; although, unlike withholding, a deliberate act of payment does accompany these other taxes.)

Withholding has been applied to federal income tax since 1943, but many states delayed implementing it until comparatively recently. By 1971, however, only three income tax states had not adopted withholding.

A 1964 study of federal withholding by Wagstaff [16] indicated withholding tax error margins of roughly the same percentage order of magnitude as the total tax errors found by Enrick. Interestingly, however, Wagstaff found that overestimation of taxes withheld was associated with lower income and underestimation with higher income. This association of the direction of the illusion's bias is consistent with the German studies by Schmölders cited above.[3]

Real Property Taxation

After a sharp fall in the immediate postwar period, state-local dependence on property taxation has declined modestly from 36 percent in 1957 to about 31 percent of general revenues in the early seventies. Property taxation is still, however, by far the single most important revenue source, especially for local governments.

The single-payment property tax could be expected to generate a high degree of tax awareness among property owners. However, a large portion of property tax liabilities are discharged through an escrow procedure whereby property tax payments are made monthly in conjunction with mortgage payments. Whatever the merits of the escrow procedure from other standpoints, this "installment-plan" payment of property taxes probably seriously diminishes taxpayer awareness.

Unfortunately, no direct empirical test of this hypothesis about tax-

3. This prevalence of overestimation at low-income levels crops up repeatedly. The same result is also reported for Britain [10].

consciousness reduction has been undertaken. Tanzi [15] points out, however, that a recent poll by the Advisory Commission on Intergovernmental Relations shows much lower popularity ratings given to the property tax by respondents in the over-60 age category. This age group presumably includes a relatively high proportion of respondents who have already paid off their mortgages and thus pay their property taxes through the single-payment procedure rather than the installment method.

It is difficult to obtain hard data on the number of households which pay property taxes to their mortgages through an escrow account. Neither the government nor any of the trade associations collects statistics on this practice. However, federal regulations require escrows for all FHA mortgages, and the American Banking Association estimates that approximately 30 percent of conventional residential loans also involve this requirement.[4] As a rough approximation, therefore, 50 to 60 percent of all residential loans provide that property taxes be collected concurrently with mortgage payments.

For the renter, of course, property taxation is really an indirect business tax, and all of the observations made in an earlier section about inclusion in product price apply to the property levy as well. Renters may not be at all aware of the costs indirectly imposed on them because of property taxation. Again, the recent A.C.I.R. poll on tax preferences [15] is consistent with this hypothesis, since renters give a relatively high popularity rating to the property tax. Paradoxically, many economists suggest that the property tax is actually a relatively high-burden tax for the income classes in which renters predominate.[5]

A final difficulty about the real and perceived costs of property taxation relates to the question of "capitalization." Since land is a relatively fixed asset, it has been argued that a portion of the stream of future property tax liabilities will be capitalized into the market price of the land. A subsequent purchaser of the land is said to have "bought free" of the tax because its discounted present value is reflected in a lowered purchase price. There is substantial argument about the degree to which tax capitalization actually occurs empirically. However, even if full capitalization does occur, it seems quite legitimate to count the current stream of liabilities as a true "tax cost" to the present owner. After all, if the tax were removed, the current owner would enjoy a windfall gain equivalent to the present value of the tax flow. Failure to count the capitalized tax as a cost involves confusion of the notions of opportunity cost and of market-induced price compensation.

4. This estimate was acquired from personal correspondence with the staff of the American Banking Association.

5. The most recent exhaustive study of property tax impact in the United States is provided by Netzer [11].

Debt Finance

Finally, it is incumbent to say something about debt finances. The mention may be brief, since the parallels with "credit illusion" in the private sector are quite obvious. Puviani noted a propensity for the public to regard a future stream of taxation as less onerous than the capitalized value of the liability stream as paid in a single lump-sum present payment. Debt finance is not, of course, necessarily bad, but the potential for illusion to operate needs no further explanation.

Perception of Tax Changes Rather Than Levels

Up to this point, the discussion has been couched in terms of a comparison between the actual and perceived dollars of tax burden on a representative taxpayer. If the illusion thesis is accepted at all, however, the actual process of tax adjustment may itself be recognized as having implications for the level of felt burden.

It is part of the folklore of taxation that "an old tax is a good tax." By this argument, changes in taxing institutions are themselves thought to impinge themselves in a special way on the consciousness of voters. If rates could be raised and revenues could be augmented without deliberate legislative action, it is hypothesized, taxpayer consciousness and hence subjective burden would be minimized.

Revenue Elasticity of Tax Systems

The secular trend of increasing real income does, of course, make it operationally practical to have major automatic revenue adjustments without any discretionary changes in the tax statutes. The sensitivity of a government's tax system to normal income growth is usually measured by the "income elasticity" of the revenue flow. Income elasticity is the ratio of the percentage of change in revenue to the percentage of change in personal income. The higher the elasticity of the revenue system, the more it will tend to generate increased rates.

An elasticity of exactly 1.0 is a notable crossover point. Below this value, income increases faster than revenue, thus implying what are (in terms of percentage of income) effective rate decreases unless statutory rates are increased. For elasticities above 1.0, the converse is true, and automatic effective rate increases would occur if the statutes remain fixed. About 18 of the state revenue systems possess estimated elasticities of less than 1.0, about 9 exceed 1.20, and the rest fall in the range from 1.0 to 1.19 [1]. In the states with high elasticities, very substantial rates of increase in the relative size of the public sector may be possible without the legislators being obliged to bear the political onus of discretionary tax changes.

A dramatic way of making this point about automatic tax increases is to ask: What percentage of the 1966–1970 state government revenue growth was due to legislative action? Based on A.C.I.R. figures, the 50-state average is only 34 percent, with a range from −5.4 percent to +71.7 percent ([1], Table 25, pp. 43–44). Thus, approximately two-thirds of the actual increase in state tax collection could have been accomplished without any deliberate public decision being made.

Even when legislative changes are enacted, the quantitative impact of the change may be difficult for individual taxpayers to assess. For instance, the adoption of personal income tax withholding is formally the equivalent of a small permanent tax rate increase as well as a temporary, one-time windfall revenue gain to the state. Other examples include (a) changes in the categories of exempted items under general sales taxes, and (b) the movement among states toward adoption of the federal tax base definitions. In each of these cases, the net effect of the changes is usually equivalent to a rate increase, but it will normally be very difficult for the taxpayer to assess his degree of personal impact with any accuracy.

Finally, one should draw a distinction between the automatic revenue increases generated by inflation (or merely nominal income) and by changes in *real* income. Where changes in real income are involved, it can defensibly be argued that the tax system should have a revenue elasticity commensurate with the income elasticity of the demand for public expenditure. However, where income changes reflect inflationary factors, revenue systems with an elasticity greater than unity will produce higher real rates of public expenditure even if real income is unchanged!

Any progressive income tax system is particularly sensitive to both real and merely inflationary income changes. An analysis of the inflationary effect on the federal income tax during the fifties and sixties has been provided by Goetz and Weber [9] who argue that, despite the nominal cuts in federal rates during that period, large numbers of taxpayers were actually subjected to higher rates of taxation in terms of real income. Extended to the state income tax content, this line of reasoning suggests that the income tax rate increases which occurred at the state level were much higher in real terms than they appeared to be in nominal terms.

Implications

This notion of deliberate tax changes as in some sense involving a higher conscious cost than automatic ones does generate some testable hypotheses. For instance, other things being equal, the observed rate of expenditure increase should be greater in states with highly elastic revenue systems than in states with inelastic revenue structures. Preliminary evidence from a study in progress by this author suggests that empirical evidence may corroborate this hypothesis.[6]

As a final comment on automatic revenue adjustments, it should be noted that the direction of the "distortion" may be arguable even if the positive existence of an effect on expenditure can be established. While it may plausibly be claimed that automatic tax adjustments are conducive to underestimation of costs, it has also been argued that the political emotionalism surrounding tax decisions causes their cost to be perceived in excessive terms. Thus if nondeliberate or automatic adjustment does facilitate higher spending levels, the effect may be interpreted either as upward distortion or as a salutary correction of a downward bias.

Federal Impact on State and Local Finance

The preceding sections have dealt with financial institutions which are essentially under the control of the states themselves. In a federal system, state-local fiscal choices may also be affected by institutional features under the control of the central government. Within the U.S. system at least two major federal practices have a notable potential for inducing fiscal illusion at lower government levels.

Conditional Grants

The relative importance of federal grants to state-local governments has almost doubled during the postwar years, accounting for about 17 percent of state-local general revenues in 1971. Almost all federal aid is conditional, i.e., requires some quid pro quo from the recipient government. For instance, a federal grant commonly requires "matching" contributions from the state or local unit which receives the aid.

Quite obviously, states and local governments receive federal aid voluntarily and any quid pro quo requirement would be regarded as (apparently) compensating the recipient for its cooperation. In some cases, however, the immediate lure of federal aid may cause a recipient to commit itself to hidden future costs which have not been fully perceived and evaluated.

Interstate highway aid may be cited as an illustration. The federal gov-

6. This study involves a regression analysis of the determinants of percentage change in state own-source general revenue during the sixties. The income elasticity of the state's revenue system enters the regression equation with a positive coefficient.

ernment pays 90 percent of the cost of such highways, with only a nominal 10 percent matching share required from the states. Nonetheless, some economists worry that, in their rush to reap the "bargain" on capital or construction costs, the states may not have fully costed out the enormous future flow of maintenance and operational costs. Framed in more general terms, this argument alleges that, when future outlays and other implicit costs are fully accounted for, certain federal grant programs may prove to be less generous than they initially appear. Under these circumstances, states commit themselves to programs which would not be undertaken in the absence of financial illusion. State aid to local governments is, of course, subject to much the same comments as federal aid to the state-local sector. State aid accounted for about 56 percent of local general revenues in 1970.

Federal Deductibility of State and Local Taxes

Under current federal law, income tax deductions are accorded to most state-local property, general sales, income, and motor fuel taxes.[7] Because of this provision, one dollar in additional state or local taxes actually reduces the taxpayer's disposable income by considerably less than a dollar, the exact amount depending on the taxpayer's federal income tax bracket. In those states where local taxes are also deductible from state income taxes, the effective impact of *local* taxes is even further reduced. To the extent that taxpayers fail to accord full recognition to these offsets, the marginal costs of state-local public goods will tend to be overestimated.

If the deductibility provisions do cause cost-overestimation errors, these are likely to be more emphatic at the higher income levels. There are two reasons for this. First, the use of any deduction requires that the taxpayer itemize on his income tax return, but lower-income taxpayers frequently use the standard deduction. Second, for taxpayers who do itemize, the effective value of the deduction is directly dependent on the individual marginal income tax rates.

Oddly enough, it is possible that failure to appreciate fully the deductibility aspects of state-local taxes is a "good" illusion. This argument depends on the recognition that state-local tax deductibility is a subsidy to state-local taxpayers which is, in essence, "paid" by federal taxpayers. On average (although not for any one individual), the gains and losses on the tax side must be exactly counterbalancing. Thus, unless some rationale can be advanced for an artificial stimulus to state-local spending, the deductibility provision in the federal tax system can be regarded

7. Although his analysis was completed in the mid-1960s, Bridges [2] provides an overview of deductibility information which still retains considerable relevance.

as inducing inefficient or distorted resource allocation. Paradoxically, then, any illusion which causes the deductibility feature to become partially inefficient in state-local fiscal decisions may be an irrational means to more rational ends.

Conclusions

Empirical evidence exists for some of the forms of illusion discussed above, but others are merely conjectural, even if they frequently seem to have a sound basis in casual experience, common sense, and introspection. Much more could and should be done to subject the various illusion hypotheses to statistical testing and quantification. In some cases, even the net *directional* effect of tax illusion is not predictable, much less its quantitative magnitude. Indeed, some of the studies cited above suggest that the direction as well as the magnitude of the illusion appears to change over different ranges of the income scale.

One of the important lessons of the new public finance is that alternative tax forms and fiscal institutions do have a potentially powerful effect on the level and composition of public budgets. This lesson, unfortunately, has only recently been learned, and as a consequence, the theory has only rarely been turned to practical application. However, in an age when such phenomena as "consumerism," Ralph Nader, and "truth in packaging" (or lending) have been able to arouse such widespread interest, it is perhaps not overly optimistic to hope for an increasing body of evidence about illusion during the next decade. In the meantime, it may be helpful to know some of the questions about fiscal illusion even if one does not know many of the answers.

References

1. Advisory Commission on Intergovernmental Relations. *State-local Finances: Significant Features and Suggested Legislation.* Washington, D.C.; U.S. Government Printing Office, 1972.
2. Bridges, Benjamin, Jr. "Deductibility of State and Local Nonbusiness Taxes Under the Federal Individual Income Tax." *National Tax Journal* 19 (March, 1960): 1–17.
3. Buchanan, J. M. *Fiscal Theory and Political Economy.* Chapel Hill: University of North Carolina Press, 1960.
4. Downs, Anthony. *An Economic Theory of Democracy.* New York: Harper & Row Publishers, 1957.
5. Enrick, Norbert. "A Pilot Study of Income Tax Consciousness." *National Tax Journal* 16 (June, 1963): 169–173.
6. _____. "A Further Study of Income Tax Consciousness." *National Tax Journal* 17 (Sept., 1964): 319–321.

7. Ferber, Robert. "How Aware Are Consumers of Excise Tax Changes?" *National Tax Journal* 7 (Dec., 1954): 355–358.
8. Gensemer, Bruce L., Jane A. Lean, and William B. Neenan. "Awareness of Marginal Income Tax Rates Among High Income Taxpayers." *National Tax Journal* 18 (Sept., 1965): 268–276.
9. Goetz, Charles J., and Warren E. Weber. "Intertemporal Changes in Real Federal Income Tax Rates, 1954–70." *National Tax Journal* 24 (March, 1971): 51–64.
10. Institute of Economic Affairs. *Choice In Welfare, 1965.* London: The Institute, 1965.
11. Netzer, Dick. *The Property Tax.* Washington, D.C.: The Brookings Institution, 1966.
12. Papke, James A. "Michigan's Value-Added Tax After Seven Years." *National Tax Journal* 13 (Dec., 1960): 350–363.
13. Puviani, Amilcare. *Teoria della illusione finanziaria.* Palermo: Sandron, 1903.
14. Schmölders. Günter. "Unmerkliche Steuern." *Finanzarchiv* 20 (1950): 23–34.
15. Tanzi, Vito. "Taxpayer Choices in Future Tax Shifts." *Tax Review* 33 (Nov., 1972): 41–44.
16. Van Wagstaff, Joseph. "Income Tax Consciousness Under Withholding." *Southern Economic Journal* 32 (July, 1965): 73–80.

11. Private versus Public Sector Growth: A Collective Choice Approach   *Winston C. Bush and Robert J. Mackay*

Introduction and Summary

Most studies in this volume examine the growth of the public sector using Niskanen's [19] hypotheses concerning the behavior of active bureaucrats. In order to have some basis for comparison, an analysis is also needed of an economy in which bureaucrats are passive. This paper provides such an analysis.

One implication of Niskanen's study is that the maximizing behavior of bureaucrats generates forces that cause excess public sector growth.[1] An alternative explanation of public sector growth and, in particular, the rapid rise in municipal budgets has been offered by W. Baumol [1]. Using a simplified production model of an economy with passive bureaucrats, a technologically progressive private sector, and a nonprogressive public sector, Baumol argues that the pressure on municipal budgets results from the fact that the public sector will tend to exhibit persistent and cumulative increases in the per unit costs of the output of the public sector relative to the output of the private sector.[2] He obtains this result, and several other propositions concerning public sector growth, using a model in which only production conditions are explicitly analyzed. Specifically, he assumes that both sectors of the economy have linear homogeneous production functions and that the one input is labor which is stationary over time. The equalization of wage rates between the two sectors along with his assumption concerning the relative rates of technical progress complete the specification of the basic model.

Baumol's propositions concerning unbalanced growth follow immediately from his model and are summarized below.

1. The cost per unit of output of the public sector will rise without limit while the cost per unit of output of the private sector will remain constant.

---

1. See Bush and Denzau [12] for a further discussion of this point.
2. Baumol applies his model to other economic services such as the performing arts, restaurants, and household servants. The present paper, however, is only concerned with the application of his model to public services. As a result, his model and propositions are restated in terms of the output of the public sector rather than in terms of general personal services.

2. If the ratio of the output of the public sector to the output of the private sector is held constant then, over time, more and more of the given labor force will be employed in the public sector. Employment in the private sector will approach zero.

3. If the ratio of the output of the public sector to the output of the private sector is held constant then, over time, the growth rate of the economy will asymptotically approach zero.

By adding an additional assumption with respect to the elasticities of demand for the output of the public sector, he is also able to establish the following proposition.[3]

4. There is a tendency for the *relative* outputs of the public sector whose demands are not highly price inelastic nor highly income elastic to decline and perhaps ultimately vanish over time.

One final point should be emphasized. Baumol's model does not imply that society is forced to consume a decreasing quantity of public sector output over time. Since the source of the problem is increasing productivity, it can easily be shown that society can consume constantly increasing quantities of both the private good and the public good. The question Baumol leaves unanswered, however, is whether society in some sense wishes to consume greater and greater quantities of both goods.

An answer to this last question obviously requires some way of representing society's wishes. Several approaches to this problem are available. For example, one might posit some social welfare function or community preference function containing both the outputs of the public sector and the private sector as arguments. The economist could then simply determine those time paths for the outputs of both sectors that would maximize social welfare subject to the production possibility curve.[4] Alternatively, one might posit some specific demand function for the public good by a representative consumer and then examine how changing prices and income effect the desired quantity of the public good.[5] In this paper, however, a third approach is chosen. A positive theory of public sector behavior is developed in which the desired quantity of the public good and its rate of growth are determined endogenously through median voter analysis.

More specifically, this paper examines the implications for public

3. See the comment by Lynch and Redman [17] for additional discussion of these elasticity assumptions. Also see Spann [22].

4. See Worcester [25] for an example of this type of analysis in the context of Baumol's model. See Uzawa [24] for an example of this approach in analyzing optimal fiscal policy in an economy producing both a public and a private good.

5. See Spann [22] for an example of this type of analysis.

versus private sector growth of incorporating Baumol's assumptions about relative rates of technical progress into a model containing explicitly specified political institutions. The economy considered has constitutional rules establishing specific institutions. These institutions are a democracy in which everyone is free to make proposals concerning the quantities of the public goods, provided everyone votes on these proposals and the majority rules. The tax structure is also specified in the constitution by assigning each individual a tax share. The members of the economy, therefore, individually purchase one bundle of goods in the private sector and collectively purchase another bundle through the public sector. Economic models based on a set of assumptions similar to these lead to what is called the collective or public choice approach.[6]

Incorporating these particular institutions into an economic model does not yield new insights into the fiscal process unless the individuals in the economy are in some sense distinct and there are more than two commodities. Given the institution of majority voting, the outcome of an election feeds back into the decision making process of individuals through their budget constraint because of the necessity of financing the public sector. If everyone in the economy is identical in the sense of having the same tastes, tax shares, and incomes, and they face the same prices, then this feedback does not raise any interesting problems since there is unanimity with respect to the provision of the public good. In the present paper individuals are assumed to have the same tastes but they are not identical since they may face different tax shares and may have different incomes. As a result, they may prefer different quantities of the public good and, thus, the feedback effect of the voting process through the budget constraint may significantly affect individual consumption and saving decisions.

This last point can be seen more clearly if the present model is specified in some detail. All individuals in the economy are assumed to have the same utility function which includes the consumption of the private good, the public good, and savings for the future as arguments. The individual maximization process can be viewed as taking place in two stages. In the first stage, each individual, given the political institutions, his income, his tax-share, and relative prices, votes for the quantity of the public good he prefers. After the voting process determines the actual quantity of the public good that is to be supplied, the second stage occurs. Given his resulting tax liability, each individual divides his remaining income between present consumption and saving for the future so as to maximize his utility. This two-stage maximization process introduces complex

6. For a thorough discussion of this approach, see Buchanan [8] or Buchanan and Tullock [11].

interdependences among individuals into the model. Of course, unless there are two or more commodities besides the public good, this last stage can be ignored.

As a result of the particular political institutions assumed in this paper, the actual quantity of the public good supplied is determined by the median voter's preferences. In other words, society's wishes are represented by the wishes or preferences of the median voter in the present paper. In order to analyze the forces leading to public sector growth, it is necessary to locate the median voter in the income distribution and to determine how his location is affected by alternative tax structures. Once the median voter is located and his preferences established, these preferences then feed back into the decision making processes of the other individuals in the economy through their budget constraint. These feedbacks have important implications for the course of the economy. In particular, it is established below that the introduction of a public good and majority rule leads to interdependent saving functions in which each individual's saving depends on the desired saving of the median voter, tax shares, and the distribution of income as well as utility parameters.

This last point also indicates that, unlike Baumol and others who looked at public versus private sector growth, the present model includes saving decisions and, hence, a capital market. Furthermore, the present model contains a more sophisticated production sector. For example, the progressive private sector uses both labor and capital to produce its output. The nonprogressive public sector, however, only uses labor to produce its output. The public good in this model, therefore, might best be thought of as some kind of public service. In addition, the model also allows for labor force growth at some constant rate per period. In short, the economy under consideration possesses three sources of growth — technical progress in the private sector, labor force growth, and growth in the capital stock.

Using the assumptions sketched out above, a dynamic collective choice model is constructed in the second section of this paper. Although these assumptions are fairly restrictive, the resulting model does yield several new insights into the fiscal process. For example, the following questions are studied in this section.

1. Under what tax structures and conditions is the median income recipient the median voter with respect to the provision of the public good?

2. Is the Bowen solution [6] an internal or feasible voting solution in the sense that each individual has sufficient income to pay his assigned share of the public budget?

3. How are individual saving decisions and, hence, the dynamic path of the economy affected by the introduction of a public good along with the institution of majority voting?

The model developed in the second section is then used in the third section to examine the implications of equilibrium growth for the relative size of the public sector over time. The major results of the third section are summarized below.

1. The cost per unit of output of the public good — the price of the public good — will rise without limit along the steady-state growth path. Furthermore, the price of the public good will increase at a rate greater than the rate of technical progress due to capital deepening in the private sector.

2. The tax-price to the median voter of an additional unit of the public good will increase over time due to the rise in the price of the public good, but this rise is offset, either in part or in total, by the decline in the median voter's taxshare due to the growth in the size of the tax-sharing group.

3. The median voter's demand for the public good and, hence, the actual output of the public good will grow at the rate of population growth along the steady-state growth path.

4. The ratio of employment in the public sector to employment in the private sector is constant along the steady-state growth path.

5. Value shares are constant along the steady-state growth path in the sense that the public sector consumes a constant share of gross national product.

6. Although the output of the public sector grows over time in an absolute sense, the output of the public sector relative to the output of the private sector declines over time along the steady-state growth path.

In a limited sense the results of section 3 are comparable to Baumol's results. The results are only comparable in a limited sense because Baumol does not provide an endogenous determination of the size or rate of growth of the public sector whereas the present paper does. Instead, he performs exercises such as fixing the ratio of outputs and then determining what happens to employment in the two sectors or what happens to the rate of growth of the economy.

Both models predict that the price of the public good will rise without limit since this is an immediate implication of the specification of the production sector in both cases. Baumol's model also predicts that the *relative* outputs of the public sector, whose demands are not highly price inelastic or highly income elastic, will decline over time. The present model also predicts that the relative output of the public sector will decline over time even though the actual output of the public sector grows over time. The present paper also clearly indicates the importance of carefully specifying the measures of relative size that are used in analyzing public versus private sector growth since, in terms of relative employment or relative value shares, the size of public sector is constant in the present model.

A Collective Choice Model

The economy initially consists of L_o individuals, $L = \{1, \ldots, L_o\}$, and three commodities, a private good, a pure public good, and saving for the future. A pure public good is a commodity for which the consumption of the commodity by one individual does not diminish the quantity available for consumption by another individual (see Samuelson [20]). The population is assumed to grow at the exogenous rate of $(1 + n)$. The private good is produced through a Cobb-Douglas production function. The private sector is progressive — production is subject to Hicks-neutral technical progress at the exogenous rate of $(1 + \lambda)$. The public good is produced through a simple linear production function requiring only labor as an input. The public sector is nonprogressive — there is no technical progress in the public sector.[7] In short, the private sector is technologically progressive and the public sector is nonprogressive. These assumptions are presented in detail below.

Each individual's preferences are represented by the same Cobb-Douglas utility function.

(1) $\qquad lnU_i(t) = \alpha \, ln x_{1t}^i + \beta \, ln x_{2t}^i + \gamma \, ln x_{3t}^i + 1,$

where $(\alpha, \beta, \gamma) > 0$ and $\alpha + \beta + \gamma = 1$. x_{1t}^i is individual i's consumption of the private good in time period t. x_{2t}^i is individual i's consumption of the public good in time t. x_{3t+1}^i is the quantity of capital individual i *expects* to own in time $t + 1$. All individuals expect the returns from capital to be the same in time period $t + 1$ as they are in time t and make their decisions accordingly. Capital depreciates at a one hundred percent rate each time period. An individual saves s_t^i in period t and expects to receive $r_t s_t^i = x_{3t+1}^i$ in time period $t + 1$, where r_t is the returns from capital.

The income of each individual in time period t, w_t^i, is his wage rate, e_t, plus his earnings from the quantity of capital he saved in time period $t - 1$, $r_t s_{t-1}^i$.

7. See Bradford, Malt, and Oates [7] and Spann [23] for empirical evidence indicating that the private sector is more progressive than the public sector. For simplicity we set the rate of technical progress in the public sector equal to zero rather than allow for a positive rate in both sectors.

Realistically one might want to allow for a disparity between the wages paid in the two sectors to allow for some lagged relationship between the wage rate in the private sector and the wage rate in the public sector. In order to simplify the analysis, however, wages are assumed to be equal in the public and the private sector. This equality is brought about by the mobility of labor between the two sectors and competition in the labor market.

In order to specify the individual's budget constraint it is helpful to first specify the production conditions existing in the economy. The production conditions in the private sector are described by the following aggregate Cobb-Douglas production function.

(2) $x_{1t} = (1 + \lambda)^t [L_{1t}]^a [K_t]^{1-a}$, $0 < a < 1$.

x_{1t} is the total output of the private good. L_{1t} is employment in the private sector in time t. K_t is the total capital stock in time t. $(1 + \lambda)$ is the rate of Hicks-neutral technical change. The production conditions in the public sector are described by the following linear production function.

(3) $x_{2t} = bL_{2t}$.

x_{2t} is the output of the public good. L_{2t} is total employment in the public sector in time t. Total employment is equal to the total population.

(4) $L_t = L_{1t} + L_{2t}$.

The total population, which is assumed to be equal to the total labor force, grows at the rate of $(1 + n)$. Therefore,

(5) $L_t = (1 + n)^t L_0$.

Because of competition in the labor market workers in both sectors are paid the marginal product of labor in the private sector, e_t. As a result, the total cost of the public good is given by the wage rate times the employment in the public sector. From equation (3), the total cost of the public good is given by

(6) $e_t L_{2t} = e_t x_{2t}/b$.

From equation (6) it is clear that the per unit cost or price of the public good in terms of the private good, the numeraire, is given by the ratio e_t/b. The opportunity cost to society or the price of an additional unit of the public good, P_t, is thus given by

(7) $P_t = e_t/b$.

P_t is the slope of the production possibility loci between x_1 and x_2. In other words, P_t is the rate at which the public good can be transformed into the private good and is given by the ratio of the marginal product of labor in the private sector to the marginal product of labor in the public sector.

Each individual is assumed to pay some share of the total cost of the public sector. In order to simplify the analysis, the set of individuals in the economy is divided into three equal size subsets, $L = \{L_1, L_2, L_3\}$ where $L_1 \cap L_2 \cap L_3 = \phi$. In the initial time period all the persons in the same subset have identical income levels. Since $U(t)$ is the same for all i and since all individuals in the same group face common prices in each time period, all individuals in a subset are identical in all respects in the present and future time periods. This result allows one to form a new subset of three individuals, $I = \{1, 2, 3\}$, by selecting a representative from each subset, and to perform the remaining analysis of the paper using this new set. If L_t is the total population and l is the number of subsets, then the number of persons in each subset, m_t, is given by $m_t = L_t/l$. Both the total population and the number of persons in each subset grow at the rate of $(1 + n)$ so that m_t can be written as

(8) $\qquad m_t = (1 + n)^t \, m_0.$

Equations (5) and (6) imply that the total population is given by

(9) $\qquad L_t = m_t l = (1 + n)^t \, m_0 l, \qquad l = 3.$

Each subset of the population is assigned a nonnegative tax share, τ_i, and $\sum_{i=1}^{3} \tau_i = 1$. In addition, each individual in a particular subset or group pays a proportionate share of the total tax liability of that group. Thus, the tax share in period t of an individual in group i is given by

(10) $\qquad t_{it} = \tau_i/m_t,$ for $i = 1, 2, 3.$

Note that although the group's tax share, τ_i, is fixed, the tax share of an individual in this group declines over time as the number of individuals in the group increases. The total tax liability of an individual in group i is equal to his tax share, t_{it}, times the total cost of the public sector, $e_t L_t$ or $P_t x_{2t}$. In symbols, the individual's total tax liability is $t_{it} P_t x_{2t}$.[8] By way of interpretation, $t_{it} P_t$, which equals $(\tau_i/m_t)(e_t/b)$, can be thought of as the *tax price to an individual in group i of an additional unit of the public good.*

Finally, using equations (6), (7), and (10) the budget constraint of individual i, $i \in I$ can be written as

(11) $\qquad w_t^i = e_t + r_t s_{t-1}^i = x_{1t}^i + t_{it} P_t x_{2t}^i + \rho_t x_{3t+1}^i$
$\qquad\qquad\qquad\qquad = x_{1t}^i + (\tau_i/m_t)(e_t/b) x_{2t}^i + \rho_t x_{3t+1}^i$

8. It is important to distinguish between the individual's tax share, t_{it}, and the individual's tax rate. The individual's tax rate is equal to his total tax liability divided by his income. In symbols, the individual's tax rate is given by

$t_{it} P_t x_{2t}/w_t^i.$

The private good is taken as the numeraire. The tax shares are viewed by all individuals as being exogenously determined. ρ_t is the one period present value factor and is equal to $1/r_t$. Hence, the last term in the budget constraint is saving in time period t, s_t^i. Furthermore, each individual is assumed to take all prices as given. In particular, it is assumed that the individual does not consider the effect of a larger public sector on the wage rate and the marginal product of capital, through an increased capital-labor ratio in the private sector, in deciding and voting on his preferred quantity of the public good.

In words, the individual divides his income in period t among purchases of the private good, his share of the expenditures on the public good, and saving. Note that at the voting stage each individual treats x_{2t} as an endogenous variable and determines how much of the public good he desires given his preferences, income, prices, and his tax share. The actual quantity of the public good supplied, however, is the outcome of the voting process; thus, at this later stage some of the individuals treat x_{2t} as exogenous in deciding how much of the private good to consume and save.

As mentioned above, the quantity of the public good preferred by each $i \in I$ can be found by maximizing the individual's utility function subject to his budget constraint while treating x_{2t}^i as an endogenous variable. The resulting optimal value of x_{2t}^i is the amount of the public good individual i prefers assuming *he alone* is making the decision of how much of the public good to provide and is given by

$$(12) \qquad \bar{x}_{1t}^i = \beta w_t^i / t_{it} P_t = \frac{\beta w_t^i}{(\tau_i/m_t)(e_t/b)}, \text{ for all } i \in I.$$

The bar over a variable indicates a preferred quantity. Note that the utility function assumed in (1) leads to unitary income and price elasticities of demand since the expression in the denominator is the price to individual i of an additional unit of the public good. The actual quantity of the public good supplied is determined through majority voting.

The set of voting institutions considered in this paper are those outlined by Bowen [6].[9] This particular set of voting institutions combined with the strict quasi-concavity of $U(t)$ implies a majority voting Bowen solution for each time period (see Bowen [6] or Bergstrom and Goodman [3]). More specifically, a Bowen solution is an outcome of the voting process in which the actual quantity of the public good supplied is the

9. These institutions are: (1) any individual can submit a proposal for a particular quantity of the public good to be supplied; (2) this proposal is paired against the status quo; (3) voting is instantaneous, costless, and all individuals participate; (4) the majority rules; and (5) logrolling and all other types of gaming are absent. See Black [4] and Denzau [14].

median of the distribution of preferred quantities. The individual who demands the median quantity is labeled the median voter.

In order to carry out the analysis of this paper, the median voter must first be located. Given the particular assumptions of this model, locating the median voter involves establishing that the median income recipient is also the median voter. The median voter is located under three alternative tax structures: progressive, regressive, and proportional. A more precise definition of these tax structures can be obtained if the individuals are indexed so that $w_t^1 \leq w_t^2 \leq w_t^3$ and if w_t^1/w_t^2 is defined as δ_t^1 and w_t^2/w_t^3 is defined as δ_t^2.

DEFINITION 1.

(a) If $\dfrac{t_{1t} P_t x_{2t}}{w_t^1} < \dfrac{t_{2t} P_t x_{2t}}{w_t^2} < \dfrac{t_{3t} P_t x_{2t}}{w_t^3}$, then the tax structure is progres-

sive. Equivalently, if $\tau_1/\tau_2 < w_t^1/w_t^2 \equiv \delta_t^1$ and $\tau_2/\tau_3 < w_t^2/w_t^3 \equiv \delta_t^2$, then the tax structure is progressive.

(b) If $\dfrac{t_{1t} P_t x_{2t}}{w_t^1} > \dfrac{t_{2t} P_t x_{2t}}{w_t^2} > \dfrac{t_{3t} P_t x_{2t}}{w_t^3}$, then the tax structure is regressive.

Equivalently, if $\tau_1/\tau_2 > \delta_t^1$ and $\tau_2/\tau_3 > \delta_t^2$, then the tax structure is regressive.

(c) If $\dfrac{t_{1t} P_t x_{2t}}{w_t^1} = \dfrac{t_{2t} P_t x_{2t}}{w_t^2} = \dfrac{t_{3t} P_t x_{2t}}{w_t^3}$, then the tax structure is propor-

tional. Equivalently, if $\tau_1/\tau_2 = \delta_t^1$ and $\tau_2/\tau_3 = \delta_t^2$, then the tax structure is proportional.

By use of equation (12) it can easily be shown that *the median income recipient, individual 2, is the median voter under all three types of tax structures.* Specifically, the following proposition can be established.[10]

PROPOSITION 1. *Individual 2 is the median voter under all three types of tax structures.* $\bar{x}_{2t}^1 > \bar{x}_{2t}^2 > \bar{x}_{2t}^3$ *if and only if the tax is progressive;* $\bar{x}_{2t}^1 < \bar{x}_{2t}^2 < \bar{x}_{2t}^3$ *if and only if the tax is regressive; and* $x_{2t}^1 = \bar{x}_{2t}^2 = \bar{x}_{2t}^3$ *if and only if the tax is proportional.*[11]

Although it is rather easy to demonstrate in the context of this model that the median income recipient is the median voter, it is more difficult

10. See Bush and Mackay [13] for a proof of this statement in the context of a similar model.

11. A Lindahl solution [16] occurs when the tax structure is such that all individuals demand the same quantity of the public good. Note that for the particular model constructed in this section, a Lindahl solution occurs only if the tax structure is proportional. This result follows from the Cobb-Douglas utility function which leads to a demand function for the public good with unitary price and income elasticities. See Buchanan [9] for an excellent discussion of this point. This solution is Pareto optimal whereas this is not generally true of the Bowen solution (see Bergstrom [2] or Foley [15]).

to demonstrate that the quantity of the public good demanded by the
median income recipient is feasible. The quantity of the public good demanded by the median income recipient is feasible if both individuals 1
and 3 have sufficient income to pay their designated share of the cost of
public sector. If $\bar{x}_{2t}^2$ is feasible, then an internal voting solution exists. That
is, if $t_{1t}P_t x_{2t}^2$ is less than w_t^1 and $t_{3t}P_t \bar{x}_{2t}^2$ is less than w_t^3, then an internal voting solution exists.

The conditions under which the Bowen solution is an internal majority
voting solution within all three types of tax structures can be stated in
terms of relative tax shares, relative incomes of the three individuals, and
the utility parameter β. Specifically, the following proposition can be
established.[12]

PROPOSITION 2. *A Bowen solution is an internal voting solution within a
progressive tax structure if and only if* $\tau_2/\tau_3 \geqq \beta \, \delta_t^2$; *within a regressive
tax structure if and only if* $\tau_1/\tau_2 \leqq (1/\beta)\delta_t^1$; *and within a proportional tax
structure always.*

Note that Proposition 2 requires that individual 2's tax share be positive.
The commonsense explanation of this result is that if his tax share is
zero he will demand an infinite amount of the public good. The conditions
set limits to which relative income and relative tax shares can diverge if
an internal voting solution, in which the median voter is the median income recipient, is to exist. Note that in interpreting these conditions β is
directly related to the utility an individual receives from consuming the
public good. Thus, the smaller β the smaller the demand for the public
good by the median voter and, hence, the less likely a corner solution.

In summary, the analysis of the growth of the public sector relative
to the private sector that follows is limited to the case of Bowen solutions
in which internal voting solutions exist and in which the median income
recipient is the median voter.

Up to this point, the analysis has dealt only with desired quantities of
the public good in the sense that at the voting stage all individuals derive
their desired quantity of the public good from a full consumer equilibrium,
i.e., given the marginal conditions for all three goods—the private good,
the public good, and expected capital. The above analysis, however, establishes that individual 2 determines the quantity of the public good actually supplied, $\bar{x}_{2t}^2$. Therefore, individuals 1 and 3, in a second stage
maximization process, take $\bar{x}_{2t}^2$ as given or exogenous. Their budget constraint then becomes, after substituting the expression for $\bar{x}_{2t}^2$ from equation (12) into equation (11),

12. The proof of this statement is rather lengthy and the interested reader is referred to
Proposition 2 in Bush and Mackay [13].

(13) $\qquad w_t^j = x_{1t}^j + \dfrac{\beta \tau_j w_t^2}{\tau_2} + \rho_t x_{3t+1}^j, \qquad j = \{1,3\}.$[13]

The constraint for individual 2 remains as that given in equation (11). In other words, individual 2 is in full consumer equilibrium — in the sense that the marginal conditions are satisfied for all three goods — but, individuals 1 and 3 are not.

The saving decisions of the three individuals can now be derived. The quantity of saving individual 2 demands in time period t is obtained by maximizing his utility function subject to the constraint in equation (11) and is given by

(14) $\qquad \bar{s}_t^2 = \rho_t x_{3t+1}^2 = \gamma w_t^2.$

Utility maximization by individuals 1 and 3 subject to their constraint in equation (13) yields saving functions that are proportional to after-tax income, $w_t^j - \dfrac{\tau_j}{\tau_2} w_t^2$, the factor of proportionality being $\gamma/1 - \beta$. These expressions can be rewritten to yield the following expressions for their desired level of saving.

(15) $\qquad \bar{s}_t^1 = \bar{s}_t^2 \left[\dfrac{\delta_t^1 \tau_2 - \tau_1 \beta}{\tau_2 (1 - \beta)} \right] = \bar{s}_t^2 c_t^1,$

(16) $\qquad \bar{s}_t^3 = \bar{s}_t^2 \left[\dfrac{\tau_2 - \delta_t^2 \tau_3 \beta}{\delta_t^2 \tau_2 (1 - \beta)} \right] = \bar{s}_t^2 c_t^3.$

It can be shown that the saving of all three individuals are nonnegative under all three types of tax structures when an internal voting solution exists.[14] Note that the saving functions of individuals 1 and 3 depend on the saving function of individual 2, tax shares, relative income levels, and preferences. Equations (15) and (16) clearly illustrate the unique features of the present model since the saving functions of the individuals are interdependent rather than independent or identical as in most dynamic models of economic growth. These features of the present model are summarized in the following proposition.

PROPOSITION 3. *The introduction of a public good and majority voting yields interdependent saving functions in which individual i's saving de-*

---

13. One advantage of basing the analysis on individual utility maximization subject to a budget constraint is that it leads to the interdependencies highlighted in equation (13). If the analysis, instead, is based on some hypothesized demand function for the public good by the median voter, these interdependencies are lost. See Spann [22] for an interesting analysis and empirical test of this latter type of model.
14. See Proposition 3 in Bush and Mackay [13] for a proof of this statement.

pends on the desired saving of the median voter, the tax shares, the distribution of income, and utility parameters.[15]

Given the description of individual saving decisions contained in equations (14), (15) and (16) an expression for the aggregate capital stock in time period t can be derived. That is,

$$(17) \qquad K_t = m_t(\bar{s}_{t-1}^1 + \bar{s}_{t-1}^2 + \bar{s}_{t-1}^3),$$
$$= m_t \gamma w_{t-1}^2 (c_{t-1}^1 + 1 + c_{t-1}^3),$$
$$= m_t \gamma w_{t-1}^2 c_{t-1}.$$

As noted earlier, capital depreciates at a rate of one hundred percent per time period.

By substituting the expression for the quantity of the public good desired by the median voter into the production function for the public good, the following expression for employment in the public sector can be found.

$$(18) \qquad L_{2t} = \frac{\bar{x}_{2t}^2}{b} = \frac{m_t \beta}{\tau_2 e_t} w_t^2.$$

Employment in the private sector is then given by the total labor force, L_t, less employment in the public sector. That is

$$(19) \qquad L_{1t} = L_t - L_{2t},$$
$$= m_t \left(1 - \frac{\beta}{\tau_2 e_t} w_t^2\right),$$

from equations (4), (9), and (18).

From equation (2) the marginal product of capital is:

$$(20) \qquad \frac{\partial x_{1t}}{\partial K_t} = (1 + \lambda)^t (1 - a) [L_{1t}/K_t]^a = r_t.$$

The marginal product of labor in the private sector and, thus, the real wage is:

$$(21) \qquad \frac{\partial x_{1t}}{\partial L_{1t}} = (1 + \lambda)^t a [K_t/L_{1t}]^{1-a} = e_t.$$

Since each individual is paid the marginal product of labor in the private sector and each supplies one unit, the wage income of individual i is given by equation (21). The returns from capital to each i in time period t depends, however, on their saving from time period $t - 1$ and may be different for each individual as a result of different income levels or tax shares.

---

15. These equations play a key role in the dynamics of the present model and the ability to explicitly derive these equations, with their complex interdependencies, possibly justifies the restrictive assumption initially made regarding the form of the utility functions.

(22) $r_t s_{t-1}^i = (1 + \lambda)^t (1 - a) [L_{1t}/K_t]^a \bar{s}_{t-1}^i.$

The income of each individual in time period t is given by

(23) $w_t^i = e_t + r_t \bar{s}_{t-1}^i = (1 + \lambda)^t a [K_t/L_{1t}]^{1-a}$
$$+ (1 + \lambda)^t (1 - a) [L_{1t}/K_t]^a \bar{s}_{t-1}^i.$$

In order to derive the dynamic equations for the income levels, it is necessary to solve for the capital-labor ratio in period t as a function of lagged income levels and/or the lagged income distribution variables. Equations (18), (19), (20), and (21) can be used to derive the following expression for the capital-labor ratio in the private sector.[16]

(24) $$\left[\frac{K_t}{L_{1t}} = w_{t-1}^2 \frac{\gamma\left(\dfrac{\beta}{\tau_2}\dfrac{1-a}{a} + c_{t-1}\right)}{1 - \dfrac{\beta}{\tau_2}}\right].$$

Note that c_{t-1} depends on the lagged values of the income distribution variables, δ_{t-1}^1 and δ_{t-1}^2. In short, the capital-labor ratio in period t depends on the median voter's income in $t - 1$ and the distribution of income in $t - 1$, i.e., on w_{t-1}^2, δ_{t-1}^1, and δ_{t-1}^2.

The basic dynamic equations for this model can now be derived. The dynamic variables are w_t^1, w_t^2, w_t^3, δ_t^1, and δ_t^2. Substituting equation (24) into equation (23) and then equations (14), (15), and (16), into (23) gives, for the case in which there is an internal voting solution, the following equations.

(25) $w_t^1 = (1 + \lambda)^t A_{1t} [w_{t-1}^1]^{1-a},$
(26) $w_t^2 = (1 + \lambda)^t A_{2t} [w_{t-1}^2]^{1-a},$
(27) $w_t^3 = (1 + \lambda)^t A_{3t} [w_{t-1}^3]^{1-a};$

where

$$A_{1t} = \left[\frac{\gamma\left(\dfrac{\beta}{\tau_2}\dfrac{1-a}{a} + c_{t-1}\right)}{\delta_{t-1}^1\left(1 - \dfrac{\beta}{\tau_2}\right)}\right]^{1-a} \cdot \left[\frac{a\left(\dfrac{\beta}{\tau_2}\dfrac{1-a}{a} + c_{t-1}\right) + (1 - a)\left(1 - \dfrac{\beta}{\tau_2}\right)c_{t-1}^1}{\dfrac{\beta}{\tau_2}\dfrac{1-a}{a} + c_{t-1}}\right],$$

$$A_{2t} = \left[\frac{\gamma\left(\dfrac{\beta}{\tau_2}\dfrac{1-a}{a} + c_{t-1}\right)}{1 - \dfrac{\beta}{\tau_2}}\right]^{1-a} \cdot \left[\frac{a\left(\dfrac{\beta}{\tau_2}\dfrac{1-a}{a} + c_{t-1}\right) + (1 - a)\left(1 - \dfrac{\beta}{\tau_2}\right)}{\dfrac{\beta}{\tau_2}\dfrac{1-a}{a} + c_{t-1}}\right],$$

and

16. See Bush and Mackay [13] for a detailed explanation of this derivation.

$$A_{3t} = \left[\frac{\gamma \delta_{t-1}^2 \left(\frac{\beta}{\tau_2} \frac{1-a}{a} + c_{t-1} \right)}{l - \frac{\beta}{\tau_2}} \right]^{1-a}$$

$$\left[\frac{a \left(\frac{\beta}{\tau_2} \frac{1-a}{a} + c_{t-1} \right) + (1-a) \left(l - \frac{\beta}{\tau_2} \right) c_{t-1}^3}{\frac{\beta}{\tau_2} \frac{1-a}{a} + c_{t-1}} \right]$$

Note that equations (25), (26), and (27) also reveal the strong interdependencies among individuals that exist in this model as a result of the existence of a public good and majority voting since the time paths for individual income levels depend on the income distribution variables, as well as tax, utility, and production parameters, and the rate of technical progress.

The ratio of (25) to (26) gives a relationship for the income distribution variable $\delta_t^1 \equiv w_t^1/w_t^2$.

(28) $$\delta_t^1 = \frac{ac_{t-1} + (1-a) \left[\frac{\beta}{\tau_2} + \left(l - \frac{\beta}{\tau_2} \right) c_{t-1}^1 \right]}{ac_{t-1} + (1-a) l}.$$

In a similar way an expression for $\delta_t^2 \equiv w_t^2/w_t^3$ can be obtained.

(29) $$\delta_t^2 = \frac{ac_{t-1} + (1-a) l}{ac_{t-1} + (1-a) \left[\frac{\beta}{\tau_2} + \left(l - \frac{\beta}{\tau_2} \right) c_{t-1}^3 \right]}.$$

Equations (25) through (29) are nonnegative. Using these equations, the complete dynamic system can be summarized by the following set of equations:

(30) $$w_t^1 = \psi^1(w_{t-1}^1, \delta_{t-1}^1, \delta_{t-1}^2),$$
          $$w_t^2 = \psi^2(w_{t-1}^2, \delta_{t-1}^1, \delta_{t-1}^2),$$
          $$w_t^3 = \psi^3(w_{t-1}^3, \delta_{t-1}^1, \delta_{t-1}^2),$$
          $$\delta_t^1 = \phi^1(\delta_{t-1}^1, \delta_{t-1}^2),$$
          $$\delta_t^2 = \phi^2(\delta_{t-1}^1, \delta_{t-1}^2).$$

Implications of Equilibrium Growth for the Relative Size of the Public Sector over Time

The model of section 2 can now be used to study equilibrium time paths for the following important economic variables: (1) individual income levels and, in particular, the median voter's income level; (2) the capital-labor ratio in the private sector; (3) the real wage rate and, hence, the relative price of the public good; (4) the marginal product of capital; (5) the tax price to the median voter of an additional unit of the public good; (6) real output in the public sector; (7) employment in the public sector; (8) employment in the private sector; (9) the capital stock; and (10) real output in the private sector. Given the above results, it is then possible to examine various measures of the rate of growth of the public sector relative to the private sector. In particular, the measures examined in this section include: (1) the ratio of employment in the public sector relative to employment in the private sector; (2) the ratio of the value of output in the public sector relative to the value of output in the private — the share of the public sector in gross national product; and, (3) the ratio of real output in the public sector to real output in the private sector. The results of this section can then be compared with Baumol's results on unbalanced growth.

This section of the paper is only concerned with the properties of a balanced or steady-state growth path along which individual income levels grow at some constant rate, say, $(1 + \mu)$.

DEFINITION 2. *A steady-state equilibrium for the income levels is a time path such that* $w_t^i = (1 + \mu)^t w_{t-1}^i$ *for all* $i \in I$.

The dynamic system can be greatly simplified if the ratios of the income of the three classes are constant over time. This guarantees that individual 2 is always the median income recipient along any stationary-state equilibrium path and, hence, the median voter.

DEFINITION 3. *A stationary-state equilibrium with respect to the ratio of income levels is a pair of ratios of income levels,* δ^{1*} *and* δ^{2*}, *such that*

(a) $\qquad \delta_t^1 = \delta_{t-1}^1 = \delta^{1*}$ *and* $\delta_t^2 = \delta_{t-1}^2 = \delta^{2*}$, *and*

(b) $\qquad 0 \leqq (\delta^{1*}, \delta^{2*}) \leqq 1.$[17]

If the income distribution is stationary — δ^1 and δ^2 are constant — then c_t^1, c_t^3, and c_t are also constant [see equations (15), (16), and (17)]. As a result, the A_{it}'s in equations (25), (26), and (27) are also constant. The dynamic system then reduces to,

(31) $\qquad w_t^1 = (1 + \lambda)^t A_1 [w_{t-1}^1]^{1-a},$
$\qquad\quad w_t^2 = (1 + \lambda)^t A_2 [w_{t-1}^2]^{1-a},$
$\qquad\quad w_t^3 = (1 + \lambda)^t A_3 [w_{t-1}^3]^{1-a},$

where A_1, A_2, and A_3 are constant.

17. See Bush and Mackay [13] for a discussion of the conditions and tax structures under which this equilibrium will exist.

The steady-state equilibrium growth rate that is of interest here is the one that reproduces itself through equations (31)—that solves equations (31). Note that the equilibrium growth rate $(1 + \mu)$ can always be expressed as some power of $(1 + \lambda)$. In fact, it can be shown that the equilibrium path for the individual income levels is given by

$$(32) \qquad w_t^i = (1 + \lambda)^{t/a}\, A_i;$$

where,

$$A_i = [1 + \lambda]^{(1-a)/a^2}\, A_i^{1/a} \text{ for } i \in I.$$

The equilibrium rate of growth implied by this equation is represented by $(1 + \lambda)^{1/a}$. Since $0 < a < 1$, raising $(1 + \lambda)$ to the $1/a$ means that the equilibrium rate of growth in individual income, w^i, is greater than the rate of technical progress in the private sector. The explanation for this result is established below; but, briefly, the cause is an increasing capital-labor ratio in the private sector.

Given these equilibrium growth paths for the individual income levels, it is now possible to determine the growth paths of the other variables in the model. Next, consider the equilibrium growth path for the capital-labor ratio in the private sector. From equations (24) and (32)

$$(33) \qquad K_t/L_{1t} = w_{t-1}^2 \left[\frac{\gamma\left(\dfrac{\beta}{\tau_2}\dfrac{1-a}{a} + c^*\right)}{1 - \dfrac{\beta}{\tau_2}} \right] = (1 + \lambda)^{t/a} B_o;$$

where,

$$B_o = (1 + \lambda)^{-1/a}\, A_2 \left[\frac{\gamma\left(\dfrac{\beta}{\tau_2}\dfrac{1-a}{a} + c^*\right)}{1 - \dfrac{\beta}{\tau_2}} \right],$$

and c^* is the value of c_t along the stationary equilibrium path for δ^{1*} and δ^{2*}. Equation (33) implies that the capital-labor ratio in the private sector is not stationary; instead, it grows at the rate $(1 + \lambda)^{1/a}$, which is greater than the rate of technical progress in this sector. Note that the rate of growth in the capital-labor ratio equals the rate of growth in individual income levels.

Third, consider the equilibrium rate of growth in the real wage, e_t. Substituting equation (33) into (21) gives,

$$(34) \qquad e_t = (1 + \lambda)^{t/a} B_i;$$

where

$$B_1 = a B_o^{1-a}.$$

Equations (34) and (7) imply that the equilibrium rate of growth in the price of the public-good—the marginal rate of transformation between the public good and the private good—is also growing at the same rate as the real wage. That is,

(35) $P_t = e_t/b = (1 + \lambda)^{t/a}(B_1/b).$

The results of equations (34) and (35) are summarized below in Proposition 4.

PROPOSITION 4. *The cost per unit of output, or the price of the public good, P_t, will rise without limit along the steady-state equilibrium growth path. Furthermore, the price of the public good will increase at a rate greater than the rate of technical progress in the private sector due to capital deepening.*

Fourth, consider the equilibrium rate of growth in the marginal product of capital. Substituting equation (33) into (20) gives,

(36) $r_t = (1 + a) B_0^{-a}.$

Hence the marginal product of capital is constant along the steady-state growth path. From equations (20) and (33) it can be seen that the technical progress in the private sector increases the marginal product of capital, but the decline in the labor-capital ratio exactly offsets this effect leaving the marginal product of capital unchanged.

Fifth, consider the equilibrium path of the tax price to the median voter of an additional unit of the public good, $t_{2t}P_t$. Note that although the opportunity cost or price of the public good, P_t, grows over time at the rate $(1 + \lambda)^{1/a}$, this effect is offset somewhat by the decline in the median voter's tax share due to population growth—due to an increase in the size of the tax sharing group. Specifically, the median voter's tax share, t_{2t}, which equals τ_2/m_t, declines at the rate $(1 + n)$. These results are summarized below in Proposition 5.

PROPOSITION 5. *The time path of the tax price to the median voter of an additional unit of public good, $t_{2t}P_t$, is composed of two elements: (a) an increase in the tax price due to the growth in the price of the public good at the rate of $(1 + \lambda)^{1/a}$; and, (b) a decline in the tax price due to the increase in the size of the tax sharing group through population growth at the rate of $(1 + n)$.*

Sixth, consider the equilibrium path for real output in the public sector. An intuitive understanding of the implications of this model for public sector growth can be obtained from a close examination of equation (12) for the case of the median voter. That is,

(37) $\bar{x}_{2t}^2 = \dfrac{\beta w_t^2}{t_{2t}P_t} = \dfrac{\beta w_t^2}{(\tau_2/m_t)(e_t/b)};$

where,

$$m_t = (1 + n)^t m_o,$$
$$e_t = (1 + \lambda)^{t/a} B_1,$$
$$w_t^2 = (1 + \lambda)^{t/a} A_2.$$

Note that the median voter's income, w_t^2, and the price of the public good, P_t, are growing at the same rate. Since the median voter's demand function for the public good exhibits unitary income and price elasticities, the increase in the median voter's income and in the price of the public good exactly offset one another. Thus, the only source of growth in the demand for the public good is due to the decline in the median voter's tax share, t_2, as a result of population growth. Since the median voter's tax share declines at the rate, $(1 + n)$, his demand for the public good grows at this same rate, given the unitary price elasticity. Another way of putting this point is that the median voter's income, w_t^2, grows at the rate of $(1 + \lambda)^{1/a}$ and the tax price to the median voter of an additional unit of the public good, $t_{2t} P_t$, grows at the rate, $(1 + \lambda)^{1/a}/(1 + n)$, so that his demand for the public good grows at the rate $(1 + n)$, given the unitary income and price elasticities. In short, the demand for the public good grows at the biological rate or the rate of population growth. That is

(38) $$\overline{x}_{2t}^2 = x_{2t} = (1 + n)^t B_2;$$

where,

$$B_2 = \frac{b m_0 \beta A_2}{\tau_2 B_1}.$$

These results are summarized below in Proposition 6.

PROPOSITION 6. *The median voter's demand for the public good and, hence, the actual output of the public good will grow at the rate of population growth along the steady-state equilibrium growth path.*

Seventh, consider the rate of growth of employment in the public sector. From equations (38) and (3) it is obvious that

(39) $$L_{2t} = (1 + n)^t (B_2/b).$$

Thus, employment in the public sector grows at the same rate as the population or labor supply grows.

Eighth, consider the rate of growth of employment in the private sector. Substituting equations (9) and (39) into (4) and solving for L_{1t} gives,

(40) $$L_{1t} = (1 + n)^t B_3;$$

where, $B_3 = (m_o l - B_2/b)$. Thus, employment in the private sector also grows at the same rate as the population or labor supply grows.

Ninth, consider the rate of growth in the capital stock. Equations (40) and (33) imply that

(41) $K_t = (1 + \lambda)^{t/a}(1 + n)^t B_o B_3.$

Since population grows at the rate $(1 + n)$, equation (41) implies that individual saving grows at the rate $(1 + \lambda)^{1/a}$ — the same rate as the real wage.

Tenth, consider the rate of growth of real output in the private sector. Substituting equations (40) and (41) into (2) gives,

(42) $x_{1t} = (1 + \lambda)^{t/a}(1 + n)^t B_4,$

where,

$$B_4 = B_3 B_o^{1-a}.$$

This rate of growth in the output of the private sector results from three sources — technical change, labor force growth, and capital deepening.

Given the results above, it is now possible to examine various measures of the rate of growth of the public sector relative to the private sector. The measures considered here include: (1) employment in the public sector relative to employment in the private sector, (2) the value of output in the public sector relative to the value of output in the private sector — the share of the public sector in gross national product, and (3) real output in the private sector.

First, from equations (39) and (40) it is obvious that the ratio of employment in the two sectors is constant. That is,

(43) $L_{2t}/L_{1t} = B_2/bB_3 = $ constant.

This result is summarized below in Proposition 7.

PROPOSITION 7. *The ratio of employment in the public sector to employment in the private sector is constant along the steady-state equilibrium growth path. That is, each sector of the economy employs a fixed proportion of the total labor force along the equilibrium path.*

Second, from equations (35) and (38) it is clear that the equilibrium *value* of the public sector in terms of the numeraire, $P_t x_{2t}$, is growing at the rate given by $(1 + \lambda)^{1/a}(1 + n)$, and from equation (42), this rate is also the rate at which the real output of the private sector is growing. Therefore, the ratio of the value of the public sector to the value of the private sector is constant along the equilibrium path and is given by

(44) $\dfrac{P_t x_{2t}}{x_{1t}} = \dfrac{B_1 B_2}{bB_4} = $ constant.

Note that since $P_t x_{2t}$ equals $e_t L_{2t}$, equation (44) also implies that the total cost of the public sector grows at the same rate as the total cost of the private sector along the equilibrium path. These results are summarized below in Proposition 8.

PROPOSITION 8. *Value shares are constant in the sense that the public sector consumes a constant share of gross national product along the steady-state equilibrium growth path. Equivalently, the total cost of the public sector grows at the same rate as the total cost of the private sector along the equilibrium path.*

Finally, from equations (38) and (42), it is clear that the ratio of the real output of the public sector to the real output of the private sector along the equilibrium path is given by

$$(45) \qquad x_{2t}/x_{1t} = (1 + \lambda)^{-t/a}(B_2/B_4).$$

Although public sector output grows at the rate of $(1 + n)$ — in absolute terms the sector grows over time — it is not growing at as rapid a rate as the private sector. This result is summarized in Proposition 9.

PROPOSITION 9. *Although the output of the public sector grows in an absolute sense, the output of the public sector relative to the output of the private sector declines over time along the steady-state equilibrium path.*

The results of this section are summarized below.

Given a steady-state equilibrium with respect to individual income levels and the resulting stationary-state equilibrium with respect to the income distribution:

(a) Individual incomes, w^i; the capital-labor ratio, K/L_1; the real wage rate, e; and the price of the public good, P, all grow at the rate given by $(1 + \lambda)^{1/a}$. This rate is greater than the rate of technical progress due to capital deepening.

(b) The tax price to the median voter of an additional unit of the public good, $t_2 P$, grows at the rate given by $(1 + \lambda)^{1/a}(1 + n)$.

(c) The output of the public good, x_2; employment in the public sector, L_2; and employment in the private sector, L_1, all grow at the rate of population growth.

(d) The output of the private good, x_1; the capital stock, K; and the value or wage cost of the public sector, PX_2, all grow at the rate given by $(1 + \lambda)^{1/a}(1 + n)$.

(e) The ratio of employment in the public sector to employment in the private sector, L_2/L_1, is constant over time. Each sector employs a fixed proportion of the total labor force.

(f) The public sector consumes a constant share of gross national product over time—value shares are constant over time. Or, the total (wage) cost of the public sector grows at the same rate as the total cost of the private sector.

(g) The ratio of real output in the public sector to real output in the private sector, x_2/x_1, declines over time at the rate of $(1 + \lambda)^{1/a}$.

References

1. Baumol, W. J. "Macroeconomics of Unbalanced Growth: The Anatomy of the Urban Crisis." *American Economic Review* 57 (1967): 415–426.
2. Bergstrom, T. "Collective Choice and the Lindahl Allocation Method." Mimeographed paper, Washington University, 1971.
3. _____, and Robert Goodman. "The Price and Income Elasticities of Demand for Public Good." *American Economic Review* 63 (1973): 280–296.
4. Black, D. *The Theory of Committees and Elections.* Cambridge: Cambridge University Press, 1958.
5. Borcherding, T. E., and R. T. Deacon. "The Demand for the Services of Non-Federal Governments: An Econometric Approach to Collective Choice." *American Economic Review* 62 (1972): 891–906.
6. Bowen, H. "The Interpretation of Voting in the Allocation of Economic Resources." *Quarterly Journal of Economics* 58 (1943): 27–48.
7. Bradford, D. F., R. A. Malt, and W. E. Oates. "The Rising Cost of Local Public Services: Some Evidence and Reflections." *National Tax Journal* 22 (1969): 185–202.
8. Buchanan, J. *The Demand and Supply of Public Goods.* Chicago: Rand McNally, 1968.
9. _____. "Fiscal Institutions and Efficiency in Collective Outlay." *American Economic Review* 54 (1964): 227–235.
10. _____. *Public Principles of Public Debt.* Homewood, Ill.: Richard D. Irwin, 1958.
11. _____, and Gordon Tullock. *The Calculus of Consent.* Ann Arbor, Mich.: University of Michigan Press, 1962.
12. Bush, W., and A. Denzau. "The Voting Behavior of Bureaucrats and Public Sector Growth," in this volume.
13. _____, and R. Mackay. "Public Goods, Taxation, and the Distribution of Income Over Time: A Collective Choice Approach." Unpublished manuscript, Virginia Polytechnic Institute, 1973.
14. Denzau, A. "Majority Voting, Residential Migration and the Local Public Sector." Mimeographed paper, Washington University, 1970.
15. Foley, D. "Lindahl's Solution and the Core of an Economy with Collective Goods." *Econometrica* 38 (1970): 66–72.
16. Lindahl, E. "Just Taxation—A Positive Solution." In *Classics in the Theory of Public Finance,* R. Musgrave and A. Peacock (eds.). London: Macmillan and Co., Ltd., 1958.
17. Lynch, L. K., and E. L. Redman. "Macroeconomics of Unbalanced Growth: Comment." *American Economic Review* 58 (1968): 884–886.
18. McGuire, M. C., and H. Aaron. "Efficiency and Equity in the Optimal Supply of a Public Good." *Review of Economics and Statistics* 51 (1969): 31–39.

19. Niskanen, W. A., Jr. *Bureaucracy and Representative Government.* Chicago: Aldine-Atherton, 1971.
20. Samuelson, R. "The Pure Theory of Public Expenditure." *Review of Economics and Statistics* 36 (1954): 387–389.
21. Seligman, E. R. A. "Progressive Taxation in Theory and Practice." *Publications of the American Economic Association* 9 (1894).
22. Spann, R. "The Macroeconomics of Unbalanced Growth and the Expansion of Government Spending." Mimeographed paper, Virginia Polytechnic Institute and State University, 1973.
23. _____. "Rates of Productivity Change and the Growth of State and Local Government Expenditures" in this volume.
24. Uzawa, H. "An Optimum Fiscal Policy in an Aggressive Model of Economic Growth." In Irwa Adelman and Erik Thorbecke (eds.), *The Theory and Design of Economic Development.* Baltimore: Johns Hopkins Press, 1966.
25. Worcester, D. A. "Macroeconomics of Unbalanced Growth: Comment." *American Economic Review* 58 (1968): 886–893.

12. The Effects on Public Spending of the Divisibility of Public Outputs in Consumption, Bureaucratic Power, and the Size of the Tax-Sharing Group   *Thomas E. Borcherding, Winston C. Bush, and Robert M. Spann*

In two recent papers by Borcherding and Deacon [8] and Bergstrom and Goodman [6] the determinants of public spending were assessed using an extremely simple model of collective choice. What is interesting about these two papers is their calculations of both the price elasticity and the degree of publicness (or divisibility in consumption) of various public services. Up to this time these parameters had been considered unmeasureable, with the possible exception of three other papers which measured only price elasticity [4, 5, 12]. The studies concluded, among other things, that (*a*) the price elasticity was indeed negative, but rather inelastic; and (*b*) the services were probably better classified as private services, not as public goods. This last finding seemed rather strange since some indivisibility (or externality) in consumptions should be present or no gains from collective provision would be realized. In other words, if there is no publicness or spillovers, why collectivize the activity?

Two not wholly inconsistent answers are possible. The first is that the goods are, in fact, purely private, Stigler's interpretation of Director's Law of Public Income Redistribution [16]. This is discussed by Borcherding elsewhere in this volume.[1] The other is that self-interested bureaucracies choose to produce private goods for their "desirable" effect on spending, i.e., for budget or output expansion reasons, and that mobile populations lead to crowding which exhausts the economies of publicness. The effect of these on public spending is a matter of some interest.

This paper will attempt to shed some light on these matters as well as to explore the question of bureaucratic power and its effect on public spending. Before doing so, however, let us briefly present the model used by Borcherding and Deacon and Bergstrom and Goodman.

---

1. See "The Sources of Growth of Public Expenditures in the United States, 1902–1970," chap. 3 in this volume.

Passive Bureaucracy and Immobile Population

In the models for both of these studies and most others in the collective choice literature, the demand and supply decisions underlying the provisions of public services are assumed to be affected by three crucial factors: the tastes of the choosers, the political method of aggregating preferences, and the opportunity cost to the chooser(s) of the activities undertaken.

The first determinant, tastes, is taken as given. Essentially, little can be said about this variable by economists, since operational models describing the theory of taste formation are conspicuously absent in the literature. Thus, both models assume tastes are identical over the political units studied.

Preference aggregation is rather a different matter, however. Following Downs [11] and Tullock [19] it is assumed that representatives are elected by informed, rational citizens via a majority rule process. The franchise is assumed to be freely available and the citizens choosing to exercise their vote mirror perfectly the entire unit's population which includes the nonvoters. Competition among elected office seekers is brisk and for well-known reasons is assumed to lead to the election of a government which accurately reflects the median citizen's preferences.

Citizens are assumed to be informed and immune to fiscal illusion and other forms of political chicanery. The median voter, since he is controlling, in effect chooses his preferred budget-tax "package" by electing candidates that bring his marginal-tax prices in line with his marginal benefits. He presumably is able to do this since the political market for selection of successful political entrepreneurs, i.e., elected candidates, is diverse in choice and as a spin-off insures the production of accurate and cheap information.

Logrolling or side-payments among voters is taken to be too costly for either voters or political entrepreneurs to arrange. Further, "Arrow problems" in platform formation are dismissed as unlikely on the basis of Tullock's theorem that the likelihood of cyclical majorities, i.e., no stable median voter, declines as the number of voters increases holding the issue space constant [18]. Thus, Downsian implicit logrolling accomplished by "piecing" together a platform of intense minority interests is also unlikely.[2]

Comparative statics in this public choice world can be accomplished by simply assuming *ceteris paribus* that as price falls the quantity demanded by the median voter increases, since the demand of each voter will be in this direction. The possibilities of aggregation problems are overlooked, just as they are for private markets in the case of differential income effects. However, Bergstrom and Goodman, and Barr and Davis

---

2. Downs [11]; also see Tullock, "Hotelling and Downs in Two Dimensions" [19].

both have theoretical sections where they show sufficient conditions for an inverse relationship between tax-price and quantity demanded.

On the cost side Borcherding and Deacon, and Bergstrom and Goodman use rather different, but not inconsistent approaches. Borcherding and Deacon assume that the median voter's percentage share of the marginal cost of the public output is the same in each political unit, but that marginal tax-prices differ because input prices are not uniform across units. They assume that the production function is Cobb-Douglas and that capital is costlessly mobile across units while labor is not. Within each unit, however, the inputs are available to government in perfectly elastic supply. Cost minimization yields a perfectly elastic supply function to each unit which in dollar terms is a constant term times the real wage rate raised to a power equal to labor's share of total cost ($p = kw^\rho$). On the other hand, Bergstrom and Goodman assume the marginal cost function is not only perfectly elastic in each jurisdiction but identical over all units. Marginal-tax prices differ between units, however, as the tax institution causes the median voter class—assumed by both studies to be the median income holders—to pay different percentages of the total cost. Cost minimization is not explicitly assumed but is implied. In both studies, the bureaucracy is considered to be of no consequence either as to determining the level of costs or by influencing the level of output chosen.

The estimation procedure for both models is developed in the following abbreviated manner. Let q equal the subjective quantity of Q, the public output, captured by the median preference holder according to the equation

$$q = \frac{Q}{N^\alpha}$$

where α is the degree of publicness ranging between 0 for the purely public good to 1 for the purely private good. α is assumed to be a technical or subjective characteristic of the good such that it does not vary with N or Q, i.e., crowding effects are ruled out. The demand for the subjective output q is assumed to be characterized by the form

$$q = As^\eta y^\delta$$

where A is some constant, s is the index of subjective marginal tax-price, y is the median voter's income and η and δ are the price and income elasticities respectively. Although neither s nor q is observable directly, by appropriate manipulation it can be shown that[3]

$$E = A'p^{\eta+1}y^\delta N^{(\alpha-1)(\eta+1)+1}$$

3. Actually to avoid problems of heteroscedasticity in estimation both Borcherding and Deacon and Bergstrom and Goodman put expenditures in the per capita form $e = Ap^{\eta+1} y^\delta N^{(\alpha-1)(\eta+1)} \mu$ where μ is an error term.

where E is the measure of total spending and p is the marginal-tax price of the observed output measured in terms of a wage function (Borcherding and Deacon) or tax-percentage (Bergstrom and Goodman). Thus, the demand relationship is made operational and is consistent with the theory of public choice.

In the next sections we will relax some of the assumptions of these models in order to investigate the effects of activist bureaucracies and mobile populations on the level of public spending.

Bureaucratic Activism

Recently Niskanen has offered a most intriguing hypothesis about the role of bureaucracy in the public sector which may suggest one possible reason why the degree of publicness has been observed to be so small [15]. He posits a model where government bureaucrats have monopoly power over supply for a number of reasons: the demise of the "spoils system"; the advent of Civil Service reform; the decline of overlapping but competing bureaus; and the tendency to purchase less output from sources in the private sector through the letting of competitive bids. This process is not countervailed by Congressional monopsony purchasing power because the key review legislative committees are controlled by those who represent constituencies or interest groups who benefit differentially relative to their tax burdens from budget expansions. In the private sector this monopoly power would lead to a reduction in output from the competitive level since the producing unit, if nonregulated, will have pressure exerted upon it through inside traders and the capital market to maximize profits. Not so the public sector where property rights to "profits" are severely attenuated. Niskanen assumes, instead, that these rents are distributed according to a function which is directly related to the budget of the bureau. Indeed, empirical evidence does suggest that bureaucrats' salaries, their status and their power are highly correlated with the budget of the unit,[4] a hypothesis offered by Parkinson several years ago. Given this monopoly supply power, Niskanen hypothesizes that at the limit the monopoly-bureaucracy will offer the elected officials all-or-none choices causing the supply to be much larger (he claims by 100 percent) than that which would be chosen under competitive circumstances.

In another context Alchian and Kessel [3] have argued that firms possessing monopoly power, but subject to regulatory constraints limiting the amount or rate of pecuniary profit that could be realized from their activities, might choose to take some of its noncompetitive returns in

---

4. See Robert J. Staaf, "The Growth of the Educational Bureaucracy: Do Teachers Make a Difference?" chap. 8 in this volume.

the form of nonpecuniary rents, i.e., soft carpets and well-appointed offices, pretty but not terribly competent secretaries, laxity in supervising subordinates, etc. The bureaucratic, governmentally owned monopoly, since legally constrained to earn no profits, may take some of the rents from the "business" in these aforementioned nonpecuniary forms as well as by raising salaries above the normal level by budget expansion. Thus, we would expect that the more monopoly power the bureau possesses the greater would be both the observable "waste" and its budget. Since the demand seems to be price inelastic it may be that bureaucrats are operating in that fortuitous range where increases in costs also increase their budgets as well.

Lately, a few studies have studied the effects of bureaucracy on budgets and costs. All seem to "confirm" or be consistent with the hypotheses of both Niskanen and Alchian-Kessel. Spann examines data on labor-output ratios for a few measureable public outputs over the period 1962–1967.[5] He concludes that the rate of productivity gains appear to be zero or even negative on average for workers employed in state and local governments. In still another study he found that unit costs were significantly lower in the private sector for garbage collection and fire services, than in those jurisdictions where such services were carried out by governments.[6] Ahlbrandt [1] has found this to be true for fire services as well. Davies's study of the two airlines in Australia, one public, one private, corroborates this too [10]. Spann also found that for those public activities which have close substitutes in the private sector the cost differentials were negligible.[7] Staaf has found that consolidation of school districts increases per pupil operating costs, and greatly increases the salaries of teachers and school administrators but does not improve the achievement levels of students at all. In fact, there is some evidence that student achievement is negatively related to the degree of consolidation. Despite the costliness of consolidation the number of school districts today has managed to fall to one-fourth of the 1949–1950 level.[8]

A few more things should be noted here before going on. It is possible that both the Borcherding and Deacon and Bergstrom and Goodman estimation equations contain specification errors from their neglect of bureaucratic supply power and its budget or output expanding character. It is possible that this is responsible for the high value of α rather than the inherent privateness of these activities.

5. Robert M. Spann, "Rates of Productivity Change and the Growth of State and Local Governmental Expenditures," chap. 6 in this volume.
6. "Public versus Private Provision of Governmental Services," chap. 4 in this volume.
7. Ibid.
8. Staaf, "The Public School System in Transition: Consolidation and Parental Choice," chap. 7 in this volume.

If, for instance, bureaucratic power is positively correlated with population, N, because of citizen disinterest, as Downs and Tullock suggest, then the term $(\alpha - 1)(\eta + 1)$ will be larger than if this force were elsewhere accounted for. Since η is algebraically larger than -1, α will be necessarily overstated.

Finally, if bureaucrats do indeed have monopoly supply power, they may prefer to produce goods with high α's rather than those with lower α's. This follows since the first (partial) derivative of E with respect to α is equal to $E(\eta + 1) 1nN$. Since $(\eta + 1) > 0$ for the observed price elasticities, it follows that as α rises so too does E. Thus, other things equal, budget maximizers should be observed to supply public services with less public qualities than those with more public service flows. Unfortunately, we have not devised a suitable test for this hypothesis though in principle it is a refutable proposition.

The Bureaucrat as Voter

The bureaucratic-monopolist model has one unfortunate characteristic which makes it incompatible with the Borcherding and Deacon and Bergstrom and Goodman models. Waste and budget (or output) "push," while explaining the endogenous forces leading to excessive outputs and budgets, emasculates, partially at least, the notion of the median voter and the competitive market in political entrepreneurship. It may be true that bureaucratic supply is cartelized, but it sells its output to only one buyer, the legislature. More importantly, the legislature is ultimately responsible for the monopolization of the activity. Why political entrepreneurs in their naturally monopsonistic positions "give in" to bureaucrats is then an important question unless we are to attribute these changes to some vague sort of legislative drift, a most unappealing explanation.

We offer the following explanation which we believe is consistent both with the role of noncompetitive bureaucracy, the median voter, and a sensitive political entrepreneur.[9] We shall only briefly outline this model here.

Consider a simple two-good world, one privately provided, X, and the other publicly distributed, Q. The budget constraints facing two types of individuals, a bureaucrat and a nonbureaucrat, are respectively:

$$Y_{nb} = P_x X_{nb} + \gamma P_Q Q_{nb}$$

and

$$Y_b = \bar{Y}_b + aQ = P_x X_b + \gamma P_Q Q_b$$

9. A more extended model is developed by Bush and Arthur Denzau, "Voting Behavior of Bureaucrats and Public Sector Growth," chap. 5 in this volume.

P_x, P_Q and γ are the prices of X, Q and the tax-share respectively and are assumed invariant regardless of the chooser's role. Y_{nb} is the income of the individual as a nonbureaucrat and X_{nb} and Q_{nb} are the quantities of the public and private goods he can consume. His income is assumed not to be affected by the community's choice of output mix.[10] Likewise X_b and Q_b refer to the bureaucrat's consumption. The crucial difference is that we assume that the individual bureaucrat's income is dependent on the output chosen. (Economy of analysis here requires such a simple model and the linear relationship between Y_b and Q is offered in a similar spirit.)

As a nonbureaucrat an individual might demand Q solely on its utility effects in consumption. But to the bureaucrat there is an extra dimension, the increased income he receives as Q increases. In short, purchase of Q by the bureaucrat is effectively subsidized and, *ceteris paribus,* more will be desired by him than by another citizen not so employed. Figure 1 illustrates this point very simply, holding the real income of a representative chooser constant.

Figure 1

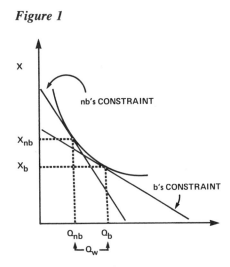

We can now examine the effects that bureaucrats have on the level of public output actually chosen. Assuming the tax-share of each individual as given, a cumulative distribution of preferred points is shown in Figure 2. With majority voting the quantity Q is chosen where the number of

10. Nonbureaucrat owners of specific inputs whose stocks or flows are sold to governments will experience larger incomes as public purchases increase since their supply functions are positively sloped. This group, e.g., the so-called military-industrial complex, is ignored here, as its inclusion would only strengthen our results.

Figure 2

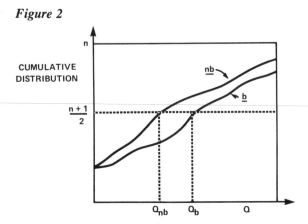

voters in favor of that level over all others is $\frac{n+1}{2}$. The curve *nb* represents the cumulative distribution with a competitive bureaucracy in the
public sector, i.e., where $a = 0$. When, however, bureaucrats are successful at pushing through Civil Service schedules such that $a > 0$, the distribution shifts to *b* assuming that bureaucrats are located more-or-less
randomly among the population.[11] Thus, self-interested bureaucrats
nudge the level of public spending to the right by $Q_w = Q_b - Q_{nb}$. In
dynamic terms the movement will be continuously toward more Q as
individuals newly hired by government bureaus will shift their preferences
toward larger public outputs. The process ends only when the gain in additional income, $a\Delta Q$, is smaller than the added taxes, $\gamma P_Q \Delta Q$, less the
marginal value of Q in consumption to the bureaucrat. At this point Q
may be so large as to have little marginal value.

A study by Martin [14] on voter participation by occupation groups is
suggestive here. Martin's data are taken during local elections in Austin,
Texas, during 1933. He found that overall voter participation was 58.1
percent whereas city employees' participation was 87.6 percent. He
concludes that "if all elements comprising Austin's population were as
election-minded as municipal employees this city would have no serious
problems. . . ." (We would predict that budgets would decrease too.) If
Martin's findings are general over time and political geography, the influence of bureaucrats on election outcomes might be nontrivial.[12] For
instance, if the ratio of bureaucrats and their families to the number of
eligible voters is 0.1, a reasonable estimate for Austin in the thirties, and

---

11. It may also be that the supply of bureaucrats is less than perfectly elastic. If this is
the case and wage discrimination is not permissable, $a > 0$. Cf. Borcherding [7].
12. Several studies cited in Lipset [13] also bear this out.

if Martin's figures are correct, bureaucrats made up 16 percent of those voting, though they consisted of only 10 percent of the working population. This suggests that nonbureaucrats voting participation rate was 0.49. Of course, this 16 percent may be minimum when it is recalled that these individuals can also be relied on to contribute in other ways to the success of candidates taking congenial platform positions on their preferred programs.

Assuming Martin is correct about the voting habits of bureaucrats and nonbureaucrats, a power-index of bureaucrats in affecting outcomes is easily computed according to the formula

$$\pi = \frac{1}{1 + \frac{V_{nb}}{V_b}(1/g - 1)}$$

where the V's are the voting participation rates of bureaucrats and nonbureaucrats (and by assumption their families) and g is the percent of bureaucrats in the labor force. Assuming Martin's participation rates are still valid, ($V_b \simeq 0.88$ and $V_{nb} \simeq 0.49$) the following table is computed:

g	π
0.05	0.08
0.10	0.16
0.20	0.31
0.30	0.45
0.37	0.51
0.40	0.55
0.50	0.64
0.60	0.72
0.70	0.82
0.80	0.90
0.90	0.94
1.00	1.00

If this is the case, it is possibly clear why at one time bureaucrats were denied the franchise in the political unit in which they worked. Consider, if it is not too close to home, those employed by nonfederal governments in the educational establishment. Though they compose only 5 percent of the work force, by our power-index, they effectively account for almost twice that percentage by their votes. It seems plausible, then, that such a group might affect public education budgets. Further, with the creation of unions which represent diverse groups of government employees the actual power-index of state and local employees in aggregate may not be much less than our method suggests. In any case, given recent court interpretations collusion among and consolidation of various diverse government unions may become easier. Perhaps this index also explains why the Hatch Act and state and local variants of this legislation prohibiting overt political activity on the part of civil servants have been so general. These act as checks in one dimension, at least, on the budget or output expanding tendencies of bureaucrats. It appears, however, that this restraint is in the process of being overruled by judicial decisions.

Two more institutional facts might be added to the analysis. Many cities and most counties and states require that an individual must reside in the unit if he is to be an employee of that government. The orthodox interpretation is that the individual bureaucrat is expected to be more "sensitive" to local preferences if he is a fellow citizen. Our interpretation would be different since the regulations are almost always Civil Service rules, not statute law. Another point to recall is the low cost of voting to bureaucrats. Most governments give anywhere from one-hour to all day off with pay on election day, even though polling hours now extend considerably outside of the ordinary working hours. Private firms are required by law in most localities to give time off, but usually not with pay. What role the bureaucrats had in instituting these rules can only be conjectured, but their potential influence on voting behavior should nonetheless be noted.

Civil Service and Budget Expansion

Just as in the private sector where any collective unit restraining the self-interested behavior of its members might lead to a higher level of wealth or utility, so too in the public sector.[13] The Civil Service mechanism could, in principle, act as a cartelizing force. It can, by various means limit entry, set wages, partially prescribe production functions, and delimit permissable political conduct of government employees. If the Civil Service is successful in such a task we should expect to find spending higher with than without its presence for two reasons. First, by restricting management choice it will cause unit costs of production to be higher. Given the price inelastic nature of demand this will be budget expanding. Second, given the budget or output expansion goal we would expect the bureaucracy's members, through their unions, to support candidates who preferred expanding government to some point, at least. To the extent Civil Service encourages unionism among public em-

13. For example, the restraining of price and quality competition can, when coupled with entry limitations, lead to higher levels of joint producer rents. Likewise firms exist to internalize the diseconomies from pure market exchanges among factory owners as pointed out by Alchian and Demsetz [2].

ployees, the effect of unionization can be looked on as ancillary to Civil Service.

In this section, the hypothesis that Civil Service has led to higher levels of spending in state and local governments is scrutinized. This hypothesis is tested by estimating state and local government expenditure functions which include a variable for the presence or absence of Civil Service regulations. The results do not refute the hypothesis that Civil Service regulations have increased the level of government spending. In almost all of the state and local expenditure categories examined, the existence of a Civil Service system leads to significantly higher levels of per capita expenditures. Within states which have had Civil Service systems for extended periods of time, per capita expenditures are positively associated with the length of time Civil Service has been in effect.

The model used to estimate the effects of Civil Service systems on expenditures is the Borcherding and Deacon model of the demand for government services, since its data permit testing this proposition and that of Bergstrom and Goodman does not. The Borcherding and Deacon model hypothesizes that expenditures per capita are a function of income, population, and the wage rate. The wage rate, under the assumptions made, is a proxy for the price of government services to the taxpayer. Its coefficient, β_1 below, equals $\rho(\eta + 1)$ where ρ is labor's share of total cost. The coefficient of income, β_2, measures the income elasticity of demand. Population is included in the model to determine the degree of publicness of the government service in question. Its coefficient, β_3, is $(\alpha - 1)(n + 1)$. If the service is purely private $\alpha = 1$ and $\beta_3 = 0$. If the government service is quasi-public, β_3 will be positive if demand is elastic and negative if demand is inelastic. If the service is purely private or if in the pure congestion range $\alpha > 1$, then this coefficient will be zero when $\eta = -1$, positive when η is inelastic, and negative when η is elastic. Formally, the model is

$$log\ e = \beta_o + \beta_1\ log\ w + \beta_2\ log\ y + \beta_3\ log\ N + \mu$$

where

      $e =$ expenditures per capita,
      $w =$ the wage rate adjusted for labor quality differences,[14]
      $y =$ average income per capita,
      $N =$ population, and
      $\mu =$ a disturbance term.

The demand function postulated assumes that government expenditures can be instantaneously adjusted in an upward or downward direc-

14. See Borcherding and Deacon [8] for a complete discussion. This adjustment attempts to keep labor units comparable.

tion. This will not be the case in an effective Civil Service system and, in particular, downward adjustments in the level are severely restricted. Except for income effects, this will not affect the quantity demand of new government outputs, since the existing level of government employment is a "sunk cost." The fact that existing programs cannot be cut back should not effect the marginal decision process on new programs (unless new programs and old programs are gross substitutes). The downward rigidity in expenditures will effect the aggregate level of expenditures, however. The effect of such restrictions is to make demand functions, based on marginal calculations, downward-biased estimates of the total expenditures function. Total expenditures, given an effective Civil Service, will be the expenditures predicted from elasticities based on marginal calculations plus the added expenditures due to the downward rigidity in existing expenditures.

This implies that the model should be respecified as

$$log\ e = \beta_o + \beta_1\ log\ w + \beta_2\ log\ x + \beta_3\ log\ N + B_4\ X_1$$

where

$X_1 = 1$ if the state has Civil Service and
$\quad = 0$ otherwise.

The mere existence of Civil Service might not be the primary effect of such systems, however. One might expect Civil Service coverage and power to grow over time. In this case, the length of time Civil Service has been in force should effect total expenditures also; both of these hypotheses are tested below.

In Table 1 estimates expenditure functions including the effects of Civil Service are presented. The effects of Civil Service are included in the model by specifying a dummy variable which is 1 if the state had Civil Service prior to 1940 and 0 otherwise. The year 1940 was used as a dividing point for two reasons. This was the year in which the federal government required states to have some form of "merit system" in order to qualify for certain kinds of federal aid. In addition, one would expect it to take some time before the full effects of Civil Service are felt. Expenditures functions are estimated for six expenditure categories using state and local data for 1962.[15]

We would expect that the coefficient of $X_1(\beta_4)$ would be positive and significant, since an effective Civil Service prevents downward adjust-

15. Higher education and local education expenditures are not included here in the analysis. Most employees in these sectors would be covered under tenure systems which usually operate independently of the Civil Service system. Thus, one would not expect Civil Service to have an effect on expenditures in these sectors. West [20] does present evidence, however, that public education in the United States has been exceedingly influenced by its major suppliers, teachers.

Table 1. Effects of Civil Service on state and local expenditures ('t' statistics in parenthesis)

Expenditure category	Wage rate (β_1)	Population (β_3)	Income (β_2)	Civil Service (β_4)	Constant	R^2
Highways	0.5110 (2.010)	-0.1954 (-5.367)	0.1235 (0.6416)	-.07108 (-0.8751)	-0.5168 (-0.3709)	.5278
Health-hospitals	-.03231 (-0.1056)	.04847 (1.128)	0.4073 (1.797)	0.1277 (1.330)	-5.141 (-3.101)	.2442
Police	.05740 (0.2192)	.08717 (2.831)	1.137 (8.354)	0.1221 (1.970)	-11.96 (-11.56)	.7742
Fire	0.2392 (0.6875)	.05241 (1.171)	1.368 (6.782)	0.3451 (3.683)	-14.48 (-9.201)	.7332
Sewers-sanitation	-0.4454 (-1.021)	0.1418 (2.479)	1.507 (4.257)	.01075 (.08360)	-14.68 (-5.951)	.4826
Parks and recreation	0.4348 (1.120)	0.1143 (1.801)	1.796 (5.553)	.07764 (0.5553)	-18.63 (-7.735)	.6224

ments in the size of the bureaucracy. The fact that Civil Service prevents the firing of employees (except under stringent conditions) will increase total expenditures, since existing employees whose value marginal product is less than their wage rate cannot be fired or demoted.

In two out of six categories (police and fire) Civil Service has a significant positive effect on the level of per capita expenditures. In the three of the four cases in which this variable is not significant, it has the correct sign (positive).

The magnitude of the impact of Civil Service varies among categories. It ranges from a 7 percent increase in expenditures to a 34 percent increase in expenditures. For the two cases in which the Civil Service variable is significant, the increase in expenditures due to Civil Service is 12 percent to 34 percent.

The results of these regressions lend some support to the hypothesis that Civil Service systems tend to increase the level of state and local expenditures. The effects of Civil Service were positive in almost all cases and significant in one-third of the expenditure categories examined.

In Table 2, the effects of the length of time Civil Service has been in force on government expenditures is estimated. Expenditure functions for the 24 states which had Civil Service prior to 1940 were estimated which included a variable X_1, the number of years Civil Service had been in existence to 1962. The effect of this variable is positive in all but one case. It is significant in two cases. On average, government expenditures increase about one-third of one percent for every year Civil Service has been in force. This implies that not only might Civil Service regulations increase government spending, but that this increase is probably greater the longer Civil Service has been in force.

The hypothesis that Civil Service regulations increase government spendings was tested in this section. The evidence was not totally in favor of the hypothesis but, on balance, the data indicate that Civil Service regulations have increased the level of government spending.

It is also interesting to note that in both Tables 1 and 2, the inclusion of the Civil Service term, X_1, did not change α from that observed by Borcherding and Deacon and Bergstrom and Goodman. To test this adequately, however, we would have to observe the α's for various classes of values at X_1. Unfortunately, we have not enough observations to make such a test statistically meaningful at this time.

Congestion and the Size of the Tax-Sharing Group

Free population migration is yet another factor that raises α, hence total per capita government spending. Buchanan and Tullock [9] have recently demonstrated that the operation of what we call the Tiebout

Table 2. Duration of civil service and state and local expenditures ('t' statistics in parenthesis).

Expenditure category	Wage rate (β_1)	Population (β_2)	Income (β_3)	Time since Civil Service introduced	Constant	R^2
Highways	.4229 (.943)	−.0464 (−.7761)	−.3022 (−.811)	−.0003837 (−.135)	1.626 (.646)	.1486
Health-hospitals	.38912 (.817)	.0225 (.387)	−.0106 (−.031)	.00766 (2.820)	−2.360 (−1.018)	.6134
Police	.865 (1.61)	−.0156 (−.275)	1.1392 (4.145)	.00083 (0.346)	−12.16 (−6.5281)	.8191
Fire	.808 (1.5491)	−.1848 (−2.693)	1.3116 (4.03)	.0101 (3.248)	−13.03 (−5.593)	.8371
Sewers-sanitation	−.4563 (−.497)	.1074 (.826)	1.3386 (1.661)	−.00053 (−.088)	−13.04 (−2.358)	.3413
Parks and recreation	1.0883 (1276)	.01237 (.110)	1.2824 (2.007)	.00243 (.476)	−14.60 (−3.306)	.6575

Effect [17] will not insure that nonfederal governmental activities will be efficiently allocated if the consumption of the service is subject to crowding, i.e., $\alpha'(N) > 0$. They develop a model where individuals compare rents from living in different localities and move to those that offer the highest utility returns. Equilibrium is established where each identical person's utility is equalized. Unfortunately, this is not an optimum, for in the migration decision the prospective immigrant considers only the marginal effect on himself, not on the community he is leaving nor on the one he is entering. Because the returns to land and other private assets that are subject to crowding costs are privately owned, no externality from their use is predicted. Such is not the case when it comes to "citizenship," however, since generally no congestion charges are levied to immigrants into densely settled cities, nor is an exit fee charged (or bribe offered) in sparsely populated areas to limit emigration. The results are an overcrowding of larger cities and too thin a population density in rural areas and small population centers. Since much of the statistical weight goest to the larger populated areas where crowding is observed, the estimated α may be overstated.

One simple test of this proposition would be to run Bergstrom and Goodman's municipal data separately for units of very different size and then compare the resulting α's. If Buchanan and Goetz are correct, as population increases past some point the α's will rise and may even pass through 1.

Theoretically, however, it is easy to find the most efficient size unit for the representative citizen. When α is less than unity, there may be some gains in joint consumption. Assuming the tax-price of Q, the objective marginal cost, is constant over output, the subjective marginal tax-price, s, will fall as N increases to the point where

$$(\alpha - 1)N + \alpha' 1nN = 0$$

i.e., where $(\alpha - 1) < 0$.[16] Unfortunately, we cannot offer the statistical relationship between α and N as the largest N in the data of Bergstrom and Goodman is only 100,000. Two things we do know, however. First, that α is observed always to be equal or greater than 1 suggests that on average political units are too populous. Second, because α probably does become larger as a result of the migration to the large American cities, the shared costs of public services therewithin actually rise. (Recent attempts by some large cities to restrict entry of new residents may reflect this diseconomy.) Given the observed price inelastic demand of these services budgets will necessarily expand. Thus, some budget expansion

---

16. This follows since $s = \gamma p N^{\alpha-1}$ where γ, the tax-share, and p are taken as fixed, hence, $\dfrac{ds}{dN} = 0$ when $\gamma p N^{\alpha-1} [(\alpha - 1) N + \alpha' \, 1nN] = 0$.

at the state-local level may, indeed, arise from the demographic movements attendant to the so-called urban crisis.[17]

Conclusion

The question whether Stigler is correct that public outputs are really divisible (private) because of Director's Law or whether the self-interested behavior of bureaucrats and migrants have caused these goods to become private has been explored. No firm conclusions have been offered. It has been shown, however, that the consideration of the Parkinson and Tiebout Effects on the level of public spending, is a potentially fruitful source of explanation. We feel that further research on both these subjects is necessary. We invite other scholars to use their ingenuity in testing these most intriguing propositions.

References

1. Ahlbrandt, Roger. "Efficiency in the Provision of Fire Services." *Public Choice* (fall, 1973).
2. Alchian, Armen A., and Harold Demsetz. "Production, Information Costs, and Economic Organization." *American Economic Review* (Dec., 1972).
3. _____, and Reuben A. Kessel. "Competition, Monopoly, and the Pursuit of Money." *Aspects of Labor Economics*. Princeton, N.J.: Princeton University Press, 1962.
4. Barlow, Robin. "Efficiency Aspects of Local School Finance." *Journal of Political Economy* (Sept./Oct., 1970).
5. Barr, James L., and Otto A. Davis. "An Elementary Political and Economic Theory of Local Government." *Southern Economic Journal* (Oct., 1966).
6. Bergstrom, Theodore C., and Robert Goodman. "The Price and Income Elasticities of Demand for Public Goods." *American Economic Review* (March, 1973).
7. Borcherding, Thomas E. "A Neglected Cost of a Voluntary Military." *American Economic Review* (March, 1971).
8. _____, and Robert T. Deacon. "The Demand for the Services of Non-Federal Governments." *American Economic Review* (Dec., 1972).
9. Buchanan, James M., and Gordon Tullock. "Efficiency Limits of Fiscal Mobility: An Assessment of the Tiebout Model." *Public Economics* (spring, 1972).

17. Actually, it appears that over the narrow range of N that Bergstrom and Goodman consider α is practically constant implying $\alpha'(N) = 0$. We hypothesize, however, the inclusion of the great American megopoli would change this. If not, students of the urban crisis are seriously misleading us. Thus, assuming $\alpha'(N)$ is an increasing function, at least at some large level of N, it can be shown that the elasticity of E with respect to N equals $1 + (\alpha - 1)(\eta + 1) + \alpha'(\eta + 1)\frac{lnN}{N}$. Since empirically it has been demonstrated that $\alpha > 1$ and $0 > \eta > -1$, it follows that a shift of N from smaller towns and cities to the great urban centers will lead to an increase in total local public spending.

228   *T. E. Borcherding, W. C. Bush, and R. M. Spann*

10. Davies, David G. "The Efficiency of Public and Private Firms: The Cases of Australia's Two Airlines." *Journal of Law and Economics* (April, 1971).
11. Downs, Anthony. *An Economic Theory of Democracy*. New York: Harper & Row, 1957.
12. Gensmerer, Bruce. "Determinants of Fiscal Policy Decisions of Local Governments in Urban Areas." Ph.D. dissertation, University of Michigan, 1966.
13. Lipset, Seymour Martin. *Political Man: The Social Bases of Politics*. Garden City, N.Y.: Doubleday and Co., 1960.
14. Martin, Roscoe C. "The Municipal Electorate: A Case Study." *Southwestern Social Science Quarterly* (Dec., 1933).
15. Niskanen, William A. *Bureaucracy and Representative Government*. Chicago: Aldine-Atherton, 1971.
16. Stigler, George J. "Director's Law of Public Income Distribution." *Journal of Law and Economics* (April, 1970).
17. Tiebout, Charles. "A Pure Theory of Local Government Expenditures." *Journal of Political Economy* (Oct., 1956).
18. Tullock, Gordon. "The General Irrelevance of the General Impossibility Theorem." *Quarterly Journal of Economics* (May, 1967).
19. _____. *Towards a Mathematics of Politics*. Ann Arbor, Mich.: University of Michigan Press, 1967.
20. West, E. G. "The Political Economy of American Public School Legislation." *Journal of Law and Economics* (Oct., 1967).

13. Economic Models of Bureaucracy: Survey, Extensions, and Evidence   *William Orzechowski*

The behavior of those who manage public agencies has been the focus of scholarly endeavor for many years. Most of the earlier contributions were made by sociologists.[1] Not until recently have economists developed economic models of bureau behavior.

Economic models of bureaucracy can be traced back to the early literature through the development of the theory of the neoclassical firm.[2] Starting after Berle and Mean's pioneering study, "The Modern Corporation and Private Property," economists developed a utility maximization theory of the neoclassical firm. These models provide an alternative to the traditional profit maximization hypothesis. An exhaustive treatment of this approach has been covered in the literature. The most notable utility maximization models of the firm are those developed by Baumol [4], Marris [16], and Williamson [31].

Von Mises in his seminal work [27] provided the first economic approach to the study of public agency behavior. His analysis was suggestive, but it has not been until recently that economists have developed an explicit utility maximization model of the public bureau. This model was developed by William A. Niskanen [22] and has been modified by Migue and Belanger [19] to incorporate elements of the utility maximization models of the neoclassical firm. Finally, less formalized and extended models have been suggested by Borcherding, Bush, and Spann [8], De Alessi [3], Parkinson [23], and Tullock [26].

Since economic models of bureaucracy provide a set of testable propositions, alternative models of bureaucracy yield different implications. Thus, it is possible empirically to discriminate among these models and in this way shed light on the general objective function and constraints faced by the bureaucrat.

There have been some empirical studies of public agencies. Works by Ahlbrandt [1], Borcherding [7], Davies [12], Parkinson [23], and Spann [25] provide striking evidence in favor of some of these economic

---

1. See Blau [6], Crozier [11], Parkinson [23], Meyer [18], Weber [28], and Whyte [29].

2. The neoclassical firm (a term coined by Robin Marris [15]) is usually defined as an enterprise where managers and owners are essentially distinct bodies (because of institutional features such as limited liability). The general hypothesis is that managers of these firms have a significant range of discretion within which they can pursue goals that maximize their own utility at the expense of the stockholders. Also see Scitovsky [24].

models of bureaucracy. Relatively little empirical work, however, has been performed and almost no statistical evidence is available which allows discrimination among the models.

In this paper I discuss the existing models of bureau behavior and propose an extended version. The implications of the different models are drawn out and their testable results are derived. Finally, empirical tests of these implications are presented. The results of those tests suggest that the bureau may be of a different nature than the firm and other institutional forms. They indicate that firms are significantly more efficient than public bureaus. The tests show that bureaucrats maximize utility by producing outputs above minimum costs. Furthermore, they demonstrate that bureaucrats may exhibit a preference for staff in their production decisions.

Existing Models of Bureau Behavior

In this section, three models are presented. The first model is that of Niskanen, who assumes bureaucrats maximize utility by producing that output level which yields the largest total budget. The public manager is, in effect, a budget maximizer. The second model is that of Williamson. He assumes that managers of neoclassical firms derive utility from staff and related expense, and he predicts that neoclassical firms have both larger costs and staff than profit-maximizing firms. It is important to note that "bureaucratic waste" is explicitly incorporated into the Williamson model. Finally, Migue and Belanger, in a forthcoming paper, develop a model which incorporates elements of both the Niskanen and Williamson models. Their model predicts that bureaus are, more than likely, to be both exchange and production inefficient.

The Niskanen Model

Niskanen's fundamental model of bureaucracy is based upon budget maximization. Niskanen assumes that all dimensions of bureaucratic utility are a monotonic function of the total budget of the bureau.

Among the several variables that may enter the bureaucrat's utility function are the following: salary, perquisites of the office, public regulation, power, patronage, output of the bureau, ease of making changes, and ease of managing the bureau. All of these variables except the last two, I contend, are a positive monotonic function of the total budget of the bureau during the bureaucrat's tenure in office (the last two variables are reduced by increases in the budget).[3]

---

3. Niskanen [22], p. 38.

Thus, Niskanen contends bureaucrats produce that output level which yields the highest possible budget as opposed to the output level which will maximize the difference between revenues and costs. The reason is bureaucrats do not have property rights to the fiscal residuum[4] of the bureau. Bureaucrats are civil servants and as such cannot hold claim to any tax dollars that remain after costs. As a consequence, Niskanen asserts, fiscal residuum can be claimed only indirectly through budget expansion.

Niskanen's important insight develops with the second feature of his model. He assumes that bureaus possess a unique monopoly advantage and asserts that bureaus can exercise monopoly power to the degree of perfect price discrimination. Bureaus are able to extract almost the full amount of consumer surplus generated by government output.

The highest degree of monopoly power is afforded bureaus because of the institutional features of the budgetary process. Bureaus bargain with appropriations committees on the basis of a total budget. Bargaining does not proceed on a per unit basis. The fiscal purchaser, in effect, is constrained to buy the output of a monopoly bureau in one large package.[5] That is, he is constrained to buy at all-or-nothing prices. To quote Niskanen: "The primary difference between the exchange relation of a bureau and that of a market organization is that a bureau offers a total output in exchange for a budget, whereas a market organization offers units of output at a price."[6] The main result of Niskanen's propositions is that bureaucrats will produce an output level far beyond the social optimum. Further, given normal elasticity conditions, such output will be produced at minimum costs.

We can illustrate the Niskanen effect graphically. This is done in Figure 1. The curve (L) represents the community demand curve for a public

Figure 1

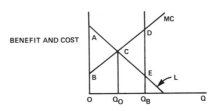

4. The difference between tax dollars collected for a public service and the minimum costs of producing that service.

5. Niskanen argues that bureaucrats obtain more information about the preferences of the constituency than the representatives of the constituency can obtain about the operation of the bureau. This relative information advantage of bureaus buttresses their extracting potential.

6. Niskanen [22], p. 40.

service, and *MC* represents the marginal costs of such a service. The equilibrium output of the bureau is located at (Q_B). At (Q_B) the largest possible budget is generated $[OAEQ_B]$ subject to the constraint that total revenues must equal total costs. Consumer surplus $[ABC]$ generated on output levels up to (Q_o) is used to expand output to Q_B $(ABC = CDE$, obviously income effects are neglected or $CDE < ABC$ and Q_B would have to be smaller). Further, the bureau provides an output level which is not Pareto efficient. The Pareto efficient output occurs at the intersection of (L) and MC or (Q_o). By contrast, the bureau vastly overproduces at Q_B.[7]

To summarize, Niskanen's basic model assumes bureaucrats reap utility solely from large budgets and possess the highest level of monopoly power. The prediction which emerges is that bureau output will be beyond the Pareto optimal level but will be produced at minimum costs. Further, the model predicts that both budgets and output levels of bureaus will expand at a rapid pace in response to increasing public demand over time.

The Williamson Model

The Williamson model assumes that managers of the neoclassical firm can, within limits, operate the firm to further their own interests. The model predicts that such firms will produce above minimum costs and operate with an oversized staff.[8]

Managers of neoclassical firms find themselves in a situation similar to that of the bureaucrat. Both the bureaucrat and the neoclassical manager are not constrained to deliver the complete difference between revenue and costs to the owners of the organization they operate because owner-

7. There is a variant of the basic Niskanen model which incorporates bureaucratic inefficiency as a by-product. If demand is relatively inelastic, the largest budget can only be gotten by producing above minimum costs. This is illustrated in panel (a).

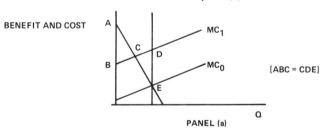

PANEL (a)

The bureaucrat can generate the largest possible budget (O, C, E, D) only by producing above minimum costs $(MC_1 > MC_o)$. Inefficiency on the part of the bureaucrat is a result of the relative elasticities of cost and demand and is not explicitly incorporated into the analysis.

8. The same hypothesis was elaborated by Alchian and Kessel [2].

ship and management functions in both types of organization are separate. Managers in both institutions are not able to directly appropriate, in pecuniary form, the difference between revenue and costs.[9]

According to Williamson, managers indirectly appropriate part of the potential residual of the organization by producing output above minimum costs. This is expressed by a preference on the part of management for larger than required expense for the staff function. Staff is an important source of utility to management for at least two reasons.

First, staff size is hypothesized to be positively related to the salary of middle and higher management. The larger the size of staff the more likely that further steps in the organizational hierarchy will be created. Given the assumption that superiors are paid more than those below them, over-staffing will then lead to higher salaries.[10]

Second, it is hypothesized that a large staff increases the security of management, and, it is argued, a large staff reduces the anxiety and in-security that large organizations generate. If the surest guarantee to the survival of the various parts of the bureaucracy appears to be size, efforts to expand the separate staff functions can be predicted. As long as the organization is able to satisfy its minimum profit constraint,[11] the tendency to value staff apart from reasons associated with its productivity produces a predisposition to extend programs beyond the point where marginal costs equal marginal benefits.

The managerial discretion model is based upon the selection of choice variables (especially staff) which maximize managerial utility subject to a minimum profit constraint. The relevant variables can be expressed in the following terms:

P = Price
X = Output
TR = Total Revenue = $P \cdot X$
S = Staff or approximate administrative expense
T = Taxes = $\bar{T} + t\pi_R$ (where t is a tax rate applied to a profit base π_R)
E = Demand shift parameter
C = Production cost (excluding staff)
π_R = Reported profit = $TR - C - S$; the amount of profit actually re-

9. In the case of the bureau, the owners are taxpayers, a widely dispersed group which is practically ignorant of the operations of the bureaus they finance. In the case of the neo-classical firm, the owners represent a dispersed set of stockholders with neither the incen-tive nor the information to adequately monitor management. They have a weak incentive because of the free-rider effect associated with large numbers, and poor information is the result of imperfections in both capital and product markets. See Alchian and Demsetz [2], Marris [16], and Williamson [31] for the theoretical arguments.

10. This is an outline of Robin Marris's so-called bureconic theory of the neoclassical firm. See Marris [16], pp. 99–103.

11. The return that minimally satisfies stockholders.

ported by management and paid out to two groups, in the form of taxes to the government and profits to stockholders

π_o = The minimum profit constraint is the amount of return which will minimally satisfy stockholders

$\pi_D = \pi_R - \pi_o - T$ = Discretioning profit. It is equal to the amount of reported profit over and above taxes and the minimum profit expected by stockholders. It is a return given to stockholders over and above what they expect. According to Williamson, this return to stockholders may yield utility to management in the form of pride in the organization, etc.

The Staff Model

In this model, management derives utility from two sources (*a*) π_D or discretioning profit and (*b*) S, the level of expense for the staff function. In equation form, the utility maximizing problems can be set up as follows:

(1)   Max: $U = (S, \pi_D)$
          Subject to: $\pi_R \geqslant \pi_o + T^{12}$

In words, the manager maximizes his utility which is a function of staff and discretionary profits subject to the constraint that reported profits be greater than or equal to taxes plus the minimum amount of return expected by stockholders.

Using the above definitions the problem can be reduced to:

Max: $U = [S, (1 - t)(TR - C - S - \bar{T}) - \pi_o]$
Subject to: $\pi_R - \pi_o - T \geqslant 0$

First order conditions are obtained by setting the partial derivatives of U with respect to X and S equal to zero.

(1) $\dfrac{\partial TR}{\partial X} = \dfrac{\partial C}{\partial X}$

$\dfrac{\partial TR}{\partial S} = \dfrac{-U_1 + (1 - t)U_2}{(1 - t)U_2}$

From (1) we observe that the firm makes its production decision in the conventional manner by equating marginal revenue to the marginal costs

12. The constraint can be rewritten as $\pi_R - \pi_o - T \geqslant 0$. Assuming diminishing marginal utility and disallowing corner solutions, it follows that the firm will always choose values of decision variables that will yield positive utility with respect to each component of its utility function. The second component is $\pi_R - \pi_o - T \geqslant 0$. If it is to be positive, then the constraint will always be satisfied as an inequality. Thus, the constraint is redundant and the problem can be treated as one of straightforward maximization.

Figure 2

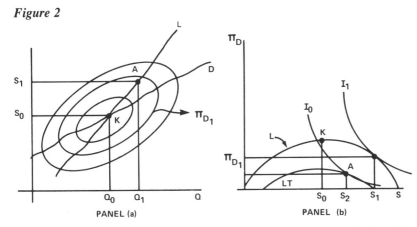

of production (excluding staff). Equation (2), however, reveals that the firm employs staff in the region where the marginal value product of staff is less than its marginal cost. That is, the firm will operate where $\left(\dfrac{\partial TR}{\partial S} < 1\right)$, whereas the short run profit maximizer would employ staff only up to the point where the equality of marginal value product and marginal cost exists.

Williamson's model of the firm yields comparative static results different from the standard profit maximizing model. An illustration of this difference is demonstrated in Figure 2.

In panel (a) iso-profit contours are drawn over two variables, staff and output. Lines (L) and (D) are ridge lines. Along (L) the marginal effect of an increase in output on profits is zero (holding staff constant). Along (D) the marginal effect of an increased staff (holding output constant) on profits is zero. These lines intersect at the profit maximizing staff-output combination (K). By contrast, Williamson's model predicts that the utility maximizer locates on a lower profit contour such as π_{D_1}, and chooses a staff-output combination such as (A).

The diagram can be further simplified. This is done in panel (b). In this diagram discretionary profit (π_D) is plotted as a function of staff. The discretionary profit contour (L) is derived by slicing across the iso-profit field along ridge line (L) where points (K) and (A) are identical in both diagrams.

The major comparative static differences between the profit maximizing model and Williamson's model is the predicted response to changes in fixed charges such as a lump sum tax. This difference is illustrated in panel (b). In response to a lump sum tax increase, the profit contour (L) shifts vertically downward to (L_T). The profit maximizer maintains the same level of staff (S_o). Whereas, the utility maximizer will adjust the size of its staff ($S_1 \rightarrow S_2$).[13]

In sum, the Williamson model assumes that managers of neoclassical firms maximize utility by producing output above minimum costs. Compared to the standard profit maximization model, utility maximizing firms will have higher costs mirrored by a large staff. Further, in response to changes in the environment, it is predicted that utility maximizing firms will make relatively large adjustments in staff size compared to profit maximizing firms.

The M-B Model

Migue and Belanger [19] construct a utility maximizing theory of the bureau which explicitly incorporates cardinal features of both Niskanen and Williamson's models. The model combines the superior monopoly power of bureaus via the budgetary process (Niskanen's assertion) with the notion that bureaucrats exhibit preferences for items beside output (Williamson's assertion). The model predicts that bureaus are both exchange and production inefficient.

The M-B model is developed on the basis of an alleged inconsistency contained within the Niskanen model. Niskanen assumes that the goal of the bureaucrat is to generate the largest possible budget. This is equivalent to saying that bureaucrats maximize output subject to the bureau's budget constraint. Carrying this to its logical conclusion would imply zero fiscal residuum remaining for such utility dimensions as salary, perquisites, and security—dimensions which Niskanen assumed were the consequences of budget maximization. "In Niskanen's model, budget maximization is equivalent to output maximization with the bureau's budget constraint. If Niskanen is right in assuming that the budget of the bureau is maximized, then no expenses other than those contributing to productivity are incurred since these would compete with output."[14]

---

13. Exogenous changes such as lump sum tax shocks are difficult to observe. However, demand changes are relatively easy to observe. Williamson's empirical studies came from observation of firms which experienced dramatic declines in demand. His studies suggest that firms with characteristics conducive to utility maximization cut their staff rather severely relative to profit maximizing firms. An illustration of these effects is given below. The profit maximizer makes the adjustment ($S_o \rightarrow S_1$) while the utility maximizer makes the adjustment ($S_2 \rightarrow S_3$), where ($S_2 - S_3$) > ($S_o - S_1$).

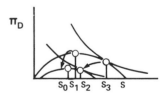

14. Migue and Belanger [19].

In order to contrast the M-B model from Niskanen's model, consider the diagrams in Figure 3.

In panel (a), a fiscal contour is constructed over output and it is equal to the difference between taxes collected for a bureau's service and the minimum cost of producing that service. The curve labeled TB is the total budget correspondent to each output level. The curves are drawn on the assumption that the bureau, in effect, is able to perfectly price discriminate. At output level (Q_o) maximum fiscal residuum is generated. It is correspondent to area ABC in panel (a), and it is the Pareto efficient output level.[15]

Niskanen's bureaucrat would produce at Q_N. Here the largest possible budget TB_N is generated. All residuum is used efficiently, in the production sense, to generate the largest possible budget TB_N. One implication of the model is that the Niskanen bureaucrat reaps zero utility from fiscal residuum. Paradoxically, the bureaucrat in Niskanen's model is as production efficient as a firm in a competitive market but takes zero rent for his effort. By contrast, the M-B bureaucrat chooses an output-residuum combination such as (Q_{MB}, FR_{MB}). The M-B bureaucrat expresses a preference for both output and residuum. The residuum represents an amount of tax revenue above minimum cost from which the bureaucrat can extract utility in the form of costly expense such as leisure, salary, perquisites, and payments to lobbyists supporting the bureau. The M-B maximization process implies that bureaucrats produce above minimum costs. In panel (b) this would serve to move marginal cost above the minimum marginal cost level (MC_0 to MC_1) and result in an equilibrium output level such as (Q_{MB}).

The comparative static implications of the Niskanen model and M-B model are also different. The Niskanen model predicts that bureaus, in response to a demand increase, would adapt by expanding both output

Figure 3

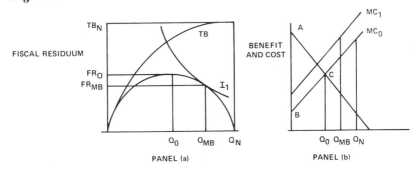

PANEL (a)   PANEL (b)

15. After Q_o, marginal cost of output exceeds marginal social benefits.

Figure 4

FISCAL RESIDUUM

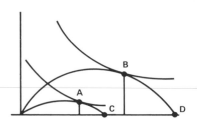

and budget in relatively large amounts.[16] By contrast, the M-B model predicts that bureaus would respond to the same demand increase with a large increase in budget but with a comparatively large increase in unit costs. Consequently, its productivity record would be poor relative to the Niskanen bureau. We can illustrate these effects in Figure 4. A demand increase can be represented by an outward shift of the fiscal contour. Niskanen's bureau moves from C to D while the M-B bureau moves from A to B. Output response is greater in the Niskanen model than in the M-B model because M-B's bureaucrat reaps utility from items which raise costs above the required amounts.[17]

In sum, M-B's model assumes that bureaus exhibit preference for items which boosts costs above required costs. Second, it assumes that bureaus have the monopoly power of a perfect price discriminator. The prediction which emerges is that the bureau will be both production and exchange inefficient.

Overview of the Models

We have surveyed four models of bureaucracy. In order to bring out the differences in these models, consider Figure 5. Two wealth contours are drawn on the assumption of identical demand and cost curves. θ_o is drawn on the assumption that the organization in question has simple nondiscriminatory monopoly power. θ_1 assumes that the organization has monopoly power of the nth degree.

Position A represents the equilibrium position of Williamson's manager where the residuum of the organization is distributed to stockholders in the form of a minimum return and to management in the form of extra

16. To quote Niskanen, "The output and budget of the bureau operating in the budget constrained region will always grow faster than those of competitive industries faced by the same increase in demand. In fact, for constant marginal cost, the rate of increase of both output and budget will be twice that of a competitive industry."

17. This effect is a consequence of the mechanics of demand expansion process. As demand rises, it has the effect of making the new budget line steeper for every level of residuum (this can be seen by comparing the slopes of two contours at A and F). This implies that the relative price of fiscal residuum falls at every level of output. Thus, a substitution effect would induce the bureaucrat to choose a residuum-output combination favoring residuum. The consequence is that output is likely to be little sensitive to changes in demand. See Migue and Belanger [18].

Figure 5

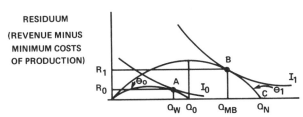

RESIDUUM
(REVENUE MINUS
MINIMUM COSTS
OF PRODUCTION)

staff and related expense. Position C represents the equilibrium position of Niskanen's bureaucrat. In this case the bureaucrat uses his superior monopoly power to generate the largest possible output and budget. Finally, position B represents the equilibrium position of the M-B bureaucrat who uses his superior monopoly power to expand output beyond the Pareto efficient point (Q_0), and who uses residuum for expense (R_1) above minimum cost.

The major difference between the Williamson approach and those of Niskanen and M-B is that the former deals with a firm which is assumed to have monopoly power of the first degree whereas the latter models deal with public bureaus which are assumed to have n^{th} degree monopoly power.

The overriding testable difference between the Niskanen and the M-B models is that M-B's model predicts that bureaucrats will produce substantially above minimum costs. The Niskanen model predicts that bureaus produce output at minimum costs. The Williamson and M-B models are similar in that both predict that output will be produced above minimum cost. The major testable distinction between the Williamson and M-B models is that the former model predicts that managers will exhibit particular input preferences in the use of the organization's wealth (staff and related expense), whereas M-B prefer to leave their analysis in general terms. They do not specify the particular input preference of bureaucrats. Consequently, their model does not allow for a test of bureaucratic bias in resource utilization.

A Public Choice Model of Bureau Behavior

The foregoing discussion of public agency behavior leads us to the conclusion that bureaucrats operate organizations which offer superior monopoly advantages. This unique monopoly position yields a relatively large fiscal residuum from which bureaucrats can indirectly extract wealth. The manner by which such wealth is extracted, however, is not made clear.

Niskanen assumed that all utility dimensions can be satisfied by maximizing output subject to a budget constraint. Migue and Belanger argued that such a maximization process involved a contradiction since it implied that zero residuum remained for the utility dimensions specified by Niskanen. On the other hand, M-B hypothesized that bureaus would maximize utility by producing output above minimum costs, but M-B find it convenient to ignore the pattern of such inefficient resource usage.

It seems reasonable to assume along with M-B that bureaucrats do use the residuum generated by the agencies they operate for their own purposes. This in turn boosts costs above the minimum. Corner solutions usually demonstrate behavioral patterns of an extreme sort and Niskanen's budget maximization hypothesis, under normal conditions, implies such a result. However, it also seems possible to push the theory beyond the limits of the M-B model by developing a model of bureau behavior which explicitly incorporates resource preferences of bureaucrats.

Input Choice

That Migue and Belanger's model does not contain a treatment of bureaucratic input preference is surprising since much of the literature on bureaucracy and managerial discretion highlights the particular input preferences of bureaucrats.

C. N. Parkinson's early studies of bureau behavior suggest that bureaucrats exhibit a strong preference for staff.[18] One implication of Parkinson's analysis is that the growth rate of staff in public bureaus would be approximately constant (Parkinson's Law). In one of his illustrations Parkinson noted that the staff of the British Colonial office had more than quadrupled in a time period over which Britain had lost most of its colonies.

Robin Marris and Oliver Williamson, in their penetrating analysis of the neoclassical firm, indicate that utility maximizing managers may have a strong bias favoring the staff function. Marris and Williamson argued that an oversized staff was a means to salary and security, two goals highly prized by management. Williamson's case studies of firms experiencing declining demand suggested that neoclassical firms made relatively severe cutbacks in staff—an implication that such firms may have been overstaffed.

Another interesting hypothesis concerning input utilization is suggested by Borcherding and Bush and Spann. They contend that bureaucrats have preferences for large staff since larger staff provides more bureaucrat-voters. The more bureaucrats there are relative to nonbureaucrats, the greater will be the voting power of the former group. This, in turn, will lead to higher budgets since the bureaucratic voting block will favor

18. See Parkinson [23].

budget expansion. The authors present data which show that voter participation is strongest among bureaucrats. For example, Martin, in a study of local elections in Austin, Texas, found that overall voter participation was 58.1 percent, whereas employees of the city participated at the rate of 87 percent.[19]

Last, theories have been presented which indicate that bureaus may exhibit an input preference for capital goods. De Alessi [13] argues that bureaus may favor production methods which use relatively more capital than labor. The basic reason is that capital intensive production methods tend to lump a larger proportion of costs over a shorter time horizon. Thus, it is hypothesized that capital intensive methods of production yield greater utility to budget-minded bureaucrats than projects which provide the same budget over a longer time period.

In sum, M-B provide a theory of the bureau which predicts that bureaucrats will indirectly extract wealth from the organization they operate, but they do not suggest the manner by which this is accomplished. Others have been more explicit in this regard and have suggested that bureaucrats maximize by using biased methods of production favoring either capital or labor. In the next section, a model is developed which incorporates elements of both approaches.

The De Alessi-Parkinson Model

In this section an extended version of the economic models of bureaucracy is presented. The model contains the assumption that bureaucrats exhibit preferences for types of inputs. This assumption is based on the observation of Parkinson and De Alessi, who claim that public managers may exhibit input preferences for either labor or capital.[20]

In the model constructed below it will be assumed that labor is a preference variable. The actual specification of input preferences is not a matter of major concern. At some levels, bureaucrats may exhibit a bias for labor relative to capital, and at other levels, the reverse may be true (this issue will be explored later). Furthermore, the bureaucrat can use the fiscal residuum generated by the bureau to buy overly-large amounts of both; however it is assumed here that bureaucrats express a labor bias for two reasons. First, the bulk of the literature on this topic suggests that utility maximizing administrators act in this fashion (see Borcherding, Bush, and Spann [8], Marris [16], Williamson [31], and Tullock [26]. Second, an empirical test for input usage is performed on private versus public colleges and universities. Public colleges and universities are usually state or locally controlled. State and local bureaus contain insti-

19. See Martin [17].
20. See De Alessi [13] and Parkinson [23].

tutional features which would tend to make them labor biased relative to the federal sector.

Thus, incorporated into the extended model is a utility function of the bureaucrat which is assumed to contain two variables. First, quantity which makes the utility function similar to the Niskanen and M-B utility function. Second, the utility function contains labor which bridges the M-B and Niskanen approach with the input theories of bureaucracy. In notational form this can be represented as:

$$MAX: U = U(Q,L)$$

It is hypothesized that the bureau is constrained by the demand function of the median voter. Additionally, it is reasonable to assume that the bureau must cover all costs incurred in its operation. These propositions can be restated in the form that bureaucrats will maximize utility by choosing two variables, output and labor, and must operate the bureau such that all costs of operation equal some finite budget.

The Bureau's Maximization Problem

The problem described in the previous section can be put in equation form. In order to do this, the following terms are defined:

Q = The output of the bureau
w = Wage rate
r = Price or rental of capital
K = Capital
L = Labor
B = Total budget of the bureau. This can be written in the form $B = R(Q)$. Following Niskanen, this says that the total budget of the bureau is assumed to be a function of output. Recall that Niskanen's crucial insight lies in his development of the superior monopoly powers of public agencies. This power exists because the bureau offers a total output in exchange for a budget, whereas a market organization offers units of output at a price. Since $Q = f(K,L)$ then $B = R[f(K,L)]$.

The utility maximization problem can be set up in the following fashion.

(1)   MAX: $U = U(Q,L)$
(2)   Subject to $R[f(K,L)] = wL + rK$

Condition (1) needs no further elaboration. Condition (2) gives the constraint which the bureaucrat must satisfy. Specifically, the bureaucrat is constrained to cover all costs of operation given the budget he is able to obtain from his sponsor.

Using the Langrangian method for problems of constrained maximization, we have:

(1) $\quad \Lambda = U(Q,L) - \lambda(R(Q) - wL - rK) = 0$
(2) $\quad \Lambda = U(Q,L) - \lambda(R[f(K,L)] - wL - rK) = 0$
(3) $\quad \Lambda = U(f(K,L),L) - \lambda(R[f(K,L)] - wL - rK) = 0$

In expression (2), the maximization problem is converted into a choice problem involving two variables, labor and capital. The first order condition for the constrained maximization problem are listed below.

(1) $\quad \dfrac{\partial \Lambda}{\partial K} = U_1 f_K + \lambda R_K - \lambda r = 0$

(2) $\quad \dfrac{\partial \Lambda}{\partial L} = U_1 f_L + U_2 + \lambda R_L - \lambda w = 0$

(3) $\quad \dfrac{\partial \Lambda}{\partial \lambda} = R[f(K,L)] - wL - rK = 0$

where R_k and R_1 denote the value of the marginal products of both capital and labor and U_1 and U_2 are the marginal utilities of output and labor.

These equations can be manipulated to yield an expression which indicates the pattern of resource usage by bureaus. This is given in equation (4). Since

(4) $\quad \dfrac{f_K}{f_L} = \dfrac{r}{\left(w - \dfrac{U_2}{\lambda}\right)}$

λ and U_2 are both greater than zero, we derive the implication that

(5) $\quad \dfrac{f_K}{f_L} \neq \dfrac{r}{w}.$

Interpretation of the First Order Condition

The implication of equation (4) is that the bureau will hire inputs in an inefficient combination. This is because the condition for optimal input usage requires that the ratio of the marginal products of labor and capital to be equal to ratio of their prices. This condition is not fulfilled in the extended model because both λ and U_2 will be most likely greater than zero.

One interpretation of λ, is that it registers the change in the objective function with respect to a small change in the constraining equation. In the extended model, this means that λ gives the marginal utility of output and labor for a small change in the budget. Given that the bureau is limited to the quantities of both labor and output it can choose, it would be reasonable to assume that it has not reached the satiation point for either variable. As a consequence, we would expect λ to be greater than zero. For the same reason U_2 or the marginal utility of labor will also be greater than zero.

The equilibrium result sketched above is a consequence of the fact that labor is both an input and preference variable. This means that labor will be chosen in quantities beyond the point where the value of the marginal product of labor is equal to its price. An implication of this result is that the labor to capital ratio (L/K) will be greater in a bureaucratic institution supplying the same service and facing approximately the same demand condition as profit maximizing firms.

The effect of bureau supply on the labor-capital ratio is shown in the equations below where it is assumed that the production function is Cobb-Douglas.

(1) $$X = L^{1-\theta} K^\theta$$

(2) $$\frac{\partial X}{\partial L} = (1 - \theta) L^{-\theta} K^\theta$$

(3) $$\frac{\partial X}{\partial K} = \theta L^{1-\theta} K^{\theta-1}$$

(4) $$\frac{MPP_L}{MPP_K} = \frac{K}{L} \frac{(1 - \theta)}{\theta}$$

Equation (4) yields a relation which expresses the labor-capital ratio as a function of the ratio of the marginal products of labor and capital. For a profit maximizing firm:

$$\frac{MPP_K}{MPP_L} = \frac{r}{w}.$$

So the equilibrium labor-capital ratio becomes:

$$\frac{L}{K} = \frac{w}{r} \left(\frac{1 - \theta}{\theta} \right).$$

By contrast, the bureau hires labor and capital such that:

$$\frac{MPP_K}{MPP_L} = \frac{r}{\left(w - \dfrac{U_2}{\lambda} \right)}.$$

So the equilibrium labor-capital ratio becomes:

$$\frac{L}{K} = \frac{r}{\left(w - \dfrac{U_2}{\lambda} \right)} \left(\frac{1 - \theta}{\theta} \right).$$

Since $\lambda > 0$, and $U_2 > 0$, it follows that a bureau supplying the same service, faced by the same demand condition and subject to the same input-price ratio will use a greater labor-capital ratio compared to a profit maximizing firm. This will be true for any linear-homogeneous or homothetic production function.

Comparative Statics

The extended model also contains comparative static implications different from the standard profit maximization models. For example, the bureaucrat's response to a decrease in the price of capital will have an ambiguous effect on the labor-capital ratio. To see this, consider the equation for the equilibrium labor-capital ratio:

(1) $$\frac{L}{K} = \frac{r}{\left(w - \dfrac{U_2}{\lambda}\right)} \left(\frac{1-\theta}{\theta}\right).$$

This can be further simplified to:

$$\frac{K}{L} = \frac{w\theta}{r(1-\theta)} - \frac{U_2\theta}{\lambda r(1-\theta)}.$$

Taking the partial derivative of K/L with respect a change in (r), the price of capital, we have:

$$\frac{\partial\left(\dfrac{K}{L}\right)}{\partial r} = \frac{\theta(1-\theta)(U_2 - \lambda w)}{\lambda[r(1-\theta)]^2}$$

The response of (K/L) to a change in (r) is ambiguous since (U_2) and $(-\lambda w)$ are of opposite signs. If (U_2) is greater than (λw) and (r) falls, the capital-labor ratio will fall also. This implies that a reduction in the price of capital may actually induce the use of more labor relative to capital.

The partial derivative of (K/L) to a change in (w) is greater than zero.

$$\frac{\partial\left(\dfrac{K}{L}\right)}{\partial w} = \frac{\theta}{1-\theta} > 0$$

Thus, the bureaucrat responds to wage rate changes in a manner similar to a profit maximizing firm.

The response of the bureau to other changes in the environment such as demand shocks is not unambiguous. Migue and Belanger's analysis suggests that bureaus become relatively more production inefficient as the budget of the bureau expands. This effect is shown in Figure 6 below. The positively sloped expansion path is the comparative static

Figure 6

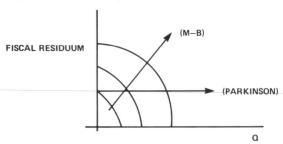

response of M-B's bureau over budgets of different size. The M-B model predicts that larger bureaus become relatively more production inefficient.[21] Assuming that fiscal residuum is labor biased, this would imply larger (L/K) as the bureau expands. By contrast, Parkinson's studies of bureaucracies indicate that the negatively sloped expansion path is representative of bureau behavior. Recall that his case studies showed that bureaus which experienced large cuts in their budgets actually expanded staff size. Thus, greater (L/K) may be associated with smaller budgets.

An account of the Parkinson expansion path is given by Niskanen.[22] He suggests that as the demand for a bureau's services fall, demand becomes relatively inelastic. If this is the case, then bureaus would be predicted to become relatively more production inefficient[23] and consequently, exhibit higher (L/K) as the demand for their services falls.

As yet, no real explanation has emerged to account for the slope of the expansion path of a bureau. However, it is quite possible that the Parkinson path is the most likely result. This is possible because of the process by which bureaus are monitored. This effect is explained below.

Most literature on the budgetary process suggests that budgeting is incremental.[24] This means that, except for uncommon events, bureaus experience only small increments or decrements in their budgets. It is argued that appropriations committees have time only to look at marginal adjustments in budgets and find it unfeasible to assess the entire budget of the bureau. This means that rational congressmen would spend most of their time monitoring those bureaus with the largest budgets since these bureaus would experience the largest marginal effects. Consequently, it might be predicted that the larger the bureau the more likely it will be monitored and the smaller the margin for slack (production inefficiency). Thus, we would expect the expansion path to be Parkinsonian.

An implication of the above is that smaller bureaus face more inelastic

21. See Migue and Belanger [19], p. 13.
22. Niskanen [22], p. 72.
23. In other words, per unit costs rise.
24. See Wildavsky [30].

demands (as Niskanen suggests without explanation). The total budget can be considered to be one giant political package which serves to help the reelection of incumbent congressmen. Each bureau's budget can be considered an input to this package. Clearly the smaller the contribution of an input to the total package, the more inelastic its demand.

An Overview of the Model

The extended model of bureaucracy is based upon Niskanen's critical assumption that public bureaus possess the monopoly power of a perfect price discriminator. Unlike Niskanen's model, but along the lines suggested by M-B, this model assumes that bureaucrats have preferences for above minimum cost expense. Unlike M-B, the model assumes that bureaucrats exhibit preferences for particular types of inputs. Following the lead of Borcherding, Bush, Spann, Marris, Parkinson, and Williamson, it is assumed that bureaucrats exhibit a bias for staff and related expense (as well as for output).

The model predicts that per unit costs of bureau supply will be greater than that of a profit maximizing firm supplying the same service. The model suggests that the output of a bureau will be greater than that of a firm facing the same demand curve. Finally, it is predicted that the labor-capital ratio will be greater for bureaus supplying the same service and facing the same demand curve as a profit maximizing firm.

The results of the model are summarized in Figure 7. For purposes of simplicity, the following assumptions are made. First, it is assumed that labor is a variable cost, and a preference variable for the bureau. Secondly, it is assumed that the firm and the bureau face the same demand relation. Thirdly, for ease of exposition constant per unit costs are assumed. Lastly, it is assumed that, in the short run, capital is a fixed factor. The extended model suggests that the equilibrium output of the bureau will be at Q_3. Further, the bureau will produce above minimum marginal cost by hiring extra staff and associated expense $[ABCD]$. By contrast, the profit maximizing firm will produce in the interval $[Q_1 - Q_2]$ depending upon the degree of competition in the market and will produce at minimum

Figure 7

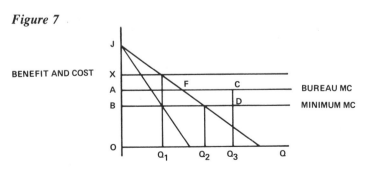

marginal costs. Finally, a nonprofit institution selling output on a per unit basis will produce in the interval $[Q_1 - Q_2]$ depending upon competition. The nonprofit institution, if it is operated to maximize managerial utility, may produce output at a marginal cost as high as (OX) depending upon the slope of manager's indifference curve between staff and output.

The following important results emerge. First, the bureau will produce a larger output compared to any of the other institutional firms. Second, the bureau will have a larger labor-capital ratio than any of the other institutional forms. Finally, except for special cases associated with the nonprofit institution, the bureau will produce at higher per unit costs and operate with less capital per unit of output than any of the other institutional forms.

Economic Theories of Bureaucracy: Empirical Results

Three economic models of bureaucracy have been presented. These are the Niskanen, Migue and Belanger, and De Alessi-Parkinson models. The Niskanen model can be distinguished from the latter two models on the basis of cost and productivity comparisons; it predicts that bureaus will operate in a production efficient manner, whereas the latter two models predict that bureaus will be production inefficient. Finally, the M-B and De Alessi-Parkinson models can be distinguished on the basis of input utilization. The De Alessi-Parkinson model predicts that bureaucrats will use labor-biased production techniques. The M-B model is input neutral.

Three sets of empirical results are presented. The first two sets of data are productivity and cost comparisons. These studies show that public agencies operate at costs above private alternatives and exhibit slow or negative changes in productivity growth. These results suggest that the M-B and De Alessi-Parkinson models may be better predictors of bureau behavior than the Niskanen model. Finally, the third set of data provides a comparison of input utilization between privately and publicly controlled institutions of higher learning. These studies indicate that publicly controlled institutions use labor-biased techniques of production, which is a result in accord with the input choice model.

Productivity Studies

Productivity measurement in the public sector is a relatively new research topic for economists. There are not many studies in this area currently available. One of the first attempts to examine productivity in state and local governments was made by Bradford, Malt, and Oates

[9]. The authors attempt to measure the rate of productivity change in four local governments services, education, police, fire, and hospitals.

The authors' studies of primary and secondary public education indicate that the rate of input expansion exceeded the increase in the number of pupils. This implies that productivity change was negative in the education sector and was reflected in the cost of a unit of education which rose relatively to the costs of other goods and services at a rate of 5.3% per year.

Their data on public hospitals indicate costs have risen at a rapid pace, and hospital employees per 100 patients have almost doubled in nineteen years between 1946 and 1965. Surely some of this cost increase represents quality increase, but it is doubtful that these quality increases are of the same order and magnitude as the cost increases.

Finally, in examining both per capita expenditures on police and fire services and employment per capita, Bradford, Malt, and Oates found that cost per capita rose faster than the wholesale price index and that police and fire employment per capita was constant, or rose slightly between 1954 and 1963. These findings indicate that the rate of productivity in fire and police is much less than productivity gains in the private sector.

Along these same lines, Robert Spann performed a comprehensive study of productivity trends in state and local governments. Spann computes changes in labor output ratios between 1962 and 1967 for six state and local government services. His primary conclusions were:

(a) The rate of productivity gain appears to be zero or negative, on average, for the state and local services examined.

(b) During the period 1962–1968, almost twenty-five percent of the growth in per capita costs of state and local government expenditures not due to increases in the general cost of living was due to a zero rate of productivity gain in the public sector.

(c) During the period 1962–1967, productivity gain appears to have been least (or productivity losses the greatest) in small states with low levels of government expenditures in 1962 and large numbers of local governments per capita in that year.

Productivity studies have been performed at the federal level also. These studies indicate that the federal government has experienced some productivity gain. These gains are overshadowed by two factors. First, the method used in computing output indices for the federal government is spurious to say the least.[25] The OMB uses close to 114 output indices.

25. See Civil Service Commission [10].

Some of these indices are in money terms and are not properly deflated for inflation; next, a good portion of the indices are not actually measures of output but are dubious proxies. For example, the number of requisitions purchased and customer orders filled is a widely used index. Yet, the number or volume of these items does not necessarily have a strong relation to actual output produced. Thus, productivity indices used for the federal government must be regarded as a crude upper bound estimate.

Second, there is the problem of relevant comparison. Some have made the argument that public bureaus are labor intense and are similar to the service subsector of our economy.[26] It is argued that the service subsector is a nonprogressive sector since there is not much opportunity for capital accumulation. This may well be true for the service sector. Available data indicates that capital per unit of worker in this sector is very low relative to the manufacturing sector of our economy.[27] However, computations for the federal sector reveal that capital per unit of worker is almost twice as high as an average of manufacturing industries and almost ten times higher than the service subsector. An illustration is provided in Table 1.

These computations imply that the relevant productivity comparison should be made between the federal sector and the manufacturing sector of our economy. This is done in Table 2. The chart indicates that the federal government lags behind the manufacturing sector in registered

Table 1. Sector differential trend in capital per worker from book values in current $.

Capital per worker	
Industry	12,030
Service	4,380
Fed. govt. (excl. DOD)	28,252
Fed. govt. (incl. DOD)	50,232

Sources: Victor R. Fuchs, *The Service Economy* (New York: National Bureau of Economic Research, 1963); and U.S. Congress, House Committee on Government Operation, Federal Real and Personal Property Inventory report, June 30, 1964.

Note: Ratios for the private sector were computed for 1960. Ratios for the Federal Govt. were computed for 1963. Book value of fixed assets per employee, 311,000 manufacturing firms 1964 (10,188), 1968 (12,407).

26. See Baumol [4].
27. See Fuchs [14].

Table 2. Productivity in the federal sector.

	Unit labor costs (1967-base year)		Output per man hour (1967-base year)	
	Federal govt.	Manufacturing	Federal govt.	Manufacturing
1967	100.0	100.0	100.0	100.0
1968	102.5	102.3	101.8	104.7
1969	108.5	106.6	103.4	106.9
1970	117.5	112.5	106.4	108.1

Source: Economic Report of the President (Feb., 1971).

productivity gain by a fairly significant amount even when it is realized that the productivity index for the federal government is probably a serious over-estimate.

Cost Comparison

In this section, a survey of comparative efficiency studies of public bureaus and private firms supplying the same service is presented. These studies provide a relatively rare opportunity to study bureau behavior because many times it is difficult to make such comparisons. One reason is that bureaus to a considerable extent have monopolies over the production of particular items. Second, when bureaus do compete with private suppliers relative price comparisons are misleading since bureaus are financed by tax revenues and consequently charge prices below true costs.

D. G. Davies [12] performed an empirical test on airlines in Australia. This test is quite remarkable in that it provided one of the relatively rare cases where a private firm and a bureau provided virtually identical services. Australia has two trunk airlines, Trans-Australian, a bureau, and Anset Australian National Airways, a private firm. Government policy is purposely designed to make these airlines similar in many important aspects. The government forces the airlines to fly similar routes, make similar ports of call, be treated equally with respect to airport facilities, to charge equal prices, and to use similar aircraft.

The data clearly indicate that the private airline is more efficient than the public airline. Consider Table 3, which reproduces some of Davies's findings. The exhibit demonstrates that the productivity of the private airline is in all cases greater than the public airline and in some cases over twice as efficient. According to Davies's study substitution of private production for public production would reduce costs by at least thirteen percent.

Table 3. Ansett productivity measures divided by TAA productivity measures × 100.

Year	Freight and mail	Passengers	Revenue
1958–59	242	130	117
1959–60	236	119	111
1960–61	242	148	123
1961–62	234	135	114
1962–63	236	124	110
1963–64	229	118	112
1964–65	242	123	113
1965–66	227	120	116
1966–67	202	110	109
1967–68	177	108	109
1968–69	179	110	112
Mean	204	122	113

Source: D. G. Davies, "The Efficiency of Public versus Private Firms," *Journal of Law and Economics* 14 (April, 1971).

Roger Ahlbrandt [1] tests for the relative efficiency of public and private fire companies. Data was gathered from cities and fire districts in the Seattle–King County area and from additional cities within the state of Washington. The fire departments studied included 14 operated entirely by volunteers, 22 by a combination of fully-paid and volunteer personnel and eight staffed by a fully-paid force. Population ranged from 900 to 536,000 and area serviced from 1.5 to 102 square miles. From this sample, Ahlbrandt devised an empirical cost equation where per capita cost of fire provision is made a function of quantity variables — population, geographic size, etc. — and quality variables where fire insurance classification is used as a proxy. Data were than obtained for a privately operated fire department serving Scottsdale, Arizona. Ahlbrandt used his empirical cost function of bureaucratic supply in Seattle to simulate costs of bureau production in Scottsdale. His estimates, which were statistically significant at the .9 level of confidence, indicate that if a bureau were to supply fire services in Scottsdale costs would be approximately twice as high.

Empirical studies have been made in the area of sanitation. This area of research is interesting because private enterprises often compete with public bureaus in providing sanitation service. Ralph Stone and Company performed a test for efficiency in garbage collection between public and private organizations. The Stone Survey covers 85 cities. The major results are reproduced in Table 4. The Stone Survey indicates that private suppliers are significantly more efficient than public agencies.

Table 4. Efficiency in garbage collection.

Public vs. private collection	Tons collected per man day	Tons collected per $1000	Residences served
Public	4.3	104	62.8
Standard deviation	2.3	53.7	32.8
Number of cities	74	71	78
Private	9.6	216	73
Standard deviation	1.9	127	23
Number of cities	6	6	5
Significant difference	Yes	Yes	No

Source: Ralph Stone and Company Survey of 85 Municipal Governments. Study can be found in *1973 Municipal Yearbook.*

Along the same lines, Robert Spann, using data from 56 cities with population between 24,000 and 400,000 in the states of Pennsylvania, New York, and Delaware, estimates labor requirements for garbage collection as a function of ownership, population, population diversity, number of trucks used, and a frequency of collection variable. His results indicate that use of a public sanitation department increases garbage employees by 97.26 percent. Spann also noted a study completed by the planning board in Monmouth County, New Jersey. The results of that study indicate that communities using private contractors have significantly lower costs. The average per capita costs of garbage collection was $8.33 for cities with municipal sanitation and $5.84 for cities using private contractors. Hence, public costs are almost 70% higher.

An Empirical Analysis of Private and Public Universities and Colleges

The previous studies indicate that private suppliers are always more efficient than public suppliers. This suggests that considerable slack exists in public agencies. In the M-B model, slack is input neutral, but as mentioned previously, a considerable literature exists which indicates that expense for the staff function is a preference variable. This implies that staff inputs would be used in greater proportion in a public production process as compared to private firms supplying the same service.

From section 2, the equilibrium factor use combination for the De Alessi-Parkinson model (assuming a Cobb-Douglas production function) is:

$$(1) \qquad \left(\frac{L}{K}\right)^* = \frac{\theta}{1-\theta}\left(\frac{w - \dfrac{U_2}{\lambda}}{r}\right).$$

The equilibrium factor use condition for a profit maximizer, however, is:

$$(2) \qquad \left(\frac{L}{K}\right)^{**} = \frac{\theta}{1-\theta}\left(\frac{w}{r}\right)$$

where

$$\left(\frac{L}{K}\right)^{*} > \left(\frac{L}{K}\right)^{**}.$$

The results above imply that a bureaucrat, who conforms to the De Alessi-Parkinson model, uses a higher labor to capital ratio, *ceterus paribus,* than the Niskanen or M-B bureaucrat. The Niskanen model predicts that bureaucrats will generally be production efficient in order to generate the largest possible output. Thus, the Niskanen bureaucrat will use the production efficient labor-to-capital ratio (equation [2]). The M-B model assumes that bureaucrats reap utility from residuum and output, but M-B do not specify the manner by which residuum is extracted. Consequently, the M-B model is input neutral.

In order to empirically discriminate amongst the three models, an empirical study of resource utilization for publicly and privately controlled colleges and universities was performed. This sample allows for an inspection of staff-to-capital ratios by state and by control of institution, and thus the study allows for a test of the hypothesis that public bureaus overstaff (especially at the state and local levels).

Private colleges and universities are largely nonprofit institutions, but the bulk of their finances came from tuition charges. Thus, private colleges and universities net most of their revenues by selling educational services at a per unit price. By contrast, public colleges and universities receive most of their budget through the "back-door." That is, they receive their finances via tax revenues bargained for through the legislative process. Consequently, the public institution enjoys the superior monopoly advantage afforded a perfect price discriminator.

Private colleges and universities must compete on the basis of the per unit price and quality of the services they offer. Further, substantial competition exists in this market. Public colleges and universities, for the most part, do not compete on the basis of price. The prices they charge are nominal and much lower than the prices charged by private institutions because the bulk of their finances are tax revenues collected from the public. Moreover, the low prices charged by public colleges and institutions are usually restricted to individuals within the particular constituency financing the public colleges or university. This has the effect of insulating the public college or university from serious regional competition from other public and private sources.

An additional factor contributing to a labor bias in publicly controlled colleges and universities in their status as state and local units. Overstaffing can provide larger budgets by adding to the voting power of the bureaucratic bloc. The greater the number of bureaucrat-voters, the larger the political power of public agencies. This effect becomes magnified at the state and local levels where the constituency is much smaller relative to the number of bureaucrats than at the federal level, and may explain why the federal government is relatively capital intense.[28]

Given the above considerations, the prediction which emerges is that the private college or university is under a greater constraint to use the optimal mix of inputs. Further, the superior monopoly advantage enjoyed by the public college or university would enable it to use factor combinations which maximize the utility of the bureaucrats that operate these institutions. This would imply that a strong overstaffing bias would be evident at the public level of provision.

Empirical Results From the College and University Sample

In order to test the propositions derived above, an empirical analysis of capital to staff input ratios is performed on thirty-one states by control of institution (public versus private) for the year 1968.[29] A large part of the data used was published by the National Education Center.

The center publishes data on the capital holdings of most of the colleges and universities in the United States. Capital is measured in value terms (current dollars) and in physical terms (in square feet). The center also publishes data with respect to employment in these same institutions.[30] The employment data make it possible to measure the number of professional staff members hired by the state and by control of institution. Additionally, an index of salaries or wages paid to professional staff was computed from pay scales published annually in the AAUP bulletin.

The sample above makes it possible to regress capital-to-staff ratios by state on the relative price of capital and staff by state and as a function of control of institution. The value of capital holdings was divided by capital holdings in square feet in order to generate a price index for capital. The relative price index was then computed by dividing the capital

28. See De Alessi [13].
29. Data for the test were obtained from the National Center for Educational Statistics [20 and 21].
30. For some states the Center's capital data were more comprehensive (covered more institutions) than its data set for staff. In these cases it was possible to identify the non-respondents. Enrollment figures for the nonrespondents were then obtained and staff figures were computed on the basis of student-faculty ratios. A student-faculty ratio of nineteen was used for public institutions and a student-faculty ratio of twelve was used for the private institutions. The student-faculty ratios were computed on the basis of national enrollment and faculty aggregates published by the Center.

prices, derived above, by an index of the average salary for a professional staff member for each state. Thus, it is possible to compute an index for the relative price of capital to staff by state. Last, although the data makes it possible to compute capital-labor ratios for each of the thirty-one states by control of institution (public versus private), the data was not sufficiently disaggregated to compute the ratios for each separate institution.

The estimating equation used in this analysis is:

$$Y = a_0 + a_1 X_1 + a_2 + X_2$$

where:

$$Y = ln \ (K/L)_1^{Pub.}, \ldots, \ ln \ (K/L)_{31}^{Pub.} \ ln \ (K/L)_1^{Pvt.}, \ldots \ ln \ (K/L)_{31}^{Pvt.}$$
$$X_1 = 1, \ldots 1, 0, \ldots, 0$$
$$\quad\quad 31 \times 1 \quad\ \ 31 \times 1$$
$$X_2 = ln \ RP_1, \ldots ln \ RP_{31}, \ ln \ RP_1, \ldots \ ln \ RP_{31}.$$

For ease of economic interpretation this equation can be rewritten as:

(1) $$ln \left(\frac{K}{L}\right)^j = a_0 + a_1 \ C_j + a_2 \ ln \ RP_{c'}$$

where

$$\stackrel{c}{\stackrel{}{\scriptstyle i} } = 1; \ldots 31; j = \text{Pub., pvt.,} \ c_{\text{public}} = 1; \ C_{\text{private}} = 0.$$

The other variables are defined as follows. K equals total nonhousing capital holdings in square feet by control of institution (public versus private) and by state. L equals the volume of professional staff members by control of institution and by state. RP measures the relative price of labor to capital by state. It is assumed that administrators, whether public or private, face the same rental rate on capital in each state. Likewise, it is assumed that administrators, whether public or private face the same wage rate with respect to faculty and other professional staff in each state. These assumptions should not be overly restrictive. For example, the estimated difference in wage rates for staff in public versus private colleges was $364.74, a rather small amount. The results of the estimation procedure are presented below. T-statistics are in parentheses below the estimated coefficients.

$$ln \ (K/L) = a_0 + a_1 \ C + a_2 \ ln \ RP$$
$$= 4.069 - .33621 \ C - .31384 \ ln \ RP$$
$$\quad\quad (8.461) \quad (2.146) \quad\quad (7.080)$$
$$R^2 = .4820,$$
$$R^2 = .6943,$$
$$F = 27.452,$$
$$N = 62, \text{d.f.} = 59.$$

For purposes of interpretation this equation can be rewritten as the following two equations.

$$ln\ (K/L)^{Pub.}_i = (a_0 + a_1) + a_2\ ln\ RP_i$$
$$= 3.633 - .31384\ ln\ RP_i;$$

and,

$$ln\ (K/L)^{Pri.}_i = a_0 + a_2\ ln\ RP_i,$$
$$= 4.069 - .31384\ ln\ RP_i.$$

The coefficient a_2 indirectly measures the elasticity of substitution. That is, σ equals $(a_2)^{-1}$. Thus, $\sigma = 1/(-.3138) = -3.15$. The two equations above can be used to measure the size of the labor bias effect – the effect of public versus private control for a given relative price of capital. Subtracting $ln\ (K/L)^{Pvt.}$ from $ln\ (K/L)^{Pub.}$ gives:

$$ln\ (K/L)^{Pub.}_i - ln\ (K/L)^{Pvt.}_i = a_1.$$

Or,

$$ln\ \frac{(K/L)^{Pub.}_i}{(K/L)^{Pvt.}_i} = a_1.$$

Taking the anti-log of both sides and rearranging gives:

$$(K/L)^{Pub.}_i = e^a 1\ (K/L)^{Pvt.}_i,$$
$$= .72\ (K/L)^{Pvt.}_i.$$

Rearranging to get a measure of labor bias gives:

$$(L/K)^{Pub.}_i = 1.4\ (L/K)^{Pvt.}_i.$$

In words, this equation states that for the same RP_i, the public colleges in a state would be expected to employ roughly 40% more labor than the private colleges for the same size capital stock. This result, coupled with the fact that there appears to be little, if any, statistical difference in the relative price ratios faced by public and private colleges, buttresses the position that the labor bias estimated for public colleges and universities is due to behavioral reasons associated with difference in ownership.

Summary

In sum, we have hypothesized that public colleges and universities are operated by administrators who are utility maximizers and that the fiscal residuum generated by these organizations will be used, to a considerable extent, for overstaffing. An empirical test was performed on public versus private colleges and universities. The results of this test show that public colleges and universities operate with significantly greater labor to capital ratios. An implication of this empirical result is that bureaucrats, especially at the state and local level of government, have a strong inclination to overstaff. This suggests that bureaucrats use inefficient methods of production as the M-B model indicates, and such methods of production will be labor-biased as the input preference model implies.

References

1. Ahlbrandt, Roger. "An Empirical Analysis of Private and Public Ownership and the Supply of Municipal Fire Services." *Public Choice* 16 (fall, 1973).
2. Alchian, A., and H. Demsetz. "Production, Information Costs and Economic Organization." *American Economic Review* (Dec., 1972).
3. _____, and R. Kessel. "Competition, Monopoly and the Pursuit of Money." In National Bureau of Economic Research, *Aspects of Labor Economics*. Princeton, N.J.: Princeton University Press, 1962. Pp. 157–175.
4. Baumol, W. J. *Business Behavior, Value and Growth*. New York: The Macmillan Company, 1959.
5. Berle, A. A., and G. C. Means. *The Modern Corporation and Private Property*. New York: Commerce Clearing House, Inc., 1932.
6. Blau, P. *The Dynamics of Bureaucracy*. Chicago: University of Chicago Press, 1955.
7. Borcherding, Thomas E. "One Hundred Years of Public Spending." Chap. 2 in this volume.
8. _____, W. C. Bush, and R. M. Spann. "The Effects on Public Spending of the Divisibility of Public Outputs in Consumption, Bureaucratic Power, and the Size of the Tax-Sharing Group." Chap. 12 in this volume.
9. Bradford, D. F., R. A. Malt, and W. E. Oates. "The Rising Cost of Local Public Services: Some Evidence and Reflections. *National Tax Journal* (June, 1969).
10. Civil Service Commission, General Accounting Office and Office of Management and Budget. *Measuring and Enhancing Productivity in the Federal Sector*. Prepared for the Joint Economic Committee of the Congress of the United States. Washington, D.C.: U.S. Government Printing Office, 1972.
11. Crozier, M. *The Bureaucratic Phenomenon*. Chicago: University of Chicago Press, 1964.
12. Davies, D. G. "The Efficiency of Public versus Private Firms." *Journal of Law and Economics* 14 (April, 1971).
13. De Alessi, Louis. "Implications of Property Rights for Government Investment Choices." *American Economic Review* 59 (March, 1969).
14. Fuchs, Victor F. *The Service Economy*. New York: National Bureau of Economic Research, 1963.
15. Kamerschen, D. R. "The Influence of Ownership and Control on Profit Rates." *American Economic Review* 58 (June, 1968).
16. Marris, R. *The Economic Theory of Managerial Capitalism*. New York: Free Press, 1964.
17. Martin, Roscoe C. "The Municipal Electorate: A Care Study." *Southwestern Social Science Quarterly* (Dec., 1933).
18. Meyer, Marshall W. "Two Authority Structures of Bureaucratic Organization." *Administration Science Quarterly* 13, no. 2 (Sept., 1968).

19. Migue, J. L., and G. Belanger. "Toward a General Theory of Managerial Discretion." *Public Choice* 17 (spring, 1974).
20. National Center for Educational Statistics, U.S. Office of Education. *Inventory of Physical Facilities: Institutions of Higher Learning, 1968.* Washington, D.C.: Superintendent of Documents Catalogue, U.S. Government Printing Office, 1971.
21. _____. *Employment Characteristics; Institutions of Higher Learning, 1968.* Washington, D.C.: Superintendent of Documents Catalogue, U.S. Government Printing Office, 1971.
22. Niskanen, William A. *Bureaucracy and Representative Government.* Chicago: Aldine-Atherton, 1971.
23. Parkinson, C. Northcote. *Parkinson's Law and Other Studies in Administration.* New York: Ballantine Books, 1957.
24. Scitovsky, Tibor. "A Note on Profit Maximization and Its Implications." *Review of Economic Studies* 40 (1943): 57–60.
25. Spann, R. M. "Rates of Productivity Change and the Growth of Local Government Expenditure." Chap. 6 in this volume.
26. Tullock, Gordon. *The Politics of Bureaucracy.* Washington, D.C.: Public Affairs Press, 1965.
27. Von Mises, L. *Bureaucracy.* New Haven, Conn.: Yale University Press, 1944, Pp. 94–97.
28. Weber, M. *The Theory of Social and Economic Organization.* New York: Oxford University Press, 1947.
29. Whyte, W. F. *Man and Organization: Three Problems in Human Relations in Industry.* Homewood, Ill. Richard D. Irwin, 1959.
30. Wildavsky, Aaron. *The Politics of the Budgeting Process.* Boston: Little, Brown and Co., 1964.
31. Williamson, Oliver E. *The Economics of Discretionary Behavior: Managerial Objectives in a Theory of the Firm.* Englewood Cliffs, N.J.: Prentice Hall, Inc., 1964.

14. Reopening the Question of Government Spending   *Cotton M. Lindsay and Don Norman*

The idea that different results obtain when activities are privately and governmentally organized is at least as old as political economy itself. Equally venerable is the notion which holds that government can therefore be thought of as too little or too large. Economists have not been singularly successful in giving substance to these intuitions, however. This paper surveys and reconsiders these arguments.

Treatment of this question has not been uniform in its various dimensions including, for example, the criteria by which the adequacy of a government budget is to be judged. Almost every government project involves taking from some who do not benefit and extending benefits to those who bear none of the costs. We would predict nontaxpayer beneficiaries of government spending to view budgets as "too small" and taxpaying nonbeneficiaries to regard them as "too large." Resolution of this question depends ultimately on the manner in which conflicting interests in society are to be resolved. Economists are of many minds on this issue.

Ambiguity does not end there, however. The issue is also clouded by questions of the composition of the budget and the efficiency with which government output is produced. A budget may contain too little financing of worthy projects and too much support of those projects which are not desired. On the other hand, if a project itself is inefficiently organized, output may be too small while at the same time spending on it is too great.

Finally, there remains the question of government involvement in wealth redistribution. There have been efforts to identify appropriate levels of this activity in terms of its effect on productivity [3 and 7] and in terms of Paretian efficiency [14]. While each of these considerations remains a plausible point of view, neither captures what appears to us to be the essence of the appeal for, nor the defense against, wealth transfer in society. The overriding issues here are ethical and ultimately unyielding before economic analysis. As economists seem to be among those least qualified by popular sanction to render (or presumably comment upon) ethical judgments, the redistributional aspect of government budgets will be ignored. Our remarks will be confined (as are most treatments of this topic) to the size of the budget in a state which already exhibits an appropriate distribution of wealth.

Colin Clark

Perhaps the most widely referenced analysis of this question is found in the writings of Colin Clark. In 1945 Clark argued that efforts to increase the size of government beyond roughly 25 percent of personal income were destined to failure [4]. He claimed that offsetting wage and price inflation would invariably follow such efforts resulting eventually in a decline in the government's share back to the 25 percent level at which it seemed to stabilize. This theory was supported by evidence from the budgetary history of several nations. Clark's explanations for this result in the 1945 paper are, however, sketchy and unsatisfactory.[1]

In a later paper [5] Clark is more explicit about the nature of the underlying factors he perceives to be producing this result. Clark assumes household consumption spending to be habitual and largely insensitive to changes in income and taxation. Changes in tax rates are thus seen to have their most immediate effect on savings. The effect of a tax increase on consumption spending comes only after old habits are broken. An increase in government spending then represents an immediate net addition to aggregate demand causing the price level to rise. If government spending and taxes increase at a faster rate than the growth of productive capacity of the economy, Clark predicts a permanent excess demand, labor shortages, and thus rising prices. In summary, even if increases in government spending are matched by increasing taxes, the effect of expenditures being immediate, while the effect of increasing taxes is delayed, will lead to excess aggregate demand and thus rising prices.

There are a number of problems with Clark's theory. First, even if the mechanics of the process worked as he describes, his theory suggests resistance to *any* increase in government spending. It fails to support the idea of a "barrier" at 25 percent beyond which government cannot grow. Second, empirical work on the determinants of consumption denies the hypothesized irresponsiveness of consumption to taxation. Third, even should such a lag in the adjustment of consumption exist, this predicted "drying up" of savings should inhibit inflation through its effect on investment via increased interest rates. Finally, Clark's predictions cannot be taken seriously today when government's share of the American net national product approaches 40 percent.

Clark's test of the desirability of government expansion is perhaps the simplest of those to be considered. According to his view, it is simply fruitless to attempt to expand government beyond the limit he identified. Increased taxation brings no more resources to government and produces price instability. Other theories, more sanguine regarding the *feasibility* of fiscal expansion, have considered its merits on other grounds. One

---

1. He seems to regard the price level as responsive through the political process to the wishes of different interest groups. Those in favor of monetary expansion are allied against those favoring contraction. At the critical limit at which taxation becomes "excessive," however, there is a "transfer of allegiance from the deflationary to the inflationary side on the part of a number of politicians, bankers, economists and others sufficient to alter the balance of power." It is not made clear why this occurs at 25% or, more importantly, why this coalition does not simply vote to reduce taxes.

possibility is to adopt the standard grounds implicit in the existing democratic system.

Anthony Downs

This is the approach taken by Anthony Downs [6]. He argues that governments are too small, that they spend too little. The appropriate level, according to Downs, is that amount which a *fully informed* majority of the electorate would adopt. He attempts to demonstrate that, because the electorate is less than fully informed, these taxpayers invariably choose less than this optimum amount of government.

The basis for this model is an axiom that political parties are primarily motivated by the desire to enjoy the income, prestige, and power of being in office. The political party "in power" thus makes both expenditure and tax decisions so as to maximize its chances of winning the next election. Voters are assumed to be rational, i.e., they vote for candidates of parties which best represent their interests. Thus if information about benefits of programs were costless, something approaching Downs's optimum might be expected to emerge from the democratic process.[2]

Downs recognizes, however, that in the real world, individuals make voting decisions on the basis of incomplete information. Quite often the benefits of programs voted on are indirect and not apparent to voters. Moreover, voters often vote, not on just one program, but rather a mix of programs. He argues that the mix of programs will often contain proposals which cause voters to reject the entire bundle, each feeling that the budget, and thus his tax burden, is too large in relation to benefits he will receive from it. Thus Downs concludes that voters will usually undervalue the programs put before them; the result being that the role of government is smaller than it would be in a world of perfect information.

Downs's analysis is not convincing, however. In essence, he asserts that a bias exists in the sort of information which affects voters. He argues that citizens, in reaching their voting decisions are more aware of taxes which reduce their purchasing power than of the "indirect" benefits of government spending. But an equally plausible argument may be made in the opposite direction. It can be argued that many taxes are themselves "indirect" and "hidden," and that almost all tax decisions are made infrequently and are divorced from any particular spending decision. Voters may feel that in supporting particular programs they are receiving "something for nothing," since if the tax receipts are not spent on a project which they favor, they will simply be spent elsewhere. Such behavior would result in a government which is "too large" by Downs's criteria.

2. Indeed, this is trivially true.

Furthermore, evidence now exists which supports this latter construction. In a forthcoming study, Craig Stubblebine reports the results of a survey of voters to determine the accuracy of their perceptions of their share of tax costs of various government programs. He discovered a systematic underestimate of these costs for every program extending across the entire income spectrum. The wealthy as well as the poor are unaware that government programs such as welfare, higher education, and police protection are costing them as much as four to five times what they believe them to be costing.

Economic Efficiency

Few economists have been willing to attach this much importance to existing voting rules in determining expenditure policy. Indeed, some have argued that economic criteria should be considered in determining appropriate democratic voting rules [2]. The explicit application of economic efficiency considerations to the level of government expenditure seems to have originated with A. C. Pigou [19]. He argued that government budgets were of correct size and composition only when the marginal satisfaction to each person of a dollar spent was the same everywhere, both inside and outside of government. As long as the satisfaction to any citizen derived from a dollar spent by the government exceeds that derived from his own spending of the dollar privately then the budget of the government may be viewed as too small (and the citizen in question's own household budget may be viewed as correspondingly too large). Although we are no longer willing to allow economists (unless they are in the government) the license to make interpersonal efficiency judgments (utility comparisons), Pigou's application of the standard efficiency to the size of the government sector still has merit. It is now recognized that as long as the allocation of resources between the public and private sector is inefficient, some shift may be arranged which leaves everyone better off. In principle, it is very difficult to take exception to the norm that such inefficiency should be eliminated.

The application of efficiency criteria to the budgeting issue radically alters the nature of the question analyzed. It shifts the focus of analysis from the size of the budget in the aggregate to individual contributions and benefits. It recognizes that the budget may be simultaneously too large for some taxpayers and too small for others. In terms of economic efficiency the budget may contain too much of one item and too little of another. Economic efficiency is essentially an individualistic yardstick.

As a benchmark for spending policy, however, Pigou's standard is not very helpful. Individual satisfactions regarding either public or private spending are not observable, hence the standard is inapplicable directly. In certain cases, however, individual citizens reveal their satisfactions in their market behavior. The "worth" of government spending on certain projects is revealed in the amount individuals would save on substitute expenditures, were the government project undertaken.

Cost-Benefit Analysis

It is this interpretation of efficiency which lies behind the concept of cost-benefit analysis. Potential government projects are scrutinized to determine whether the benefits derived from their provision are worth their cost in terms of resources which might be diverted to other activities. In essence cost-benefit analysis entails a quantification of expected future costs and benefits which are to result from the adoption of a project, coupled with a conversion of these future values into present values.

Cost-benefit analysis has serious limitations, however. The first, mentioned earlier, is the problem of identifying the value of many government projects. While the benefits of certain government activities may be estimated with considerable precision, the values of others are virtually undiscoverable. This is especially true of projects which yield intangible costs and benefits. These aspects of projects are usually dismissed as unquantifiable thereby lessening the exactitude and objectivity supposedly exhibited by cost-benefit analysis. Activities like pollution abatement and space exploration are examples of projects which are clearly of value to some if not all citizens, but for which we can only speculate as to their value.

Other practical problems of cost-benefit analysis are the choice of the appropriate discount rate and the lack of objectivity of those performing the study. Economists agree that no single discount rate is appropriate to all government projects [13, 1, and 21]. Coupled with this "subjectivity" of the discount rate choice is another problem which further serves to reduce the credence which can be placed in such estimates. Those upon whom government must rely for cost-benefit analysis are rarely disinterested in the results. Bureaus developing these studies often perceive a vital interest in the adoption or rejection of the projects under consideration. By appropriate manipulation of benefits estimation or the discount rate, the attractiveness of such a project may be dramatically altered.

Perhaps the most crippling defect of cost-benefit analysis, however, is that the advice is too general. This approach tells us that certain activities are worthwhile, i.e., that the benefits derived from a flood control project or a new airport exceed the costs. But the same results could quite plausibly follow from cost-benefit calculations applied to the production of automobiles, food, or clothing. All profitable private production is cost effective. The question then becomes which cost effective activities should be privately organized and which should be publically organized. Cost-benefit analysis does not inform this decision. Cost-benefit analysis at best informs us when a project is undesirable. A convincing demonstration that benefits of particular programs are not worth the cost may be interpreted as prima facie evidence that such spending by government is not justified on efficiency grounds. The contrary finding that benefits exceed cost does not indicate that government involvement is warranted, however. Cost-benefit evidence may thus be regarded as necessary but not sufficient grounds for expansion of government activity.

Another way of stating the problem is the following. If economic efficiency is to inform us regarding which activities government is to organize and at what levels, then the theory must say something about the comparative cost of organizing privately and governmentally. For example, a demonstration that the same beneficial activity currently provided by government can be provided at lower cost privately would suggest that government spending, at least in this case, is excessive. The opposite conclusion would, of course, follow from the alternative demonstration. Unfortunately economists have not been particularly successful in these efforts.

Public Goods

The most significant development along these lines has been Samuelson's identification of a class of goods (collective or "public" goods) which, when privately produced for sale, are not purchased in efficient amounts [20]. If the cost of excluding others from enjoyment of such a good prohibits any exclusion, then, it is argued, the private sector produces too little. When exclusion is costless, on the other hand, the private sector produces too much [22]. Many economists have leapt from these arguments to the conclusion that efficiency requires that public goods be produced by governments. Though widely accepted, this view has recently been challenged by Lindsay [16].

First, these demonstrations of "market failure" allude to a caricature of the private sector. Such arguments, at most, demonstrate the superiority of collective rather than individualistic financing of the provision of such goods. They do not even address the question of whether such collective organization exists in the private sector, or whether we should expect collective organization to be any more compatible in a government than in a private environment. Lindsay argues that given a property rights enforcing government, (1) collective organization for the provision of public goods in the private sector is predicted to be spontaneous (i.e., no coercion is necessary), and (2) such private organization will yield efficient amounts.

The exclusion argument featured prominently in much of this discussion is essentially a property rights issue affecting transactions in both public and private goods. Arguments purporting to derive from lack of excludability the implication that government provision of public goods is efficient are fallacious. Government enforcement of the terms of private agreements (including collective agreements involving financing of public goods) is the only apparent role arising from these considerations.

Moreover, as Margolis [17] pointed out at the nascency of the public goods discussion, little state or federal spending can be explained or justified on these grounds since few of the goods or services which these governments provide are public goods. National defense, a plausibly "impure" public good, represents a diminishing proportion of total government outlays, while outlays for ostensibly private goods such as education, income security, transportation, health, and public welfare are coming to dominate government budgets. Outlays on lighthouses are insignificant, and television is privately organized.

Theorizing which focuses on technological properties of goods has failed to date to provide us with plausible advice regarding the efficient size of government. More promising terrain for this sort of exploration may be the nature of allocative decision-making processes in government and in the private sector. The public good discussions of the past two decades have, by their narrow focus on the alleged "market failures" of the private sector, subverted interest from the question which must ultimately be answered if efficiency is to inform us on the appropriate role of government. Those questions are (a) what intrinsic properties does government as an organizational form have that private firms lack? and (b) in what ways do these properties suggest organizational cost advantages for government or the private sector?

Milton Friedman

Friedman is perhaps the best known proponent of the view that government is inferior to the market system as an organizer of economic activity. In his highly influencial book, *Capitalism and Freedom* [8], he argues that government should "play the role of the umpire" in our economic system. Government should limit itself to providing national defense, police services, the court system, and aid to those who are unable to care for themselves.

Though the generation of this list of "appropriate" government activities is largely eclectic, the reasons for Friedman's aversion to increasing government influence in the economy are straightforward. The decision, according to Friedman, on how large the role of government should be comes down to whether we want resources and production directed by the market or the political system. The difference in the outcomes of these processes is predicted on the basis of their differing susceptibility to the influence of special interest groups.

When activity is organized by private markets, the profit motive guides resource owners to employ these resources in their most valuable (hence most efficient) uses. Dollar bids by individual members of society attract resources toward those activities where they contribute most to the value of the economy's output. When the same activity is organized by government, it is not dollar bids which attract resources, but political influence. Interest groups which stand to gain substantially from particular projects organize and bring pressure to bear on decision makers, while the masses of citizens who will bear most of the cost of these programs remain uninformed and therefore unorganized to oppose them.

The beneficiaries stand to gain much through their support; hence well-financed lobbies push for their adoption while the expected loss to the average taxpayer does not warrant the investment of energy, time and resources to mount effective resistance to these programs. The result is that resources are devoted to projects which would not meet a market test of their efficiency, were the activity organized privately.[3]

Those who disagree with Friedman argue that the market is the cause of problems such as monopoly, unemployment, and the extent of inequality of income in this country. If it were not for the government, it is argued, these problems would be worse. In *Capitalism and Freedom* Friedman examines those allegations and finds that typically the problem is political interference with or supersession of the market.

James Buchanan and Gordon Tullock

A similar argument has been advanced by James Buchanan and Gordon Tullock in their now classic book, *The Calculus of Consent* [2]. This pioneering study of democratic processes considers the behavior of representative government where decisions are made on the basis of less than unanimity (usually majority rule). Such decision rules, they argue, lead to an overextension of the public sector in terms of economic efficiency. The argument here is quite close to Friedman's discussed

3. Examples of behavior consistent with Friedman's view are commonplace. See Hirshleifer, DeHaven, and Milliman [12] for a discussion of government handling of water resources and the adoption of economically wasteful but politically attractive water projects. D. Gale Johnson's careful analysis [15] of the agricultural supports program reveals some remarkable examples of results when a politically potent group is able to influence government to promote its interests. For Friedman's own dissection of other "special interest" government programs, see his collected *Newsweek* articles in *An Economist's Protest* [9].

above. Here, however, it is the voting rule rather than the costs of being informed and organizing to influence policy which produce inefficiency. Such results are predicted to obtain even where information and organizational costs are negligible.

Beneficiaries of particular programs (special interests) form coalitions to secure passage of these programs financed at levels beyond the point where marginal benefits cover costs. By virtue of the fact that most taxes are levied on the whole taxpaying population, the beneficiary-coalition bears less than the full cost of incremental additions of these programs. Rationally behaving coalitions of this type may be expected to fund such projects to the point where the marginal benefits just cover the marginal cost to themselves. As the coalition bears only a portion of the cost (part is borne by those who do not benefit at all), political processes are predicted to produce too much of these types of services. Further, as the extent of this "pork-barrel" coalitioning is likely to be inversely related to the proportion of the lawmaking body required for passage of these projects, Buchanan and Tullock argue that adoption of more inclusive decision rules (i.e., rules requiring stronger majorities) are likely to increase the efficiency of budgetary decisions.

William A. Niskanen

One final argument may be considered in terms of conventional efficiency considerations. That is the analysis of William A. Niskanen in his recent book, *Bureaucracy and Representative Government* [18]. His analysis focuses on the behavior of government bureaus in organizing the production of goods and services. He notes that heads of such bureaus cannot keep the profits which accrue to efficient operation and thus have no incentive from this source to operate them efficiently. On the other hand, their prestige, the amenities of office, and often money income itself are positively associated with the size of the bureaucracy which they control. Niskanen argues that, given such influences, budgeting behavior of bureaus may be predicted on the basis of efforts of those in charge to maximize bureau size.

Congress, in purchasing services from any of these bureaus, confronts an effective monopoly intent, not on obtaining maximum profits, but on maximizing the revenue from its sales. Niskanen argues that such behavior, if actually descriptive of bureau behavior, may imply spending at as much as *twice* the amount necessary to provide the level of output of government services currently being produced.

Little testing of the validity of the Niskanen model has yet been performed. Its implications, as is the case for the theories reviewed earlier, carry only the conviction which the reader is willing to invest in the descriptive accuracy of these models. Much more work must be done, particularly in the area of empirical validation, before economists can speak with authority on the question of the comparative efficiency of private and public organization of economic activity.

Decisions will not wait on the development of economic science, however. If one is willing to presume that advice based upon theory alone is superior to no advice at all, then that advice suggests that government is "too large" in efficiency terms. The widespread belief that economic theory supports the proposition that governmental financing of "public" goods is superior to private contractual arrangements for their provision is mistaken. Consideration of governmental decision making regarding both financing and organizing production suggests that governments will "overspend." Both the costs of organizing lobbies to influence legislation and majority rule decision processes of government imply an excess of "pork-barrel" spending on special interests at the expense of the public at large. A large scale voter sampling suggests informational biases which lead taxpayers to underestimate their personal portion of the cost of government programs. These results may imply that, were voters aware of the real cost of such programs, they would demand substantial cut-backs. Finally, the incentive structure within bureaucracy leads us to predict that government *organization of production* is inferior in efficiency terms to private production.

In summary, the theory suggests a rather distressing picture. Governments are predicted to provide inefficient pork-barrel programs to produce excess amounts of those goods providing benefits to all, and to organize the production of everything with an eye toward maximizing its cost.

John Kenneth Galbraith

Analysis of the level of government activity in the economy may not be closed without considering one final and extremely influential discussion of the topic, the "institutionalist view" popularly associated with Ralph Nader and John Kenneth Galbraith, but having antecedents in the writings of Thorstein Veblen and Clarence Ayres. These views obtained wide currency in the early sixties through publication of Galbraith's phenomenally successful *The Affluent Society* [10]. His hypothesis is that a "social imbalance" exists; that private wants are being gratified to satiety and beyond while the government sector is starved of resources. Though superficially similar, the social balance sought by Galbraith is not identical to Pigou's concept of efficient division of resources between government and private sectors. Economic efficiency is defined given individual wants. That is, people's tastes are instrumental in determining the parameters of an efficient organization of economic activity. Without these data the concept of efficiency is meaningless. It is to this particular *Weltanschauung* that Galbraith takes exception. He feels that individuals cannot be relied upon to decide what is best for them. He argues that consumers are victimized by their own susceptibility to the highly developed marketing technology of producers and would be better off if more of their income were taxed away and spent for them by the government.

This position is not debatable. That is, one cannot refute the logic of an argument that social imbalance prevails when the standards of this balance exist — not as objective criteria against which reality is to be measured — but as personally held beliefs in Professor Galbraith's heart. Nevertheless, we may reexamine the rhetoric by which he wishes to convert us to the same faith.

Galbraith attempts to disparage the desire for increasing amounts of private goods with the following arguments. First, he argues that a distinction exists between "necessities" and "luxuries"; that the goods purchased with low income (the former) are more urgent than the items we add as our incomes increase (the latter). Galbraith points out that theorists have developed economic theory in such a way that we can't say, scientifically, at least, that the purchase of chrome hubcaps is less urgent than the purchase of sanitation. The mere statement of this shortcoming of theory does not, of course, fill the lacuna.

Galbraith moves to the rescue by arguing that if income-elastic goods are to have the same urgency placed on their acquisition as "necessities," then demands for them should originate within the individual. Urgency is seen to be associated with innateness in Galbraith's view. "(Wants) cannot be urgent if they must be contrived," he argues. Wants for income-elastic goods are not innate, however, but the creation of producers themselves. Galbraith asserts, "Production only fills a void that it has itself created." This relationship between production and creation of effective demand is labeled the "dependence effect." Galbraith continues, "the fact that wants can be synthesized by advertising, catalyzed by salesmanship and shaped by the discreet manipulation of the persuaders shows that they are not very urgent."

If individuals made truly independent choices between private and governmentally produced output, then, presumably, resources might be allocated between the two sectors in appropriate proportions. The dependence effect operates to prevent such an "independent" choice, however. Galbraith denies that this same phenomenon affects public sector production; only private sector output is advertised and promoted. "Advertising operates exclusively, and emulation mainly, on behalf of privately produced goods and services. Since management and emulative effects operate on behalf of private production, public services will have an inherent tendency to lag behind." The result is social imbalance; resources are devoted to whimsey in the private sector while more urgent needs in the public sector are ignored.

Galbraith believes that it is incumbent on government to redress the social balance. His solution is a system of taxation which automatically makes a pro rata share of increasing income available to the government for this purpose. He calls upon rational liberals to resist tax reductions in the future, even if they seem like they will help the poor, if the tax cuts are at the price of social balance.

When do we know if we have achieved social balance? According to Galbraith there's no way in which we can really tell when an exact balance has been reached, but a precise balance isn't of primary importance. One benefit of an affluent society is that there's considerable margin for error. As long as we are sure there is an imbalance, it's plain we should expand the role of government.

Galbraith's thesis has been criticized on a number of points. Friedrich A. Hayek [11] attacks one of the pillars of Galbraith's analysis: the dependence effect. Hayek contends that very few wants, aside from the desire for food, shelter, and sex, originate within the individual. Most desires are formed by numerous influences associated with the culture in which we live. Hayek agrees with Galbraith that the desire for cars and fur coats is not innate, but asserts that neither are demands for arts, music, and more public parks. All such wants are to some extent conditioned by our culture. Galbraith may want to take the position that more parks are superior to more cars, but he is not justified in using this notion of the dependence effect to do this. According to Hayek, the dependence effect is a complete non sequitur.

Another criticism concerns Galbraith's analysis of advertising. No one questions that advertising is directed towards stimulating demands for products, but Galbraith wishes to argue more than this. Galbraith seeks to convince us that advertising affects demand by operating on tastes directly; that is, by creating wants where none existed previously. There are, of course, other explanations of how advertising affects demand. Advertising has been alleged to provide information to potential purchasers about products offered for sale or to create brand-name capital in the selling firm which serves to reassure purchasers of product quality. As neither of these latter functions represent the sort of wasteful activity depicted by Galbraith's dependence effect, he must be arguing implicitly that most advertising may be explained as want-creating.

This is an empirical question, and Galbraith offers only the most casual evidence. In fact, the argument as he states it is so incomplete that it defies empirical analysis. If firms may create demand for their output simply by advertising, one must ask why any firm or product ever fails when demand might be bolstered by more advertising. Indeed, one must question why firms do not abound in the business of selling highly advertised empty boxes, if advertising alone is sufficient to assure sales. Galbraith would doubtless respond to these queries by replying that a firm's ability to enhance demand for its output is not unconstrained, and that advertising must be directed at *some* germinative and unsatisfied want in the public if it is to be effective. To make these admissions greatly weakens the impact of Galbraith's argument, however.

The constraints on a firm's ability to enhance demand for its product may in fact be the extent to which it can supply potential customers with information which they value pertaining to characteristics and the quality of its product. Such information may include ways in which the product may serve consumers' basic wants more satisfactorily than previously available products. Indeed, it is very easy to interpret Galbraith's comments on advertising in this light, i.e., that some of these advertised products serve to satisfy consumers' desires for emblems of prestige, virility or social rank. And it is Galbraith himself who regards these particular wants as less urgent than those which exist for government services.

If this is really what Galbraith is saying, then we may discard his constructions, both the dependence effect and the concept of social balance, as excess baggage. For all Galbraith is telling us is that he believes that people, if left to spend their own earnings without his advice, will do it unwisely. That primitive societies devote much of their meager resources to the production of baubles and costume, testifies convincingly that such "waste" is not the invention of advertisers. It also shows the absurdity of attempting to construct some urgency-based hierarchy of wants from the budget information of poor and "affluent" societies, as Galbraith wishes us to do. It is not social balance which Galbraith seeks but simply increased government spending of others' money on the amenities which he wishes to see them enjoy.

Concluding Remarks

This paper has attempted to deal with the question of the "adequacy" of government financing from several points of view. That vantage point occupying the largest part of our discussions applies the test of economic efficiency to spending proposals. Economic theory and the concept of efficiency offer no "answer" to this question. Theory can tell us only whether to expect particular institutional arrangements to foster "efficient" allocation of resources where efficiency is defined in objective, not normative, terms. Whether efficiency is a suitable objective of government policy, each reader must decide for himself.

Several theories were considered from this point of view. The technological properties of goods were considered as having some relevance to a theory of what activities are efficient for governments to engage in. It was noted that conventional arguments to this effect (i.e., that "publicness" in goods implies government financing) were defective.

Government budgeting was also considered from the point of view of the allocative processes of democratic government. Several theories were considered. The views of Milton Friedman, William Niskanen, James Buchanan, and Gordon Tullock were analyzed. This theoretical analysis suggests the hypothesis that government is inefficiently large in several dimensions. Government is predicted to be producing too much of what it produces and producing that level of services inefficiently (i.e., at higher than necessary cost).

Finally, arguments unrelated to efficiency were considered. The "taxable capacity" theory of Colin Clark was considered wherein it is argued that a sort of natural limit exists on the real size of government as a proportion of net national product. This limit is alleged to operate through the insensitivity of consumer expectations for disposable income to changes in tax rates. This argument was rejected on both theoretical and empirical grounds as was the information cost based argument of Anthony Downs. The Galbraithian thesis of social imbalance was also considered.

There remains to be answered the question of how policy makers and the public may respond to these results. Of major importance is the issue of the validity of these hypotheses which suggest that the budget is too large in efficiency terms. Almost no empirical testing has been done to verify these propositions. Second, there may be overriding ethical or ideological considerations which render the objective of economic efficiency inappropriate in this application. Finally, even if the objective of efficiency is accepted in principle, there remains the question of political viability. Most of the theories suggesting that government is too large infer this outcome to be the result of the normal processes of democratic government, the very institution through which reform is presumably to be achieved. Reform in the direction of more efficient results must therefore take the form of change in these political institutions themselves. Discussion of the sorts of reforms likely to produce these results is beyond the scope of this paper. We may note in closing, however, that the very definition of efficiency implies that reform in this direction may increase the welfare of some without reducing the level of well-being of others. Well designed reform should therefore prove capable of achieving the broadest possible electoral support.

References

1. Baumol, William J. "On the Discount Rate for Public Projects." In *The Analysis of Public Expenditures,* U.S. Congress Joint Economic Committee, 91st Congress, 1st Session, 1 (1969): 489–503.
2. Buchanan, J. M., and G. Tullock. *The Calculus of Consent.* Ann Arbor, Mich.: University of Michigan Press, 1962.
3. Carver, T. N. "The Ethical Basis of Distribution and Its Application to Taxation," *Annals* 6 (July, 1895).
4. Clark, Colin. "Public Finance and Changes in the Value of Money." *Economic Journal* 55 (Dec., 1945): 371–389.
5. _____. *Taxmanship: Principles and Proposals for the Reform of Taxation,* 2nd ed., Hobard Paper 26. Institute of Economic Affairs, Ltd., 1970.
6. Downs, Anthony. *An Economic Theory of Democracy.* New York: Harper & Row, 1957.
7. Edgeworth, F. Y. *Papers Relating to Political Economy,* Vol. 3. London: Macmillan and Co., 1925.
8. Friedman, Milton. *Capitalism and Freedom.* Chicago: University of Chicago Press, 1962.
9. _____. *An Economist's Protest.* Glen Ridge, N.J.: T. Horton, 1972.
10. Galbraith, J. K. *The Affluent Society.* Boston: Houghton Mifflin Co., 1958.
11. Hayek, F. A. "The Non-Sequitur of the 'Dependence Effect.'" *Southern Economic Journal* 27 (April, 1961): 346–348.
12. Hirshleifer, J., J. C. DeHaven, and J. W. Milliman. *Water Supply: Economics, Technology, and Policy.* Chicago: University of Chicago Press, 1960.
13. _____, and D. Shapiro. "The Treatment of Risk and Uncertainty." In *The Analysis and Evaluation of Public Expenditures.* U.S. Congress Joint Economic Committee, 91st Congress, 1st Session, 1 (1969): 505–530.
14. Hochman, H. M., and J. D. Rodgers. "Pareto Optimal Redistribution." *American Economic Review* 59 (Sept., 1969): 542–557.
15. Johnson, D. Gale. *Farm Commodity Programs.* Washington, D.C.: American Enterprise Institute for Public Policy Research, 1973.
16. Lindsay, C. M. "Impurities in the Theory of Public Expenditure." Discussion Paper No. 20, Department of Economics, University of California, Los Angeles (rev. Aug., 1972).
17. Margolis, J. "A Comment on the Pure Theory of Public Expenditure." *Review of Economics and Statistics* 37 (Nov., 1955): 347–349.
18. Niskanen, W. A. *Bureaucracy and Representative Government.* Chicago: Aldine-Atherton, 1971.
19. Pigou, A. C. *The Economics of Welfare,* 4th ed. London: Macmillan and Co., 1932.
20. Samuelson, P. A. "The Pure Theory of Public Expenditure." *The Review of Economics and Statistics* 36 (1954): 387–389.
21. Somers, Harold M. "On the Demise of the Social Discount Rate." *The Journal of Finance* 26 (May, 1971): 565–578.

15. What Is To Be Done? *Gordon Tullock*

It is only relatively recently that economists have turned to the study of bureaucracy and, even now, only a few economists are interested.[1] The cost-benefit ratio on this rather small amount of research has been very favorable, but I think it must be admitted that we still know relatively little about bureaucracy. Nevertheless, it seems sensible to attempt to redesign the institutions to take advantage of what information we now do have while we attempt to increase our knowledge by further research.

The word *bureaucracy* traditionally was a sort of swear-word. Saying that someone was a bureaucrat or that some type of activity was bureaucratic was a criticism, albeit a criticism without any very strong denotative content. On the other hand, many people thought that government agencies were motivated to maximize the public interest. I trust that one aspect of the recent work in bureaucracy and, in particular, this book will be to eliminate both of these myths. If we consider a bureaucracy as simply a fairly large hierarchical organization and make no preliminary assessment of whether it is doing good or ill, we will get further in our understanding of the world.

Looked at in this way, *bureaucracy* is a very general term and covers General Motors, the AFL-CIO, the Postal Service, Virginia Polytechnic Institute and State University, and the Roman Catholic Church. There are some characteristics that all of these organizations share and these are the most general characteristics of bureaucracy. On the other hand, there are differences according to the particular situation in which we find the bureaucracy. It is clear that the Postal Services does not function as efficiently as General Motors. It is highly probable that the Department of Health, Education, and Welfare does not function as efficiently as the Postal Service. It is likely that the Ford Foundation functions less efficiently than any of the above.

Let us, however, put these problems aside for the moment and consider what we know about the broadest conceivable category of bureaucracies. In general, today the bureaucracy is in essence a black box. Like the WANG calculator, we know something about the constraints on it and something about the basic components of which it is manufactured, but we do not understand how they go together. Consider a large corporation. We know that the basic components of its bureaucracy are human

---

1. There is voluminous literature on bureaucracy in sociology and in that branch of political science called public administration. I think the most favorable thing you could say about this work is that it has involved the collection of a fair amount of empirical data.

beings, much like any other human beings. In any discussion of the performance of the bureaucracy of the corporation we must take into account the fact that the human beings will behave in the human manner. They will attempt to achieve their own goals as far as possible and will be led to achieve goals of other people only so far as the structure in which they operate is arranged in such a way that achieving their own goals is best done working the will of other people.

Since we are human beings, we can get by introspection some idea of the type of goals that other human beings will have, although the fineness and precision of this view of their motives of course leaves much to be desired. On the other hand, it does turn out that one of the characteristics of human beings is that, generally speaking, they have a desire for certain rather broad-gauge qualities which increases their power to achieve their specific goals. Normally human beings would like to increase their income and/or their power. Assuming that human beings are income maximizers or power maximizers or want to maximize some function does not do a great deal of harm in general. No individual is entirely an income-power maximizer, but that assumption is a good approximation. Further, it is statistically testable. The fact that individuals have other motives turns up as random noise in a statistical test and therefore the hypotheses based on these assumptions can be tested. It should be said that hypotheses based on other assumptions can also be tested, although in most cases the other assumed motives are of less importance; hence, the R^2 can be expected to be smaller. Most people, for example, have at least some interest in the well-being of others and are willing to devote at least some effort and wealth toward that end.

The most important characteristic of individuals when designing a bureaucracy, however, is not that they are to some extent interested in the well-being of others and, hence, to some extent are public-spirited, but also that to a large extent they will seek their own selfish goals. This means that simply telling them what is good or what is wanted by their superiors is of little benefit in obtaining their cooperation. Arrangements must be made so that carrots and sticks are present to control their actions. Descriptions of bureaucracies in which the carrots and the sticks are not mentioned are not accurate. Unfortunately, there are a very large number of ways of arranging the reward and penalty structure; therefore, though necessity rules out many possible bureaucratic organizations, many still remain.

In addition to our knowledge that the bureaucratic black boxes are composed of individuals and computers are composed of transistors, we also have some idea of the restraints to which they are subjected. Consider again our large corporation. It must, of necessity, sell its products for enough to pay for its input including the salary of its employees. Preferrably it will also produce interest on its borrowings and a dividend for its stockholders, but at the very least it must pay its operating costs. If the corporation is selling its services in the market, there is a fairly stiff set of constraints imposed upon it. The more competitive the market, the tighter these constraints; but they are quite tight even in a monopoly. Indeed, they appear to be quite tight even in companies whose principal customer is the federal government.

In addition to these constraints imposed by the product market, there are others imposed by the capital market. If the company fails to pay the interest on its borrowed debt, it may find its existing management replaced by a receiver in bankruptcy. If the company is unable to produce enough profit to please its stockholders, the stockholders may throw out the present management and introduce another. The process by which this occurs normally involves the sale of stock by people who are unhappy with the management; as a consequence, there is a depression of stock prices and the purchase of stock by people who are interested in changing the management and, hence, getting a rise in prices. In those fortunate cases where the president owns the company, this final constraint is not operative. There is a sort of simplification of it in which the owning individual may decide to sell out, but that is basically different. Clearly these financial constraints are tighter than the pure market constraints. Further, they are little, if at all, affected by monopoly position, except insofar as a monopoly position is newly acquired and not known to the stockholders.

Even if we consider a corporation operating in a highly competitive market with a highly competitive market in its stock, it is clear that the management has at least some discretion. (Indeed, study of this discretion has, to a considerable extent, been initiated by that most capitalistic of economists, Armen Alchian.) Having said this, however, we immediately are brought to realize how little we know about bureaucracy. What do we mean literally when we say "management has some discretion"? That "management" is not completely constrained is clear; but how does "management" make the decisions as to how it shall use its discretion? Who decides who will get the blonde secretary? Who, indeed, decides anything? What does the interior of the black box look like? Normally the closer we look at any given corporation, the less we feel we know about the answers to such questions. It is clear that some kind of a collective decision process is going on in the sense that, with very rare exceptions, there is not one man who always gives orders; but what this collective decision process is is not clear.[2]

We have here, then, an enigma—the decisions of higher corporate managers—and we have some idea as to the constraints on the black box

2. The lack of clarity is even stronger in governments, particularly those governments that make no pretense to be democratic, like the present governments of Peru or China.

and the components within it; but we do not know how the interactions among them operate. We can go a little further, however, still staying with our corporation in a competitive industry. It is clear that insofar as management is subject to the external constraints we have been describing, it is under pressure toward efficiency in the pure, capitalistic sense of maximum returns on resources. What is the mechanism by which this pressure is transmitted from a general desire to such specific decisions as: we will build a new plant in Keokuk, increase our advertising budget, and change the color of our package from red to green?

Such problems, in a way, can be factored away from the top management. The top management can perhaps divide its company into "profit centers" and then simply put pressure on each profit center to make profit and ignore specific decisions. In general, however, this simply moves the black box problem down a step. Now we have the question of how the individual manager of a division converts his desire to maximize profits, and hence keeps his job, into specific decisions by his subordinates on the kinds of issues I have listed above. He wants to increase profits, but he has to be able to motivate behavior among his subordinates which is not easily attached to a given change in the profit ratio. Indeed, he may find it necessary to spend much of his time preventing his subordinates from carrying out successful conspiracies against him.

There are two partial solutions to this problem. First, *The Politics of Bureaucracy* contains a very abstract theory of the internal functioning of bureaucracy [4]. Since this theory is not presented in mathematical terminology, it seems to have escaped the notice of some of the readers of the book, but it does exist. Unfortunately, the theory is so abstract that it only places some extreme limits on the type of detailed institutions we might anticipate finding in a given hierarchy. Still, I think it should have been given more attention than it has been by students of bureaucracy. Unfortunately, it is too long to detail here.

There is a second theory which has never been made explicit, but which is implicit in many of the writings about bureaucracy. This theory is that the black box of a big hierarchy in essence is composed of a set of smaller black boxes which are contained within it. In other words, we can take any subsection of the bureaucracy and treat it as a black box, subject to constraints put upon it by the remainder of the bureaucracy. The Department of Defense is a big bureaucracy, composed of a set of black boxes called the services (and certain other independent areas) which in turn are composed of further black boxes. Not only can we look at the Department of Defense on the whole as a hierarchy which maximizes some type of goal subject to some kind of constraint, we can consider each of the individual internal black boxes in the same way. Under these circumstances, the Department of Defense in essence imposes certain constraints on the inner black boxes which they then maximize against.

This method, which is implicit in a very large number of discussions of bureaucracy, normally is applied by deciding what are the constraints to which some black box or bureaucratic subordinate organization is subject, and what that organization is attempting to maximize. It is then possible to make a number of calculations, sometimes quite detailed, as to how it will behave. William Niskanen's *Bureaucracy and Representative Government* [2] is an example of this technique, although he assumed that a very large number of bureaucracies are all attempting to maximize the same thing, subject to the same set of constraints; hence, a theory covering many bureaucracies is derived.

This description of the existing state of the study of bureaucracies in the widest definition immediately suggests desirable directions for further research. Clearly what we mainly need is a good theory (preferably well tested) of the internal functionings of bureaucracies. Although this is what we most need, it is not clear that this is the area where we should put most of our research. In choosing research areas, we not only choose important ones but also ones with which we can deal reasonably. I suppose most of us would agree that eliminating the aging process in human beings beyond the age of 21 would be perhaps the most important improvement medicine could achieve. We put very little research into it because we believe that the probability of achieving this goal is so low that even the great value of success does not pay for the investment. Similarly, it is hard to argue for a great deal of research being devoted to attempting to understand the internal functionings of bureaucracy.

If it is hard to argue for a great deal of research in this area, it is nevertheless highly desirable that all students of bureaucracy continuously keep in mind the desirability of learning what goes on inside the black boxes. It is not terribly likely that a formal research program will solve this problem, but the cost of keeping it in mind while doing research on other aspects of bureaucracy is comparatively low, and continued attention to the problem may lead to the sudden inspiration that solves it.

Turning from this highly important but very difficult problem, there are a number of more mundane matters which we can consider. The obvious one is a more careful specification and then careful testing of the constraints to which the various bureaucratic black boxes are subject. Detailed investigation of human motivations insofar as they are relevant to these constraints also would be worthwhile. I must say that the latter field, which would depend on psychological work, seems to be almost as difficult as the general theory of bureaucracy to which I referred above. Still, once again it should be kept in mind. Altogether, it seems likely that the most promising line of research is the investigation of the type of constraints to which bureaucracies actually are subject. This, of course, will involve careful investigations of such things as the type of information available to people who would like to exercise control over bureaucracies or subbureaucracies, the preference orders that are imposed by the external environment upon them, and the possibility of the bureaucracy to misinform its superiors and therefore actually conform to a different set of constraints than the superiors anticipate.

The last should be perhaps elaborated upon a little bit. Suppose that the superior of some bureaucracy wishes the bureaucracy to maximize a variable, A. Maximizing variable A is difficult, but there is another easily maximizable variable, B, which can be misrepresented to the superior as being A. Under these circumstances, the bureaucracy will be maximizing B rather than A. Note, however, that this does not mean that it is not maximizing subject to constraint; it merely means that the variable it is maximizing is different from what the superior intends. It is probable that this type of thing, although not quite in the pure form I have given above, is omnipresent throughout bureaucracies. Indeed, the Niskanen theory of bureaucracy is an example.

So far I have talked about bureaucracy in a very general sense. Indeed, I have talked mainly about business bureaucracies because in a way they are the optimally efficient bureaucracies in the present world. When we consider different types of bureaucracies, the first observation is that the constraint set under which bureaucracies may operate can be of varying degrees of tightness. In some cases (shall we say the Ford Foundation?) the bureaucracy in essence is subject to practically no constraint. Decision as to how it will invest its portfolio does have some effect on how much money it can spend, but subject to that constraint it can do substantially anything it wishes. This is an unconstrained bureaucracy. Most bureaucracies lie somewhere between such an unconstrained bureaucracy and the bureaucracy of a company operating in a highly competitive market and with active trading of a highly significant portion of its stock.

Government bureaucracies in particular fall along the continuum between them; and it is notable that most discussions of bureaucracy tend to concentrate on the government sector. There are two good reasons for concentrating on the government sector, the first of which is that policy decisions are most likely to have a payoff if we concentrate there. The second is that it is likely that the inefficiency introduced through badly designed bureaucracy is of much greater magnitude in our society in the government sector than anywhere else. The book to which this essay is appended as a final chapter is almost entirely devoted to a discussion of government bureaucracy. In common speech, the government is regarded as *the* bureaucracy and the term *bureaucracy* is only applied to other areas, such as corporations, as a sort of poetically pejorative way of speaking.

All of this is quite appropriate, granted the importance of government bureaucracy, but it should never be forgotten that it is merely a special (albeit a very important) subcategory of a more general phenomenon. The difference between the government bureaucracy and a corporation in a highly competitive business is essentially the difference in the type of constraints and the strength of the constraints to which the bureaucracy is subject. It may be that somewhat different people are attracted to the two types of bureaucracy, but surely this variable is of much less importance than the difference in the constraints.

The weakness of the constraints is partially due to the absence of competition. There is not even the type of very remote competition one normally gets in a monopoly in which the individual could refuse to purchase the monopolized product and purchase some totally different product with his money. Characteristically the individual is compelled to purchase the government product whether he wishes to or not. Further, characteristically there is only one government supplier.

Not only is this characteristic of government bureaucracy, but most government bureaucracies fight hard to keep it that way. Robert Spann's study (appearing earlier in this book) indicates that in those cases in which government bureaucracies face even potential private competition at a fairly significant level (i.e., those areas of local government where some local governments have private contracts and others have public provision), the bureaucracy functions very much more efficiently than elsewhere; in fact those are the areas in which he is unable to find great differences in cost between private and public bureaucracy.[3]

Needless to say, government bureaucrats normally object to this situation. The objection to the introduction of the voucher system for paying for education has come mainly from the professional school teachers in the government service, not from parents or taxpayers. Government employee unions are very rapidly introducing into their contracts clauses prohibiting contracting out to private companies. Legal prohibitions on private service are quite common.

In a democracy, the weakness of the constraint starts at the very top; the voter is not motivated to acquire very much information about the performance of various parts of the bureaucracy because his vote is such a small portion of the total number of votes that improving its quality pays off almost not at all. This is, of course, less true with small local government, but information may be harder to get at that level. Presumably, in any event control over bureaucracy could be tightened up by moving it to smaller governments. Not only would the individual voter's vote count more for him, the various smaller governments are in implicit competition with each other. Nevertheless, examination of the actual performance of the small governments does not indicate that this is any

---

3. His figures are not adjusted for the difference in tax treatment.

magic solution to the problem. They seem to be more efficient, but still not very efficient.

The weakness of constraints at the top is the probable reason that constraints are similarly weak throughout the pyramid. Various officials, not being carefully supervised by the voters, find it is not necessary to carefully supervise their inferiors who, in turn, find it unnecessary to carefully supervise *their* inferiors, etc. The difference from private industry is quantitative rather than qualitative, but it is a very large quantitative difference and the effects superficially look qualitative.

There are a number of aspects of this general weakening of supervision. First, a very important aspect, and one which is both a result and a cause of the weakening of supervision, is that it is frequently impossible to fire government employees. Thus, only positive incentives can be used to obtain their cooperation. Further, these positive incentives are frequently administered in an almost automatic way, with the result that even they are not very significant. It is sometimes said that the Italian civil service gives service only as an act of pure charity. The American civil service is not quite that bad, but there certainly is a strong charitable element in the performance of work by government employees.[4] On the other hand, the rewards for the civil service employee are not very great, with the result that it is probable that most civil servants live a relatively low-pressure existence. They have a fairly secure income and a great deal of freedom in planning their own activities. Since the literature is full of examples of the use of this freedom for bad causes, let me suggest that it has some advantages, too. The individual whose behavior is not likely to affect his future income very much is free to devote more of his effort to maximizing his own utility function. One argument in this utility function is normally a desire to benefit others which, in a government servant, may involve the public interest. Thus, the individual civil servant may do what in his view is the right thing for the government simply as a way of maximizing his own utility.

Unfortunately, although this is an advantage of the present system, it should be emphasized that one individual's views of the public interest may not be another's. This chapter is being written at the time of the Watergate investigation and in the last week two alleged memoranda from high-ranking officials of the Nixon administration have been published. In one of them a high-ranking official complained that the civil servants operating the Internal Revenue Service were not willing to assist President Nixon by harassing his opponents. In the other, a high-ranking official requested another such official to stop the Internal Revenue Service from harassing friends of the president. I do not know whether either of these allegations is true, but there seems to be nothing particularly im-

---

4. Robert Staaf, in an earlier chapter in this book, points out that this aspect is particularly strong in elementary and grade school teachers.

probable about them. Note the described behavior of the Internal Revenue Service supervisor. He is refusing to harass enemies of the president and is harassing his friends instead. He is described as a liberal Democrat in one of the memoranda, and there is no doubt that if he is a liberal Democrat, he would regard this policy of refusing to harass enemies of Nixon and harassing his friends to be in the public interest. So far as I can see, this is also the attitude of the *Washington Post,* which showed no signs of interest at all in the behavior of the head of the Internal Revenue Service and a great deal of interest in the behavior of the political officials who were trying to change it.

This is simply one example of the type of freedom to advance what they think is the public interest given to civil servants in our system. It should be noted that many elected officials have somewhat the same power. Congressmen are gradually developing more and more security of tenure. This is, to a large extent, the result of their own efforts in increasing the amount of money spent by the federal government in campaigning for them, and putting more and more restrictions on money available to their opponents for the purpose of campaigning against them. As a result, various members of Congress are free to pursue what amounts to hobbies. Whether this hobby is promoting the B-1 bomber or Head Start makes little difference; it is clear that the activity in at least some cases is essentially an effort to maximize what the individual thinks of as the public good. In many other cases, of course, it is an effort to appeal to some potential source of support.

Whatever the use to which an individual in government puts his greater freedom from constraints, it is clear that the phenomenon of such a reduction in constraint is important. Further, one of the results of this may be that some of the constraints are in fact perverse. At various levels, the weakness of constraint may lead to behavior at a lower level that is contrary to the desires of the people at the upper levels. Take the expansion of bureaucracy for the expansion's own sake, for example. It may be that this arises largely through the fact that the high-level supervisor in the bureaucracy pays relatively little attention to its behavior and, in making decisions, tends to use indices which lead to perverse results. When the salary of supervisors is simple multiple of the salary of teachers, then it is most unwise to entrust a supervisor with negotiating wage claims with the teachers. Nevertheless, Staaf finds that this particular pattern of behavior is quite common. Anyone familiar with the federal government can find innumerable other examples, and indeed Niskanen's book *Bureaucracy and Representative Government* is based on a somewhat similar phenomenon.

Once again, let us consider areas for future research. It seems to me the important problem here is one of specifying the *real* constraints under which government bureaucracies operate. It is clear that if we make up the usual pro forma statement of what some given government agency is *supposed* to be doing, this is only in a very mild and indirect way related to the actual constraints upon that agency. On the other hand, the constraints themselves are surely more complex that the simple maximization/size-of-bureau hypothesis which has been a foundation of much of modern work. This does not mean that maximization of the size of the bureau may not be a very important maxim and that the constraints upon it may not be those which are currently being described, but only that there must be other things, too. The nature of these other things varies a good deal from bureau to bureau, and investigation both of the type of general constraints that exist and the specific constraints for each bureau would be worthwhile.

Once again, the problem of the black box contained within the black box is important here. One of the reasons maximization of size is significant is that it is probably a characteristic of all of the black boxes. Further, if the large bureau organization wants to increase its size, then it will be particularly willing to cooperate with subsections that wish to increase in size. Conflict between the bureaus in objectives is less likely on this variable.

On the whole, if we would like to improve the efficiency of our government bureaucracies, investigations as to what might be described as optimal constraints are also an important area. Such investigations are difficult because the objectives of bureaus are so widely varying and so hard to measure. It seems possible, however, that we may follow the market here. The objectives individuals would like to get from market goods and services are also widely varying and hard to measure. What we do is give a number of entrepreneurs the opportunity to satisfy these widely varying demands and pay them off in money. Thus, they maximize income and the constraints are whatever desires the customers actually have. Doing somewhat the same thing in the government seems to me at least feasible. Instead of hiring soldiers, the Army might hire regiments; instead of hiring policemen, a small city might hire a police force; and a state government might deal with its financial problems by hiring an accounting firm rather than by hiring accountants.

It should be emphasized that this would improve efficiency at the lower level. Errors, and there are many, or imposition of inappropriate constraints at higher levels would not be dealt with at all. We can get an idea of the consequences if we compare the purchase of weapons from private producers in a reasonably competitive market with government provision for most of the services involved in military activity. Clearly, in the former area we are more efficient; but no one would argue that we are highly efficient. Still, although I think not a great deal could be expected from this kind of reform, something can and should be tried.

Last, we come to an underlying theme of this entire book: why do bureaucracies grow? As the reader may know, I am associated with the view that it is to a very large extent because the factor suppliers are permitted to vote. Indeed, they are permitted to exercise political influence in many ways. Thus, the growth of the bureaucracy to a large extent is self-generating. An expansion of the bureaucracy or government purchases of other factors pay off the present suppliers in the sense that they receive somewhat higher prices than they would if the market were not expanding. At the same time it pulls further people into the market and they combine their political power with the original participants to produce a further step upward.

This theory of mine is, to put it mildly, not accepted by all scholars. Nevertheless, it seems to me a useful hypothesis and I should like to see it tested. However, there are several other hypotheses and any test of mine should, I think, run in parallel with tests of the others.

Perhaps the most famous alternative hypothesis is William Baumol's service hypothesis. To say that this is Baumol's hypothesis is rather an oversimplification. Baumol's actual position is much more sophisticated than the hypothesis I am about to propound under his name. Nevertheless, this is the "oral culture" version of the hypothesis among economists, and it is certainly true that Baumol set it in motion, regardless of whether he intended to do so. According to this hypothesis, it is less possible to reduce labor inputs in the service industries than in the nonservice industries, and the government has an exceptionally high percentage of service activities. If it is indeed less possible to introduce labor-saving devices to the service industries, one would anticipate a gradual increase in the price of such activities in comparison to other types of activities. If we have two sectors of the economy, one which is progressive in the sense that costs fall and the other which is not, then as the economy grows in wealth as a result of the improvements in the first sector, there could be a gradual shift of resources from the second to the first.

For this argument to explain the growth of government, it would have to be true that labor inputs into government services grow faster than non-labor inputs. This does not appear to be true. If we look at the capital-labor ratio, we find that in the federal government it is very much higher than that in most industries [3]. Far from being as low as that in services, it is many times as high. Thus, it would appear that government activity absorbs both more labor and more capital as time goes by. Indeed, there are special theories to explain why government tends to overinvest in capital.[5]

It should be noted, however, that there appears to be a difference here.

5. See Niskanen [2] and De Alessi [1]. Baumol himself, in fact, has contributed a general survey of the social discount rate problem, which is relevant to this issue.

The federal government seems to accumulate a great deal of capital per unit of labor. The state-local governments, on the other hand, have an increase in labor and not in capital. The federal government is capital intense and the state-local governments are labor intense.

This is hard to explain on the "service" hypothesis, but fairly easy to explain on the factor-supplier pressure group hypothesis. As a general rule, civil servants live where they are employed whether by a local government or the federal government. Therefore, they are always available to apply political pressure for the expansion of their market share. Producers of capital goods, on the other hand, do not have this characteristic. Due to the economies of large-scale production, most producers of capital goods that are used in local government activities are not located in the local government which is their consumer. The police are spread across the entire United States, with some of them in all local government areas. The police cars they drive are produced in only a few places.

Under these circumstances, one would anticipate that there would be little in the way of direct voter pressure on local governments to purchase additional capital equipment and a good deal of pressure to hire more civil servants. The federal government, on the other hand, is subject to pressure from both the civil servants and the manufacturers of capital goods. As a consequence, we would anticipate a differential capital intensity between these two levels of government and, in fact, we do observe such a difference. Once again, it is hard to see how this could be explained by the service hypothesis.

While I have been considering this subject, the possibility has occurred to me that perhaps there is no particular tendency for modern societies to increase their service sector and reduce their manufacturing sector. Perhaps what is happening is simply that the size of the labor input in those areas that are heavily unionized is shrinking. It may be that manufacturing is shrinking because it is a particularly suitable area for unionization. This is, however, a hypothesis that is offered without anything in the way of statistical investigation. It should be fairly easy to test.

Other possible explanations are harder to test. There is one which holds simply that, as we get into "modern" governments, it is necessary to increase the government share. Since so far as I know there is no particular correlation between the size of per capita national income and the size of government, I doubt this hypothesis. Further, if this were the cause of the growth of the government, then one would anticipate that the *structure* of government expenditures in different countries would be much the same if they were about the same level of economic development. Japan and Italy should have about the same structure of expenditures. Although there has been no careful investigation of this point, I believe that it would turn out to be untrue.

Another basically untestable hypothesis, to which I can only suggest indirect approaches, is simply that people's tastes have changed and we now want more government services. Here we can think of an easy test of an experimental nature, but one that has not been run. A good many of the current services performed by the government are private in nature. For example, if I purchase a car I am compelled to purchase with it certain safety equipment which protects no one except myself and those who accept invitations from me to ride in my car. If we made these non-compulsory, we could find out whether people actually had any great demand for them. Since people who advocate this type of equipment are very vigorously opposed to making it noncompulsory, I take it *they* think people would choose not to consume much of it. Until the experiment is run, however, we could hardly be certain. There are, of course, other areas. The Postal Service, for example, receives a very substantial subsidy for generating private goods by transmitting letters back and forth between people. We could rearrange things so that the Postal Service charged the full cost, permit other people to compete, and see what the experiment led to.

Another possible explanation for growth of government has been presented by William Craig Stubblebine in a paper as yet unpublished. He argues, on the basis of a rather careful survey, that the average individual gravely underestimates the cost to him of individual government services. Under the circumstances, thinking the price is much lower than it is, he chooses to consume more. Of course, in order to explain the growth of government services, we would have to assume that people have been gradually increasing the size of their error, but with the growth of government this is not totally impossible.

Another rather similar argument might be that people are correctly estimating the true opportunity costs to themselves of government services. They may feel, rationally, that the political costs to them of obtaining a general reduction in taxes is very high because the constitutional restrictions on special tax privileges make it difficult, albeit not impossible, to arrange. On the other hand, they may feel that it is politically fairly easy to expand the number of government services individuals receive. Making a cost-benefit analysis of the return on political activity in these two areas, they may quite correctly come to the conclusion that they can do better by investing resources in efforts to improve special privileges for themselves, rather than in an effort to obtain special tax reductions. They would, of course, be relatively uninterested in either increasing expenditures or reducing taxes which were of a pure public good nature.

Once again we have a series of questions for research. The government must have some reason for growth, since we observe it growing; but it is astonishing that the issue has received so little attention. Perhaps the basic reason is simply that most economists profit from the growth of at least two aspects of government: developing federal and local bureaucracies that consume economic "research," and the educational system. Biting the hand that feeds one may be dangerous and, in any event, surely an unprofitable activity. We are, in the end, all bureaucrats, even if we do not like to admit it.

References

1. De Alessi, Louis. "Implications of Property Rights for Government Investment Choices." *American Economic Review* 59 (March, 1969): 13–24.
2. Niskanen, William A. *Bureaucracy and Representative Government.* Chicago: Aldine-Atherton, 1971.
3. Orzechowski, William P. "Labor Intensity, Productivity, and the Growth of the Federal Sector." *Public Choice* 19 (fall, 1974).
4. Tullock, Gordon. *The Politics of Bureaucracy.* Washington, D.C.: Public Affairs Press, 1965.

Index